A parting gift
to
Henry C. Granger
from his affectionate
Sabbath School Teacher
Chicago April 26th 1858
George S Lord

SKETCHES FROM LIFE;

OR,

ILLUSTRATIONS OF THE INFLUENCE OF CHRISTIANITY.

PUBLISHED BY THE

AMERICAN TRACT SOCIETY,

150 NASSAU-STREET, NEW YORK.

This volume consists wholly of articles selected from the successive numbers of the "AMERICAN MESSENGER," to the middle of its thirteenth volume. No other changes have been made, than to adapt the phraseology in a few instances to a permanent volume, and to classify its subjects so as to add, it is hoped, to the interest and profit of its readers. As presented to the public in this form, it is believed, that by the divine blessing, the labors of the respected writers of these narratives may be more widely and lastingly extended. The signatures of the estimable authors being in many instances well known, will add interest to their papers.

CONTENTS.

DOMESTIC REMINISCENCES.

THE NEGLECT OF RELIGION.

SKETCHES FROM LIFE.

CONVERSION.

GEORGE TAYLOR.

In the years 1820–21, Princeton, New Jersey, was blessed with a precious revival of religion. The work was still, solemn, and powerful. Among the subjects of it were some who became useful ministers of Christ. Others besides college students felt its power. The distress of many before attaining settled peace of mind was pungent, and often continued for days. There are pangs as well as joys in the new birth. He who believes the contrary, deceives himself. He who teaches the contrary, deceives others. The degree and duration of this anxious concern are determined by Him who doeth all things well, and "giveth not account of any of his matters." He knows what best suits each case.

In the village at that time was an Englishman whose name was George Taylor. He was poor, feeble in mind and body, and much afflicted with rheumatism. He was honest, but very ignorant of divine things. He felt the powers of the world to come.

He had a deep sense of his sinfulness, and awful apprehensions of the wrath of God. At first his case was not distinguished from that of many others. But while others obtained relief, and were begotten to a lively hope, he sunk into deeper distress. His state of mind excited the affectionate interest of the pious around him. He manifested a solemn attention to every thing that showed him his vileness. His sleep was short and disturbed. His burden of guilt was "a vast oppressive load." His appetite almost left him, and like David, he "forgat to eat." "His bones waxed old through his roaring all the day long; for day and night God's hand was heavy upon him; his moisture was turned into the drought of summer." He often feared that it was too late for him to repent and turn to God. Yet he could not give over seeking.

His chief difficulty was to conceive *how* a just and holy God could forgive sin, and particularly *his* sins. He saw that the law was holy, just, and good, in its precept and penalty. But he could not see how such a God, with such a law, could consistently forgive such a sinner as he was, or indeed any sinner. Many conversed with him, and tried to show him how God can be just, and yet justify the ungodly who believe in Christ. He also heard some excellent sermons on the work of Christ as a Redeemer. Still all was dark. "How should man be just with God?" was the perplexing question. Such phrases as are commonly and very properly used to teach the nature of the offices of Christ in behalf of sinners, conveyed no idea to him. He knew not the language of Canaan. The effect of his distress was plainly perceptible in his face. The pious deeply commiserated his state, and the more so because no one had been able to afford him any relief. At last one explained to him some of the sacrifices under the law. He told him how a lamb was brought by a guilty man, and laid bound on the altar, and how he who had sinned laid his hands upon it, confessing his sin, and how its blood became the blood of atonement, and how he was thus set free from the guilt of breaking the ceremonial law. His friend then said, "Christ is our lamb," and, suiting the gestures to the words, repeated these lines of Watts :

"My faith would lay her hand
On that dear head of thine,
While like a penitent I stand
And there confess my sin."

This was enough. To poor George it was life from the dead. The day-spring had visited his soul. He said, "I understand it now. All is plain. Christ is the lamb to take away our sins. Why did not some one tell me this before?" His friend said, "We have been telling you the same thing all along, but in different words. Did we not tell you that Christ is the way, the truth, and the life ; and that no man cometh unto the Father but by him?"

George Taylor was received into the church of Princeton, August 10, 1821; and for a few years, till his death, led a devout, consistent life. He held fast his integrity, and is now, I trust, singing the song of Moses and the Lamb.

This short narrative is not intended to illustrate the whole of that great change which must pass upon men in order to salvation. Nor is it given as a type of conversions. God deals variously with men. But it may teach some useful lessons.

1. The use of learning is to make things plain.

2. There is milk as well as meat in the word of God, milk for babes and meat for strong men. Let each have his portion in due season.

3. Whoever would come to Christ, must be taught of God. Jesus said, "No man can come unto me, except the Father, which hath sent me, draw him." Reader, if God is drawing you, now is your time. If he is calling you, rise and follow him. He will not always call. Left to yourself, you will never find the way to God. You must be led by the Spirit. Pray like David, "Take not thy Holy Spirit from me?"

4. God works when, how, and by what means he will. He offers salvation to the rich and the poor, to the learned and the rude. But how often are we reminded of those words of Christ, "I thank thee, O Father, Lord of heaven and earth, that thou hast hid these things from the wise and prudent, and hast revealed them unto babes; even so, Father, for so it seemed good in thy sight." Let us thank God that he reveals these things to babes, to the weak-minded and ignorant, who are willing to learn. "The entrance of thy word giveth light." "It maketh wise the simple."

5. Let none despise the gospel because it is preached to the poor, nor because the child and the simple can understand enough of it to be saved. Pride is as damning as murder, and pride of intellect is as ruinous as pride of person, family, or estate. "The wicked, through the pride of his countenance, will not seek after God." "God resisteth the proud, but giveth

grace to the humble." "The proud, and all that do wickedly, shall be burned up." You must humble yourself as a little child, if you would be saved.

6. It is always safe to tell of Christ and his love, of his death and his grace. This theme has awakened thousands, and brought millions to salvation.

7. How transforming is the doctrine of the cross, whenever understood and received. It is life and it is spirit. It cheers, it purifies; it puts men to praying; it makes them zealous of good works. Such were its effects on George Taylor, as many saw; on the Greenlanders, as the Moravians testify; on the Indians of New Jersey, as Brainerd declares; on the people of Kilmany, as Chalmers states. The cross at once subdues and wins. "God forbid that I should glory, save in the cross of our Lord Jesus Christ."

8. And now, dying mortal, you too are a sinner, and you too need a Saviour no less than poor Taylor. Unless you are brought to strive to enter in at the strait gate, you will never be saved. Unless you are brought to loathe and abhor yourself, you must perish. You must find the Lamb of God, by whose blood alone your guilt can be washed away. "He that believeth not, shall be damned." It is said of a poor Greenlander, that the first time he heard the love and death of Christ explained, he said, "If this Saviour died for me, he shall be my Saviour." If you will rest all your weight upon the precious blood of Christ, your soul shall be saved, your sins shall be blotted out, and heaven shall be yours.

O repent and believe; for why will you die?
Since God in great mercy is coming so nigh—
Since Jesus invites you, the Spirit says, Come,
And angels are waiting to welcome you home.

If you die in your sins, many will rise in the judgment and condemn you. If you now receive Christ, you will be safe for eternity. Will you not receive him? Will you not receive him *now?* The Bible presents no alternative but NOW OR NEVER.

AN INFIDEL BLACKSMITH.

SCENE I. THE PASTOR'S STUDY.

"Have you conversed with our infidel and scoffing friend Mr. R——, on the subject of religion, to-day?" said the venerable pastor to Mr. B——, an aged neighbor.

"I have, and at great length, but was unable to make the least impression upon his mind. You know that he is a man of extensive reading, and is master of all the ablest infidel writers. He regards the fortress in which he has intrenched himself as impregnable. You know his ready wit, and when he finds he cannot talk you down, he will laugh you down. I can say no more to him. He made my errand the butt of ridicule for the whole company."

"Then you consider his case hopeless?"

"I do, indeed. I believe him to be given over of God to believe a lie; and I expect to see him fill up his cup of iniquity to the very brim without repentance, and die a hardened and self-ruined man."

"Shall nothing, and can nothing more be done for him?" And the pastor arose, and walked the floor of his study, under the influence of deep agitation.

It was now a solemn time in the congregation. The preaching of the pastor, for many Sabbaths, had been full of earnestness and power. The church was greatly quickened. The spirit of prayer prevailed. Many were inquiring what they should do to be saved. Many, too, were rejoicing in hope, and the whole community were moved, as with one silent, but mighty impulse.

But unmoved, unconcerned, stood the infidel, amid the many changes of heart and mind in those around him, proud of his position, and confident in his strength, and able, as he believed himself to be, to resist every influence, human and divine, which might be brought to bear upon him. The pastor had often approached him, and had as often been repulsed. As a last resort, he had requested his able and skilful neighbor, a lawyer of piety and talents, to visit Mr. R——, and endeavor to convince him. But it was like attempting to reason with the tempest, or soothe the volcano.

SCENE II. THE CHRISTIAN'S CLOSET.

There was a fire blazing upon the hearth in that little room. The wind was howling without; the snow was whirled in eddies, and was swept with violence against the casement. It was a cold night in January. In that secret and retired chamber, where none but God could hear, was poured out a voice from a burdened soul. The aged Christian was upon his knees. His bosom heaved with emotion. His soul was in agony. That voice of prayer was continued at intervals through the livelong night. In that room was a wrestling like that of Jacob. There was a prevailing like that of Israel. It was a pleading with the Most High for an unwonted display of his power and grace, with the confidence that nothing was too hard for the Almighty. It was a night of prayer, of entreaty, of importunity. It was prayer as a man would pray for the life of a friend, who was on the eve of execution.

SCENE III. THE PRAYER-MEETING.

The meeting was still and solemn as eternity. The house was crowded to its utmost capacity. It was a cheerful evening, and the astrals threw their mellow light over the dense assembly. Now the song of praise resounds from all parts of the room, and there is a heart in the utterance which belongs not to other times. Now the voice of one and another ascends in prayer, and such prayer is seldom heard except in the time of genuine revivals of religion. The silent tear steals down many a cheek. The almost inaudible sigh escapes from many a bosom. An intense interest rests on every countenance, and the voice of prayer is the voice of all. One after another arises, and tells the listening company what "the Lord has done for his soul." There stands Mr. R——, once the infidel—now the humble believer in Jesus. He is clothed in a new spirit. His face shines as did the face of Moses when he had seen God face to face. He is a new creature in Christ Jesus.

"I stand," said Mr. R——, "to tell you the story of my conversion." His lips trembled slightly as he spoke, and his bosom heaved with suppressed emotion. "I am as a brand plucked out of the burning. The change in me is an astonishment to myself; and all brought about by the grace of God, and that *unanswerable argument*. It was a cold morning in January, and I had just begun my labor at the anvil in my shop, when I looked out and saw Mr. B—— approach-

ing. He dismounted quickly, and entered. As he drew near, I saw he was agitated. His look was full of earnestness. His eyes were bedimmed with tears. He took me by the hand. His breast heaved with emotion, and with indescribable tenderness he said, 'Mr. R——, I am greatly concerned for your salvation—greatly concerned for your salvation,' and he burst into tears. He stood with my hand grasped in his. He struggled to regain self-possession. He often essayed to speak, but not a word could he utter; and finding that he could say no more, he turned, went out of the shop, got on his horse, and rode slowly away.

"'Greatly concerned for my salvation,' said I, audibly, and I stood and forgot to bring my hammer down. There I stood with it upraised—'*greatly concerned for my salvation.*' Here is a new argument for the truth of religion, which I have never heard before, and which I know not how to answer. Had the aged man reasoned with me, I could have confounded him; but here is no threadbare argument for the truth of religion. Religion must be true, or this man would not feel as he does. 'Greatly concerned for my salvation;' it rung through my ears like a thunder-clap in a clear sky. Greatly concerned I ought to be for my own salvation, said I—what shall I do?

"I went to my house. My poor pious wife, whom I had always ridiculed for her religion, exclaimed, 'Why, Mr. R——, what is the matter with you?' 'Matter enough,' said I, filled with agony and overwhelmed with a sense of sin. 'Old Mr. B—— has rode two miles this cold morning to tell me he was greatly concerned for my salvation. What shall I do; what shall I do?'

"'I do not know what you can do,' said my astonished wife; 'I do not know what better you can do than to get on your horse, and go and see him. He can give you better counsel than I, and tell you what you must do to be saved.'

"I mounted my horse, and pursued after him. I found him alone in that same little room, where he had spent the night in prayer for my poor soul, where he had shed many tears over such a reprobate as I, and had besought God to have mercy upon me.

"'I am come,' said I to him, 'to tell you that I am greatly concerned for my own salvation.'

"'Praised be God,' said the aged man. 'It is a faithful saying, and worthy of all acceptation, that Jesus Christ came into the world to save sinners, even the chief,' and he began at that same scripture, and preached to me Jesus. On that same floor we knelt, and together we prayed—and we did not separate that day till God spoke peace to my soul.

"I have often been requested to look at the evidence of the truth of religion, but, blessed be God, I have evidence for its truth *here*," laying his hand upon his heart, "which nothing can gainsay or resist. I have often been led to look at this and that argument for the truth of Christianity; but I could overturn, and, as I thought, completely demolish and annihilate them all. But I stand here to-night, thankful to acknowledge that God sent *an argument* to my conscience and heart, which could not be answered or resisted, when a weeping Christian came to tell me how greatly concerned he was for my salvation. God taught him that *argument*, when he spent the night before him in prayer for my soul. Now I can truly say, I am a happy man. My peace flows like a river. My consistent, uncomplaining wife, who so long bore with my impiety and unbelief, now rejoices with me, that, by the grace of God, I am what I am—that whereas I was blind, now I see. And here permit me to say, if you would wish to reach the heart of such a poor sinner as I, you must get your qualifications where he did, in your closet and on your knees. So it shall be with me. I will endeavor to reach the hearts of my infidel friends through the closet and by prayer."

He sat down overcome with emotion, amid the

tears and the suppressed sobs of the assembly. All were touched; for all knew what he once was, all saw what he had now become.

"Time, on his noiseless wing, pursued his rapid flight." Years passed by, and the faithful old man was numbered with the dead. But the converted infidel still lived, an earnest, honest, faithful, humble Christian.

A GENTLEMAN IN BOSTON.

A few years ago, a gentleman in Boston having a leisure hour, sauntered into the court-room, where an interesting trial was in progress. Directly over the head of the judge there was suspended a large clock. The broad face of the brass pendulum, nearly a foot in diameter, vibrated to and fro in a solemn measured movement which arrested his eye. For a moment he looked listlessly upon the precision of its oscillations, and the idea gently occurred to his mind of the lapse of time—its ceaseless, rapid flow, marked off so solemnly by the tickings of the clock. The train of thought thus suggested, gradually and silently absorbed his attention. His eyes were fixed upon the pendulum. He was entirely insensible to the scene passing around him, as he thought of the events occurring over the world in the interval marked by the vibrations: now some are sinking into a watery grave—now the assassin plunges the dagger—now comes the fiend-like shock of armies—now the cry of remorse ascends from the pillow of the dying sinner—what multitudes die during each vibration! How rapidly the vibrations cut off the moments allotted to me. How soon will the clock strike my last hour? Where shall I then be? In heaven, or in hell?

Thus he stood, lost in reverie, while that noiseless pendulum preached to his soul in tones such as he had never heard before. He left the court-room, and mingled with the thoughtless crowds in Washington-street, but the barbed arrow of religious conviction had pierced his heart, and he could not extract it. He sought his closet. He fell upon his knees, and in anguish offered the prayer which, sincerely offered, never is refused, "O God, be merciful to me a sinner." He soon found the peace of pardon, and went on his new way heavenward, rejoicing. "The wind bloweth where it listeth, and thou hearest the sound thereof, but canst not tell whence it cometh, and whither it goeth; so is every one that is born of the Spirit."

A RATIONAL SCEPTIC.

Mr. H——, an eminent lawyer of Western New York, who died a few years since in the triumphs of Christian faith, when a student in the office of Judge H—— was inclined to sceptical views. His moral character was unsullied, but in his ambitious aspirations he cherished that dislike to the gospel which is the hidden source of nearly all infidelity. The eloquent ministrations of the sanctuary failed to remove the deepening gloom of unbelief.

One day, while absorbed in the study of law, his eye rested upon a copy of the Bible lying on the table before him. He paused, and the thought came like the voice of an invisible spectator to his soul, *What if that book is the word of God?* Then conscience inquired if he had, with earnestness and honesty becoming the momentous question, examined its claims to his faith. He was condemned at the bar of that inward judge and monitor, and resolved to begin a careful perusal of the sacred volume. The duty and propriety of *prayer* to the "Father of lights" for illumination were impressed on his mind. For the first time in his life, he solemnly entered on the reading of the Scriptures, and closet communion with God. In a few days, he was an anxious sinner, and he soon rejoiced in the love of Christ. He made a full consecration of himself to the Redeemer, in a written covenant copied from Doddridge, and found among his papers after his death; and for more than twenty years was an active, growing Christian. In the court-room and social circle, his consistent piety revealed itself, calm and clear beneath the excitements and pleasures of life.

Truly, "atheism is a crime, rather than a mere intellectual error;" and so is all fatal unbelief. The heart is wrong, and the head refuses to receive or seek the light of the cross. This view of the sceptical and scornful gives fearful import to the prophet's question, "What wilt thou say, when he shall punish thee?"

P. C. H.

A SCOFFER.

In the village of W—— a missionary meeting was announced, at which the lamented Rev. Dr. Armstrong was to be present. Attracted by the lighted church and the unusual crowd, young Robert L—— entered, to see what was going on, and to find new themes for his powers of ridicule and mimicry. He took a seat near the door, that he might not be recognized, and that when weary, as he anticipated he should soon be, he might pass out unnoticed.

The interest of the meeting was increased by addresses from a returned foreign missionary and a colporteur from one of our western states. These servants of God portrayed their fields of labor, their love for their work amid the trials and difficulties they had encountered, the encouragement they had in laboring for such a Master, and the hope that they might live and die with the harness on.

Robert became deeply interested in their narrations. He felt that they were sincere, however deluded in their belief; and conscience whispered that "it was no delusion; that they had an aim in life worthy of an immortal being; that the gospel which they hazarded all to bear to their dying fellow-men, was true; that they had no mercenary motives to lead them to a life of toil and hardships, unrequited by earthly rewards." And while this truth was rankling in his heart like a barbed arrow, the faithful colporteur drew his portrait to the life, as in very simple language, he portrayed a class of young men whom he often encountered, that threw off the restraints of early religious education when beyond the influence of home.

Robert recognized the likeness, and felt it was his own. The first emotion was that of resentment, that he should be thus held up to public view by an ignorant stranger; for he had when a lad left the parental fireside, where a pious mother had instructed, and a praying father had counselled him, to mingle with a class of men of loose habits, and still looser principles, till he had imbibed their infidelity, and renounced his belief in God's word. But he remained till the meeting was closed at a late hour, and then went from the sanctuary of God a convicted man.

His conviction did not leave him till he was brought to the foot of the cross. The life which God had mercifully spared in the midst of his rebellion, he consecrated to his Saviour, and he lived to adorn his profession. Those devoted servants of Christ knew not, and probably never will know until they both are gathered with their sheaves into the garner above, that their simple narrations that evening, and the testimony they bore, that their Master's "yoke was easy," was instrumental in doing a work that caused joy among the angels in heaven. G.

A MERCHANT IN BOSTON.

It was immediately after the great fire of 1835 in New York, that I was at Boston, in company with a Christian friend. We put up at the Tremont hotel. On the succeeding Sabbath we were walking in the parlor conversing on the afflictive providence with which our city had been visited; in the course of which, reference was made to the power and sovereignty of God. There was but one other person in the room, and he was seated silently near the fire. As the above remark was uttered, he stepped up to us, and inquired whether he had the happiness to address those who loved the Lord Jesus Christ. With some surprise at the sudden and *uncommon* inquiry, we replied with pleasure that we trusted it was so. He then apologized, with much courtesy and in a gentlemanly manner, for the intrusion upon our conversation; remarking that he was a stranger in Boston, where he had come a short time previous, having business with eminent merchants there. He further stated that he had, as he hoped, been led to taste the wonders of redeeming love, and to rejoice in that liberty wherewith the Lord makes his people free.

We had become by this time greatly interested in his remarks, and encouraged him to give us a history of the hope that was in him, to which he readily assented; and the following is a brief account of the dealings of the Holy Spirit with his priceless soul.

He was a native of Great Britain, and a son of a pious mother. Early in life he had been instructed in the way of godliness; but he had disregarded the admonitions and teachings of parental love, and given himself up to utter worldliness. He engaged in mercantile business in a foreign country, in the midst of an irreligious population, who were also sunken in the follies and superstitions of Romanism; and to all appearance, he entirely forgot the Lord God of his fathers.

During the year in which we met with him, he was providentially led to the city of New Orleans, where he had large transactions in business. Here the Holy Spirit led him, while walking the streets one Sabbath morning, to enter a church, in which the Rev. Mr. P—— was then preaching. His attention was so led to a consideration of the holiness of the Lord's day, and the sin of desecrating it, that immediately after service, with a frankness and promptitude which appeared to be characteristic of the man, he went to the counting-room of a French merchant with whom he had engaged to dine that day at his country-seat, and told him that he must be excused from dining with him. Upon being asked the reason, he unhesitatingly replied, that at church that day he had heard what had convinced him that it was wrong so to do, and although the invitation was again urged with great importunity, he steadily refused. The transaction, however, did not appear to make any lasting or saving impression on his mind.

Shortly after this he went to New York, and from thence to Boston. While there, walking one evening past where a number of persons were at the moment leaving a prayer-meeting, a lady handed to him a tract, and politely requested him to peruse it. He took it to his room, and read it. The title was, "*Quench not the Spirit.*" Its perusal made him solemn, awakened in him emotions to which he had hitherto been a stranger, and led him to commune thus with himself. "R——, how foolish and inconsistent has been your conduct. You have provided yourself with whatever is conducive to your comfort and convenience while travelling. You have around you all the appliances needful for the body. But what of the immortal soul? What have you done for its happiness and welfare? Nothing; nothing! You have not even a Bible in your trunk, to direct your soul to its Author and Preserver." Without delay he went to the nearest bookstore and purchased a copy of the word of God, and at once set about its perusal. The truths, the warnings, the invitations there found, only fastened the arrow of conviction more deeply in his wounded heart, and the effect was not lessened by a reperusal of the tract. The Spirit of the Lord had found him out, and was making known to him his sinfulness, the holiness of God's broken law, and his own inability to cleanse away the pollution within.

This state of mind continued for some days, and although compelled daily to mingle in business with those who could not sympathize with him, yet in the retirement of his room, and in deep communing with himself, he continued to have before him "a certain fearful looking for of judgment."

On the morning of the next, or the succeeding Sabbath, in deep agony of spirit, he wandered from his hotel without any settled purpose. He came in front of a church into which many persons were flocking, and he entered with them. The Rev. Mr. S——, of the Methodist church, addressed the audience from the words, "Quench not the Spirit," and powerfully unfolded the sin and danger of so doing. The words pierced the very soul of the stranger, and taught him more and more the total depravity of his heart, and his need of an all-sufficient Saviour to satisfy that holy law which he had fearfully broken. He returned to his room, and again engaged in earnest prayer, in reading the Scriptures, and in self-examination. I think he stated that it was on the succeeding Thursday evening when, having obtained no relief, he took the word of God, laid the sacred volume open upon a chair, and upon it the tract, and kneeling down, prayed for divine mercy with an earnestness which could not take a denial. Thus engaged, he continued upon his knees until nearly the dawn of day, when it pleased

HIM, with whom is boundless compassion, to speak peace to his soul, and enable him to rejoice in Jesus Christ our Lord.

"And now," said he, "my soul is filled with joy and peace, and I bless God that an unknown friend handed me that blessed tract, by which I have been led to Christ, and which I shall keep with me while life lasts;" saying this, he opened his vest, and we perceived that he had laid it next his heart. He repeatedly apologized for thus intruding upon our attention, but stated again, that being a stranger in the city, except to a few who were of Unitarian sentiments, he had had no one with whom he could hold converse on what was so dear to his heart, until meeting providentially with us.

It was a fitting sequel to this interesting event, upon visiting the tract depository in New York, a few weeks after, to purchase some copies of the above tract, that we heard the respected depositary observe that his stock of this tract had been lately greatly reduced, as one gentleman had purchased no less than six hundred copies for distribution in the West Indies; and upon inquiry we found that he was the warm-hearted brother whose story is here narrated.

G. T.

A PROFANE STUDENT.

At a time of general religious solemnity some years since, in ——, the students of the old and venerable college were blessed with one of those visitations of the Holy Spirit which are truly seasons of refreshing in Zion. Among them was a youth of fine talents and polished manners, eminently popular among the votaries of the world; but with such pleasing qualities he united a sad disregard of the teachings of the word of God, and the oath and biting sarcasm levelled against the consistent followers of Jesus often fell unrestrained from his lips. His mode of life, his sources of amusement, and especially his associates, were such as apparently to preclude the possibility of a change, and to render him least likely of all that numerous concourse of students to feel the power of religious truth.

Among the personal efforts made at that time by the professed disciples of Christ, it was not the will of Him who toucheth the hearts of men that L—— should be passed by. A sincere and deeply pious member of his own class called at his room one day, and finding him alone, entered into a faithful and earnest conversation with him on the value of his soul, and the necessity of immediate preparation for the eternal state. The interview was concluded with prayer, and the kind visitor departed. L—— was deeply enraged at this "unwarrantable intrusion," as he deemed it; and in the bitterness of his malignity, upon entering the room of a fellow-student and narrating the occurrence, he deliberately cursed the friend who had sought to point him to the Lamb of God.

But the arrow of conviction had accompanied the word of truth, and in the silent chambers of his heart the upbraidings of conscience were not easily to be appeased; and having to prepare a rhetorical exercise on the following day, the mind of L—— was directed, providentially it would seem, to that shortest verse in the Bible, which is, nevertheless, so expressive of the divine sympathy for our fallen mortal race—"Jesus wept." His ignorance of the word of God forced him to apply to a pious student to find the verse; but his mind had scarcely began to dwell upon its touching theme and the sacred scenes of the Redeemer's mission, when he burst into a flood of tears. The arrow of conviction had pierced his heart. The recollection of his contempt of God evinced in his treatment of the kind friend who sought his highest good, filled him with remorse; while a deep sense of the wondrous love of Him who not only wept over our sin and sorrow, but died to secure us mansions of immortal joy, pervaded his soul. The enormity of his transgressions rose in terrible array before him, and the strong-minded seeker of pleasure, the despiser of truth and righteousness, was bowed in sorrow for sin.

The stated prayer-meeting of the few who loved God in that institution came round, and one, hitherto a stranger to its very being, was seen wending his way towards the place "where prayer was wont to be made;" and when the words of supplication and the notes of praise had ascended on high, he who had been so prominent in ungodliness arose and declared his purpose of leading a new and holy life. None who were present at that prayer-meeting will ever forget the scene. Louder than before swelled the song of praise and thanksgiving for the "lost" that was "found," for the "dead in trespasses and sins," whom the all-pitying Jesus had called to life.

And may not some who read this paper realize for the first time, that "Jesus wept" for man? Let them, like L——, receive in the inmost recesses of their hearts this blessed truth, and joy shall fill the angelic hosts at the spectacle of another sinner turning unto God.

And, Christian disciple, who art mildly, yet perseveringly bearing the all-important message to those who know not its value, care not though reproof and contumely fall to thy lot. Even when thou art despairing, the providence of God may be impressing some stubborn heart. He will not suffer thy faithful labors to fail of a glorious reward. L. V. R.

AN INFIDEL STUDENT.

In the year 18—, a young man from the South entered a New England college. He was the child of infidel parents. The influences of home had all been adverse to the religion of Christ. He went to college quite young, and was a frivolous, inconsiderate youth. He had no religious or moral principle to guide him, and to seek his own present pleasure was his only object in life. He was quick and passionate in his disposition, easily taking offence, and not hesitating to resort to a challenge to mortal combat, as the proper method of settling the difficulties of a ball-room.

In becoming a member of a puritanic New England college, he found himself in a new world. He attended prayers regularly, because it was required by the laws of college; but when he stood up in that consecrated chapel, and heard the venerable president address an invisible Being, he said to himself, "What folly! There is no God to listen to this prayer." He said in his heart, "There is no God."

As one looked over that assembly, no one among those hundreds of young men seemed in so hopeless a case as that young infidel. But God had said of him, "He is a chosen vessel unto me, to bear my name before the Gentiles, and kings, and children of Israel." He was affected by the Christian influences about him. The Spirit of God touched and softened his heart. He began to ask himself, "Am I mistaken? Is it possible that there is a God?" The president of the college took much interest in him, and gave him, in private, such instruction as he thought would benefit him.

One evening the president talked with him very earnestly and affectionately. He talked long and faithfully, and when —— left him, he said to him, "When you return to your room, you will find it occupied by gay young men; and if you go in and join them in their amusements, all these impressions will be effaced from your mind: but do not go there; go away alone, and pray earnestly that God will enlighten and teach you." He left the president and went to his room; but did he enter it? No. He heard the loud laugh of his companions, and he remembered the words of the president. He went away alone, and perhaps for the first time in his life, he communed with his Maker.

He told me that he distinctly remembered the moment when the truth of the existence of a God was first impressed upon his mind. He was in the chapel at college-prayers, and when the president rose to pray, his old disbelief passed away, and he felt that there was a God. He could truly say, "Lord, I believe; help thou mine unbelief." He could hardly restrain his emotions during the service, and as soon as the prayer was closed, he seized the arm of a pious young man, saying, "Do you believe in a God?" He wondered that, if the Christian young men about him did believe, they did not manifest the excitement and deep feeling which he experienced at that moment. A light had suddenly shined into his soul from heaven, and like Paul, he trembled and was astonished.

During the last two years of his college life, he associated but little with his former companions. He roomed alone, and spent a portion of each day in the study of the Bible and prayer. He was greatly changed in his external character.

When he left college, the Holy Spirit accompanied him. He placed himself under the influence of a Christian minister and Christian friends, and he made his Bible his constant study. He became a pupil, and afterwards a teacher in the Sabbath-school. At length he ventured to hope that he had been brought out of nature's darkness into God's marvellous light. He entered a theological seminary, and having completed his course of study, he returned to the scene of his college life, and performed divine service upon the Sabbath.

He commenced the exercises of the day by reading that beautiful hymn by John Newton, commencing,

> "Mercy, O thou Son of David!
> Thus blind Bartimeus prayed—"

And among the children of God who had known him while in college, not a tearless eye, I am sure, could have been found in that house. His text was, "Except a man be born again, he cannot see the kingdom of God;" and truly the hearts of those listeners "burned within them," as they heard the evidence which he so strikingly gave, that he had become a new creature in Christ Jesus.

I never felt more humbled and reproved than by this living epistle. When —— left college, I might have been his teacher. I was more familiar than he with the words and the doctrines of the Bible; but he returned as my teacher, and I found, with surprise, what a change those few years had wrought in him; how diligent he had been, how much he had learned, how familiar he had become with the word of God, and with all its teachings.

And now this young man is a missionary of the cross, the Rev. E. J. P——, in a dark and benighted part of the world.

"DO LET ME ALONE."

Mr. T. S—— resided near the western shore of Lake Champlain. As a husband and father he was kind and affectionate, but the whole subject of religion he treated with neglect. His wife, two daughters, and a son were devoted Christians. He never opposed them in any of their religious views or duties, but seemed ready to assist them whenever they wished to attend a religious meeting, either on the Sabbath or during the week; and yet, for more than twenty years, he did not attend a religious meeting of any description.

Being called to the pastoral care of the congregation, in 1828, I could get no opportunity, for more than a year, to converse with him on the interests of his soul; nor would he allow any of his family to converse with him on the subject. He would say to them, "If you wish peace in the family, if you wish unmolestedly to enjoy the privileges of your religion, you must be quiet towards me, and let me and my belief alone." I thought him a troubled man, by no means at ease in his spirit; but whenever I entered his house, he was sure to leave before I could converse with him.

At one of my Wednesday evening meetings, some one of the family informed me that he was to start the next morning for a short journey. I had before arranged to go that morning into his neighborhood for pastoral visitation; and as I came in sight of his house, which was about forty rods from the road, knowing that he had not seen me, I dropped at his gate the tract, "Danger of Delay," and passed on, still unobserved, when I felt inclined to pause and see how he would treat the little message I had laid in his way. When he came to the gate, he took it up, looked about him, and seating himself upon a rock, commenced reading. I soon observed him wipe his eyes; and when he had read it through, he held his handkerchief to his face for some time, and then arose, returned to his house, and relinquished his journey.

The scene took such hold on my feelings that, after making a few visits, I returned and called at his house. On inquiring for him, I learned from his weeping wife that the tract had so alarmed him, that he dared not go on his journey; and that he had fastened himself in his stable, and refused admittance to any one. I went to the stable; but in agony, and with an emphasis which I can never forget, he begged me, if I did not wish to increase his misery in hell, not to talk to him on religion, or even pray for him; "for," said he, "I am sure of damnation; for me, who have so long rebelled, and who have so wilfully slighted such infinite mercy, there can be no hope." I tried to convince him that God was willing to be gracious even to him, however great were his sins. But his constant and agonizing cry was, "Do let me alone; there is no hope for me." I left him, and returned to the family, whom I found all engaged in prayer for their distressed husband and father. After uniting with them in a season of prayer, I returned home; calling on one of my deacons, and requesting his family to spend the evening in joining their prayers with those of the family of Mr. S—— and mine, for that poor awakened man.

On Friday afternoon I called again, and found him still in his stable, and in as deep agony as when I left him the day before. He still begged me not to talk with him, or even to pray for him, lest it increase his condemnation in the coming world. After praying with the family, I again returned home, but never felt a heavier burden on my heart. On Saturday morning I again called, and still found him in his stable, having utterly refused to converse with his family, or to receive any food.

I went to the stable, and said to him, "Mr. S——, are you determined to increase the long catalogue of your sins by self-murder?" He replied, "Mr. B——, how can you think that of me? No, no, I will not add that sin to the dark catalogue." "But," said I, "you are doing it as surely as though you were to cut your throat; for you can no more live without food, than you can without blood. The best thing that you can do is to come out of your concealment, and act like a rational man."

He finally came out, and after taking some refreshment, seemed more calm. I conversed with him; and after praying with him, I told him that it would be better to attend meeting the following day, than to stay away, even were he finally lost; for then the sin of turning away from the sanctuary and the means of grace would not rest upon his soul. He promised me that if able he would attend; and he did. And as he entered our large school-house, every Christian seemed to drop the head as though in silent prayer.

On that morning I preached from the words, "Come unto me, all ye that labor and are heavy-laden, and I will give you rest." Near the close I proposed the inquiry, "Who of you will come to Christ? *He* is *ready*, he *waits*, he *calls*, yes, he *urges you*, poor *sinking*, *burdened*, and *dying* sinner, to come to him and find *rest*, and *peace*, and *joy*, and eternal salvation. Will you come; and come now?" Persons who sat by him afterwards informed me that they heard him distinctly say, "Yes, I will come, and I will come now."

He soon after made a public profession of religion; and in relating his experience, he remarked that when he felt the resolve in his heart to yield to Christ, the removal of his burden was so sudden, and his joy was so great, that he could hardly refrain from shouting, "Glory to God," for so wonderful a display of the riches of grace. A deeper sense of guilt, or a more exalted view of the power and grace of God, than he expressed, I never witnessed. His family altar burned morning and evening, he was punctual at the prayer-meeting, and was one of our most consistent, active, energetic, and devoted Christians. Thus he continued to live for many years, when he died in the triumphs of faith, and went to join the church triumphant in the song of redeeming grace and dying love. O. B.

A DARING OPPOSER IN PENNSYLVANIA.

Never had such a revival of religion been witnessed in all that region of country, as was enjoyed in —— valley, Eastern Pennsylvania, in the years 1832 and '33. It extended many miles in various directions, and hundreds were brought under its blessed influence, and made savingly acquainted with the Lord Jesus. The now large and flourishing churches in the boroughs of N—— and W—— C—— were planted as a part of that gracious work.

The enemy of all righteousness was not inactive while these inroads were made upon his kingdom. He aroused the enmity of the human heart, and much and bitter opposition was arrayed against the power and the progress of the gospel. Bands of men, young and old, were formed to strengthen each other in resisting the truth; military parades, parties of pleasure, balls, and various other means of dissipation were arranged to occupy the attention of the young, as the ranks of the enemy were thinned by the triumphs of the cross.

Foremost in reckless daring, among the number of those who arrayed themselves against the work of the

Lord, was F——, a young man whose social position gave him an extensive influence.

One after another of his most intimate friends and companions had forsaken him and his associates, and had united with the church. This irritated him, and led him to indulge in a series of petty persecutions; urged on and supported by older men, he sought by every means to cast contempt upon the cause of Christ, and especially upon his ministers. It was no unusual thing for him to visit the house of God on the Sabbath, hear with undivided attention the preached word, and after his return home, gather his associates together, and in mockery repeat the sermon and engage in prayer.

He was known many miles around for his opposition to the truth; and there was an almost universal desire among Christians, that God might convert him, as he did the persecuting Saul, and make him a herald of salvation. We have good reasons for believing that much prayer was offered to God on his behalf, and that very many who had never seen him united in these supplications for the divine mercy.

He for whom they supplicated was not without his "convictions for sin," although none suspected it. More than once, after having boldly declaimed against religion and religious people, did he retire to a solitary place, and there, trembling with fear, beseech God to pardon his great wickedness; and yet he would return again to the commission of the same sins. Thus months passed on, and F—— was still "breathing out threatenings" in "great swelling words;" and still the people of God were earnestly pleading that God would "stop him in his mad career," and make him a "trophy of his victorious grace."

Upon one occasion he was induced to accompany some young friends to a small school-house, situated in a retired spot among the G—— hills. In this obscure and lowly spot the power of God had been signally displayed. Scores of the inhabitants had been converted, and that humble school-house had been made "the house of God and the gate of heaven" to many a weary and heavy-laden sinner. At this time the work was moving forward with power, the house was crowded with eager hearers to its utmost capacity, every window was full, and rows of men were standing on the writing benches arranged around the walls of the house. F—— was one of the latter number; the sermon had closed, and no impression had been made on his mind. Before offering the closing prayer, the minister stated to the congregation that on entering his study the day previous, he had found upon his table a note signed, "A female friend," requesting the special prayers of the church on behalf of a certain young man, whose case she described. Every one knew who was meant, and so did F——, and the announcement was an arrow from the quiver of the Almighty to his hardened heart. Chills crept over his frame, his knees trembled and smote together. During the time that prayer was offered for him, he wished he were out of the house, but he had no power to move; he was overwhelmed with shame and confusion of face; his sins rose before him like a mighty cloud, and his guilt in the sight of God weighed heavily on his spirit.

At the close of the meeting he returned home in

an agony of soul; what to do he knew not; he sighed and groaned in the deepest anguish; he vowed and prayed; he would have wept, but could not; he resolved to seek the salvation of his soul, or perish in the attempt; and many sorrowful days and gloomy nights passed before he was brought to submit himself to Christ as a poor lost sinner, and to accept salvation as the gift of God, "without money and without price." It was with great difficulty that he could realize that there was mercy for one who had sinned against so much light and knowledge, and had so long resisted the "riches of grace," and despised the "goodness of God."

But at length with the apostle he could say, "It is a faithful saying, and worthy of all acceptation, that Christ Jesus came into the world to save sinners; of whom *I am chief.*" Light broke by degrees into his darkened mind; the clouds were dispersed, and every thing within and around him was rejoicing; the rigor of midwinter was relaxed, all nature smiled, "the trees of the field clapped their hands," and "December was as pleasant as May." Great was the rejoicing when it was reported of him, "Behold, he prayeth," and many a thanksgiving ascended to God for what his grace had wrought.

In the course of time he entered the Christian ministry, and for many years he was found laboring to build up the cause he once sought to pull down, and hundreds through his ministry have been brought to the knowledge of the truth as it is in Jesus. For several years F—— made earnest inquiry to learn who the "female friend" was that had presented him as the subject of special prayer; but all his efforts were unavailing. In eternity he will doubtless meet her, and unite with her and with all the redeemed in praising God for making him a "trophy of grace" in answer to special prayer.

Reader, united prayer "moves the hand that moves the world;" ask, and ye shall receive. Davies.

A DEAF MUTE.

During a revival of religion in one of our New England villages, a son of the clergyman returned home for a brief visit. The lad was a deaf mute, and had spent his first term in the asylum just then commencing its history. His parents having no knowledge of the language of signs, and the boy being an imperfect writer, it was almost impossible to interchange with him any but the most familiar ideas. He therefore heard nothing of the revival.

But before he had been many days at home he began to manifest signs of anxiety, and at length wrote with much labor upon his slate, "*Father, what must I do to be saved?*" His father wrote in reply, "My son, you must repent of sin, and believe in the Lord Jesus Christ." "How must I do this?" asked the boy again, upon the slate. The father explained to him as well as he could, but the poor untaught boy could not understand. He became more than ever distressed; he would leave the house in the morning for some retired place, and be seen no more until the father went in search of him. One evening at sunset, the boy was found upon the top of the hay, under the roof of the barn, on his knees, his hands uplifted, and praying to God in the signs of the mutes. The distress of the parents became intense. They sent for one of the teachers of the asylum, and then for another, but it seemed that the boy could not be guided to the Saviour of sinners. There were enough to care for his soul, but there were none to instruct him.

Days passed—days of parental fear and agony. One afternoon the father was on his way to fulfil an engagement in a neighboring town, and as he drove leisurely over the hills the poor inquiring and hopeless son was continually in his thoughts. In the midst of his supplications his heart became calm, and the long distracted spirit was serene in the one thought that God is able to do his own work. The speechless boy at length began to tell how he loved his Saviour, and stated that he first found peace on the very afternoon when the spirit of his agonized father on the mountains was calmed and supported by the thought, that what God had promised he was able to perform.

The converted mute became an instructor of others, and every Sabbath-day found him in one of our large cities, with a gathered congregation of fellow-mutes, breaking to them the bread of life, and guiding their attentive souls to that God who has power to do his own work. C.

AN INDIAN'S GIFT TO CHRIST.

In a portion of the southern territory from which the red man has now been driven, I once attended a large protracted meeting held in the wild forest. The theme on which the preacher dwelt, and which he illustrated with surpassing beauty and grandeur, was "Christ and him crucified." He spoke of the good

Shepherd who came into the world to seek and to save the lost. He told how this Saviour met the rude buffetings of the heartless soldiers. He drew a picture of Gethsemane, and the unbefriended Stranger who wept there. He pointed to him as he hung bleeding upon the cross.

The congregation wept. Soon there was a slight movement in the assembly, and a tall son of the forest, with tears on his red cheeks, approached the pulpit, and said, "Did Jesus die for me—die for poor Indian? Me have no lands to give to Jesus, the white man take them away; me give him my dog, and my rifle." The minister told him Jesus could not accept those gifts. "Me give Jesus my dog, my rifle, and my blanket; poor Indian, he got no more to give—he give Jesus all." The minister replied that Christ could not accept them. The poor, ignorant, but generous child of the forest bent his head in sorrow and meditated. He raised his noble brow once more, and fixed his eye on the preacher, while he sobbed out, "*Here is poor Indian, will Jesus have him?*" A thrill of unutterable joy ran through the souls of minister and people as this fierce son of the wilderness now sat, in his right mind, at the feet of Jesus. The Spirit had done his work, and he who had been so poor, received the earnest of an inheritance which will not fade when the diadems of earth shall have mouldered for ever.

J. S. G.

THE BIRD IN THE CHURCH.

The town of E—— is embowered in trees. Its ancient and spacious church, with its chiming clock and towering steeple of beautiful proportions, although in the centre of the town, is yet in the centre of forest-trees, which nearly conceal it from view; and what is more, it is the centre and home of the affections of a people whose ancestors for nearly two hundred years have there worshipped God in spirit and in truth.

And that ancient church is associated with many and wonderful displays of sovereign grace. It has been the birthplace of souls, the house of God, and the gate of heaven to multitudes. Under its ample roof thousands have consecrated themselves to God, and amid the ordinances there dispensed, have ripened for glory.

In the year 18—, the people of E—— were favored with perhaps the most signal work of grace they ever enjoyed. The whole community was moved to its deep foundations, and persons of all ages and classes were in the pursuit of salvation as the great end of their being. Many, the blessed fruits of that revival, continue until the present day.

On a Sabbath of that year of unusual brilliancy, in the late spring, that church was crowded with multitudes anxious about their souls, and hanging upon the lips of their beloved pastor, who with earnestness and tears was expounding to them the way of reconciliation with God. Every thing in the external world—the balmy and reviving breezes—the new and beautiful dress which fields and forests were putting on—the trees budding or in blossom—the blossoms setting in fruit, were in sympathy with the feelings of this worshipping people, and were but emblems of the spiritual transformations which were in progress among them.

On this Sabbath the doors of the church were open, and the windows were all closed. During the progress of the service a bird entered by the door and flew up to the vaulted roof, and alarmed by the voices which it heard, gave every evidence of anxiety to make its escape. There sat in one of the pews a female under deep conviction for sin, and who for months had been seeking without finding peace for her soul. Her eye soon lit upon the fluttering bird, and followed him from window to window, in his vain

efforts to escape. It sought an exit at every window, and almost at every pane of glass; and as it fluttered from one window to another, this female would say in her heart, "O foolish bird, why strive to get out there; is not the door wide open?" It would now rise to the ceiling—now renew its vain attempts at the vindows; this female repeating to herself, "O foolish bird, why strive to get out there; is not the door wide open?" And when its wings were weary, and when all hope of escape seemed to be abandoned, and as if unable to sustain itself longer, it lowered itself into the body of the church, caught a view of the door, and was out in a moment, singing a song of triumph over its release, amid the branches of the trees.

When the bird was gone, the thoughts of this female reverted to her own state and doings. The voice of the preacher was unheard amid the conflicts of her own thoughts. "I have been acting," said she, "like that foolish bird. I have been seeking peace in ways in which it is not to be found, and to go out from the bondage of sin through doors that are closed against me. Christ is the door; through him there is escape from the dominion of sin. I have acted like that foolish bird long enough. What the door was to it, Christ is to me. As it escaped through the door, so may I through Christ." And she found peace in believing. And almost as soon as the bird commenced its melody in the trees, rejoicing over its escape, she commenced making melody in her heart unto the Lord.

Years passed away, and her peace flowed like a river whose gentle stream is never excited into a ruffle. Subsequently she had her periods of occasional depression, but without ever forgetting that Christ is the door. Threescore years and ten passed away, and amid the infirmities of age Christ was yet precious as the door. She has put off her earthly tabernacle; and from the day that she saw that bird in the church, until the day that she passed in, through Christ the door, to the spirits of the just made perfect, she never gave ground for a reasonable doubt that Christ was in her the hope of glory.

How infinitely diversified are the ways and instrumentalities by which sinners are led to be reconciled to God. "The wind bloweth where it listeth, and thou hearest the sound thereof, but canst not tell whence it cometh, or whither it goeth; so is every one that is born of the Spirit."

And how truthful the application of the folly of that bird, by that female, to her own case. And is not its folly the folly of every sinner? The first right feeling of a sinner returning from the error of his ways, is a sense of his deep sinfulness in the sight of God. If this feeling is never felt, then, in ordinary cases, there is no return to God—we must die aliens to God, and continue outcasts from the light of the universe for ever. But when the Spirit convinces and convicts of sin, how often is deliverance sought from it in the ways that the bird vainly sought to escape from the church. The sinner flees to every thing that gives hope of deliverance but to the right thing. The Bible is read—prayer is made—sin is abstained from—the worship of God is frequented—the advice of Christian people is sought; but there is no escape from the dominion of sin—none from a sense of guilt, nor from the fear which it inspires. All these are but as the windows to the bird, which gave it hope that it might escape through them because they admitted the light. When it failed at one, it flew to another; each window in its turn excited hope, and in every case the hope excited was dashed by the trial to escape. When all is done, the weight of sin yet hangs upon the soul. And the reason is, there is yet no recourse to the remedy for sin, to the door of escape from its power and guilt. CHRIST is that remedy. Christ is that door. And so prone are men to do something to save themselves, that until all they can do is tried in vain, they will not look unto "the Lamb of God, that taketh away the sin of the world."

The great central truths of Christianity, so far as men are concerned, are these: we are sinners—Christ Jesus has died to atone to law and justice for the sins of sinners, and whosoever believes on the Lord Jesus Christ shall be saved. Reader, do you hope you are a Christian? If so, you know all this by experience. Never cease telling these truths to all men as you have opportunity. Are you a sinner convicted of your sin, and seeking deliverance from it? Then imitate not the bird which sought an exit through the closed windows, to the forgetfulness of the open door. Waste not your time, and spend not your strength for naught in seeking relief at sources that never can yield it. Go at once to Christ; ponder this one truth, until it is written in letters of living light upon your soul, "He that believeth on the Lord Jesus Christ shall be saved." Faith in Jesus Christ will save you; nothing else can.

N. M.

THE SEA-CAPTAIN.

Captain T—— was a noble specimen of the American sailor. Independent in thought and action, well skilled in his profession, combining gentleness in manner with firmness in action, a better officer never walked the quarter-deck. Frank and open-hearted, his social qualities gave him a ready welcome into every family in the neighborhood where he resided; and his influence over a large circle of friends was almost unlimited. Possessing an inquiring mind, he read on all subjects, and was particularly fond of argument and debate.

In the winter of the year 18—, Captain T—— was providentially at home, employing his leisure time in the study of elocution, preparatory to the public debates before a literary society of which he was a prominent member.

It was a season of peculiar interest in the church. After a long period of coldness and apathy, God visited them with the rich outpourings of his Spirit, and the church was humbled and revived; the word of God, preached in great plainness and simplicity, was "in demonstration of the Spirit, and of power." Sinners on the right and on the left were, with sobs and tears, asking, "What must we do to be saved?" The wife of the captain was among the first of those who passed into the kingdom of God, and were enabled to rejoice in a "good hope through grace." Hitherto she had come alone to church, but now it was perceived that about the hour for preaching the husband would enter the house of the Lord, quietly find a seat in a corner of the room, and give undivided attention to the messenger of God. None knew the exercises of his mind, and we were afraid to approach him upon the subject of personal piety, knowing his fondness for debate, and fearing it might lead to an unprofitable discussion. Great anxiety was felt by the awakened church on his behalf, and many fervent prayers were offered to God for his conversion. As the revival widened and deepened, the captain attended the morning service as well as the evening; and the hearts of Christians were cheered with the hope that God was truly drawing him "with cords of a man, with bands of love."

At the close of one of the morning services, as the minister descended from the desk, Capt. T—— came up the aisle and met him, evidently inviting conversation. The offer was not slighted, and a most interesting conversation ensued. There was no desire for argument or debate, but as a learner he desired to know the truth. He frankly confessed that he was deeply concerned about the salvation of his soul, but had difficulties in his mind arising from mistaken views of the plan of salvation; he could not feel the "terrors of the law," which he had heard others describe, and which he supposed he must of necessity feel, before he could "find peace in believing;" he could with truth say that his sins gave him pain and anguish of mind, but his distress was in consequence of his guilt in having abused the mercy of God, and despised his love in giving his only begotten Son to die for such a sinner as he felt himself to be. The goodness of God had followed him all the days of his life, while he had done naught but sin against Him: the remembrance of these things overwhelmed him with shame and confusion of face. What must I do to be saved? was now his earnest inquiry. With tears of gratitude the servant of God taught him the "way of the Lord more perfectly," directing the trembling sailor's attention away from himself, a guilty creature, away from every earthly help, away from the works of the law—leading his wandering eye to the cross of Christ, and to his atoning sacrifice; the fulness of Christ was presented to him, and the efficacy of his blood; the sovereignty and freeness of grace were shown, and he was directed to lift up the trembling eye of faith, to look and live, to believe and be saved.

In the evening the inquirer was found again in the temple of God, but under what different circumstances! *Then* he was wretched, *now* he was unspeakably happy; peace had come in like a river, and he could rejoice in hope of the glory of God. In the spirit of a little child he was seeking direction in the path of duty, desirous only to consecrate himself, body, soul, and spirit, to the service of his divine Master, and to promote the glory of Him who had saved him by his grace.

"When the meeting commenced," said the captain, "I resolved to attend every night, not that I might be spiritually profited, but in the hope of receiving some instruction in elocution from the delivery and gestures of the visiting minister; I was delighted the first evening, as I felt assured that the speaker had studied my favorite author, and that I now should have the benefit of a living model for my imitation. The next evening I was at times so much interested in the subject of discourse, as to forget the manner of the preacher; and on the subsequent evenings I lost sight of what first brought me to the house of God, in the interest I felt in the truth which was preached. I felt very uneasy; I quarrelled with myself; I lost my own esteem; my vile ingratitude to God rose up before me, and I was self-condemned. I was now under instruction, not in elocution, but in things of a higher and holier nature, 'the mystery of grace;' the law of God was now my schoolmaster to lead me to Christ. The 'motions' of the preacher did not now interest me; but 'the *motions of sins* which were by the law, did work in my members,' and the Spirit of God convinced me of sin, of righteousness, and of judgment. I bowed my knees in prayer to God, for the first time in many years. I called upon him to have mercy upon a guilty creature; but no relief could I obtain, until to-day, while the minister was unfolding the way of salvation through faith in a once crucified, but now risen Saviour, I was enabled to exercise faith on him. My burden of guilt was removed, the storm within my soul was calmed, my fears subsided, and I was unspeakably happy in the love of God."

When the inquirers were invited to meet the ministers and deacons for instruction, the first to rise from his place was Captain T——, who walked deliberately from the rear of the house, and with a face glowing with peace and joy, took a seat near the pulpit. A thrill went through the house, as mysterious as the electric influence; tears filled nearly every eye, while thanksgiving to God went up from every pious heart. The influence of his decision was felt on every side. Many, very many men and women followed his example, were found as humble penitents sitting at the feet of Jesus, and afterwards "witnessed a good confession before many witnesses."

Captain T—— was eminently useful. Wherever he went, he carried the gospel of peace. His ship was a Bethel; many a desponding heart did he comfort by his counsels and his prayers, and many a proud caviller was silenced by his arguments, enforced by the power of a consistent life.

This narrative illustrates two points:

1. The importance of being found in the house of God, under the influence of the means of grace. Multitudes have come to the sanctuary with no higher motive than did the subject of the above sketch, but who, "being in the way," were made to realize that the "word of God is quick and powerful."

2. Christians should not regard the case of any one as hopeless, nor cease to labor for their salvation. The Spirit of God can soften the hardest heart, can subdue the most stubborn will. Many apparently thoughtless persons feel more on the subject of religion than they are willing to confess. We should follow them with our prayers, and in "due season we shall reap, if we faint not." Davies.

THE LAST RESOLVE.

It was a cold, raw evening in March, when the Rev. Mr. B—— had just returned from visiting some of his parishioners, and was gathering around him his little family for evening worship, that a loud ring was heard at the door, and a young man was shown into the parlor. Wishing to see Mr. B—— alone, they retired together to his study. He soon returned, saying he had been sent for to see Sarah J——, a member of his congregation, who had for a long time been anxious about her soul, and now desired to converse with him.

He left the house with the messenger, and a walk of a few moments brought them to her door. Inquiring where he should find Sarah, he was told by her father that she was in the library alone. Mr. B—— quickly found her, seated on the sofa, her face buried in her hands, and apparently unconscious of every thing around her. He was silent a few moments, hoping that she would open the conversation; but finding that she remained silent, he said, "Jesus Christ came into the world to save sinners." "I came not to call the righteous, but sinners to repentance."

She started up suddenly, and fixing her eyes upon him, said, "Mr. B——, I have not sent for you to mock my misery, but to tell you of my *last resolve.* I have been wretched for more than a year and now, at all hazards, I shall banish the subject of religion from my mind. I wish you to promise me that you will never again speak to me on the subject, for it will do no good, and will only increase my misery."

"It is asking a great deal, Sarah, of one whose mission it is to preach the glad tidings of salvation to *every* sinner, to keep silent when he sees one in such a state as you are. It is asking too much; and I cannot, either as a minister or a Christian, make such a promise. But may I ask what has caused this change in your feelings since I saw you last? I have thought you seemed almost persuaded to be a Christian."

"Yes," she answered, "I did feel so then; but now God has forsaken me. I am left to myself, and the only thing for me is to forget the past, and seek my pleasure in the world!"

"But, Sarah, you *cannot* forget the danger of your immortal soul. You cannot forget that you must soon appear before God, and answer for the manner in which you now treat the offer of his grace. You cannot, you *must not* forget that the Saviour has died for you; and will you not *now* accept the proffered gift of life?"

"No," she said hastily; "I did not send for you to argue with me. I only wished to tell you of my decision, and that you need trouble yourself no further about me."

"Certainly I shall not insist upon conversing with you against your wishes; but before I leave you, let me urge you to consider well what you call your *last resolve*, and ask yourself if you think it will be satisfactory to you when on a dying-bed, or at the judgment-day. Still there is hope for you. 'Now is the accepted time, now is the day of salvation.'" Mr. B—— paused, hoping she would make some reply; but finding she remained unmoved, he said, "Sarah, shall I pray with you?"

"No," she said, coldly; and seeing he could do nothing more for her, he bade her good-evening, and left the house.

Long and earnestly that night did the man of God pray for the renewal of that obstinate heart, and when he retired to rest, it was with a weight upon his heart which every pastor, yes, every Christian, must sometimes feel. The next day he heard nothing from Sarah, and thinking that after what had passed his presence might only increase her opposition, he refrained from calling upon her. In the evening there was public service, and as he entered he was surprised to see Sarah in her accustomed seat. Before dismissing the congregation, he requested any who desired to converse with him to remain after the services were closed.

Much to his astonishment, Sarah remained. Extending her hand to him, she said, "Last evening, Mr. B——, I told you of *one* resolve I had made. I hope I have been brought to a very different one. I can think of nothing but my own dreadfully wicked heart. I feel that I must be a Christian. Mr. B——, do tell me how I can find my Saviour?"

Gladly did her pastor point her to "the Lamb of God, who taketh away the sin of the world," and eagerly did she listen to the gracious promises and invitations of the Saviour; and with her eye filled with tears, and yet her countenance beaming with holy joy, she exclaimed, "Lord, I believe; help thou mine unbelief." Her subsequent life gave evidence that she had indeed found "the pearl of great price."

"*I must be a Christian!*" This was Sarah's last resolve. Shall it not be yours also? S.

POOR WILLIAM.

The grace of God is displayed no less in the depths of poverty and ignorance to which it descends, than in the higher walks of life of which it forms the brightest ornament. This truth has a pleasing illustration in the following narrative of poor William, whom the writer well knew, and who was born in ——, Conn., about the year 1740.

He was lame and deformed, and could never stand upright or walk unless supported by two staves. His parents were poor; he had not strength of limb to use the implements of husbandry; his speech was so indistinct as scarcely to be understood by strangers; and his mind and memory were so weak that all efforts to teach him to read seemed to be unavailing. His condition was also apparently rendered more hopeless by the fact that, in the inability of his parents to support so helpless a child, he was early separated from them by the authorities of the town; but he was happily placed in a religious and worthy family.

Here he early discovered uncommon depravity. He was cross, intractable, mischievous, perverse. He seemed almost destitute of reflection or consciousness of right and wrong; he gave way to an uncontrolled appetite, whether for food or strong drink; and often used the most profane, obscene, and opprobrious language, and thus exhibited without restraint, and in its most fearful aspects, the native depravity of the human heart. He gave no indications of religious influence on his mind, or any just apprehension of God or the future world, and could be controlled only by the fear of corporeal punishment.

Young children, who were weaker than himself, it was his pleasure to annoy by running after them as he could with his two staves and bent body, or throwing sticks or stones at them, so that he became the terror of the neighborhood. Few human beings, probably, have had less in them that was attractive or hopeful as to the present or the future world. Thus poor William continued till near middle life, loving no one, beloved by no one, deformed in soul and body, and verifying the appalling description of the apostle, "hateful and hating one another."

"Can the Ethiopian change his skin, or the leopard his spots?" "Then may they also do good who are accustomed to do evil;" and by the power of superabounding grace, vile, degraded William may yet "shine above the brightness of the firmament, and as the stars for ever and ever."

A little before the war of the Revolution, when the state of religion throughout the country was generally low, the presence of the Spirit was enjoyed by the people among whom William dwelt; many promising young people were brought to Christ, and in the fervor of their love and joy they sometimes, between the public exercises of the Sabbath in summer, gathered under the shadow of a tree near the house of God, where they conversed, read, and sung hymns of praise. One day poor William, who it seems often attended the sanctuary, strolled in among them, and whether by what he saw, or by any special warnings addressed to him, is unknown, but the Holy Spirit there reached his heart, arousing his conscience, alarming him on account of his sins, and drawing his attention to the concerns of his soul.

Now his feeble mind, which had been unstable as water, and never before was known to be permanently affected by any thing that did not appeal directly to his senses, became fixed on the subject of his salvation and preparation to meet his final Judge. He was terrified at the view of his dark and hopeless condition as a sinner, and earnestly implored instruction; nor was he satisfied with any thing until Christ, the great atoning sacrifice for sin, the "one Mediator between God and man," was clearly set before him. His pastor spared no pains to pour the simplest gospel truths into his dark mind; and most evidently the

Holy Spirit gave peace to his soul through faith in a crucified Redeemer.

From that time no profane or irreverent language escaped his lips; he was no longer perverse and mischievous; he was now easily controlled in respect to the evil habits he had formed, and became submissive and gentle as a child. He feared and loved God. Nothing delighted him more than to hear Christians talk of Christ, the riches of his mercy, and all he has done to save lost men. His wild countenance assumed a milder aspect; his temper became peaceful and happy, and little children flocked to him and delighted in him as a companion in their harmless sports. The transformation was observed by the older and more discerning with astonishment, for they saw in him marked evidence that he had indeed become a "new creature in Christ Jesus."

It was at first doubted by some whether one so weak in mind should be received into the church; but he professed his faith in receiving baptism, and was admitted to full communion. He showed a peculiar love to the people of God; and when he learned that others were seriously inclined, would visit them, and inquire after their state with a simplicity and seriousness often truly affecting. His faithful pastor was especially endeared to him. Hearing of the good man's death, William, though then many miles distant, hastened to attend the funeral, saying to the mourning son of the deceased whom he met at the door, "They tell Mr. S—— dead; I be glad on 't;" that is, he rejoiced that he had "kept the faith," "finished his course," and gone to receive the "crown of righteousness reserved for him against *that day*."

William's Christian walk was generally consistent. In a few instances he was known to exhibit a wrong temper, but his sorrow for it was most sincere. On one occasion, before the present principles of total abstinence from intoxicating liquor prevailed, a designing young man, being alone with him, gave him a sweet mixed liquor, by which he was intoxicated. When he came to himself, and knew what had been done, he cried and wept bitterly, and gave the most satisfactory evidence of true repentance before God and man.

Generally he was happy in the enjoyment of God and the anticipation of heaven. Sometimes he was clouded with fears and temptation; but he would say, "The devil comes, picks me all to pieces—I cry—pray hard to my blessed Master—and the devil then goes away." Thus William pursued his course till the Master called him to sit down in his kingdom.

Can the deniers of the Bible and of the truths distinguished as *evangelical* produce, in all their annals, such an example of moral elevation as was effected in poor William? Did Deism or Universalism ever work such a change? Such results are effected only by the word and Spirit of God.

Is the reader, with all his superior advantages, living "without hope and without God in the world?" Let not poor William stand in the judgment a witness against you. "Christ" must be formed "in you the hope of glory," or to the heaven where poor William's stammering tongue now lifts the song of praise you can never come; but like him, "Seek the Lord while he may be found," sincerely and with all your heart, and your salvation is secure. T. S.

POOR DINAH.

Early one Monday morning, more than thirty years ago, in the height of the most powerful revival that I had ever witnessed, a colored woman called and wished to see me. I invited her into my study, and saw at once that she was in trouble. Great anxiety was depicted in her countenance, and I suspected the cause, or rather *hoped* she had come to inquire what she must do to be saved. "Dinah," I said, "I am glad to see you; but you seem to be unhappy. What is the matter?" With an utterance almost choked by her struggling emotions, she answered, "I don 't know. I feel *dreadfully.*" "How long have you felt so?" "Ever since yesterday afternoon." "And what made you feel dreadfully then?" "I can 't tell. I was to meetin'; and when you was preachin', somethin' struck me here," smiting upon her breast, "just as if a knife had gone right through my heart."

Never in my life was I so *struck* myself as by this answer. Here was a poor colored woman who had been brought up a slave in a neighboring state, who could not read a word in the Bible or any other book, and who had never, I believe, received any religious instruction from her master. I had seen her a few times in the gallery, but never dreamed of such a visit from her, and still less of such an illustration, almost in the very words of scripture, of the power of truth upon the heart of one so ignorant of its nature and effects.

"I felt as if a knife struck right through my heart." Had she ever heard of Peter's sermon on the day of pentecost, and how his audience were "pricked in the heart" by it? Probably not. Certain it is, she never had *read* it; and so ignorant was she, that if she had, she might not have understood what being pricked in the heart meant. But she felt it, and unconsciously expressed herself just as if she had been one of the three thousand. And then that other scripture in the letter of blessed Paul to the Hebrews came to my mind: "The word of God is quick and powerful, sharper than any two-edged sword, piercing even to the dividing asunder of soul and spirit, and of the joints and marrow, and is a discerner of the thoughts and intents of the heart." Also that in Ephesians, "Take the sword of the Spirit, which is the word of God."

Here was an example and illustration before my eyes of what those scriptures mean; for I soon found, upon further inquiries, that though Dinah could not tell what ailed her, she for the first time felt that she was a great sinner; and O how eagerly she listened, while I told her, as well as I could, what she must do to be saved. Poor creature, it was all new to her. "How could she find her way to the cross?" And she went away as sorrowful as she came.

She did not remain in that state a great while; but while it lasted, it bowed her to the earth. "She went mourning all the day," scarcely daring to hope that such a poor ignorant sinner could be saved. And when the burden was taken off, she was about as much at a loss to account for its removal as she had been to tell what ailed her at our first interview. She knew there was a great change of some sort in her feelings, but what to make of it she did not know, unless it was that she was becoming stupid again.

She did not for some time seem to imagine that it could be a change of heart, and I thought it safer to let her gradually find out by the teaching of the Spirit, than to tell her at once that I hoped she had "passed from death unto life;" "being confident of this very thing, that He which had begun a good work in her, would perform it until the day of Jesus Christ."

As may well be supposed, Dinah needed a great deal of instruction, and she most thankfully received it, giving increasing evidence that Christ was formed in her the hope of glory. When the first-fruits of the revival were gathered into the church, about four months after it commenced, she stood up and entered into covenant with God and his people, with nearly a hundred others, among whom were lawyers, physicians, merchants, and altogether a large majority of the first men in the town. There was poor Dinah in the midst of them, and none more welcome than she. She had thought for years that she was too old to learn to read; but now she was eager to be taught, and some of the young ladies in the neighborhood as eagerly volunteered to instruct her.

To all human view she adorned her profession, "walking humbly with God." She is now dead, and I believe she has gone to heaven, and that her garments have been washed in the blood of the Lamb, and made as white as any of our robes will be. Multitudes of such will be found in heaven; and what greater privilege can ministers enjoy than leading them to Christ? It is worth more "than thousands of gold and silver." I am sure the conversion of poor Dinah is and will be one of the happiest reminiscences of my pastoral life. H. H.

AUNT DELPHY.

Perhaps no region of our country, in fertility of soil, scenery, and climate, surpasses that portion of Virginia which stretches for hundreds of miles along the eastern slope of the Blue Ridge. Nowhere are the poet's lines more true :

> "Hills peep o'er hills, and alps o'er alps arise."

The scenery of this region is solemn and elevating, and lifts the thoughts of the devout mind which sees God in all his works, in adoration to Him who "setteth fast the mountains, being girded with power."

But our object is not so much to give a description of this region, as to speak of a visit we paid to an aged colored woman by the name of Delphy, of whose case we heard through a pious physician who sometimes visited her. In company with him we found our way with some difficulty by a bridle path through the woods to her cabin, which was far distant from any other dwelling. Its outward appearance was comfortless and neglected ; built of unhewn timbers, plastered with mud ; the floor of dirt, and uneven ; no furniture but two bedsteads and an old chair ; no window, the light being admitted through the door and from the wide and low chimney. A shelf nailed against the wall held a few vials of medicine.

Upon one of the beds near the chimney lay the woman we came to see. She had received an injury in her youth, which paralyzed her lower limbs, so that they had been incapable of motion for more than *forty years*. During all that time she had suffered acute nervous pains shooting through her limbs. She had been for many years entirely blind. Her few and simple wants were but scantily supplied. But notwithstanding this complicated suffering, she had, we were repeatedly assured, never been heard to murmur, and her faith and patience had been the admiration of all who have known her. For more than twenty years, as she told us, she had not heard the Bible read, nor did she remember ever having been visited before by a Christian minister.

We found her quite ignorant of every thing except the simplest truths of the gospel—that she was a great sinner, and that Christ was a great Saviour—in the strength of which she had gone through the long period of this dreadful affliction. She spoke of her alarm and terror in her conversion at the sight of her sins, which, she said, were as great as the mountain near by, and as black as charcoal. When asked if she was willing to endure the same suffering for ten or fifteen years longer, she replied, that though she desired to depart, yet she was willing to wait "as long as God loved it." To the question, whether she ever doubted the love of her Saviour in thus leaving her to suffer so long, she answered that she could not, after he had died to save her.

In her experience she had, as she supposed, a trance, in which she went to heaven; and when wishing to stay there, lest, if she went back to this world, she should sin again, was told that she must return and warn her fellow-sinners. She was once, we were credibly informed, for some time in a state of suspended animation, when she had, as she thinks, this vision. However this may be, it does not affect the reality of the rest of her religious experience, nor should it cast any suspicion over the genuineness of her conversion. Such trances are very often spoken of among colored persons, and with them form almost a necessary part of true conversion. She had certainly been faithful in warning, or as she called it, *pleading* with those around her. She evidently possessed the substance of true piety—most unfaltering trust in God; she could say with Job, "Though he slay me, yet will I trust in him;" and there was in her case the most constant and simple looking to Jesus' fulness of grace and strength.

As I looked round her neglected dwelling, and upon her countenance radiant with the deepest submission to the will of God, I thought of the light afflictions over which so many Christians think they have cause to murmur, compared with Delphy's mighty trial for forty years. They would have done well to visit her dwelling, and witnessed her "sad variety of pain," that they might learn a lesson of patience. Deprived of sight and of the use of her limbs, in the sordid hut of cheerless poverty, her food and clothing insufficient, she never murmured, but took pleasure in suffering God's will.

We might learn, too, from this case of "long-suffering with joyfulness," how unimportant our condition is in this world, compared with that in the world to come. In this mean cabin lay one of God's hidden ones, an heir of glory who is to possess all things. Her piety hallowed her home, though poor indeed, and converted it, in the eye of faith, into a palace which kings might covet.

Her case, too, proves that God is no respecter of persons. He had evidently revealed unto her what is hid from "the wise and prudent" among men, as if to show the sovereignty of his grace, and how little truth, if it be received "in an honest and good heart," can carry a soul to heaven. Let us hope that many such cases of piety, far more than we are wont to imagine, may be found, especially among our colored population, in the remote cabins of our mountains and valleys. J. P.

A VAGABOND.

Some years since, as a congregation in one of the beautiful and retired villages of Connecticut were assembled on Sabbath morning, a well-known abandoned character, to their great surprise, came in among them. He was a friendless, homeless, wandering vagabond, possessed originally of a strong mind and retentive memory. His intemperance had become so excessive that he was subject to the most violent attacks of *delirium tremens;* and when the fits were upon him, he resembled the demoniacs in the gospel. To escape the devil, he would rush down precipices, throw himself into the water, and wander through fields and woods and swamps, fancying that his tormentor was ever at his heels.

It is not surprising that the worshippers of a staid New England church should be startled by the entrance of such a vagrant. Many whispered, "What has brought him here?" In answer to a similar question at the close of the service, he replied, "I have come to get good to my soul." Grace had reached the heart of the outcast. He was then sitting at the feet of the Saviour, in his right mind. The dress of

a vagabond was soon changed for one becoming a disciple. He immediately abandoned not only his cups, but his tobacco, lived for years a dignified, devoted, consistent Christian, and died beloved and lamented. Scepticism taxed its ingenuity in vain to account for the sudden and wonderful change in the character of this man, but his devoted piety for years disarmed all cavilling.

As this is a very unusual instance of God's dealings with men, it is well to consider the means employed in his conversion. It was not one of the blessed results that attend the pledge of total abstinence, in its great work of reform for the abandoned.

It was not amid revival scenes. It was not the ordinary preaching of the gospel, for he did not visit the sanctuary. The ladies of the church, in their monthly tract distribution, had given him the tract, "*The Amiable Louisa*," at a house where he called. He read it, and God blessed it to the salvation of his soul.

How striking the fact that this vagabond, who had always been a stranger to the saints, was immediately found in the sanctuary seeking the society and sympathy of God's people. He appeared to be moved almost by an irresistible impulse to go where Christians were to be found, and where they worshipped.

We should not hastily determine that any man is abandoned of God, or presume that God has said, "Let him alone," to any fellow-being this side of a miserable eternity.

There is a "patient continuance" in Christian efforts, with which "God is well pleased." "In the morning sow thy seed, and in the evening withhold not thy hand." The grand characteristic of a steward of God is, that he "be found faithful." K.

A PUPIL AT MOUNT HOLYOKE.

A young lady possessing a very sweet religious spirit, gives the following account of her first serious impressions:

I entered the seminary—the Mount Holyoke, then under the care of the lamented Mary Lyon—a very gay and thoughtless girl. I expected I should have to become religious some time or other, in order to save my soul from destruction; but it was the last thing I desired to do, and I hoped for long, long years of enjoyment first.

Among other regulations which were made known to us, we were informed that every pupil was required to spend half an hour in her own room alone, each day. In compliance with this requisition, I entered my little apartment; all was silent, solemn; I could almost hear the beatings of my heart, and an unaccountable awe stole over my spirit. I could not trifle with or ridicule the regulation. I could not even spend the time in common reading. I tried to do so, but I dared not. Conscience lifted up her voice in that deep silence, and made itself heard. It told me I ought to pray; and I felt as if the Almighty himself stood by, commanding me to pray, and listening to hear if I complied. And yet I had no desire to do it. My heart was cold and hard; I was distressed, but not melted—afraid, but not penitent. Slowly the time wore away; I gazed out of the window on the noble range of mountains visible from that beautiful location, and beheld the glorious works of the great Creator; but while my heart kindled into a kind of poetic enthusiasm at the sight, I had no desire to become the child of that divine and holy Being; there was an opposition to the very idea rising up in my breast. At length the bell summoned me to the recitation-room, and I gladly fled from that dreary solitude.

Day after day passed in a similar manner. I sometimes read a little in my Bible, but it did not interest me; yet I never *dared* read any thing else, so thoroughly was my conscience awakened. After some days it occurred to me what a wicked creature I was, to be thus unwilling to pray, and to seek Him who had done so much for me, and who alone could save my soul. I dwelt upon the thought, and for several successive days a sense of guilt accumulated, till the burden was very heavy upon my soul; and the first sincere prayer I ever offered in my lonely room was wrung from me by a deep conviction of my sinfulness. Almost unconsciously I cried, "God be merciful to me a sinner!" And he was merciful. He heard my feeble cry, and before any one had spoken to me individually upon the subject of religion, I had been convinced of my great guilt, and of my need of Jesus for a Saviour. Much excellent instruction was given to the pupils generally, and when I had begun to cherish a faint, trembling hope that my sins were forgiven, my class-teacher one day asked me if I hoped I was a Christian.

The principal afterwards had a conversation with me, and I need not say to any one who has known her faithful earnestness and tender anxiety for her pupils, how replete that conversation was with sound, practical wisdom. When I told her how I was first led to feel upon this subject, she said, "Oh yes, it is because we do not *think*, that we are so unconcerned. It is Satan's great device to keep souls from God, to occupy them so completely with other things, that they have no time nor opportunity to *think;* when we think, the Holy Spirit can gain entrance, and it leads us to see things as they are.

The pupil thus led to Christ removed to a distant land; and thousands of miles away from her New England home, she diffused the light and peace acquired in those half-hours of solitary meditation and prayer. G.

A RETURNING PRODIGAL.

Returning from a western tour during the spring of 185–, the writer providentially became a travelling companion with the Rev. Mr. K—— of B——. Our passage from Detroit was taken on board the "new and splendid" steamer Ocean. Amidst the throng that crowded the saloon, was a youth whose forbidding exterior and evidently troubled thoughts attracted special observation. His tattered garb, squalid appearance, dejected mien, and haggard features, were impressively suggestive of the *prodigal's* history.

To avoid unpleasant annoyances, we had secured a state-room, though fitted with accommodations for three persons. After some time, however, the vacant berth was claimed; and as if to render the intrusion the less welcome, the claimant was none other than the unpromising and forlorn youth spoken of above.

"The hand of God is plainly visible in this intrusion on our favorite arrangement," said my companion subsequently; "this stranger needs religious counsel; go, converse and pray with him, as I have endeavored to do." Feeling reproved by his promptitude in ascertaining the spiritual condition of a fellow-traveller, especially of one so apparently degraded and repulsive, I went immediately. The youth, who had scarcely reached his seventeenth year, was sitting in the state-room bathed in tears. The following is his history as given by him, interrupted by sobs and exclamations against himself. His pious mother, living at Kingston, Canada West, had dealt with him faithfully and tenderly. Chafing under the restraints imposed by her admonitions and prayers, he had three years previously forsaken his home, and "taken his journey into a far country." Employed as a driver on the Illinois canal, he had fallen upon vicious courses, and made himself "very wicked indeed." But God, not willing that the child of so many prayers should perish, but should rather be brought to repentance, had sent upon him sickness, want, and finally a disaster which fastened on him for life a distressing lameness. Now with shame and tears he had set his face homeward.

"What do you propose to do on reaching home?" "Beg forgiveness of my kind mother for having deserted her so shamefully." "Is this all?" "I ask God to pardon my sins; may I hope he is willing? Do pray for me that he will." "Do you think you deserve his forgiveness?" "No, I deserve no mercy." "Do you think God is unjust in inflicting upon you this series of calamities, especially this afflictive lameness?" "No, sir. It was kind in him. But for them, I should have gone on in wickedness, and come to some dreadful end." "Do you not fear that you shall return to your roving and abandoned courses?" "Not if God will show me mercy, for Jesus will be precious to me, and will help me to live a Christian life."

He seemed truly to have "come to himself;" and having formed the resolution to "arise and go to his Father," he carried it into instant execution; "he arose and came." And his Father was evidently welcoming the penitent prodigal, and sending into his soul the spirit of adoption.

The encounter with this wanderer was to us instructive, and we would hope not without use to him.

His humility, tenderness, and filial spirit; his child-like simplicity, uttering as it were in lisping accents the "language of Canaan," rendered those interviews with this mendicant prodigal more refreshing than the most genial companionships. At Buffalo we separated—he returning to his Canadian home, and we to the land of the pilgrims, in the hope of meeting yet again in the house of our common Father.

1. The seed planted by faithful parents, and watered with many prayers and tears, may be expected sooner or later to spring up and produce saving results.

2. Souls burdened with spiritual anxieties are round about us when we least think it, in our family, in our social circle, or among our travelling companions.

3. Providence sometimes thrusts upon us as it were persons of unattractive, perhaps repulsive exterior, for the express purpose of benefiting them through our influence. "The poor ye have always with you, and *when ye will*, ye may do them good."

4. Christians may easily unite happiness and usefulness in their journeyings, if they but have an eye open to opportunities of doing good, and a heart ready to seize upon them and delight in them.

A MODEL OF MORALITY.

There had been no revival of religion for many years in the neighborhood of the T—— meeting-house; the word of God seemed to be preached in vain. While all who heard paid respectful attention to the message of grace, few received it into good and honest hearts. It was a discouraging field, and the servant of God often had occasion to "weep between the porch and the altar," and to say, "Lord, who hath believed our report?" The people were not infidels, they were not profane or grossly wicked, far from it; very few neighborhoods could be found where the standard of morality was higher; but here was the difficulty, they were building their hopes of salvation on their morality, "going about to establish their own righteousness," and refusing to submit themselves to the righteousness of Christ.

As is usual in such cases, there were some who were regarded as "models" for their morality, and among them the subject of this sketch, L—— T——, stood in the front rank. He was the youngest son of his mother, "and she was a widow," and a devoted child of God, who had long prayed for the conversion of her dear boy, so dutiful and affectionate in all the relations of life.

In 1843, the pastor felt called to hold a "meeting of days;" but L—— did not attend, he was away from home. Having heard of the meeting, he resolved to attend only on the Sabbath; and to avoid the solicitations of his pious friends, he laid his plans to be absent from home through the week in a distant cedar swamp, procuring rails. But many hearts offered up fervent prayer to God on his behalf; and the prodigal son was so unhappy in the cedar swamp, that he was compelled to return home. He then resolved not to attend the meeting, but to go down on the "sound," for the purpose of procuring fish and oysters. But here he was more wretched than he had been in the woods; the Spirit of God was striving with him; his sins began to rise before him, and to press upon him like mountains. What could he do? This man who "had been zealous to keep the law," felt himself a poor miserable and lost sinner, ready to sink into despair; he fell upon his knees, and called upon God to have mercy upon him.

Speedily he returned to his mother's house, resolving to attend the meeting, and to seek the salvation of his soul Surprised and delighted, we saw him enter the house of God next morning, with sorrow written upon his countenance. Fervent prayer was offered to God on his behalf. Soon he was found among the few inquirers who sought counsel and instruction. His soul was bowed within him, his heart was wrung with anguish; and though a large athletic man, he wept like a child and trembled in every limb. We prayed with and for him; we directed his attention to the cross of Christ, to the efficacy of his blood, to his boundless compassion, to the riches of his grace; we besought him to yield himself to Christ, to give up every thing, and to trust in his all-sufficient merits. "Oh," said he, "I am such a sinner; I have sinned so long against so much light, against so much love. Oh, my poor old mother, how I have resisted her prayers and entreaties. I am ready to yield, I withhold nothing. O Lord, have mercy on me a poor sinner."

Thus he wept, and thus he prayed. He invited Christian friends home with him; they agonized together around the family altar; he walked his chamber all the night, weeping and crying for mercy. In this state of mind he continued for several days, neither eating or sleeping: we became apprehensive that the violence of his grief might unsettle his reason; but we could do nothing but pray to God for him.

On the afternoon of the third day of his anguish, he felt that if he did not find relief soon, he must die. He went to the barn, ascended the haymow, threw himself upon his face, and prayed, but no relief could he find; he thought he had not become humble enough: he descended to the stable, where again and again he called upon God to save him. No response was made to his cry, but to increase his anguish, and to drive him still nearer to despair; his heart was ready to break. "O Lord, what wilt thou have me to do?" was his cry; and in answer to his own question, he said, "There is one thing more I can do: I can pray before my poor old mother." Strange as it may seem, while he was willing to pray everywhere else, he felt that he could not pray before his pious mother; but now he was willing to do any thing, to do *even this.* He started to the house ready to sink beneath his load; he opened the door, he fell upon his knees, and cried, "O God!" and at once his load was removed, darkness vanished, light streamed in, rapture filled his soul; he sprang up, threw his arms around his mother's neck, praising and blessing God; he was unspeakably happy.

At once he set out to tell to all around what a dear Saviour he had found. On the way he met an intimate friend; he threw his arms about him, saying, "Oh my dear friend, morality will not do, you must love Jesus."

God was now in the midst of the people, the whole place was aroused, and the work went on with power; between forty and fifty souls professed conversion, most of whom lived to testify the gospel of the grace of God.

The race of L—— T—— was short, but while he lived he was a most valuable member of the church, humble, self-denying, and laborious; his light was shed on all around. He early ripened for heaven; cut down by a fever in the midst of his days, he passed away from the toils of earth to the rest of heaven: his end was triumphant; his death-cry was victory—"victory through our Lord Jesus Christ." Davies.

AN UNEXPECTED INQUIRER.

One day, as we were just rising from the dinner-table, a young man knocked at the door. He had lived but a few months in the town, and my acquaintance with him was very slight indeed. I believe we had never spoken together but once, when I was making a pastoral visit to the family in which he boarded. The thing that most struck me then was his extreme diffidence. I was not aware that any particular impression had been made on his mind. Hence, it did not occur to me that his call, especially at such an hour, was connected with the state of his feelings on the subject of religion.

Judge then of my surprise, as he took his seat by the fire in the midst of my family, and looking up, said, "I have come to talk with you about my soul." The words thrilled through my heart. Such a remark, from a modest, retiring youth who had never entered our door before, could not but awaken tender emotion. For a few moments I hardly knew what to say. Soon, however, I found utterance, and in a few simple sentences gave him such direction as seemed suited to his circumstances. It was a word in season. God had evidently been moving upon the mind of the diffident young man, and he was in a short time led to the knowledge of the truth as it is in Jesus. Years passed away, but no one had reason to doubt that this was a genuine conversion.

Is there no reader of these lines who might be benefited by such an interview with his pastor? You can imagine what it cost a retiring timid youth to bring his mind to make a visit like this. But had he not done so, it might have proved a fatal resistance of the Holy Ghost. The direction is, Seek the Lord while he may be found; call upon him while he is near. And ministers are appointed to guide souls to the Saviour. The young man that takes such a step, is using means which God may bless to his spiritual and eternal good. Pastor.

A MISTAKEN SINNER.

Mr. W—— had received a religious education. I resolved to call on him, and use all my influence as his pastor, to persuade him to seek an interest in Christ. He assured me that there was nothing he so much desired, that he would give all the world to be a true Christian; but that he knew not what more could be done than to continue his attendance upon the means of grace, and keep his mind open to conviction.

I asked him if he had carried his case before God in importunate persevering prayer.

He replied, "I have been accustomed to say my prayers from early childhood. I do not even remember when I began to pray, and I never lay my head upon my pillow without saying my prayers. I hope I am not such a heathen as to neglect it."

"But, my friend, have you taken up this great question, the conversion and salvation of your soul, and carried it before God, and pleaded with him earnestly to show you the way of life?"

"Why, no. How could I? I have no faith. It seems to me that it would be a sort of sacrilege. The sacrifice of the wicked is an abomination to the Lord. Is there not such a declaration in the Bible?"

"Yes, there is such a statement in the book of Proverbs; but what does it mean? I have no doubt that the allusion is to those who continue in sinful ways, but who say their prayers either for the purpose of deceiving men, or to quiet their consciences by setting off their devotions as a compensation for continuing in wicked courses. When our Saviour says, 'Enter into thy closet, and when thou hast shut the door, pray to thy Father who is in secret; and thy Father, who seeth in secret, shall reward thee openly,' he intends to summon such as you to the duty of earnest prayer. This exhortation is not made to disciples as such, but to men as sinners. Such a gospel call, like the decalogue, is not designed for a class, but for all who are really in a state of dependence on their Maker. So when our Saviour says, 'Come unto me, all ye that labor and are heavy-laden, and I will give you rest,' he addresses himself not to the disciples as being already pious, but to all that are in want."

"Still," rejoined my friend, "if I am an unconverted sinner, are not my prayers sinful?"

"Doubtless," I replied, "you are a sinner *while you pray*, but not *because you pray*. You know that unconverted men often send forth a supplicating cry when in distress; yet they do not afterwards accuse themselves of wickedness for having cried to God for help. So, when the appeals of the gospel have sometimes come home to your own heart and conscience, and you have found yourself instinctively sending up a desire to God for the gifts of his grace, and promised yourself that you would seek earnestly the salvation of your soul, and yet the impression has passed away, it may be your conscience has accused you of being guilty for not keeping your promise, but you do not blame yourself for having prayed. You may have seen a sinner on his death-bed, and heard him utter unavailing cries, but I venture to affirm that you never thought of blaming such a one for praying.

"That is enough," said Mr. W——, "that is enough. I will never make that objection again. But after all, it *seems* to me that my prayers can do no good. I do not feel as if I could pray. I am such a sinner, and yet have so little sense of my guilt. My prayers will not be acceptable. There will be no holiness in them."

I further replied to him, "Suppose here is a young man who is like the prodigal of our Saviour's parable. He has abandoned his home, and is stubborn in his ingratitude to a kind father. His father has proposed a reconciliation. The young man has come so near his home, that his eyes often behold it. He casts wishful glances towards it. He says to me, as you say in respect to becoming reconciled to your heavenly Father, that he would give all the world if the controversy between himself and his father were settled. I urge him to go and present himself to his father, and ask his favor. He hesitates, and says, I am not in a proper state of mind; my father has penetration enough to discover the least defect: if I should make a request in this state of mind it will be unacceptable, and I shall be spurned from his presence. To this I answer, your father desires a reconciliation. Any indication of a disposition on your part to return, interests him. Besides, how do you know but that the very attempt to approach him will soften your heart. As you see yourself coming near to him, as your eye falls upon his benignant countenance and reads in its expression a readiness to forgive, it may have a most subduing influence upon you. Come, I say to him, come, go in and present yourself to your father. In my earnestness I pull him by the sleeve, still repeating my urgent exhortation, Inquire for your father; go to him. He enters, and is seen to put back his hand and close the door after him.

"Suppose now, my friend, you have witnessed this interview, and seen the young man enter. What do you expect will be the result of his thus going to his father? You perceive, at once, that there was something very ungracious in his reluctance to go. But you expect to learn that a reconciliation has taken place. If not at once, you think this may lead to another interview, and that ultimately a reconciliation will result. And may not such be the consequence, if you go to your chamber and approach your heavenly Father in earnest prayer? It is most unworthy and ungrateful in you to manifest the least reluctance. Will you do it?"

"You have satisfied me," he replied, "that I ought to do it. But how can such a man as I am pray?"

"Go and try. Go with humble trust that God, through the merits of Christ, will meet you as a forgiving Father."

"But how can I? Must there not be a divine influence?"

"Yes; but is there no divine influence now acting on your heart and conscience? Do not resist the Holy Ghost. Do what you confess your conscience urges you to do."

We parted. He went to his home, and I to mine.

I was engaged in prayer for him. A gentle tap on my door called me to open it. It was W——. His lips were quivering with emotion, and his eyes streaming with tears. "Can you sing?" said he.

"Yes, come in. Did you go home to pray?"

"Yes," said he, "I went resolving that I would go to my chamber to pray. It seemed strange. As I walked up the stairs, I said to myself, it is strange. I am going to my chamber to pray. Shall such a man as I am pray? Yes, I am going to my chamber to pray. I opened the door. I had no more than begun, when the room seemed full of light; and I could only praise God for his mercy in Jesus Christ to a poor unworthy sinner."

We sung the praises of God together, wondering at the richness and freeness of divine grace. A quarter of a century has elapsed since the conversion of W——, and the result has confirmed my conviction, that it is right to direct a sinner to go to God in prayer, in the name of Christ; and that plain gospel appeals to individuals, are among the most effective modes of preaching. P. J.

WILLIAM WIRT.

The power of religion in promoting happiness in this life, and in disarming death of its terror, has seldom been more beautifully illustrated than in the example of William Wirt, Attorney-General of the United States. When a young man, just commencing his professional career, he was distinguished for his genius, his eloquence, his fascinating powers of conversation, and his polished manners. In every circle his society was courted. Fond of pleasure, and the centre of attraction of every convivial party, he was living for the joys of this short life; and was in great danger of being ingulfed in that vortex of worldliness and fashion where so many thousands have perished.

While thus living, as he was on one of his professional circuits as a lawyer, he passed a Sabbath where the celebrated Blind Preacher of Virginia was to preach. Mr. Wirt having no other way to pass the Sabbath, entered the humble church with the congregation. He has himself described, in his own forcible language, the scene which ensued. The primitive simplicity of the preacher, the subdued pathos of his tones, his unaffected piety and fervid eloquence, all combined, through the influence of the Holy Spirit, to touch the heart of Wirt. He felt the emptiness of his own joys, and the unprofitableness of his own life. He reflected and wept and prayed. "God, be merciful to me a sinner," became, for many days and nights, the anxious supplication of his soul. Forsaking his thoughtless companions, and his dangerous habits of gayety, he commenced a new life of Christian usefulness. True peace visited his heart. And his benignant countenance proclaimed that he had sought happiness and found it, where alone happiness can be found. He became the advocate of Christian missions, and to every object of philanthropy he consecrated the energies of his noble mind.

Though necessarily called to move in the highest circles of opulence and intellect, and to encounter the temptations with which those circles are always filled, he humbly, yet fearlessly sustained his character as a disciple of Jesus Christ, and gave his commanding influence unreservedly and constantly for the promotion of piety. Revered by the community, and loved almost to devotion by a wide circle of friends, he spent his days in doing good. And when the dying hour came, hope and joy beamed from his eye, brilliant with almost celestial vision, as the glories of his heavenly home were unfolded to his view. His body has long ago mingled with the dust, and his spirit has long dwelt, we trust, with the God who gave it.

Such are the effects of religion. Infidelity can show no such triumphs. Who will not utter the prayer, "Let me die the death of the righteous, and let my last end be like his?" A.

HOLY OBEDIENCE.

A DYING GIRL.

NOT long since, a pastor whose parish lay among the hills of New England, entered his study one Sabbath evening with great heaviness of heart.

He had been unusually interested in the labors of the day, and had spoken with great tenderness of feeling, and with an energy that surprised him. His discourses had been prefaced in prayer. They were delivered to his congregation with an earnest desire that they might deeply stir the souls of those who listened, and incline them in the way of life.

His own heart was warmed and quickened in spiritual things, for God was leading him through the furnace of severe affliction, bringing darkness upon his home and heart by the ravages of disease and death; and this way in which God was leading him was good for him, though every step was attended with anguish of spirit; it led to the throne of God, and brought his soul into blessed communion with the only adequate and satisfying good.

At the close of the services in the evening, as he looked over the assembly, it seemed to him that the solemn truths which he had been communicating had failed in doing service—they had not reached the heart—he had been preaching in vain. He was overcome, and pronounced the benediction with a tremulous voice. He hastened to his home; thick darkness came over him, his faith was exceedingly small. That night was a restless one, sleep departed from him, and he was sorely troubled in the multitude of his thoughts which there rolled tumultuously over him : "It was of no use for him to preach. His labors were not blessed. God had not called him to the work of the ministry, else he would favor him with more frequent and signal tokens of his gracious presence and power." Should he abandon his chosen profession? It might be well to do so.

The morning came, but the cloud had not withdrawn; there it hung, with its dark folds obscuring his whole sky. He could never preach again—this was for other men, not for him.

But suddenly he was called to visit a young girl who was rapidly sinking to the grave. She sent a special request for him. He hastened to her bedside, and found her sweetly confiding in Jesus as her Saviour, and God as her friend.

As the pastor held that fevered hand in his, and listened to that sick girl's story, how did his darkness clear up, and what tears of repentance and joy fell from his eyes!

Some weeks before, she had heard him preach on the duty of immediate submission to God. This sermon, through the blessing of God, led her to conviction, which resulted in her conversion. As she told this to the pastor, her face gleamed with sacred joy, as if light shone thereon from the throne of God and the Lamb. She felt that her sickness was unto death, and was strongly desirous of being received to the communion of saints on earth, that she might take at the hands of that pastor the sacramental bread and cup.

After several satisfactory interviews, it was decided to receive her into the visible church. This was done one bright Sabbath morning in August; the sky was serenely fair, and the air vocal with the melody of birds. In the presence of a few friends, the young and dying disciple gave herself to Christ in the act of public consecration. There were tears in that parlor on that bright summer morning, and no one felt more deeply than that pastor. A sweet smile rested on those features of the dying one; and when asked, at the close of the ordinance, if she was fatigued, she replied, "O no, I have had such satisfaction, and have been so happy." A few days after, she calmly fell asleep, and we believe that she is now white-robed among the angels of God, with "the general assembly and church of the first-born."

That pastor often visited her grave, and as he stood by that grassy mound, he rejoiced "with joy unspeakable and full of glory" at the thought of meeting her on mount Sion, as one whom God in infinite mercy has given him as a seal of his ministry. It was enough that he had been instrumental of saving one soul, and while he strove to win more, he struggled against falling into that slough of desponding thought to which allusion has been made.

The ministers of Christ should not be discouraged—they are God's laborers, and he will let none of their words fall to the ground. They do not always know the amount of good they are accomplishing; it is not best they should. They have their gracious reward in another world. Let them bide God's time, and not be weary in well-doing; for in due season they shall reap, if they faint not.

F. B. W.

A TEMPTED YOUNG MAN.

In the year 1845, there lived in F——, New York, a young man about seventeen years old. Trained in the Sabbath-school, his knowledge of duty was too great and the voice of conscience too strong to allow him to indulge in an open course of wickedness, to which his heart was by no means opposed. He was frequently moved to tears by the sorrows of his fellow-men, but the goodness of God, his wonderful kindness and mercy, had never impressed his heart. He had always regarded God as a holy and pure being, who hated sin, and therefore must hate him. This led him to hate God's perfections, and to dread his power.

At this time a plain, instructive discourse of his pastor, showing the nature of sin, the justice of God in its punishment, and the way opened by Christ, in which God may be "just, and the justifier of him who believeth in Jesus," disclosed to him the riches of the divine method of the sinner's salvation. He saw and felt the enormity of sin, as committed against the mercy of God; and while his heart broke in repentance, he felt that Christ was able and willing to save him from his guilt and reconcile him to God; and placing his trust in his Redeemer, his mind calmed into love and confidence, with a peaceful assurance of God's forgiveness. Such is the blessing that may attend the plain and faithful preaching of the great doctrines of the cross.

The conversion of this young man was thorough, but there remained one step to manifest its sincerity—his publicly uniting with the church. Here Satan advanced to contest the movement. The communion-season was approaching, the invitation to meet the officers of the church was given out, and the young man was considering the duty of presenting himself, when the evil thought was suggested, "Perhaps you do not rightly understand your situation and the nature of your recent feelings; perhaps you will be better prepared if you wait until the next occasion." He waited. Again he considered the point, but with less inclination to duty, and Satan suggested, "Remember how inconsistent it would be to make a profession of religion after your conduct of last Thursday." Yes, last Thursday's conduct was inconsistent, and again he must wait. In this manner season after season went round, until for *four years* this young man was kept away from the precious privileges of the true Christian. He had not yet been able to take up the cross.

At length another plain discourse of his pastor upon these very suggestions of Satan, and the effect which they produced upon the converted, but lingering, hesitating sinner, disclosed the true nature of these suggestions, and the only manner in which to overcome them, which was by resolving to perform every duty, however trying, in humble dependence upon God, seeking his assistance in sincere and earnest prayer. By this he was instructed, and as the communion-season again approached, receiving in answer to prayer the assurance that Christ was with him, he was enabled to present himself as a candidate for admission; and after passing a full, but most kindly conducted examination, was received to full communion, and joined in the commemoration of his Saviour's death.

There may be others in the state of this young man at some portion of his career. His advice is, that you go to your pastor, and disclose to him your state of feeling. He loves you, although you may not think so, and he will be able to instruct you how to avoid this young man's errors, which caused him to lose four precious years of Christian peace and active usefulness, upon which loss he will ever look with regret. The writer and your adviser is that young man. R.

NANCY AND HER PASTOR.

MY FIRST VISIT.

I had been reading Baxter's Saints' Rest. I had studied that part of it that describes the condition of those who lose that rest. My soul burned within me. I had an indescribable desire to do something to save the impenitent from that condition. I felt my commission from the Most High renewed; that my commission as a messenger from God to sinners was as good as any angel's. I visited the house of two ladies who had for a long time supported themselves with their needles. The elder one was a professor, but the younger had no hope. "If you should die as you are," said I, "do you think you should go to dwell with Christ in heaven?" "I suppose I should not," replied the younger. "How then can you rest until you have made your peace with God? If you were doomed to hell only for twenty-four hours, and tears and cries could rescue you, you would weep day and night until the pardon came." Then turning to the older sister, I said, "I will pray with you, if you have no objections." "None, none," said she; "I desire it." I took from my pocket my Bible, and after reading, I commended them to God, praying for the younger especially. As I arose, I saw that she turned away her face, as if to conceal her tears.

MY SECOND VISIT.

She wished to get me upon some puzzling doctrine. "How do you understand *election?*" she said. "In this way," said I: "if you ever are so happy as to get to heaven, you will give all the glory to God. But if you go to despair, you will bear the blame for ever." A solemn pause ensued. "Well, I do not see," she continued, "that *I* can do any thing." "There is one thing," said I, "you can do. You can go on in sin, as you have done; grieve the Holy Spirit; put off the matter until death overtakes you. Then, if you perish, will God be to blame?" A pause again. "I have tried a great many times," she said, "to find what you recommend, but I have come to the conclusion that all my efforts are an abomination in the sight of God." "Well," said I, "if your prayers are offensive to God, how do you think the rest of your life appears in his sight?" She wept, and her sister wept. Then I took her Bible from the stand, and read the parable of the prodigal son, applying every point of it to her as I went on. I went to prayer. Both of them fell on their knees. After prayer they said, "Call again." The next Sabbath they walked a long way to find our meeting. As I reasoned of sin and of righteousness, the older one prayed and the other trembled.

MY THIRD VISIT.

"I saw you last evening at the prayer-meeting. I was glad to see you: and now, Nancy," said I, "have you given that hard heart to Christ?" "I fear not," she said, and covered her face in her handkerchief. Then her sister spoke, and said, "She thinks she has done all she can. I have told her every thing that I can think of, but she has remained right there. She has said over and over again, how I wish Mr. —— would come." "Yes," said I, "and as soon as ever I knocked, she asked me in: but my Saviour may knock at her door all day and all night, 'until his head is filled with the dew, and his locks with the drops of the night,' but she keeps her door locked against him." I took my hat and went out to a solitary place, and there that poor sinner was by no means forgotten. But she thought then that she was lost—that I despaired of such a wretch as she was. In a few hours I went in again. Every tear was dried. She looked despair itself. She wanted to know if I had given her up. I told her, "No. But there is a work between you and God that I cannot do. I have prayed for you, and shall continue so to do." "But can I give my heart to God now?" she asked. "Why not?" said I. "Cannot you love God, and commit your soul to Christ? Has he not done enough for you? What objection have you to loving and trusting in a kind Redeemer, who has bled on Calvary for the chief of sinners?" "It is my hard heart: I know I am a hardened sinner," she said. "But," said I, "you are a greater sinner than you are aware. If you should see *all* your heart in the light of God's law, you could not live. You would sink. But Christ is as great a Saviour as you are a sinner." I prayed and left them.

MY NEXT VISIT.

"Well, Nancy, I have come once more to see if that hard heart relents. Do you keep up your rebellion against God?" "I fear I do. I have done every thing I can. It all does no good. I fear I am given over for ever." "This acknowledgment turned into a prayer, would be a good one," said I. "Go and say, O Lord, I am a desperate sinner. I have gone this way and that, and am only in the dark. My feet are in 'the horrible pit and miry clay,' and every struggle only sinks me the deeper. I am sinking. *Lord save; I perish.* Other sinners," said I, "are one after another coming in, and here you are fighting against God. He is more willing to pardon you, than you are to repent. Why not repent, and believe in Christ?"

THE CRISIS PASSED.

I knocked. Nancy was at the door. She took me by the hand. Tears stood in her eyes; but a partial smile shone through them, like the sun after a shower, shining through the last rain-drops. "How is your mind this morning?" To describe her mind, she gave me the hymn, "Rock of ages, cleft for *me*." "Can you accept that first line?" said I. "I think I can." "Does the Saviour seem near and precious?" "O, 'the chiefest among ten thousand;' but I have not as much light as I could wish." "Hav'n't you as much as you *deserve?*" said I. "O yes; more." "Walk softly, then," said I, "and rejoice with trembling."

THE COMMUNION.

She was there and looked on. She looked at the bread and wine. She thought on Calvary, and on the resurrection. She had loved her money; but now she was ready for the contribution. She wanted to do something for the missionaries; and every time there was an opportunity to help the Tract Society, she did it. Now she is on missionary ground, where her tender sympathy and her benevolence have room for action. When her sister was pining on her death-bed, it seemed hard for them to part; but after *she* had gone home, Nancy had nothing more to give up. She bade farewell to friends, and the dear church she joined, for a home among strangers. S. M.

A FARMER'S DAUGHTER.

In the autumn of 18— I spent a week with friends at their beautiful country-seat, on the —— river. The avenue to the house crosses a spacious meadow, skirts a ravine partly concealed by a thicket of evergreens and forest-trees, and winds around among beds of perpetual roses and flowering shrubs, to the broad verandah of my friends' abode. The prospect towards the river is charming. A natural terrace, with ample lawns and parks, threaded by shady paths, form the foreground. In the distance, villages with their church spires and domes; farms cultivated to the water's edge; the glassy river, with here and there a vessel or a steamer to give life to the picture; and the immense mountain ranges, which constitute the background of the whole, present a scene of great loveliness and grandeur.

It is the fit residence of an intelligent wealthy and benevolent Christian family. Were it proper to delineate the admirable mode of instruction at morning prayers; the cheerful religious conversation, interspersed with anecdotes gathered from world-wide travel and extensive reading; the ingenious plans for blending amusement and instruction for the evening hours; the mild, yet strict control of children; the generous-hearted hospitality—it would furnish a picture of a refined Christian household on which wealthy worldlings and envious agrarians might gaze with profit. All titled or purse-proud aristocracy is contemptible, compared with the nobility of grace.

This lovely family, though reared in the circles of fashion, and related to the élite of the land, have been taught of God to respect true worth in every station, and to regard piety of heart and purity of life as the passport to confidence and affection. Among the number of those who shared their affectionate interest, was *the farmer's daughter* whose brief history will occupy the remainder of this sketch.

My friends were very ready to gratify the curiosity their frequent allusions had awakened, and took us in their carriage one afternoon to the home of Miss ——. The house, which is nearly three miles from town, is hardly visible from the road. Around the turnpike-gate, where the lane to her father's house diverges from the highway, are clustered several small dwellings, occupied by poor white and colored families. The appearance of the neighborhood is not unlike thousands of those intermediate settlements, found all over the country, presenting the aspect of poverty and neglect. Too small to sustain churches;

too distant to admit of convenient attendance on the means of grace in the towns on either side; too careless to invite the labors of religious teachers around them, these half-village, half-rural settlements are the waste places of Zion—the strong-holds of Satan.

The small farm-house which we found at the end of the lane, was plain and neat. We were received by Miss —— with great cordiality. Her dress was simple and appropriate; her manner ingenuous and unaffected; and her conversation was unconstrained and highly spiritual—though betraying sufficient defects in early education to excite our wonder at her present attainments in divine knowledge.

During our conversation, I expressed a desire to know something of the manner of her conversion. "What was it," I inquired, "that led you to the cross?" "Sin!" she replied. "Our house used to be a very wicked place. The young people from —— were in the habit of coming out here to dance and play cards. I was a very wild girl. One night in February, eleven years ago, a gay, noisy party were here, and there was music and dancing. They became very boisterous, began throwing the plates about in their frolic, and behaved very badly. In the midst of the noise and confusion I sat down by my sister, and said, 'Sister, what do you think of all this?' 'I'm tired of it; a'n't you?' she replied. 'Yes; and I mean to live a different life.' I thought of the sad prospect before me if I should die that night; and I determined to seek the Lord, and perish, if perish I must, at the foot of the cross."

"But had you no previous religious impressions?" I inquired.

"Yes; three years before that ball, when at the West, I was under conviction for sin, and there was much prayer for me in a revival of religion. I began then to study the Bible; but I returned home soon after, and our house was such a wild place that I could not read except on the Sabbath. I had nearly read the Bible through, when the Spirit of the Lord met me at the ball I spoke of. The pastor of the church at —— soon heard what was passing in our family, and came to see us; but I feared it was nothing but excitement, and knew that I must repent before the Lord for myself; so I refused to see him. Five members of our family were rejoicing in the hope of pardoning mercy within two months of that period; but I was the last of the five to yield to the claims of God and take refuge in Christ Jesus."

"Why were you the last to give your heart to the Saviour?" I asked.

"Oh, I was so jealous of myself," she replied, "I did not dare to hope."

"Were your convictions deep?"

"They were overwhelming. I saw that I was a great sinner—all vileness and pollution. My heart seemed a fountain of corruption."

"Have you enjoyed constant peace since you began to hope?"

"Yes; although I have had occasional doubts, my peace has been like a river. I have not known what it was to be free from bodily suffering for years; yet I have not lacked divine support, and I don't see how I could have lived through my trials but for the grace of God and the hopes of the gospel."

"I love the word of God!" she exclaimed in this

connection; and her features lit up with a smile that was full of spiritual joy, as the conversation turned upon the Bible. In reply to the question as to the frequency and manner of reading it, she informed us that she had "*read the Bible through several times on her knees before God.*" "I have *meditated* the Scriptures through three times," said she, "with the exception, for the third time, of the last eight chapters of the book of Revelation."

"Do you mean, Miss ——, by '*meditating*' the Bible through, that you have read distinct passages, and meditated on them at the time of reading?"

"No," she replied; "it has become so familiar that I don't need to do that. I recall the historical, biographical, or prophetical portions of God's book, in the order they stand, and bring all the incidents to mind, and then trace out the connections of the scene or event before me with other and parallel passages in the word of God. I take Genesis, and think of all that is recorded there; then Exodus, etc. One book of the Pentateuch will last me two or three months in subjects for meditation. What a beautiful book Deuteronomy is! Then I take the Psalms and the prophets, etc.; and in this way I meditate through the Bible. I do not generally attempt to commit the words, but try to make the scenes, characters, incidents, and events all my own. Ezekiel is delightful. Sometimes, when meditating some of the visions, types, or seals, I seem half taken to heaven. I think the last nine chapters of Ezekiel are the most difficult to understand in all God's book." Turning to her friend, she inquired with affectionate interest, "You meditate in this way, do you not, Mrs. ——? You'll be a growing Christian if you do. And there is no lost time; one can be thinking of the exodus, or of the offering of Isaac, or of the captivity, when about household duties."

"Let me inquire, Miss ——, if you read a commentary with the prophetical writings?"

"Not now," she replied; "I have read the Comprehensive Commentary until I have learned the views of the different writers. I find so many opinions expressed, that it is rather confusing. So I confine my reading now chiefly to Scott, or meditate on the prophecies till I understand them, with what light I have received from the helps I have enjoyed, and from above."

"But do you not find the New Testament most profitable and delightful of all?"

"Yes; the Old Testament, however, explains the New, and makes it clear. The types and prophecies relating to the Saviour are so striking, and their fulfilment so complete, that you cannot understand the New Testament fully without them. I love the whole of the word of God. Matthew and John are my favorite evangelists—though you can find all of Matthew, with the exception of thirty-eight verses, in the other gospels. Then there is so much in Luke! It is a beautiful gospel to meditate upon. All of the Bible is beautiful."

She conversed in this strain for an hour, as naturally as one would speak of the common affairs of life. How precious did the Bible seem, as the daily, hourly companion of this humble, suffering disciple—its lessons of wisdom her constant study; its consolations her perpetual support; its joys her only possession; its hopes her abundant and everlasting reward! Alas for the folly of those who possess, but undervalue or neglect the word of God; the blindness of those who reject its divine claims; the wickedness of those who withhold it from the poor. Could any book of man become to the farmer's daughter what the Bible is?

We were impressed with the facility and artlessness with which a personal, practical inquiry was thrown out, now and then, as the conversation advanced. Thus, when speaking of "meditation, self-examination, and prayer, as three of the most important Christian duties," and explaining the value of meditation, among other things, as an aid to self-examination, she turned to Mrs. —— and said with great tenderness, "You examine yourself every night, of course, Mrs. ——; *every Christian does that.*"

In answer to a direct inquiry on the subject of prayer, she said, "I have been in the habit of retiring to my room for the study of the Scriptures and prayer soon after family devotions in the morning; then at noon, and at sundown. *Of course*, I commend myself to God before I go to-bed at night, and when I get up in the morning. All Christians do that, don't they?"

Would that I could have answered, "Yes," to this simple-hearted inquiry. Thus, "seven times a day" does this child of sorrow seek divine light and support of the great Source of blessing. "Seven times a day," says David, "do I call upon the name of the Lord."

"Do you find any occasions for ejaculatory prayer?" I inquired.

"O yes; I go to God with every thing. When I

am about the house, or baking, or washing, or when a troublesome neighbor is here, or any thing goes wrong in the family, or I am suffering pain, I can lift my heart to God, and he hears me just as well as in the closet. When I am in church, and the minister is preaching, I can fix my mind on some impenitent sinner, and entreat God to bless his word to that soul; and yet I can hear all he says, and profit by preaching all the more."

Happy Christian! Would that the wealthy, and the learned, and the distinguished of this world had thy riches, and knowledge, and honor! A prayerless soul is a Christless soul; and a Christless soul can never be a happy soul, "for the wrath of God *abideth*" on it.

We took our leave of this interesting female, after a protracted interview, with a deepened conviction of the truth of the Bible, and with a more profound admiration of the gospel for this renewed illustration of its adaptation to the wants of the soul.

The next day was stormy and unpleasant; but I could not deny myself the satisfaction of another interview with Miss ——. An hour's familiar conversation concerning the precious gospel, the experience of its power on her own heart, and the means she employed for imparting it to others, only increased my interest in her history, and my gratitude for the grace of God displayed in it. When I expressed a desire that she would remember in her prayers one who was ready to sink under the weight of public responsibilities and private bereavements, she replied, "I have prayed for you ever since the day you were here." It was but the previous afternoon—frequent prayer made it seem longer. "I pray for all my friends. When I think of the —— family on my knees, they seem to be right before me. O, how I love them!"

Can it be that such a tree bears no fruit? Is the piety of the farmer's daughter simply meditative; and is there nothing more than the "unconscious influence" which every spiritual Christian exercises, but with which no truly devout disciple can be satisfied? The grace of God in the heart will as surely manifest itself in the life, as the living branch will produce its fruits when united to the living vine. Says the Saviour, "He that abideth in me, and I in him, the same bringeth forth much fruit. Herein is my Father glorified, that ye bear much fruit; *so shall ye be my disciples.*" But how can the poor, suffering farmer's daughter *do* any thing for the glory of the Redeemer, or the spiritual benefit of those around her? Is it not enough for her to suffer the will of God in patience and meekness?

For several years after her conversion, her health allowed little more than the cultivation of her own graces, and occasional efforts for the salvation of others. About three years since, however, she was so far restored as to be able to commence more systematic and efficient plans for the spiritual benefit of her neighbors. The population around her was very wicked. The Sabbath was a holiday; profanity and intemperance abounded. No Sabbath-school gathered the children from the streets; no church called the people from their houses.

She called on two families, and invited the children to come to her Sabbath-school. The kitchen was arranged for the purpose, and has since been the scene of her patient toil. By denying herself the morning service at church, she gains the quiet hours when the family are away. One by one the families around sent their children, until the number increased from twenty-seven the first year, to forty-eight at the time of our visit. From one family, residing on the hill three miles distant, five children, the youngest but five years old, walked to the school. With the exception of such aid as was rendered by two of the oldest of her pupils, in teaching the younger children to read, she was the only instructor. Sometimes, from illness, she has been under the necessity of laying her head upon her pillow, while carrying forward the instruction of nearly fifty pupils. The arrangement of her school-room must be done chiefly by her own hands. The government of her untutored charge all devolved on her. But with these disadvantages she has persevered, until that humble school has become the centre of religious light to all that district.

The results of such an attempt to do good under difficulties, with the divine blessing, are suited to encourage the humblest of Christ's disciples to like efforts. The Sabbath is now honored where it was profaned; religious books, which she constantly loaned to families through the children, furnished a substitute for preaching, and did much to promote Sabbath observance, temperance, and piety; the children were gaining a knowledge of the Scriptures, and were often in tears while the gospel was unfolded to them; and although there were as yet no marked instances of conversion among her scholars, it was no source of discouragement to her. She lived in daily expectation of a visitation from on high, which should quicken the seed she was sowing in hope. The harvest-time is coming.

On Sabbath morning, my friends from the mansion accompanied me to the Sunday-school of the farmer's daughter. Perhaps one-half of the more distant pupils were prevented from attending, by the rain. In the small neat kitchen were gathered about twenty children and youth between the ages of four and eighteen, including three or four little black boys. A few older persons had also come to enjoy her instructions. The order of the school was perfect. Though a little embarrassed by the presence of strangers, she proceeded calmly with the lesson, which related to the character of Judas, and the betrayal of the Son of God. She gave a clear exposition of the passage, and added remarks of a practical nature adapted to the comprehension of her youngest hearer. After this exercise, she requested the scholars, in order, to repeat the Commandments. A young woman, perhaps seventeen years of age, repeated the command, "Thou shalt have no other gods before me." The teacher addressed her in the most solemn and direct manner, "Sarah ——, you have broken this commandment of the Lord. You have an idol in your heart, which keeps you from the love of God. What is it? Is it dress? Is it pleasure? You know. It will ruin your soul, if it is not renounced. Will you give it up? To-day? Now?" This was said in a tone of affection, and yet with a solemnity that was dreadful. Sarah's conscience was roused; she covered her face with her book, but, for many minutes, the tears trickling down her cheeks, and the heaving of her breast, betrayed the emotion which these simple words awakened. This must serve as a sample of her manner.

After the commandments were repeated and commented upon, she began a review of her "lists," as she termed them, or a series of questions in manuscript, which she had prepared, embracing the principal events in biblical history, and the more prominent doctrines of the word of God. These were answered with great promptness, in turn, even by the youngest scholars. A class of the smallest children was then examined in the "Scripture Catechism." In such ways were these young minds familiarized with the word of God, and with such a living exemplification of its spirit and power before them as to impress every truth on the mind and heart.

Within a few months after this, Miss —— commenced visiting the parents of these children, and other neglected families in her vicinity, distributing tracts and books, conversing on personal religion, and endeavoring to bring all under the influence of the gospel. Besides being a Sabbath-school teacher, she became, in this sense, a colporteur. She also sustained a school for colored people, embracing several adults, after the service on each Sabbath afternoon.

Such are some of the ways in which piety in the heart works out in the life. This feeble, suffering female laid the foundations of pure morals and vital religion in that ignorant, destitute neighborhood; and became as truly a missionary as was Harriet Newell or Harriet Winslow. Her efforts were appreciated, and her religious character respected by all around her. She was "a light shining in a dark place," and the judgment-day may reveal many an heir of glory led to the cross by the consistent example and self-denying labors of the farmer's daughter.

This humble narrative teaches some important lessons.

1. It furnishes an illustration of the power of a spiritual faith in moulding the character and directing the influence of a family of wealth and refinement.

2. It shows that the Spirit of God can deal with the conscience even amidst seasons of gayety and folly, and in its sovereign power can make the wicked pleasures as well as the "wrath" of man to praise him.

3. The Bible furnishes sources of knowledge and of support that are unfailing. It is the poor man's book. Woe to him who would deprive the poor of this rich boon of heaven!

4. Vast attainments may be made in divine knowledge by studying the Scriptures with prayer, even by the unlettered invalid. Is there not a criminal neglect of the *study* of God's book by those in health, and with every help to understand its sacred pages?

5. There is such a thing as "praying without ceasing," and he who attains nearest to it is the happiest Christian.

6. Pious females dwelling in destitute settlements have here an example of active usefulness which should stimulate them to kindred labors. It is not great talents, nor favoring circumstances, so much as ardent piety and a willing mind, that secures results like those here delineated. "Go, work in my vineyard," is the voice of this example, echoing the voice of the great Vine-dresser.

7. The infidel may scoff at the Bible and the religion of the cross; but one such character as that here described is a proof of the divinity of the Scriptures, and of the power of the gospel of Christ in changing the gay worldling into the meek and devoted follower of Jesus, elevating and ennobling the intellect and the heart, supporting under trials, and stimulating to beneficent labors, which nothing can gainsay. Can infidelity point to one such triumph of its principles? Account for such a change, with such fruits, on any other principle than that the religion of the Bible is the religion of God, and we will concede that all is delusion which seems like truth in the experience of divine grace in the life and history of the farmer's daughter. R. S. C.

A FAITHFUL ELDER.

The following sketch is from memory, and relates to the last century:

J—— L—— was the son of pious parents in humble circumstances. He was brought up to labor on the farm, and was restrained from open vice by his religious education, and by a regard to the authority and feelings of his parents. On a certain Sabbath, there being no preaching in the immediate neighborhood of his father's residence, he had formed the purpose to attend a great meeting at the distance of twelve or fifteen miles. He owned a young horse, on which he intended to ride to the place, but on going to the pasture in the morning to bridle the colt, he eluded all his attempts to catch him, and he was obliged to return to the house foiled, disappointed, and much chagrined. How to spend the wearisome day he knew not.

At length the thought struck him that he would take a book and go out into the woods and amuse himself with reading. He stepped to the book-case and seized the first book which came to hand, which happened to be Doddridge's Rise and Progress of Religion in the Soul. It being summer, he sought out a cool, shady, and sequestered spot, where he lay down and began at the beginning of his author; and the Holy Spirit accompanied every truth which engaged his thoughts with a divine influence, for he was deeply convinced of sin on reading the first chapters; and when he came to the expiation of Christ and the method of salvation, the whole plan was opened to his believing mind, and he deliberately embraced the Saviour as offered in the gospel, and was filled with peace and joy. Thus this young man went out into the woods in an unconverted and condemned state, and in a few hours returned a renewed man, freely justified by the grace which is in Christ Jesus. In due time he entered the communion of the church, and became an active, zealous professor at a time when great lukewarmness had taken possession of the church. He married an intelligent woman, who by the force of his example and instructions embraced religion, and became as zealous and more communicative than her husband. They lived happily, and were blessed with three sons and two daughters.

About middle age he was elected a ruling elder in the church to which he belonged, and in this office he received grace to be faithful. He held up the hands of his minister, and defended his character from calumnies attempted to be heaped upon him. He visited the poor, and contrived methods of relief; wherever there was sickness, J—— L—— was to be found sympathizing with the sufferers, and offering up fervent prayers for the recovery of the sick, and for a blessing on the rod of affliction. By this means prayer was introduced into families where the voice of supplication had never before been heard.

When a boy I had an awful dread of this man, and shunned him for fear he would speak to me about religion; but a little sister being very sick, I was pleased to see this faithful man come to the house. He sympathized and advised with our parents, and spent the night in watching with the sick child; but what affected all most, was his prayer, so fervent, so affectionate, so appropriate. It was felt as if surely the Lord would hear and answer such a prayer.

When few professors kept themselves unspotted from the world, this man and his wife stood firm in their adherence to truth and duty. Worldly amusements were introduced by some influential professors; strict religion was scorned, and the *liberal* professor was lauded; but our elder could not be moved to favor dancing and cards. He set his face resolutely against all such practices as inimical to the spirit of true religion. He faithfully warned professors against the deadening influence of these *innocent amusements* as they were called; and when private exhortation and remonstrance failed, he had the fidelity to present the cases of such professors to the session to be dealt with, as acting inconsistently with their Christian profession. This exposed him to a load of obloquy; and he was clamored against as an enemy of all cheerfulness and enjoyment. Some ministers also took sides against him, and their opinions and example were published by multitudes who never remembered any of his pious sayings. J—— L——, however, went on his course unmoved; and though hated and dreaded by the wicked, whenever any one became serious he was immediately sought out, and his counsel and sympathy and prayers were always cheerfully bestowed. The state of religion in the land seemed to grow worse and worse just after the close of the Revolutionary war, until he and his wife and a few others seemed to be left alone. But even in this time, the presence of this tall, gray-headed elder would strike an awe into the minds of the most careless. One day he had business with a man who was at a dancing party in a private house, and when he approached the house consternation seized the company, and at once the fiddling and dancing ceased. He, however, administered no reproof to the company, but transacted his business and departed.

It pleased a gracious God about the year 1789 to revive religion with extraordinary power in all the country around where he lived. It was what he had prayed for night and day, but scarcely hoped to see, for he had never before witnessed what is called a revival. Almost his whole time was now spent in conversing with the new converts. I have known him often to ride six or seven miles to see persons under religious impressions. And he would labor with them in the most earnest and affectionate manner, and would bring to them suitable books, for he was much conversant with the most spiritual and experimental authors. Many were deeply indebted to his faithful labors, and none more than the author of this paper. Senex.

THE ELDER'S ELDEST SON.

Perhaps there has scarcely existed since the fall a family in which there was less to corrupt youth than in that of the faithful elder described in our last paper.

In this family there were no servants, but the elder's wife performed all the work of the house, except that, when sick or unwell, some woman of good character from among the neighbors assisted her; and the elder himself did the whole work of the farm, except in the more busy seasons, when a man was hired for a few days. In this house, purity, peace, and order prevailed. As soon as the children were capable, their aid was used both in the house and out of doors. The oldest child was a son, a fine healthy boy, large and handsome. This boy was carefully instructed in the principles of religion both by his mother and father, and he appeared remarkably docile, and learned so well, that his parents felt a strong desire to devote him to God in the work of the holy ministry, if it should please God to make him early a subject of his grace, for which blessing they ceased not to pray daily.

When the boy had arrived at the age of sixteen or seventeen years, it was thought advisable to send him to an academy at no great distance, to commence a course of liberal education under an approved teacher, a man of piety as well as learning. And it was hoped the young man's morals would be safe, as he would board in the house of an aunt who lived near the academy.

The youth had scarcely ever lodged out of his father's house in his life, and had never been exposed to any temptations from bad company, and was perhaps as innocent as any of Adam's children in a natural state. He had, however, much natural susceptibility of impressions from without, and a sociable disposition.

At this time there were some young men in the academy who belonged to wealthy irreligious families, and from their parents and the company which frequented their houses, they had imbibed a spirit of hostility to religion, and had picked up some objections to the Bible, and learned to make a jest of sacred things. These young men, as soon as the elder's son entered the school, determined to do what they could to seduce him from the path of morality and innocence. They began by throwing out hints and inuendoes against revealed religion, and expressing pity for such as were held under the restraints of religion, or were conscience-bound, as they expressed it.

These ideas were entirely new to the elder's son, and he drank in the poison greedily, for he had a strong inclination to sinful indulgences, which was only restrained by his religious education. These sceptical opinions were exceedingly agreeable to his corrupt nature, but he was not sure that these objections to Christianity had a solid foundation. He, therefore, sought for books which would have the effect of confirming him in his infidelity, and the works of Hume, Voltaire, and others were obtained by means of the young men before mentioned. And being now in a great measure freed from the restraints which had been on him, he rushed forth into a course of dissipation and licentiousness in emulation of his new comrades. Indeed, it was not long before he went beyond any of them in boldness in sinning. Those who become vicious in opposition to the restraints of a religious education, commonly run to greater lengths than others in transgression, because the strength of passion necessary to overleap this barrier is sufficient to drive them on far in the paths of iniquity.

For some time he was careful to conceal his irregularities from his parents; but ere long this was impracticable, and he began to appear boldly in the ranks of the greatest transgressors. He was a leader and corrupter of others, and seemed to have lost all sense of religion, and to be confirmed in his infidelity. It is impossible to describe the disappointment and anguish of his pious parents. They could do nothing for him but weep and pray in secret. The young man had gone on in this way for several years, growing worse and worse, until his character was ruined and all respectable people shunned his company.

About this time a young man, a cousin of his, came in from the west, where he had lived for some time, and had recently experienced a great change. He had also been very wild, and having been somewhat suddenly converted, he was full of zeal, and spoke freely to his old acquaintances of the necessity of religion, and did not neglect the elder's son, to whom he addressed himself in a very earnest but affectionate manner; and it was apparent that his example and solemn exhortations produced some impression. As he was now on his way to college, he asked the elder's son to accompany him and bring back his horse. Indeed, the plan was secretly agreed upon between his cousin and his father to get him to go, for at that time a powerful revival was in progress in the college and vicinity; and the father being acquainted with the president of the college, wrote him a full account of his son's unhappy state of mind, and entreated him to try to bring him off from his infidelity. This letter he did not put into the hand of his son, but of his cousin, with a request that he would not let his son know that he had written. The reverend president on receiving this letter invited both the young men to his house, and after some general remarks he commenced a conversation on the subject of the causes of the prevailing infidelity, and took up in order the arguments of deistical writers; he refuted them with a clearness and force which overset the system which the elder's son had long been building up. He never hinted that he had any suspicion that the young man belonged to this unhappy class, and, indeed, directed his discourse mainly to his cousin. The device answered the purpose intended. The young man not only renounced his infidelity, but fell under deep conviction of sin before he returned home. What a comfort to his pious parents. His mother had always entertained a confident hope of his conversion, and her prayers were about to be answered.

It was some time before the young man could be persuaded to entertain any hope that his sins could be pardoned. He evidently felt that he was the chief of sinners. Never was a change more manifest in outward appearance. He now became deeply serious at all times, and under the impression of his exceeding wickedness he seemed little disposed to go into company of any kind.

After much prayer and deliberation, he felt constrained to think it a duty to enter the holy ministry. But before he commenced the study of theology, he undertook to teach a classical school for a year. He had scarcely commenced his school when he was seized with a violent bilious fever. His case from the first was considered dangerous. His parents made haste to see him, though he lay at a considerable distance from their residence. While the issue hung in doubt, the father, a man of strong mind and sober principles, suffered one of those hallucinations to which pious persons are sometimes subject. Having been earnestly pleading with God for the life of his son, the text of Scripture, "This sickness is not unto death," was impressed so forcibly on his mind, that he was fully persuaded that this was an answer to his prayer, and rejoiced in the prospect of receiving his first-born from the verge of the grave. But alas, the young man in the midst of his days was cut down. Thus again the hopes of these good people were sadly disappointed; but there was now comfort mingled with their sorrow, for they had hope in his death.

Senex.

A SABBATH-SCHOOL TEACHER.

M. S. L——, the subject of this sketch, was an amiable and much respected young woman. Though living in a community where the Sabbath sheds its hallowed light, and where the doors of the sanctuary are open night and day, inviting the weary and heavy-laden to enter, where they may hear of Him who can give rest to their souls, yet she grew up in almost total ignorance of the teachings of God's word and of all spiritual duties. By precept and by example she was taught to believe that all that was required of her, as an accountable being, was faithfully to perform her domestic duties and lead a moral life. She had never bowed her knee in prayer; and it was not until she was eighteen, that she heard for the first time the preaching of the glorious gospel of the blessed God.

The death of a friend of her own age, who like herself was thoughtless on the subject of religion, and a lover of worldly pleasure, produced for a time deep and pungent feeling, and led her to desire to be a Christian, and to resolve to lead a different life; but surrounded by worldly companions, and having no Christian counsellor to guide her, the serious impressions gradually wore away, and Miriam became as careless as ever, with the exception of occasional hours of bitterness, when conscience would lift up her voice and utter her warnings.

It was about this time that she came to reside in our beautiful village, and became connected with a family in which there was but one professor of religion. He was a young man, who, two years before, during a most precious work of grace, had been plucked as a brand from the burning. He was a humble, devoted Christian, whose life was a commentary on his profession. Being naturally diffident and reserved, he was a man of few words, but his consistent example preached more eloquently than words could. On the Sabbath, while the other members of the family were spending its precious hours in vain pursuits, this young friend was found diligently engaged in the Sabbath-school, and in the sanctuary of God; and while at home, his time was spent in the careful study of God's word. His zeal and devotion deeply impressed the mind of Miriam; his example was a constant reproof to her; she felt that she was wasting her life and ruining her soul, and that he had a source of comfort which she had not, and her heart longed to enjoy what she believed he did.

Not long after this, while some drops of mercy were descending upon us, Miriam was present in the house of God and heard an earnest appeal from the pastor. She felt that every word he uttered was meant for her, but she could not pray; she could only weep and tremble. She left the sanctuary in great agony of soul, realizing that she had lived in vain; that she had been all her life sinning against God with a high hand; that she was a lost sinner, for whom there appeared to be no mercy. Overwhelmed with distress, she sought her chamber, and in the anguish of her soul she fell upon her knees, and for the *first time* in her life offered up a prayer to God. She slept little that night, and for a number of days the weight of guilt upon her soul was almost insupportable. She could not see the cross, nor realize how a sinner could be saved by believing on Christ. She was almost in despair, and felt that it was of no use to seek any longer, and that she must perish, the very thought of which filled her soul with agony. How could she endure the thought of being separated from

Christ, whom she desired to love; how could she endure the thought of being shut up in the prison of despair? Her soul struggled within her, while her cry went up to God, "Have mercy on me, a poor lost sinner." At this moment, while the "pains of hell gat hold upon her, and she found trouble and sorrow," her eye fell upon the tract, "The Troubled Conscience," and rested on the words, "Desponding sinner, dry up your tears, and doubt no longer. The greatest sin you can commit is to disbelieve God's promise to forgive your other sins." She felt that by cherishing unbelief, she was adding to all her other sins, and she resolved to cast herself on the mercy of Christ *just as she was;* and that moment hope spanned the heavens, a "great calm" succeeded the storm, and her soul was filled with "peace in believing, and joy in the Holy Ghost." As she sat in the circle of prayer, her face was illumined with brightness, and

> "Her tongue broke out in unknown strains,
> And sung surprising grace."

Did Christians realize, as they should, the *power of example,* they would be more careful to live "unblamable in holiness," and "shine as lights" in the midst of the moral darkness by which they are surrounded. The silent influence of a young man led to the conversion of the subject of the above sketch; and shortly after her conversion she met with a younger sister, to whom she told what the Lord had done for her soul, and the result was, that she too was soon "brought to Jesus," and is now "happy in the Lord." Who can trace out *all the results* of that young man's consistent conduct, even in this one instance? Davies.

SIGHT OF PRAYER.

THREE PRAYING FRIENDS.

I WAS invited to aid a pastor in Delaware Co., Pennsylvania, during a revival about eleven years ago. A young man, afterwards a missionary in New York, also assisted in the meetings for prayer. When

I was about to leave, I was accompanied on my way for a mile or more by the pastor and the young man.

We parted at a spot surrounded on three sides by woods; from the open side a field could be seen at some distance on a hill. Full of solemn feeling, we could not part without prayer. An old tree-top lay before us, and one of the company proposed to kneel down among its branches, not wishing any but the all-seeing Eye to rest upon us. All three prayed. We parted.

Three months afterwards, a letter from the pastor informed me that among the persons received into his church, the fruits of the revival, was one who traced his first serious impressions, which resulted in his conversion, to the scene above described. While ploughing on the hill-side, he had seen three men bow together in prayer in the fallen tree-top, and the *sight* of prayer had so affected him, that he could find no peace until he became himself a praying man.

Thus is "praying in secret" rewarded "openly." Thus varied are the ways in which the Holy Spirit carries conviction to the conscience. Were Christians more frequently found on their knees, in their closets, in parting hours, and in social gatherings, there would be more converts to trace their religious impressions to the sight and hearing of prayer. G.

AFFLICTION.

A POOR WIDOW.

"I HAVE nothing to live for," said a widow, who had buried her husband some years before. Subsequently she followed a beloved son to the grave, who had died in the midst of life and usefulness; and now she had been called to part with an only daughter, the mother of two children. As she returned from the grave of this loved daughter, she went up into her bed and lay down to die. "Why should I desire to live?" she said to herself; "I am left alone, my family are taken from me; what have I to live for?"

While in this despairing frame, she was aroused from her repinings by the voice of a little granddaughter, who could not realize the greatness of her loss in the death of her excellent mother, but was affected to find her grandmother in tears. "Don't cry, grandmother; I will take care of you." This tender voice scattered the clouds of grief, and brought her to her right mind. She felt the reproof. She realized in a moment that she had sinned against God; she felt that she had something to live for. She arose from her bed, and on her knees humbled herself before God, and like David took food and addressed herself to the work of life.

Those two motherless children were to be trained for God. In a few days they were sent to school, and when some of the children in the school desired the eldest to remain and play with them, she refused, and said, "I must go home and take care of my poor sick grandmother." When this expression of love and gratitude was mentioned to her, she could not refrain from weeping. "Surely," she thought, "I have enough to live for. If I can bring these dear lambs to Christ, and place them in his arms, I shall not have lived in vain."

She was permitted to see them grow up in the fear of God. This good woman might have adopted the words of David, "Thou, which hast showed me great and sore troubles, shalt quicken me again, and shalt bring me up again from the depths of the earth." Psa. 71 : 20.

Many in the midst of bereavement, stripped of friends, are ready to exclaim, "We have nothing to live for;" but such language is unbecoming a Christian. Nothing to live for! Is the glory of God nothing? Is the church of Christ nothing? Is the salvation of souls nothing? Is prayer nothing? Nothing to live for! If we were on a barren rock, or shut up for years in a sick-room, we should have enough to live for. "I have chosen thee," saith God, "in the furnace of affliction." True Christian submission—submission springing from confidence in God, and love to his character, promotes the divine glory as much as active service. Let us feel, whatever be our circumstances, that it is a blessing to live; it is a privilege to suffer, as well as do, the will of our heavenly Father. T.

HENRY L——, THE DEFORMED BOY.

Many years ago, in a quiet little village on the sea-coast of New England, lived a poor boy whose name was Henry L——. He was an only son, whom his parents had fondly hoped would be their support and their joy; but a sad accident in early childhood had made him deformed for life, and they looked forward with dread to the mortifications and helplessness which they feared awaited him in the future. Poor Henry felt his misfortune most keenly, and often stole away by himself to shed bitter tears over his blighted prospects. He was unlike all the other boys, and he always would be. It seemed to him that every one regarded him with contempt, and that though some might pity, no one could *love* him. He became hopeless and desponding, and shrank from observation, feeling that though life offered many joys to others, it had none for him.

But a change came over Henry's life, and the consolation he had so long sought in vain from the world, he found in the love of his Saviour. He was no longer hopeless, for was not *heaven* before him? His fears for the future were dispelled, for had not Jesus promised to be with him to the end? Even his deformity he could now regard without a murmur or a regret, for he knew that it had been sent upon him by his tenderest Friend, and he was willing to suffer, if in that way he might grow in grace. Jesus loved him, even *him*, and he was satisfied.

Henry's new hopes immediately began to influence his life. Hitherto he had lived *for himself*, he must now begin to live for others. He felt that as there was a work for each one to do, he had no excuse for sitting idle, and the thought of his aged parents, who would soon be entirely dependent upon him, was a sufficient stimulus to exertion. By patient application he soon learned a trade, and though his earnings were small, he cheerfully devoted them all to their comfort, and by his kind and assiduous attentions did all in his power to promote their happiness. He *had* become their staff and their stay and the joy of their hearts, and they blessed God for giving them so excellent a son.

Henry L—— became one of the most active young men in the church, and his amiability and self-sacrificing spirit made him a general favorite; indeed, his acquaintances hardly thought of his deformity, it was so overbalanced by the loveliness of his character.

When I first saw him, I pitied him; but when I heard his intelligent conversation, and saw his cheerful face beam with benevolence and happiness, my pity was exchanged for admiration of the courage and energy which through grace had enabled him to triumph over his infirmity.

It is a sweetly comforting thought, that the physical defects which so often depreciate us in the eyes of the world, make us only larger sharers in the tender love and sympathy of our Master. To him there is no deformity but that of sin, and this he is ever ready and willing to remove.

A DYING MAN.

A beloved friend, who was converted to God in 1838, in the same precious college revival with the writer, settled in Baltimore, where he inherited from his father much property, which he cheerfully laid at the foot of the cross. The following fact was related by him in my hearing. In the suburbs of Baltimore he found a poor man dying of consumption. During the former part of his sickness he was without hope and without God. Two young ladies came to his wretched dwelling and presented him a tract. He threw it on the floor, despising the gift. It lay there till it became soiled and torn, but in a few days he asked his wife to hand it to him. The title of the tract caught his eye, "Do you want a Friend?" His heart told him, "Yes, I do want a friend." He read the tract, and by the blessing of God, it led him to read the Bible, to pray, and to believe on Christ with all his heart. And this minister of the gospel said he had often seen the sick man take that tattered tract from the leaves of his Bible, and hold it up, thanking God for it.

Perhaps those young ladies never knew the blessed result. Their joyful reward may be reserved till the day of judgment. Can we not do likewise, and visit the sick to win souls to Christ, and prepare jewels for the Redeemer's diadem? I have often thought that if by waiting upon the sick for a few hours on the Sabbath, we could enable some wearied friend, long detained at home by the sickness of some member of the family, to go and fill our wonted seat in the sanctuary, it would be a noble work. Thus we could do a double service, by reading a tract or a chapter in the Bible to the sick, and at the same time sending some one to the house of God who could not otherwise hear the gospel. Let us seek "by all means to save some." T. S. M.

MOTHER FROM WALES.

"O my God, my soul is cast down within me; therefore will I remember thee from the land of Jordan, and of the Hermonites, from the hill Mizar." Psa. 42 : 6.

A case occurred recently which may prove a salutary lesson to some sinking heart, and I will relate it.

I called the other afternoon upon a Welsh friend of mine, an eminently pious woman, and found her very happy. She said to me in the sincere and simple-hearted manner of her people, "I have been in the depths. My son Tom, who you know shipped as a sailor last summer, has not written for a long time, and when he left me, he seemed not very far from the grave with some hidden disease. He may now be dying of the consumption, and his friends unwilling to alarm me. But as I sat thinking of this a while ago, I remembered all the way the Lord had led me through the wilderness. I spent some time in Wales, looking at my Ebenezers there, and then I came back again to America, and reviewed my deliverances here. And now I know that the Lord will keep his covenant with me. Oh, blessed be his name, he brings light out of every cloud. I am so happy." And this joyful Christian's face kindled up anew with the glow of her believing heart.

As we sat talking of God's faithfulness, rap, rap, rap went a fist on the door, and in rushed Tom—not the poor emaciated, deathly-looking boy of last summer, but a stalwart sailor-lad, entirely recovered, and throwing himself into his bewildered mother's arms with a hearty cry of joy.

As we were uniting our hearts in mutual salutations and thanks to God for his goodness, coming as it did in a way so marked with the stamp of peculiar providence, there seemed but one thing lacking to make our family-meeting and its joy complete. The father, a noble and true-hearted old Welshman as ever lived, had gone to the interior of Illinois some months previously, in search of a home for his dear ones and himself. He had been very anxious that this son when he returned should no longer go to sea; and Oh, if he could know that this wish of his heart was realized by the assent of the young man; if he could have met and rejoiced with us over the hope of seeing his family undivided around their western hearth, and mingled his voice and his tears with ours as we sat overflowing with happiness, what could we have wanted more?

But the realization of the present mercy would not permit its vividness of pleasure to be destroyed by any repining considerations like these, and our happy and grateful group sat communing together until—hark! another rap shook the door: it opened, and there stood the father himself. The father and the son meeting from opposite sides of the world! Oh, the gladness that filled that house, that welled from those hearts that night! They could hardly believe that they were not in some beautiful, but unnatural dream.

Yes, it was all real. The father had a story to tell of a home made ready for them in the West; the sailor-boy recounted to them his perils and deliverances; the young children mingled their glad clamor with the voices of both; and the mother, with a face that shone still brighter than all, looked tearfully up to heaven, and gave silent thanks to her Father's new manifestation of light out of darkness.

A Pastor in New York.

THE FAITHFUL NURSE.

Mrs. N——, a lady of eminent piety, was remarkable for her great attention to an aged domestic. On being asked the reason, she said, "I owe her a debt of gratitude which I can never repay. Under God, she was the instrument of my conversion. I was brought up regardless of God, ignorant of his word, always mingling in gay, fashionable society. At an early age I was married, and gave myself up more than ever to a life of pleasure. For a few years every wish of my heart seemed gratified, when my little only son, three years old, was seized with a sudden and severe illness. A few days of extreme suffering, and he was snatched from me. I was almost frantic; I raved against God as unmerciful and unjust, shut myself up in my apartment, and refused all consolation, even the sympathy of friends.

My health became so impaired, that my physician advised my husband to take a tour in Europe with me, and try what change of climate and scene could do. My old nurse was sent for to accompany me. Since I had seen her she had become a faithful follower of Christ, and was prepared not only to administer to my physical wants, but to my still greater spiritual need.

Ellen knew that the great Physician of souls could alone restore me, and she took every opportunity to lead me to him. At first I would not listen to her, and requested her to stop canting, but she was not discouraged, and patiently bore my fretfulness. I was not unobservant of the great change in her character. Sometimes with tearful eye she would repeat a precious invitation from God's word, as, "Come unto me, all ye that labor and are heavy-laden, and I will give you rest."

One day, feeling more gloomy and desolate than ever, I consented to her earnest entreaty that she might bring her Bible and read to me a few passages. It was a new book to me. I had a Bible, though always unopened, and occasionally I attended upon the service of a fashionable church.

As Ellen read verse after verse, I became interested; she explained its truths with so much simplicity, and made the way of salvation so clear and plain. The Holy Spirit carried the truth home to my heart, my darkened understanding became enlightened, and I found sweet peace in believing. It was not long before I could exclaim with the patriarch Job, "Though He slay me, yet will I trust in him." I could bless my heavenly Father for the stroke that had brought me to him. Oh the preciousness of a new-found Saviour. With peace of mind my health was gradually restored, and I was soon permitted to return home and unite myself with the people of God.

A SICK MAN OF THE SOUTH.

During the winter of 184– the writer was residing in the city of S——, whither he had gone to enjoy the advantages of a southern climate.

In the month of December, the minister of one of the churches requested him, with a companion, to visit a sick person whom he had discovered in the outskirts of the city. We promised to comply with his request, and forthwith set out on our mission. Passing the residences of the better classes, we at length came to a wretched suburb, whose miserable huts were to all appearance the abodes of poverty and vice.

In a low shanty we found the object of our search, a man about forty-five years of age. We learned from him that he had once been quite athletic, but from his occupation as a wood-cutter, he had often stood in the water in the swamps, and thus, some ten years previous, had contracted a disease which had wasted his body, and was now fast hurrying him to the grave. His mind was weak and uncultivated; he could not read, and as he had seldom, if ever, been to church, he seemed to have not the slightest knowledge of the gospel plan of salvation. Besides, he had been in a great measure deprived of his hearing, and it was only by placing the mouth close to his ear, and speaking in a loud tone, that any communication could be made to him. In addition to this, there was an utter indifference to the subject of religion, and as if to get rid of us, he said it was of no use to talk to him, for he had not sense enough to understand about the Saviour. Our only plan was to teach him orally, and this we did by having him repeat after us the great truths of the gospel.

Week after week we visited him, and were almost disheartened to perceive how mechanically he repeated our words, and how little he understood of their meaning; it indeed seemed that he had not mind enough to comprehend the way of salvation, simple as it is. By degrees, however, he understood more of our teachings, but then was manifested that disposition so natural to the carnal heart, a reliance on his own righteousness. Again and again did we explain its insufficiency to meet the law of God; but to our question, "Can you reach heaven by doing good?" he invariably answered, "Yes."

After some two months the light dawned in that darkened heart; the Spirit revealed to him his vileness, and led him by faith to rely on his Saviour, and on him alone. He obtained a hope of pardon, and enjoyed that sweet peace which flows from a sense of acceptance with God. From this time his views were clear and his evidences bright; he became like a little child; such was the simplicity and sweetness of his piety, so naturally did he express the feelings of the renewed heart, that, in the language of a Christian friend whom we took to visit him, it was a pleasure and a privilege to converse with him. He was permitted publicly to profess Christ, and was received into the church of God.

On one occasion, when asked where he would look to obtain the deepest sense of the odiousness of sin, he replied, "To the Saviour." Doubting whether we understood him, he was requested to explain, and we found that he indeed meant that on the cross was the guilt of sin displayed in its blackest hue.

By the month of April his disease had progressed so far that it prevented his lying down at night; he said to us that as he sat sleepless by his fire, "All my study is about Christ." In expressing the preciousness of his hope, he said he would not part with it for the whole city of S——.

I. F—— lived about a year after this, manifesting in his life the reality of his conversion, and then, we cannot doubt, fell asleep in Jesus. His body rests among the graves of the poor; no stone marks the spot, no inscription tells of his humble piety, but his record is on high, and he shall be the Lord's in that day when he makes up his jewels.

We have in the history of this conversion a triumph of divine grace.

1. A triumph *over circumstances most unfavorable*— a man ignorant, enfeebled in mind, cut off in a great measure from conversation, yet changed and exhibit-

ing a degree of intelligence which seemed hardly possible in his case. Truly this scripture was fulfilled, "The entrance of thy words giveth light; it giveth understanding to the simple." "Here was an enlargement and elevation of thought in an uncultivated and unintellectual mind—an earnest of the restoration of man to his original glory, when every intellectual power, as well as every spiritual faculty, is filled with 'all the fulness of God.'"

2. A triumph *over the power of sin and Satan.* For nearly fifty years had the strong man armed kept his palace and his goods in peace; but a stronger than he came upon him and overcame him, took from him that ignorance and indifference in which he trusted, enlightened the dark mind, softened the hard heart, and made this precious soul a trophy of redeeming love.

3. A triumph *over doubtings and unbelief.* More than once had we almost despaired of doing this poor man any good, so difficult seemed the work. God rebuked our want of faith, and glorified the power of his grace. There is no ignorance, obstinacy, or hardness of heart which is beyond the mighty power of the grace of God.

And lastly, we have an illustration of the importance of *the aggressive principle in religion.* Had not Providence led us to search out this poor man, to visit him repeatedly, to tell him of the Saviour, in all probability he would have perished in his sins. He is but the representative of a large class in cities and in the country who are unable or unwilling to read the Bible and to hear the gospel, and who, if they are ever to be benefited, must be sought out in our lanes and alleys and unfrequented neighborhoods. The gospel must be carried to their houses, and Christian men and women, with hearts of love and words of kindness, must tell them of their perishing need, and point them to "the Lamb of God that taketh away the sin of the world." Reader, here is a field of usefulness open to you. Though you have but one talent, it may here be so employed that it will bring a rich return. "To him that knoweth to do good and doeth it not, to him it is sin." This is the field occupied by the American Tract Society; thus "to the poor the gospel is preached." I. A. S.

THE FIRST AND LAST COMMUNION.

It was a chill morning of the first Sabbath in November, when the —— congregation assembled to obey the last command of their dying Lord, "Do this in remembrance of me." The table was spread with the emblems of his broken body and shed blood: still the pastor deferred entering upon the service; there were anxious looks towards the door, while a pew evidently prepared for an invalid was still unoccupied.

It was generally known, that among the candidates for admission, Sarah D—— had been received, and it was much feared that she would not be able to attend this her first, and in all probability her last communion; and all who knew her, hoped that she would not encounter such weather, with her slight hold on life. But they were not long kept in doubt. The door opened. For the first time in many months she entered the sanctuary of God. Supported by her brother, she came feebly up the aisle. Every eye turned involuntarily upon her, but as quickly was inverted. Not one, I am sure, in that large assembly was tearless, as they saw the ravages disease had made upon that once blooming face, and how death had marked her for his own. She alone was composed, for she knew it all. There was a calm, sweet expression, which bespoke an inward joy and peace unshaken; for now the long desire of her heart was to be gratified. She was to confess her Saviour before men.

The pastor rose, and after looking to God for a blessing, requested those who were to take upon themselves their covenant vows to come forward. There was an effort to rise by the young invalid, but the pastor beckoned her to remain seated. While with solemn though tremulous voice he proceeded with the forms of admission to the church, much he feared that she might even then pass up to the marriage-supper of the Lamb. He had heard her oft-repeated prayer for this privilege, and the expression of her confidence that the sure promise would not fail, "My strength is sufficient for thee." How many hearts went up to God in her behalf—not that her life might be spared, for God had settled that point, but that his presence might continue with her, and bear her rejoicing through the dark valley, and bind up the bleeding hearts of her afflicted parents, and that devoted only brother.

The service, always deeply impressive, was now peculiarly so. She seemed to stand a link between the living and the dead. Never did I realize the preciousness of a Saviour's love so fully, as when I sat at his table with that dying girl, and with the eye of faith saw her spirit, washed in the blood of Jesus, passing the portals of heaven. I had been much with her through her long sickness, knew how she had clung to life, how strong were its ties for her, the child of affluence, and an only idolized daughter. I had often pleaded with her to commit all into the hands of God—had watched with intense interest the struggle going on in her own mind, and God's dealings with her; at last had seen grace triumphing over doubts and fears, and heard her sweetly submissive, yea, rejoicing, utter the words of the psalmist, "Before I was afflicted, I went astray; but now keep I thy word." Oh, how much had a pious mother's instructions and wrestling prayers been instrumental in it. God seldom fails to bless such means.

After this precious communion-season was over, and the benediction had been pronounced, no one ventured to approach the young invalid, feeling that she must be too much exhausted. She sent her brother, requesting me to come to her. When I went, she said, "Will you go without welcoming me as one of the lambs of the flock? Oh, what a precious, precious privilege, that God should have permitted me to come as one of his own chosen ones!"

Months passed, and again we gathered to renew our covenant vows around the table of our common Lord. Sarah was not there; she had gone to the upper sanctuary, to the marriage-supper of the Lamb,

> "Where the smile of the Lord is the feast of the soul."

She had lingered long on the confines of the tomb, and even so far revived as to be carried to a balmier clime, her friends hoping to prolong life; but they were compelled to hasten back to gratify her last wish, of looking once more upon the home of her childhood, and to be laid in the village graveyard beside one to whom she had given her first affections, and who had gone before her a victim to the same insidious disease which was cutting her down. Much she hoped once more to enter the sanctuary of God and commemorate the Saviour's love, but he had ordered otherwise. Her first was her last communion. S.

A DYING SON.

Mrs. —— was the widow of a prosperous merchant; his life, after he made a profession of religion, was exemplary and eminently useful. His conversion could be distinctly traced to the prayers and faithfulness of his wife. When left a widow, she devoted herself with great earnestness to the spiritual interests of her family. She had two sons and a daughter. Her influence was also felt in the church; she was a mother in Israel. Many, it is believed, will rise up and call her blessed. Her eldest son became a highly respectable and useful minister of the gospel.

The younger son became a merchant in the city where he grew up. In a revival of religion he became a subject of grace, and united with the church. He settled in life under favorable circumstances, became eminent in his calling, and filled a large place in the community. His respected mother lived near him, and never failed to aid him by her counsels, for she was endowed with great good sense as well as deep and living piety.

Some years ago she was called to part with this her youngest son. When she saw that he must die, the trial at first seemed too great for her to bear. He had an interesting family. But she was enabled to roll her burdens on the Lord. This son had always been sober-minded and moral. She had reason to hope he was pious; he had been a man of prayer. But when he was visited with his last sickness, the anxious and faithful mother did not feel fully satisfied. She took her seat by his sick-bed, and held the following conversation with him.

"My son, we may fear for the result of this illness. Are you prepared to exchange worlds?"

He paused to reflect, and replied, "I hope I am."

After some remarks upon the solemnity of dying, and the fulness of Christ, she said to him with great seriousness, "J——, I have never been quite satisfied with your appearance as a Christian. I fear there is something wanting. You do not seem to have a *lively* hope, a joy in believing. There has not been enough of Christ in your experience; you do not seem to make enough of Christ; he is all in all, the chief among ten thousand. I want you to look into this matter. I have found no fault with your outward deportment, your external duties; but morality cannot save you, you must trust in Christ alone."

He said he understood her, and would give attention to the subject. She withdrew and poured out her soul in prayer in her closet, that Jesus would reveal himself to her dying son. Early the next morning she was called into his room. A change had come over him; his countenance no longer bore the marks of gloom; the dark cloud had passed away. "Mother," said he, "you were right. I see there was a great deficiency. I have been enabled to give myself anew to Christ, and he has revealed himself to my soul. I have a joy I never knew before, I see a glory in the gospel that is new. Christ is my all."

After a pause, he said to his mother, "When I was young, I used to think you were too strict with me. I was kept in at night against my will; I was not allowed much spending money, and was prevented from mingling with rude boys. I often complained, but I see you were right; I knew you were at the time, but was unwilling to acknowledge it. I thank you for your faithfulness; if I have ever done any good in the world, I owe it to your prayers and fidelity." Placing his arms around her neck, he exclaimed, "O mother, blessed art thou among women!" These were among his last words. T.

DEATH.

A WIFE AND MOTHER.

ADDISON has remarked, that there was nothing in history which interested and affected him more deeply than the conduct of eminent persons in a dying hour. "If I were a maker of books," says Montaigne, "I would compile a register, with comments on various deaths; for he who should teach men to die, would teach them to live." There are few who cannot sympathize with these sentiments, for every reflective mind will linger around the dying bed:

"Death only is the fate which none can miss."

In the course of a ministry of nearly twenty years, it has been often my privilege to stand by the bedside of the dying, and to witness scenes, both of remorse and of triumph, which no pen can adequately describe. One scene of joy, where the king of terrors was transformed into a smiling angel of mercy, I will endeavor, though it must be faintly, to portray.

It was a beautiful afternoon in August, when I entered a rural dwelling adorned with all the comforts and refinements of abundant competence, to call upon a lady who for several months had been sinking in a decline. I had often, during the progress of her lingering disease, visited her and prayed at her bedside. A glance of the eye as I entered the room, assured me that this was my last call, for she was evidently dying. She was reposing pillowed upon her bed, with an unnatural lustre in her dying eye, and with cheek and brow of almost marble whiteness. The windows of the room were open, and a gentle summer breeze breathed softly over the fragrant flowers and shrubs, which with their luxuriant verdure partially veiled the light of the sun, and threw in beautiful tracery upon the bed the shadow of twig and leaf and blossom. It was a silent summer's day. There was not even a sigh in the zephyrs which wafted grateful odors over the dying bed, and not a sound could be heard, save the plaintive notes of the birds, nestling in the abundant foliage with which the dwelling was almost embowered.

Every voice with which nature speaks is in harmony with those scenes of decay and death to which all nature is consigned. The song of the bird, the chirp of the insect, the murmur of the stream, the sighing of the wind, are all plaintive in their character. Nature is pensive in all her utterances. The swelling and dying tones of the Eolian harp seem to be the musical expression of the Author of nature in view of these scenes of time.

The husband and the children of the young wife and mother were gathered around the dying bed. The beauty of youth was still spread over those features, upon which the pallor of death was fast passing. I had often been struck with the fluent, melodious, and accurate diction with which my dying friend could give utterance to all the emotions of her heart, and the peculiar richness of all the intonations of her voice. As I entered the room she raised her eyes, and extending her hand to me, with the sweetest smile exclaimed, "You have come to see me die." And then, with a renewed smile of almost preternatural peace and loveliness, she added, "It is a very pleasant thing—*a very pleasant thing to die.* And when, after my spirit has passed away, you hereafter speak to my children of their departed mother, I hope that you will always speak with a smiling countenance and in cheerful tones, that they may have pleasurable ideas associated with my death; for it is a pleasant thing, a very pleasant thing to die."

She was gently breathing, with no pain and no agitation. Her mind was as calm, clear, and vigorous as ever. Though she spoke in tones soft and subdued, every word she uttered came from her lips with the utmost distinctness and precision. Turning her eye to her husband, whose hand she held, she remarked, "I know perfectly that I am dying. I feel the peculiar separation which is taking place between the body and the spirit. My sensations are such as cannot be mistaken. I have never experienced such before; no language can describe them. But I am fast going. I shall soon be gone. Farewell, farewell;" and her eye was fixed, and nothing remained but the lifeless clay.

This was indeed falling asleep in Jesus. She had chosen the Saviour for her friend in early life. She had been cheered by those consolations which piety alone can give, through all the trials of her earthly lot. And when the dying hour came, faith disarmed the king of terrors, and enabled her to exclaim, "O death, where is thy sting? O grave, where is thy victory?" Who, in view of such scenes as these, will not breathe the prayer, "Let me die the death of the righteous, and let my last end be like his?"

J. C. S. Abbott.

A SUFFERING CHRISTIAN.

Now and then there have been experienced leaders in the host of God's elect, who, like Payson, have written as from the land of Beulah, with the celestial city full in view; and with powers of expression perfected by use, they have been able to tell us much of the joy set before them, and already filling their enraptured souls.

But these cases are rare. And when the death-scene of one in obscure life, a private only, and not a standard-bearer in the army of the Lord of hosts, is such as preëminently to glorify God, the memory of it ought to be preserved as the sacred property of the church, while we are following those who through faith and patience have inherited the promises.

It was in an obscure upper room in the rear, secluded from observation, that she of whom we record these particulars fell asleep in Jesus. But as the happy saint lay dying, that homely, uncommodious apartment seemed to me to shine with the splendor of holiness, and it was graced with a spiritual presence which the gorgeous palaces of the rich seldom know. They that are said in Scripture to "minister unto those that shall be heirs of salvation," were beside that humble bed. They show their radiant forms to the ravished eyes of the dying one; they chant sweet music in her ears; they drop blest influences around the couch:

> Hark! they whisper; angels say,
> Sister spirit, come away.

It was meet that angels should thus come to make death triumphant and happy to one who had been so long a sufferer, even as it was that they should carry poor Lazarus to Abraham's bosom. Adeline C—— had been for many years a helpless sufferer, unable to walk. But though shut up from the Sabbath-school, and the innocent sports and studies of youth, she was a patient, even a cheerful sufferer. For more than three years she had been loving the Saviour, and at her request she had been baptized when she was so weak as scarcely to be able to support her own body.

Since that profession of her faith, though before uniformly timid and diffident, her soul had been evidently growing into the likeness of her Saviour, and he had often manifested himself unto her as he does not unto the world. His name was music to her ear; and a few friends would often call and sing those songs of Zion which she loved, when her large bright eyes would grow brighter, and her interesting face assume a more animated and intelligent glow.

As her disease advanced, she told her mother she felt glad at the appearance of a certain symptom, "for she knew now it could not be long before she should be released." Three days before she expired, it was observed by those with her that she was suddenly growing very ill, and her mother, not ready to part with one she had so long attended and become the more endeared to by her patient suffering, with a burst of sorrow left the room. Adeline observed it, and judging that they thought her dying, asked if it were so. Being answered that death must be very near, she seemed for a few minutes discomposed and uneasy. But the cloud soon passed; and on her mother's coming again to her bed, she said, "Mother, why should I shrink or fear to die? I think I have loved the Saviour. He will take me to himself. It was the enemy that made me for a moment doubt. I have no fear now."

The Sun of righteousness after this shone clear upon her. Her peace was like a river, full, flowing, unruffled. Not an anxiety or doubt for the future once interrupted her holy rapture. It was "joy unspeakable and full of glory." Whether in the body or out of the body, it seemed, like Paul, she could hardly tell; but evidently the spiritual world was opened to her; its unutterable glories beamed upon her soul; its music caught her ravished ear; its spirit was breathed into her heart; and her face became, as it were, transfigured, and it shone with a heavenly radiance and benignity, noticeable by all that looked upon her.

She lay looking upward, her dark eyes glowing with an unearthly but beautiful lustre, seemingly absorbed with subjects that gave her the most exquisite delight; and she would say, "Oh, could you see what I see! 'T is unspeakable. Oh, what beautiful brightness! 'T is Jesus and the angels."

When Christian friends called, she would look on them with benignity, and speak to them with great gentleness and cordiality, and then become absorbed again in holy contemplation. Once as her attention was called off, she looked with an expression of astonishment upon her bed and person, and said, "Mother, am I in the body? I thought I was with my Saviour." When asked if she would not be moved, "No, no," said she, "I lie as on down—

'Jesus can make a dying bed
Feel soft as downy pillows are.'"

Again, when asked if she did not suffer, "No," said she, "my body is dead; my arms have no feeling. Oh, this is spirit, this is spirit. Would I could tell you what I enjoy; but you will know it soon." To her mother and another friend she said, "It will be but a short parting; you will join me soon." And then she sang,

> "When we 've been there ten thousand years,
> Bright shining as the sun,
> We 've no less days to sing God's praise,
> Than when we first begun."

A short time before her last breath she said, "My lips grow stiff; I cannot speak plain. The room is growing dark now; I cannot see your faces. But Oh, that brightness, that brightness! There will be no night there. Tell me, my soul, can this be death? Oh, how peaceful, peaceful! Death has no sting. No, mother, there is no sting. Oh, if I could tell what I feel!"

A minute or two before expiring, she was heard to say, "Come, come," and something more that was lost in a whisper; and she sweetly fell asleep in Jesus, with a countenance of calm delight, the last impress and suffusion of that happy spirit upon its shell of clay.

> "Night-dews fall not more gently to the ground,
> Nor weary, worn-out winds expire so soft."

"Let me die the death of the righteous, and let my last end be like his."

It was the afternoon of the holy Sabbath when this dear disciple was taken to glory. She had said in the morning, "the angels would take her home before night." And when it was proposed to move her head, thinking it might give relief, "Oh, no, no," she replied; "don't you see the angels by me?" Then she told her mother, "To-day I shall be with father and Mary." There they now are in heaven, with crowns of gold, and palms in their hands, singing with angels, WORTHY IS THE LAMB.

A single remark is all that need be added to these brief notices of one of God's hidden suffering saints. How desirable to the Christian pilgrim is such an end—desirable as a significant seal of Christ's presence and favor; as a proof to the world of the power of religion; and as the most satisfactory consolation to surviving friends. Christ, so manifesting himself to the dying, seems the more precious to the living. Faith triumphing over the agonies of dissolution, preaches a sermon to beholders that none can deride, gainsay, or resist. And friends willingly part with their loved ones when they thus enter into the joy of their Lord. The dying of the unreconciled is dreadful to them and their friends, whether it be with severe physical pains or not. For them we weep bitter tears. But lamentation and death are swallowed up in victory through faith in Christ. "For if we believe that Jesus died and rose again, even so them also which sleep in Jesus will God bring with him."

H. T. C.

A POOR WIDOW'S SON.

There is so admirable a diversity in God's methods of bringing sinners to himself, together with so marvellous a uniformity as to that which is essential, that we can never fail of deriving some instruction from authentic narratives of conversion. If those who have the care of souls would oftener make records of remarkable facts in their pastoral experience, they might contribute largely to this fund of evangelical information. The little narrative which follows may be relied upon, as containing no colors of fiction; indeed it has been prepared on the principle of understating, rather than exaggerating the events recorded. For obvious reasons all the names have been concealed.

In the early part of the year 1847, I was called to visit a man whom I shall call Gordon. He was "the only son of his mother, and she was a widow." They were extremely poor, and lived in an attic in Bridge-street, in the city of New York. The aged mother had been a professing Christian for many years, and had brought up her son, during his childhood, in the knowledge of divine truth. But he afterwards went very far astray, wasted his substance, and at the time when I came to know him, was entirely dependent on this decrepit and feeble parent. He seldom attended any place of worship, and was in all respects a worldly, careless, and unbelieving man.

For a year or two, I had seen him only at rare intervals. At length his mother informed me that Gordon was confined to the house with a cough. I found him emaciated, feeble, and with marked symptoms of consumption. The disease came upon him with steps so sure and rapid, that he soon gave up every hope of recovery. In this state, racked with a dreadful cough, and with bones almost piercing his skin, he sat in his chair from day to day, being scarcely able to move about the room.

I early began to talk with him on religious subjects. He generally heard me with a kind of sullen respect, which showed that the topic was unwelcome. As he afterwards acknowledged, he felt my visits to be an annoyance, even while he admitted them to be tokens of friendship. To Mr. Gale, a pious friend, who also went to see him, Gordon said plainly, "Mr. Gale, I know the kindness of your intention, but all this talk gives me pain, and does me no manner of good. Indeed, so distressing to me is it to feel unable to fall in with your views and those of my minister, that if I were a rich man, I would take ship, go to the ends of the earth, and die there among strangers, where no one should concern himself about my spiritual state."

This perverseness and obstinacy of mind remained for some weeks. I continued to see him, as other duties allowed, and Mr. Gale went more frequently, spending hours with him in reading the Scriptures, in conversation, and in prayer. Such was his hardness, that all this seemed for a time to both of us very much like laboring against hope. Meanwhile, his poor mother was in an agony of soul for his salvation, which she expressed so constantly and so strongly that we sometimes feared it might even frustrate the end she had in view, by confirming him in his disgust. But God had purposes of mercy which we did not comprehend. By imperceptible degrees, the truth which he was continually hearing, made an impression on his heart. His ear was opened. One degree of interest succeeded another, till at length it was evident that Gordon was under the enlightening and convincing operations of the Holy Spirit. It would be difficult to give any distinct account of this gradation of feeling, extending as it did through months; but we were fully persuaded that now he was eagerly and importunately seeking the pardon of his sins. Now he listened with surprising earnestness; and though he could speak but little, he joined with unwonted fervor in the prayers which were offered. Still, he had attained to no comfortable light as to the way of access to an offended God.

At this stage, I was called away some hundreds of miles, and was absent about five weeks. During this period, Mr. Gale was faithfully and affectionately employed in laboring with the poor sufferer, who declined in body day by day. On returning to New York, in the early summer, the first thing I did after meeting with my family, was to hasten to Bridge-street, to ascend the narrow stairway, and to enter that attic chamber. I had not even made inquiry whether Gordon was alive or dead. On entering the room, I saw him seated in his accustomed place by the window. He was even thinner and more pallid than before. But there were smiles on his sunken cheeks, and a radiance in his countenance, and a beaming from his eye, which told me the change which had been wrought, and which I surely can never forget. His greeting was full of tenderness and love; and so far as his failing organs allowed, he proceeded to tell me the story of his redemption. From time to time, his old mother, pouring out tears of joy, took up the narrative, and supplied the deficiencies of his account.

Shortly after I had left him in the spring, his distress became more poignant, his sense of sin was more overwhelming, and he greatly feared lest he should not find mercy. Yet his mind was continually directed by Mr. Gale to the person and work of Christ; to his glorious obedience; to his death on the cross for sinners; and to the full and free offer of his righteousness to all who hear the gospel.

One night, as he lay alone in a little room adjoining that of his mother, she was led to go in, as she was wont to do, to see that he was in comfort, when he called her to him, and declared that God had revealed to him his love. He beheld Christ as his Saviour. He saw the way of salvation open, and the promise made good to *him*. His sins were pardoned, and he joyed in God, through our Lord Jesus Christ, by whom he was now receiving reconciliation. It was a change from night to day, from death to life. His strength was insufficient to express his joyful triumph. He wished all in the house to be called up, that they might hear what God had done for his soul. In a word, weak as he was, he passed a large part of the night in blessing and praising God for his distinguishing grace.

From this time forward, Gordon was, without any intermission that I remember, one of the happiest creatures I ever beheld; whereas I had formerly considered him one of the most miserable. As long as his voice held out, he was never weary of magnifying the love of Christ.

Nor was this a blind or enthusiastic joy. I looked anxiously to observe, during the few weeks which remained, how far the fruits and evidences of regeneration might be manifested, after so marked a revolution of feeling. And to the best of my knowledge and belief, there is no mark of genuine sanctification, allowed by his circumstances, which did not shine in him. A few of these, from among many, shall be mentioned.

In the earlier part of his illness, and under the irritating influence of disease, Gordon was fretful and impatient to an extraordinary degree. I have been filled with indignation at the manner in which he spoke to his mother, even when with trembling limbs she was attempting every thing for his relief. But now he was one of the gentlest and most tender sons. Words could scarcely express his gratitude and affection.

When we first addressed him on religious subjects, he was so dull and lethargic as to make us think his malady had rendered his mind incapable of deep emotion. But now, both his griefs and his joys overflowed. His penitence for a life of sin was never so melting as *after* he saw his sins forgiven through Jesus Christ. His mouth was full of God's praise all the day long, for having borne with him, and for having sent spiritual advisers to him. He once said to me, with memorable solemnity, "My dear pastor, let my case teach you never, never to give up striving with a poor hardened dying sinner, however impenetrable he may appear. If you and Mr. Gale had given me up, my soul had been lost."

Though poor Gordon could not go abroad to seek the salvation of souls, and though his painful and debilitating malady might naturally have concentrated his thoughts on himself, he was much exercised for the impenitent around him. He sent for such as were within his reach, and solemnly exhorted them to turn to the Lord. He sent messages to others. He desired that as many as possible might hear of the Lord's mercy towards him. And during a few days in which he was deprived of all use of his voice, he wrote sentences of Christian warning on a slate, to be read by visitors who might enter the room.

As his end approached more nearly, he was of course less and less able to make known what was passing within him. Yet his smile and his eye, and his significant gestures, especially in reply to inquiries, showed that he had peace, and sometimes exultation. So that when, after struggles for breath, he expired, we all felt the fullest assurance that he had fallen asleep in Jesus. J. W. A.

THE DYING REGRET OF HARRIET.

Harriet B—— was a teacher in my Sunday-school; and although not a professor of religion, she was far more punctual and faithful to her duties than many that were. She was a member of my Bible-class, and was among its most intelligent and interested members. Soon after I became her pastor, attracted by her serious deportment and intelligence, I sought an interview with her for religious conversation. Although remarkably diffident, she expressed a feeble but intelligent hope in Christ. She thoroughly understood her demerits as a sinner; she had clear views of the way of salvation through the atonement and righteousness of Christ; she fully comprehended the great truth, that *faith is the saving grace*, and she hoped she did believe in Christ.

Having ascertained this to be her state of mind, I

placed before her her duty to connect herself with the church of God. She expressed her great unworthiness of such a privilege, and her great unfitness for communion with the saints. She spoke much of her remaining corruption, of her varying feelings, of her besetting sins; and she expressed it as her conviction, that none should attach themselves to the church until they were assured of their good estate. I strove to instruct her upon the difference between *faith* and *assurance*. She soon comprehended me; and feeling that I had gained my point, and that at the next communion, which was then near, she would profess faith in Christ, the interview closed.

The communion-season came and passed away, and Harriet, as usual, was only a solemn spectator of the solemn scene. Repeatedly had I interviews with her similar to that now narrated, and at the close of which I indulged the hope, that at the next communion-season she would connect herself with the church. But these hopes, often indulged, were as often disappointed. Her fidelity to her Sabbath-school class, her regularity in attendance upon all the means of grace, her readiness to labor for the cause of Christ, never intermitted; but communion-seasons and years passed away without her confessing Christ before men.

Late on a summer evening, I was called from a social circle of Christian friends to see Harriet before she died. She was seized with a fever, which, before it was feared, had almost extinguished life; and before she passed away from earth, she desired one more interview with me. Her dying chamber presented a scene never to be forgotten. The family, except her mother, who had previously passed into the skies, was around her bed; and with a mind clear and collected, she was rapturously speaking to them about Jesus, and the glory, honor, immortality, and eternal life, which he had purchased for all that believe in him. And with a propriety and earnestness that I have never known surpassed, she exhorted them all to believe and to obey Christ. Never did I witness such a change. The diffident, retiring female was now all confidence; the tongue that was almost dumb, now sweetly and delightfully sung; the trembling hope was exchanged for assurance and joy; and the hand which she dared not put forth to partake of the elements of the broken body and shed blood of Christ, was now extended to grasp the crown of glory.

When the excitement of addressing her impenitent friends had passed, and she had recovered a little from the exhaustion, I took my seat by her side, and held with her my final interview, until we meet in heaven. Her confidence in Christ was strong and cheerful. The clouds which, like dark curtains, had so long hung around her mind, had all passed away, and the light of the Saviour's countenance shone upon her with the brightness of the sun in its strength. And after requesting me to preach a sermon to the young, after her burial, on the text, "Prepare to meet thy God," she uttered with the deepest emotion the following memorable sentiment: "Would, would, O would that I had taken your advice, and that I had confessed Christ upon earth. I hope to enjoy him for ever in glory; but from the joy, and from the bliss of having confessed Christ before men, I am now, and shall be for ever excluded. Warn all not to do as I have done." I prayed with her, and bade her farewell.

Soon afterwards the silver cord was loosed, the golden bowl was broken, and her spirit rose up to the God that gave it.

This narrative has deeply impressed upon my mind a few truths, which I desire to place upon record, for the prayerful and serious consideration of every reader.

1. Many, very many are prevented from professing Christ before men, because they discriminate not between *faith* and *assurance*. Here was the practical error of Harriet, and which for years kept her from the communion of the saints. *Faith*, is believing what God has said to be true, and treating it as true; *assurance*, is the persuasion that I do believe—that I am a Christian. These are very distinct. Faith, is trusting in Christ for mercy; assurance enables us to say, I know I believe. The great prerequisite for professing Christ before men, is a cordial belief in Christ, and not the assurance that we are Christians. Reader, are you in the state of mind of her whose brief narrative I have here placed before you? Do you believe in Christ? Then wait not for assurance, to profess Christ before men. With the delightful persuasion, that Christ is mighty to save, willing to save, waiting to save, *all* that believe, go and devote yourself to his service, and follow him in the way; and assurance, and all the other graces which grow along the path of obedience, will be yours in due time.

2. Many are prevented from professing Christ because of *wrong views of the prerequisites* to such a profession. It is the superficial and unconverted that usually press their way into the church: the serious

and sober, to whom God has revealed what is in their hearts, usually, like Harriet, are found waiting at the gates, and watching at the posts of the doors, anxious to enter in, but yet afraid, lest all may not be right. She felt her unworthiness of such a privilege; but who are worthy? She felt unfit for the communion of the saints; but who are fit? And are not the best and holiest members of the church, like ourselves, imperfect? She spoke of her remaining corruption, but so did Paul; and of her varying feelings, but so did David; and of her besetting sins, but these had all the saints. It is far better to feel unfit, than fit; unworthy, than worthy. Christ came not to call the righteous, but sinners to repentance. It is they who are sick that have need of the physician. It is the weary and heavy-laden that Christ invites to himself for rest. Reader, is the question before your mind, "Shall I, or shall I not profess Christ before men? As you would do duty intelligently, and follow Christ truly, I implore you to permit nothing to enter into its settlement but that which truly belongs to it. Do you feel that you are a sinner? Do you feel that Christ alone can save you? Do you feel that you can rest alone upon him for salvation, as he is offered to you in the gospel?

> "Let not conscience make you linger,
> Nor of fitness fondly dream."

Go and join yourself to the people of God, and follow Christ in all the paths of duty, and your light will become brighter and brighter even unto the perfect day. To profess Christ before men, the great prerequisite is a true and lively faith in him. Let all of whom believing and doubting Harriet is the representative, ponder this truth, until they see it in the broad light in which it is written on the pages of the New Testament.

3. Let none think that they can *serve Christ as fully, and possess the joys of salvation as abundantly,* without professing him before men, as by so doing. This position, though often asserted, is utterly false. It involves a general principle which lays the axe at the root of the church as a divine institution. If one may serve Christ fully away from the church, so may all; and if all adopt this principle, what becomes of the church? It passes away from the earth in two generations.

Besides, obedience is better than sacrifice; and the test of true obedience is to follow the Lord fully. Can we so follow him, away from his church and people, when we have the opportunity to join them? Is there a solitary case to be found among all the records of men, in proof of this? Who, on their dying bed, have ever rejoiced that they served Christ disconnected with his church? I have known many who attempted to do this, and in every case I could trace it to a latent desire to serve God and mammon. And the Saviour tells us this is impossible.

The dying Harriet felt, when trembling on the confines of eternity, that her failing to confess Christ before men would subtract from her joy for ever. And she felt truly. One of the most precious promises of the Saviour is made to those who confess him before men. And I feel that I should be disobedient to her dying injunction unless I lifted my voice, warning all men everywhere against those errors which dying she deplored. There are consolations in Christ which none can truly know, here or hereafter, but those that follow the Lord fully.

4. Harriet died in her youth, and while putting off a present duty to a future day. That future day she never saw, and the duty was never performed. And before she entered the chariot which conveyed her to heaven, she felt, and she said, that her song of praise to the Redeemer must be lower than the song of those who confessed Christ amid many tribulations, who washed their robes and made them white in the blood of the Lamb. Reader, do your duty to-day. Your highest duty is to follow Christ. So follow him as you will wish you had done when you come to die. These truths are addressed to you from the death-bed of Harriet. N. M.

THE SLAVE JOHN.

Few things shed so sweet an influence over the mind as the memory of the pious dead. It connects the past with the present, and both the past and present with the future, when kindred souls shall rejoin each other. We reason thus: Did they conquer? So may we. Did they fight hard with sins, and doubts, and fears? So must we. Was God faithful to them? So will he be to us. Was their victory by the blood of the Lamb? We must conquer by the same.

One whose memorial was never written by man, I specially love to think of. He was not rich, nor highly gifted. He was born and died a slave. All his wisdom came from above. Yet the hours I spent in his cabin were more precious than any I ever passed with the gay, or even with the pious in prosperity.

His name was John. He hired his time; and, besides working by the day as he could, he was sexton at the church where I worshipped. I was often attracted by his peaceful countenance, no less than by his obliging behavior. At the beginning of the services he took his seat in a back pew, and seemed devoutly to unite in each act of worship. Perhaps no one who saw him, doubted that his heart was engaged. For a time he attracted attention only as a pious and polite man.

At length he was missing for two Sabbaths. I then heard that he was very sick. I went to see him, and found him suffering greatly from an attack of his old disease, asthma. Still I hoped he would soon be well, and go with the voice of joy and praise to the house of God. But God's plan was to put him into the furnace of affliction, there to show what divine grace could do. For more than two years his sufferings were constant and severe. Seldom could he lie down. He commonly sat in a chair, leaning a little forward, and having an aspect of the most quiet submission. A more serene countenance I never saw. I still remember it. Often each breath was a gasp. Yet he never uttered a murmuring word. Some things in his past history had been very afflicting, but he never alluded to them. His song was all of goodness and mercy. It was my privilege to read to him Baxter's Saints' Rest. It was manna to his soul. Often, as I read, have tears of joy run down his face. While he heard the chapter on the nature of the heavenly rest, his feelings almost overcame him. Peace, hope, joy, and a sweet sense of his interest in Christ, and his nearness to heaven, bore him far beyond his pains. He exclaimed, "Glory! It is mine! Jesus bought it for poor me. Oh, how sweet it will be!" I often paused, fearing that his strength would fail. But he would ask me to read on. When I was obliged to leave him, his heart was still full of glad emotions. Laying his head in my hands, and holding them, with sobs and tears he ascribed glory and honor to the Lamb, and bade me farewell.

Thus the winter passed away. The body was failing, but the inward man grew stronger and stronger, and the spirit was pluming its wings for its upward flight. Spring brought but slight alleviation to his sufferings. My own health failing, I went away in search of health. With deep regret I left this humble child of God. I had earnestly desired the privilege of smoothing his passage to the tomb, and of having my own faith strengthened by witnessing the grace of God in him. When I left him, I thought I should see his face no more. But on my return, after an absence of several months, I went to his cabin, and finding him still there, I said, "John, how have you got through the summer?" He replied, "Your poor servant would have perished, but the Lord has held him up; I have passed through deep waters, but they have not overflowed me, and through the fire, but it has not burned me. My poor wife was ready to sink; I had to hold her up with one hand, and buffet the waves with the other. Out of the depths I cried unto the Lord, and he heard me, and delivered me. Praised be his name!" On inquiry, I found that his little earnings were all gone; that the industry of his wife could not supply his and her necessities, and that he had been in want. Yet he had told no one. Nor did he utter any complaint against God or man. I said, "What do you most need?" He replied, "Grace, more grace." Many comforts were sent him, but he daily grew weaker. Every act of kindness from man called forth his gratitude to God, who had put it into the hearts of his people to send so timely relief.

One afternoon a message came that John was dying, and wished to see me. It was cold and stormy. John's cabin was remote. As I went past the abodes of the rich, I contrasted their state with his, and I was troubled, until I remembered that "whom the Lord loveth he chasteneth." I found John on his bed, supported by pillows, and in agony. In broken syllables he said, "I am going, and I wanted to bid you farewell." I opened my little Bible, and read to him the twenty-third Psalm. I also repeated the hymn commencing,

"The hour of my departure's come,
I hear the voice that calls me home."

The word of God was always a well-spring of joy to him, and he soon forgot his pain in view of the rest before him. His humble home became the house of God and the gate of heaven. Many things suitable to his state he said, the sum of which was, that he was happy in God through Jesus Christ. But the hour of deliverance had not yet come. Every day his sufferings increased, but patience, hope, and faith abounded. At last, He who sat by the furnace said, "It is enough." With two Christian friends I went to see him. He had failed rapidly. We inquired how he was. A pious colored friend replied, "Dark, dark.

The enemy has come in like a flood, and he has let go his hold of Jesus, and is sinking, sinking." I went to his bedside. Deep gloom sat upon his brow. Every feature expressed agony. The quiet, peaceful look was gone. I said, "John, Jesus is with you." With anguish he said, "Oh, he has left me; he has left me. Must your poor servant perish?" We felt that vain was the help of man, and, falling on our knees, we offered united prayer. While we yet spoke, God heard, and bade "the lion of the evening" to cease his roaring. Gradually the groans ceased. For a time all was quiet. Then the soft whisper, "Peace, glory, glory, precious Saviour," was heard. When we arose, all was changed. Darkness was turned into light, and the glory of the Lord was revealed in him. Prayer was turned into praise, and we sang,

"And let this feeble body fail," etc.

That precious hour! Can it ever be forgotten? Around that bed were gathered the bond and the free, Methodists, Episcopalians, and Presbyterians. All joined to sing, with the departing saint, hallelujah. Though he had long been a member of the Episcopal church, yet all names were forgotten in view of the cross and glory of Christ, and all rejoiced with joy unspeakable and full of glory; while the sufferer forgot his pains, and often said, "Bless the Lord, O my soul; and all that is within me, bless his holy name."

At length we were compelled to leave this mount of privilege, and we bade farewell to our dying brother. I never saw him more. Two hours after, his spirit

"Burst from the thraldom of encumbering clay,
And sprang to liberty, and light, and life."

More than twenty-six years have passed since that happy night. They have brought with them joys and sorrows, cares and comforts; but never have I forgotten that hour and its scenes. All who knelt around that bed, except myself, have now gone to be partakers of the joys above. All bore testimony that Jesus Christ is faithful to his promises. One of the loved sisters who was there, died as she had lived, but, as I was told, with joys greatly increased. As I sat by the death-bed of another, she said, "You know what a poor timid Christian I have always been; but now I have no fears, no, not one. All is peace." And so she too departed, to be for ever with the Lord.

"Who is wise, and he shall understand these things? prudent, and he shall know them? for the ways of the Lord are right, and the just shall walk in them; but the transgressors shall fall therein." Reader, I ask not, are you willing to die; but I ask, Are you prepared to die? Is Jesus Christ all your hope and all your salvation? Have you been born again? If not, your death must be followed by an eternity of woe. Flee for refuge to the gracious Saviour. Glory will not follow death, unless death is preceded by *grace reigning* in your heart, through Jesus Christ. G.

JOSEPH, THE MINISTER'S SON.

About the middle of December, a group of young people were gathered in the dwelling of their godly minister for conference and prayer. A few of the number had been for some weeks the subjects of deep religious impressions, and two or three were cherishing lively hope in the mercy of God through Jesus Christ. Perhaps twenty-five were present, and by no one of them can the scenes of that evening have been forgotten. God the Spirit was there, and his power was felt, and his efficiency was manifested.

In an adjoining room lay one of the sons of the minister, an interesting lad of twelve years, who was ill of an incurable disease, and expecting very soon to be in eternity. Though a great sufferer, he was happy. Grace had renewed his heart, Christ was precious to him; death had no terror; he looked to heaven as his home. At his request the meeting was held, for he wished, from that border-land which he was treading, to say a few words to the young whom he was leaving. After the services had proceeded about one hour, he was brought into the room, and placed in an easy-chair. The light from the stand shone full upon his features. He was pale and emaciated, and, but for the glow of holy animation that lighted up his eye, he would have seemed ready for his shroud.

In a few short sentences, articulated with difficulty, he told the silent listeners what great things the Saviour had done for him, and how bright was his prospect of that better world whose glories were already opening to his view. Then, as if special strength had been given him, he raised his voice, and said, "My dear young friends, I am going to Jesus; he calls me home, and I go joyfully. May I not hope to meet you *all* there? Will you not *now* give your hearts to the Saviour, and so serve him all your days as to be prepared to dwell with him for ever? O do not put off so important a work. Look on me, and see how necessary it is to repent and believe in early life. Had I now no hope in Christ, what should I do—where should I go? When you lay me in my grave, remember my words." He was exhausted, and his brother bore him to the bed from which he never rose again.

The scene was indeed tender and affecting. The words of the dying youth sunk into the hearts of the impenitent. Exhortations and prayers followed that had the very unction of heaven. The place was a Bochim. Nearly all bowed before the gentle pressure of the divine influence, like willows before the summer breeze, and yielded without resistance to the Redeemer's claims.

Among the attendants at that meeting, was a young man who had just commenced teaching the district school. He had been religiously educated, and was regarded as "piously inclined." But his heart was opposed to God, and he endeavored to brace himself against all the appeals and influences of that impressive occasion. He was far from easy; he knew his duty; but he shed not a tear, he exhibited no sign of emotion. He held up his head, looked gravely, and determined to appear unaffected. But after the services were concluded, while the few converts were singing,

> "Stop, poor sinner, stop and think,
> Before you further go,"

the inward springs were touched by an invisible Agent. He felt what never can be described. A friend whispered to him the inquiry, "Have you no interest in this great subject?" This opened a sluice for the pent-up emotion. He too confessed the power which he could no longer resist. He became an inquirer, and for a week writhed under the anguish of conviction, when, by the grace of God, he found relief at the foot of the cross.

During that week the amiable young Joseph breathed his last. Many lamented the early transfer of such a plant of promise; all believed that he had gone to unfold his graces in the paradise of God. The night before his funeral, the school-teacher and two associates watched with his remains. It was a dark night, and bitterly cold. The sky was overcast, and every thing portended a storm. No tramp of feet or rumbling of wheels was heard without. All was solemn and awful within. The air pressed with mournful cadences through the casements. The large fire of maple lighted up the apartment where the watchers were sitting—the very apartment where the "young people's meeting" had a few evenings before been held, and connected with which were touching associations. The door was open into the room where slept the youth in placid repose. The three young men sat near together, and conversed upon solemn themes. Their feelings were similar; they had no hope of future glory; they were seeking the Saviour, and fearing they should fail and be lost. Timid as children, every sound made them hold their breath, and quiver with solicitude. Occasionally the ground would crack with a loud report, so intense was the cold, and the doors and windows shook with the concussion. It was a long dreary night to those awakened sinners, watching with the dead.

The next day the house was filled with sympathizing neighbors. The sleeper lay in his coffin, with a face like polished alabaster, his eyes perfectly closed, his hair laid smoothly over his temples, and his lips a little parted, as if he would give one more exhortation. The spectators came one after another, and looked and said, "How sweet the expression!"

A hymn was sung—the very hymn for the occasion:

"Why do we mourn departing friends?"

and never did that inestimable tune, China, sound more impressively, or more deeply thrill all hearts. A sermon was preached that contained many a graphic picture of the blessedness of the righteous, and many a melting appeal to the young to honor the Saviour's claims. The bearers took up the body, and a large procession followed to the place of sepulture. It was a lonely spot, enclosed by a stone wall, and overrun with ferns and briars. As the bearers passed in with their light burden, the school-teacher, who was one of the number, stepped near the grave of his father, who had two years before found there his resting-place. O, what a rush of emotion was there, when he thought of paternal counsels and prayers! The body was lowered into its narrow home, the earth fell with a hollow sound upon the coffin, the grave was filled, the sods were laid over the little hillock, the weeping father thanked his friends for their kindness, and the people dispersed thoughtfully to their homes.

From that time the religious interest spread, and soon became general through the town. More than two hundred souls were the happy subjects of renewing grace. The churches were greatly refreshed and strengthened, candidates for the ministry were multiplied, and honor accrued to the Redeemer's name.

Years have since passed away, but many of the fruits of that precious revival remain. That school-teacher is the pastor of a Christian church, and his labors have been largely blessed by the applying influences of the Holy Spirit. Whoever may forget young Joseph, he will not. S.

A STUDENT FOR THE MINISTRY.

It is sometimes said that college influences are unfavorable to growth in grace. But this is by no means universal. The most remarkable instances of growth in grace the writer has ever known, have occurred within the walls of college.

A young man entered one of our colleges. He had the ministry in view. For some time he was scarcely noticed by his fellow-students, he was so modest and retiring. He first attracted attention by his regularity in attending religious meetings, and next by the accuracy of his recitations. Before the close of the year, he was regarded as one of the best scholars in the class, and yet he did not seem to be ambitious. No indication of a desire to excel others appeared. He studied from a sense of duty.

To a friend he once said, "When I first came to college, I felt a desire to stand high in my class, and to be popular; but I found that the spirit of ambition and the spirit of prayer could not dwell together. I came to the conclusion that I must seek to do my duty and to please God. When I had fully made up my mind to that, I found very few difficulties in my way. I believe there are fewer temptations in college than anywhere else."

His growth in grace was rapid; his path was as the shining light. It was suggested by some of his friends that one so ripe for heaven would not be permitted to remain long on earth. A fellow-student once asked him, "Have you ever thought respecting your life, whether it would be long or short?" His reply was, "I do not think it will be a long one; I used to have a great dread of an early death, but that is over. I shall go when infinite wisdom and infinite love determines. I have but one Master to serve, wherever I am."

Before his collegiate course was half completed, he suffered an attack of bleeding at the lungs. He went home and remained some months, when having partially regained his strength, he returned to college. He was cheerful, but his manner was still more gentle and subdued. There was the same devotion to duty, though his ability for study and Christian effort was impaired. In the summer of the Junior year, he bled again, and was with difficulty conveyed home. His strength again rallied, and it was hoped that a change of climate and an active life would prolong his days. As winter approached, arrangements were made for removing him to the South; but he was to remove to a brighter land than that of the palm and the orange. Before the first frost fell on the flowers he bled again, and it was evident that he would never more rise from his bed.

For several days he had spoken only in a whisper: one afternoon, to the surprise of friends who were around him, he spoke audibly and with animation. He testified of the grace of God, and exhorted his friends to strive for eminent holiness. He then asked them to unite with him in singing a hymn. He selected the one beginning with the line,

"There is a fountain filled with blood,"

and sung it with a clear, full voice. "Now," said he, "I am going to sleep, and shall awake in heaven. Farewell all." He soon fell into a gentle slumber, which passed insensibly into the slumber of death. No doubt his spirit-voice was mingling with those of the redeemed in heaven a few moments after he had finished his last song on earth. He had fulfilled his allotted course; he had finished the work which had been given him to do.

How is it with the reader? Has he but one Master to serve; and is death, in his view, simply the door by which he will pass from one scene of service into another? If he should be called from earth now, would he have finished the work given him to do?

A.

EMMA.

Emma had been reared under worldly influences. Beautiful and accomplished, and with brilliant worldly prospects, she knew nothing of true happiness—who does?—till she found peace in believing. Her piety developed under the faithful counsels of a godly companion, and the blessing of the Spirit on the reading of the Scriptures, with a freshness and vigor that admitted of none of the trammels of human philosophy: her faith was as simple as a child's. It received the divine promises as meaning just what they imported, and as being made to her. Though she was the light of a refined and wealthy circle, and bound by all the ties that attach to earth, she "desired to depart and be with Christ." The hand of disease was laid upon her. Affection and science exhausted the aids of soothing and healing. Foreign travel brought no relief. Youth and beauty withered before the destroyer. Days and nights of suffering wasted her vital energies. The struggle with death had commenced.

How did she meet the mysterious messenger? As his victim, or his conqueror? With the calmness of matured faith—with the triumph of assured hope. The trusting soul leaned on the arm of the Beloved, and all was peace and joy. Hear the dying soliloquy: "No more pain—no more suffering—no more sin. *O, how nobly Jesus reigns!* and I shall be like him, and see him as he is."

Yes; "the government shall be upon his shoulder, and he shall be called Wonderful, Counsellor, the mighty God, the everlasting Father, the Prince of peace." He reigns in wisdom: "His understanding is infinite." He reigns in righteousness: "the sceptre of his kingdom is a right sceptre." He reigns in love: "altogether lovely." He reigns *nobly*: "Worthy art thou; for thou wast slain, and hast redeemed us to God by thy blood." O, for Emma's faith, for Emma's Saviour, for Emma's blessedness! R. S. C.

RELIGION IN THE DOMESTIC CIRCLE.

A CATHOLIC HUSBAND AND WIFE.

A FEW years since, a young merchant with his accomplished and beautiful wife, located himself on one of the frontiers of our country. He was educated for a Catholic priest, but the providence of God hedged up his way to that profession, and he entered on mercantile business, in which he was very successful. His wife also had always lived with Roman-catholics, and though her friends mingled in the higher classes of society, and had free intercourse with Protestants, yet in their religious views they were bigoted.

The lot of this young and interesting couple, in their new location, was cast in the vicinity of a missionary station, and their politeness and acquaintance with the forms of society led them to treat the missionaries with kindness and attention. Thus they lived for some time, each enjoying their own religious views. The system of colportage was not then known *in name*, but the missionaries were tract distributers, and scattered the precious messages of love and mercy wherever they went. One of them was returning a call to these Catholic friends, and left on the table the tract of Baxter, entitled, "Heaven Lost." It lay some time untouched, but at last, to while away a lonely hour, this young and interesting woman took it up, and the perusal awakened a new train of reflections. She saw and felt that the course she was pursuing endangered her eternal happiness, and this led to a conviction that she was a sinner in the sight of God, and needed something more than the forms of Catholic worship to change her vile nature, and fit her to dwell in the presence of infinite purity.

But what should she do? She feared to tell her husband what were her feelings, for he had ridiculed the practice of the missionaries in thus scattering their books. She dared not go to the missionaries for instruction, for that would expose her not only to the disapprobation of her husband, but also to the anathemas of her own church; and this she considered an evil next in degree to that of the displeasure of God. Struggling with these feelings, and her heart ready to break with a sense of its own vileness, she one night retired to her bed before her husband came in from his business.

After a while he entered the house, and going into the room where she was tossing on her sleepless pillow, he opened the bookcase, and that same tract fell from off one of the shelves. He had before several times thrown it aside, and now taking it up, vexatiously remarked, "I can go nowhere but what I must be tormented with this tract; but I'll be troubled with it no longer—I'll burn it." He caught it up impatiently, and was about putting his threat into execution, when his wife ventured to say, "I would read it first, Samuel." Influenced partly by politeness to the friend who had left it, and partly by complaisance to the wife whom he loved as his own soul, he turned, seated himself at his desk, and began to peruse it. Although his position at the desk was such that his wife could not see his countenance, yet she watched his movements with almost breathless anxiety, and soon perceived he was devoting himself with earnestness to its contents.

He soon inquired, "Have you read this, Maria?" She tremblingly answered that she had. He became more and more absorbed, and at last said, with much apparent solemnity, "Maria, I don't believe you have read this attentively; shall I read it to you?" She assented; and he, changing his position, turned to the commencement of the tract, and began reading it aloud. As he proceeded, anxiety was manifest in his countenance, his voice grew tremulous, and as the fear of his disapprobation was swept from her mind, her own bursting heart found vent in sobs and tears. Thus they proceeded through the whole tract, and when the last page was finished, he was not only convinced of sin, but of the inefficacy of his false hopes to relieve his burdened soul; and was ready to unite with her in inquiring the way of deliverance.

But they knew not what to do. Neither of them had ever offered a prayer to God through the Saviour who died for sinners. Neither of them knew any thing of the Bible, which will direct the inquiring soul aright; and that night was spent in such agony as can scarcely be conceived by a mind which has been instructed in the way of salvation. The morning dawned, but thick darkness reigned in that dwelling; and before the middle of the day their inward agony had so conquered not only their pride, but their fear of Catholic anathemas, that they unitedly ordered their carriage, and were taken to the mission-house. The scenes of that interview will long be remembered by all who were present. The husband, who carried there a rebellious heart, returned with a broken one, pleading with his still agonized wife to yield herself into the hands of the Saviour, whom he had found willing to receive him. A few hours only intervened before she could rejoice with him, and unite in heart at the family altar he had established. From that time their efforts in the cause of Christ were progressive, and many were led by their spirit and conversation to exclaim, "What hath God wrought!"

Years have since passed, and the beloved Maria has, we trust, received from her Saviour her everlasting crown, and is now praising him in the heaven she *did not lose;* while her husband still lingered on the shores of time, to glorify God by an active Christian course, and to train their babes for immortality.

Anna.

MY WIFE IS THE CAUSE OF IT.

It is now more than forty years ago, that Mr. L—— called at the house of Dr. B——, one very cold morning, on his way to H——. "Sir," said the doctor, "the weather is very frosty; will you not take something to drink before you start?" In that early day, ardent spirits were deemed indispensable to warmth in winter. When commencing a journey, and at every stopping-place along the road, the traveller used intoxicating drinks to keep him warm.

"No," said Mr. L——, "I never touch any thing of the kind, and I will tell you the reason: my wife is the cause of it. I had been in the habit of meeting some of our neighbors every evening, for the purpose of playing cards. We assembled at each other's shop, and liquors were introduced. After a while we met not so much for the purpose of playing as drinking, and I used to return home late in the evening, more or less intoxicated. My wife always met me at the door affectionately, and when I chided her for sitting up so late for me, she kindly replied, 'I prefer doing so, for I cannot sleep when you are out.'

"This always troubled me, and I wished in my heart that she would only begin to scold me, for then I could have retorted and relieved my conscience. But she always met me with the same gentle and loving spirit.

"Things passed on thus for some time, when at last I resolved that I would, by remaining very late and returning much intoxicated, provoke her displeasure so much as to cause her to lecture me, when I meant to answer her with severity, and thus by creating another issue between us, unburden my bosom of its present trouble.

"I returned in such a plight about four o'clock in the morning. She met me at the door with her usual tenderness, and said, 'Come in, husband; I have just been making a warm fire for you, because I knew you would be cold. Take off your boots and warm your feet, and here is a cup of hot coffee.'

"Doctor, that was too much. I could not endure it any longer, and I resolved that moment that I would never touch another drop while I lived, and I never will."

He never did. He lived and died practising total abstinence from all intoxicating drinks, in a village which intemperance has ravaged as much as any other in this state.

That man was my father, and that woman my mother. The facts above related I received from the doctor himself, when on a visit to my native village, not long since.

May we not safely assert, that were there more wives like my blessed mother, there would be fewer confirmed drunkards? My father was a man of generous impulses and social instincts, just the man to be led into habits of inebriation, and just the man also to feel the impression such gentleness was calculated to make.

Let those wives who witness with agony the commencement of any evil habits in their husbands, be encouraged to try what patient, persevering love can do. Let their motto be, "She openeth her mouth with wisdom, and in her tongue is the law of kindness." L.

A GAMBLER AND HIS WIFE.

In the village where I am a pastor is a gambling-house, to which multitudes resort to play billiards and cards. It was kept, a few years since, by a Mr. ——, whose wife, a most interesting and amiable young woman, who was in the habit of attending my church, became hopefully converted, and made a public profession of religion. He *never* visited the sanctuary, and studiously avoided all means of grace, devoting himself entirely to his miserable business. Indeed, he had been trained to it from his childhood, having from early years been employed as a rider at horseraces, and always mingled in the society of the profligate.

From the moment the Spirit touched her heart, the Lord poured out upon her the spirit of grace and supplication for him; and she pleaded earnestly, and fainted not, that he might see his sinfulness, and flee from the wrath to come. Often would she await his return from the billiard-room at midnight, upon her knees; sometimes expecting when he opened the door to see him under conviction of sin, and disappointed when she found it otherwise.

Month after month rolled by, and no cloud of mercy seemed to gather about her habitation, and yet, like the prophet Elijah's, her eye of faith saw the rain descending.

Much to my surprise, I was summoned one morning to the house of Mr. ——, to converse with him on the subject of his salvation. I found him in the deepest agony under the pressure of his guilt, and earnestly inquiring, "What must I do to be saved?" His sense of sin was very vivid, and his apprehension of the perfect justice of God in his perdition very clear. Among the burdens which crushed him, was that of having taken money from others which did not belong to him. I advised him to make immediate confession and restitution, and at the same time abandon his ruinous business. I then prayed with him, and left him weeping bitterly.

He instantly set about the work of repentance in good earnest. Going to his partner, he said, "I shall never enter that billiard-room again." To those whom he had wronged, he made a full confession and offer of restitution. That evening for the first time I found him at our weekly prayer-meeting, when he requested the people of God to pray for him. From that day he became a burning and a shining light among us. His trials were very great, but his faith never failed, nor did he lose his first love.

But it may be asked how, under his peculiarly unfavorable circumstances, was he awakened? The answer will add another testimony to the truth of the sovereign grace of God, as conclusive as that which the conversion of Saul of Tarsus furnishes. Mr. —— was awakened at the billiard-room and at the card-table. Two men had been playing, and one, by false shuffling of the cards, had been plundered of his last cent. Filled with despair, he rose, caught a chair, and dashed it in his agony through the window. A sight of his countenance was the sermon which the

Holy Spirit blessed to the conviction of Mr. ——. He resolved that hour to seek the Lord, and he sought him with his whole heart.

How naturally do reflections such as the following arise in view of such a fact.

1. Never despair of the salvation of any man, so long as he is spared by God to live in the world of mercy.

2. All things are possible to him that believeth, and who prays in faith.

3. Let wives who have ungodly husbands who will not attend the sanctuary, hope in God, and pray on.

4. How rich is the distinguishing grace of God. What would have become of Paul, or Mr. ——, or you, or I, or any one else, were it not true that God "hath mercy on whom he will have mercy, and compassion on whom he will have compassion?" L.

THE DOOR WAS SHUT.

Mrs. F—— was educated as "a Friend." When she married, her residence was several miles from any meeting; but though out of the reach of the ordinary means of grace, she was not out of the reach of the colporteur, nor of the Spirit of God. On one occasion, when she was alone in the house, as she was looking at her expense-book, indifferent to her soul, the tract with the title, "The Door was Shut," which had some time before been placed in the family by Rev. Mr. P——, fell from the book: she stooped to pick it up, and as she did so, her eye fell upon the title. It was quaint—it was short—it was startling—*The door was shut.* Her attention was arrested; she began to read, and as she read she began to tremble. For the first time in her life she *felt* herself a sinner, and began to realize that she was in danger of being lost for ever. Her distress was very great. What must she do—what could she do?

She had no one to converse with—no Christian friend near to advise her; her mind was in midnight gloom; she had heard of prayer, but hardly knew what it was, for she had never prayed in all her life; however, she could but try: she bowed herself before God, and cried to him for mercy, but without avail; no relief could she find. All through that day and night, and through all the next day, did her distress continue.

When her husband entered the house on his return from a journey, he noticed her distress, and inquired the cause. On learning it, though not himself a professor of religion, he bade her not to be discouraged, but to read the Bible, and she would there find direction. She took his advice, and opened the sacred word, and her eye fell upon a delightful passage in Romans which God blessed to her, and she became unspeakably happy in the love of Christ.

She now longed to find some of the people of God, to tell them what he had done for her; and in a day or two she rode twenty-seven miles to converse with the minister who married her, with whose church she afterwards united. E. D. F.

A PROUD HUSBAND AND HIS WIFE.

Many years have passed since it was my privilege to mingle in the scenes connected with the gracious work of grace in C——, M—— county, New Jersey. One incident that occurred during the revival, illustrating the influence of a praying wife, made a lasting impression on my mind, which I am induced to communicate, in the hope that its publication may encourage other wives to "thank God, and take courage."

Mrs. —— became deeply impressed upon the subject of personal religion, and the duty of yielding her heart to God and securing an interest in the "great salvation." With a decision of mind characteristic of the lady, she cast away the weapons of her warfare, made an unconditional surrender of herself to the Lord, and speedily found "peace in believing," and "joy in the Holy Ghost."

Before making a public manifestation of the change which had been wrought in her by the grace of God, she felt that she must open her mind to her husband, who was not a professor of religion, and ask his permission to unite with the church. He was anxious to have the good opinion of the church-going people, and to be considered a strict moralist; yet he spent his Sabbath, not in the sanctuary, but in visiting from house to house, or in looking over his farm. He was accustomed to "measure himself by himself," and to compare himself with others, and especially with halting professors, and to conclude that he was considerably better than those who made a profession of religion.

With some apprehension of a refusal, Mrs. —— informed her husband that she felt it to be her duty to serve God and to unite with the church, and wished his consent to her so doing. He heard her request in silence, his countenance indicating a severe mental conflict, and at length, with an effort at composure, said, "I have no objections. I do not wish to act the part of a tyrant over you; unite with the church, if you feel it to be your duty, but I cannot go with you." Grateful to God that he had put it into the heart of her husband to give his consent to her uniting with the church, she hastened with joyful steps to the temple of God where the saints kept "holy day." Upon her return from the meeting in the evening, she found that her companion had retired for the night. She entered the chamber softly, supposing him to be asleep, and bowing by the bedside, poured out her soul to God in prayer on the behalf of her much-loved but unconverted husband.

When the time arrived for those who proposed uniting with the church, "to give a reason for the hope within them," Mrs. —— was one of the many who presented themselves as candidates for membership; but her husband was not there, he had voluntarily remained at home, "to keep the children."

During the introductory exercises of the morning, to the wonder and surprise of all, Mr. —— the husband entered the house, and with a calm and cheerful countenance went forward and took a seat by the side of his wife, near the pulpit. At a proper time, he rose and said as follows: "Christian friends, I have come to tell you what God has done for my soul. I remained without any interest concerning my soul up to the time when my dear wife asked my permission to unite with the church. Her request fell upon my ears like a thunderclap, and went to my heart like a dagger. I felt that the peace of my family was destroyed, and my proud and rebellious heart rose up in opposition, and had I followed my own inclination, I should have forbidden her to make a profession of religion. But I feared public sentiment; I did not wish to be thought a tyrant, and I gave a reluctant consent. I was very unhappy; I knew I ought to be a Christian, but was too proud to confess it, and I resolved that I would not confess to any one how I felt upon the subject of religion, but would privately seek God and have religion, and none should know it. I resorted to secret prayer; but the more I prayed the worse I felt, and yet I could not forego prayer. I assumed a cheerful aspect, but there was a crushing weight upon my heart. On the occasion of my wife's praying for me by my bedside, on her return from meeting, I was not asleep, but lay like a guilty culprit, trembling with fear, while she pleaded with God on my behalf. A more wretched being did not exist than I felt myself to be, but I was not humble enough to own it to my companion: I slept but little during that night. The next evening I was induced to attend the house of God, while she remained at home: upon my return, and entering the house, I found that she had retired to her chamber; but there lay the Bible open upon the stand where she had been reading, and there stood the chair by which I felt assured she had knelt and prayed for my guilty soul. I trembled with emotion. What must I do? was the language of my throbbing heart. I read the book of

God. I bowed my knees where my wife had bowed before me, and with tears I sought the mercy of God; but no relief could I find, because I was not satisfied to take salvation without any conditions. I spent another restless night. This morning, after my wife had left me to come to this place, my anguish increased; I felt that I could not live, I must yield or die. I could not find relief in my business, I could not take comfort in my little children; I was of all men most miserable. I felt a drawing to the house of God, and after asking God to direct me, I resolved to come to his temple. I went out among my neighbors, and left my little children in their care, and with eager steps I pressed my way to this place, sighing and groaning, like Bunyan's pilgrim, beneath my burden, until, as I was ascending the hill upon which this house stands, my mind was led to Calvary, to Christ and his finished work, and I was enabled to believe on him with all my heart; my burden was loosed and rolled away, and my soul is filled with the love of Jesus. And now, as a brand plucked from the burning, I wish to unite with my dear companion in serving God, and when the proper time shall come, to unite with the church as one who has obtained mercy of the Lord as the chief of sinners."

During the relation of the above incidents, tears of gratitude filled every eye, while smiles of joy irradiated every countenance, and all were solemnly impressed with the conviction

——— "that praying breath
Is never spent in vain."

Christian wives, be encouraged; offer unceasing prayer to God, he will not turn a deaf ear to your cries; encircle your dear companions in the arms of your affection, pray *for them* and *with them*, and be not faithless, but believing, and your husbands will have occasion, like the subject of this sketch, to thank God for a "praying wife." Davies.

THE YOUNG WIFE'S PRAYER.

Harry B—— was a wealthy young planter in one of our southern Atlantic states, uniting in himself all those amiabilities and excellences which in the eye of the world make up the gentleman and the good companion. He had lately married a gentle, loving maiden; and their days were speeding by in the enjoyment, as they fondly fancied, of every thing that could confer pleasure or add a greater zest to life. But in the midst of their round of dissipation, the young wife felt an undefined longing for something purer, holier, than she had yet experienced. The Spirit of God was gently leading her, though she realized it not, to the possession of real pleasure, and the prospect of unending bliss.

In this feeling of dissatisfaction with worldly joys, her steps were providentially directed to a religious service attended by the poorer class of her neighbors. The deep seriousness of the humble throng, the fervid earnestness of the preacher, and the inward monitions of the awakening Spirit in her troubled breast, told her that here was to be found the lasting joy she sought, even in the ennobling service of Christ. The conflict was short. She found repentance and submission sweet. She found her Saviour gracious.

The news fell like a thunderbolt upon the ear of

the astonished husband. She so gentle, so winning, the idol of the festive throng, and the acknowledged queen of every gay assemblage, a humble follower of Jesus? Was she to forsake the world, of which she had been so long a bright and shining star? Was she who had lived so long for him alone, to give up all for Jesus? How the deep malignity of his evil heart burst forth! But though she trembled and wept at his angry expostulations, she faltered not.

At length the time drew near when the new convert, with other fruits of the pastor's faithfulness, were publicly to avow their renunciation of the world. B——'s anger was now fully excited. Had his wife been willing to connect herself with any of the more fashionable congregations of the neighboring city, he could have the better endured it; but to behold the shrinking form of her he loved, with those of a lower grade of society, and even in company with slaves, profess faith in Christ, was most galling to his proud spirit. In his anger he sent word to the minister that he would publicly castigate him, if he dared to baptize his wife.

But a short time had elapsed, when, as he returned one night from a scene of revelry and mirth, his noiseless step was unperceived; and as he approached the door of his room, the tones of a gentle voice, in earnest pleading before the throne of grace, fell upon his ear. It was his threatened, ill-used wife, bending in prayer for her erring husband's salvation. His heart was touched; the sword of the Spirit pierced its adamantine sheath of rebellion and sin; and silently, with the tears streaming from his eyes, he too knelt beside her—he too joined in the prayer for mercy.

What a change had God wrought! He who in his pride had despised the humble followers of Christ, was now foremost in deeds of humility and love. Instead of being engrossed in the pursuit of pleasure, the ordinances of God were now his delight, the story of redeeming love his changeless theme; and husband and wife, sundering the ties that bound them to the gay world, pressed in singleness of mind "toward the mark for the prize of the high calling of God in Christ Jesus." S.

WOMAN'S FAITH AND PATIENCE.

In the year 18—, I knew a beautiful young girl, whose father lived near the village of A——, South Carolina, and who was early wedded to the man of her heart. With the accomplishments of education, refinement, and wealth, she had also, by the grace of God, that of sterling piety.

At the death of her father, the husband found himself in possession of a very handsome estate; but it is hard to resist the smiles of fortune and the sunshine of prosperity. He at once became a devotee of the world, and a lover of pleasure. He soon loved to tarry long at the wine, then to follow strong drink; he became involved in debt, and was forced to sell much of his property to pay his creditors. After a while, he removed and settled in the county of I——, where he purchased a piece of land for cultivation.

At this time I went to live with him, and remained with the family about thirteen months. And during this period I never knew him to go to bed, the night of Sunday excepted, without needing assistance, from the effects of partial intoxication. It was a remarkable fact, that though this evil habit held him with a giant's grasp, and had led him to degrade himself, to disgrace his children, and almost to break his poor wife's heart, yet such was the indelible impression made on him in childhood by pious parents, in regard to the sacred observance of the Sabbath, that I never knew him to break it by getting drunk on that holy day.

That devoted woman--Betsey, he called her--I have seen meet that drunken husband more than one hundred and fifty times, laying aside her work, or putting down her child from her arms, to assist him, reeling and tottering, from his horse, and conduct him safely into the house. And during all this, and indeed while I was there, I never heard her use an unkind word, or give him a rebuke.

One fine bright morning, I saw him start for court dressed from head to foot in a neat suit, every thread of which Betsey had spun and woven with her fingers. Alas, I saw him return home again—how changed, sadly changed! He was not only beastly drunk, but one skirt of his new coat was torn nearly off, and he was almost covered with mud and dirt. His wife met him as usual, only saying, "Never mind, Billy, I can sew the skirt of that coat so that it can hardly be seen, and to-morrow I will see what I can do towards taking that mud off."

But again, from the intemperate habits of the father and husband, their little farm was sold, and they removed further back, into the wild, rough mountains of G——. I did not go with them, but I heard that there they rented a poor piece of land, bought an old house, and by this time they had a son large enough to plough. He ploughed the land, Betsey sowed the oats and wheat, and planted the corn, pulled the fodder, and helped to gather in the crop in the fall. A delicate woman, reared in the lap of luxury and refinement, brought to such toil and drudgery! And yet it is said that at the harvest-time she would sing and praise God for his mercies in blessing her handiwork, and giving her family "daily bread."

Time passed on. Being in the village of C—— on Saturday, I met a circuit preacher of the Methodist church, with whom I had been long acquainted. He asked me to accompany him into the mountains, and preach at an appointment which he had promised to fill on the morrow. After some hesitation, I consented to do so.

When the hour of worship arrived, and I preached from the words, "Come unto me, all ye that labor and are heavy-laden, and I will give you rest," while I was pointing out to the sinner the happy results of coming to Christ, though he might have to labor, though sin wearied him, and though it oppressed him as a heavy burden grievous to be borne, I heard a voice which seemed to come from the corner of the congregation, saying, "Thank God, I have experienced all that; I came to Christ 'laboring,' 'weary,' and 'heavy-laden,' and I found relief." I paused to listen, for I thought I had heard that voice before. It was Billy's voice. And soon, in another part of the house, I heard a female voice thanking God for his goodness and faithfulness in hearing and answering her prayers. That was Betsey's voice. Then I heard the voice of children weeping, and saw them raise up their hands to heaven in adoration. They were Billy's and Betsey's children.

To my great joy, I learned that Billy had for some time been a consistent member of the church, and it was now no more a cursed, miserable family, but they were all journeying towards heaven. Betsey long had been, and now Billy was, a pilgrim and a traveller to that "better country." Their home was blessed with peace and joy.

See the power of woman's faith and patience. For thirty years had Betsey been besieging the throne of grace. And all this while she staggered not at the promises of God, and he at last heard her, and sent her heart's desire. Prayer opens heaven. "My soul, wait thou only upon God, for my expectation is from him."

A Pastor.

THE FAITHFUL WIFE.

God had revived his work in many churches in the city of B——; multitudes of weary sinners had sought and found rest in Him who is exalted to give repentance and forgiveness of sins. J—— H—— was a sceptic and scoffer, but one evening was led by his affectionate, pious wife to hear the gospel. On their return home, he solemnly asserted his intention to go no more. "Why not, my dear husband?" said the alarmed lady. "I was both provoked and insulted," said he; "that entire sermon on infidelity was preached at me; and scarcely one in the house but knew it. I have for ever done with church-going and preaching."

Weeks elapsed; the wife prayed, and friends prayed for this deluded man—and God heard their cry. Said the deeply concerned Mrs. H—— one evening, "Dear, will you grant me one little request?" Being unwilling to promise till he knew its purport, she continued, "Go with me to-night to meeting." "I will go to the door, but no further," said he. "That will do," said this amiable Christian. They went together, parted at the entrance, her heart absorbed as she took her seat in fervent prayer for her beloved partner. Some minutes elapsed, and service had commenced, when suddenly the door opened, a heavy step advanced, and to her unspeakable joy, her husband calmly seated himself near her.

That night Mr. H—— was interested and affected. Hope beat high among his friends. The next evening after tea, as Mr. and Mrs. H—— sat conversing at their pleasant fireside, he rose, and while a tear dropped from his cheeks, "Wife," said he, "*is it not time to go to church?*" She sprung from her chair, and though it was early by an hour and a half, she feared delay; and taking hat and cloak, they went. That was the happiest night of her life, for Mr. H—— presented himself a humble inquirer for the way of salvation, and numbered many years in his Redeemer's service. All who knew him believe that, under God, he owed what he is to the sweet influences of a loving, patient, meek, Christian wife: "For what knowest thou, O wife, whether thou shalt save thy husband?" 1 Cor. 7 : 16. D.

A MINISTER'S SON AND HIS WIFE.

If the son of a minister turns out badly, some are ready to say it is so with all ministers' sons. E—— R——, the son of one of the best pastors in New

Hampshire, was fast confirming the false proverb. He grew up, and left home with no religion. All the faithful instruction and prayers of his devoted parents seemed to fall powerless on his rocky heart. His father, on his death-bed, wrung with grief that his son had outbraved all parental tears and warnings, prayed most fervently for his salvation; but left the world with nothing in him to encourage his hopes.

When I first saw him, it was in Northern Vermont. He had married an amiable lady, and lived on a farm. I gave him the tract, "Quench not the Spirit;" saying to him, that if he was yet a stranger to God, he might find it contained a message for him. At length, I noticed him at a meeting where I was to preach. He had come a long distance. At the intermission, I made my way to him, and soon found that his mind was tender—that his great concern was for his soul.

Not many weeks after, I went to see him. He was rejoicing in hope, and his wife was in distress of mind for herself. I asked him to tell me what awakened him. He went into the other room, and brought me that tract. "When I first read it," he said, "it seemed a message from God." He read it again and again. "Then," said he, "all the warnings and prayers of my good old father came before me. I felt that I had slighted them all, and had grieved the Holy Spirit to leave me for ever. But I took up my long-neglected Bible, and read and begged for mercy. And now I rejoice in the Lord."

In a few days, his wife too was led to Christ; and both rejoiced in the great salvation. They became members of the church, and adorned their profession.

Brethren in the ministry, let us at all times be furnished with tracts; and after having read and pondered the burning truths they contain, let us boldly, yet courteously, approach the sinner on all suitable occasions, giving him a word of warning. Many, in the great day, shall we meet in heaven as the final result.

S. M.

THE TROUBLED CONSCIENCE.

Mrs. Frances L—— was an intelligent lady, a diligent reader of the Scriptures, and a regular attendant upon the ministry of the word; yet she was not a Christian. In my pastoral visits, I urged upon her the duty of immediately and earnestly seeking an interest in the Saviour of sinners, that by his grace she might be enabled to rejoice in hope of the glory of God, and be better qualified to discharge the solemn obligations of a wife and mother. Sometimes she would plead, that in early life she had made the attempt to be a Christian, and had failed, and it would be useless to try again: at other times, she would urge that her time to serve God had not yet come; and not unfrequently, the imperfections of professing Christians furnished her with an excuse, lest she, like them, should be a stumbling-block to others.

On one occasion, after a season of prayer, I asked her if she would not then promise me before God to make one honest effort for the salvation of her soul, and paused for a reply. After a few moments of profound stillness, she said, with characteristic firmness and decision, "I will." Having made this solemn promise, she felt bound to keep it, although at times she regretted having made it. She sought the Lord earnestly by prayer, and while she did so, her sense of guilt became overpowering, and the anguish of her soul indescribable. In vain she read the word of God, in vain she prayed for relief; no rest, no comfort, no peace could she find; hope died within her, no promise fell upon her ear, no light shone into her soul; she thought her case was peculiar, that never was any poor sinner so miserable as she.

While thus distressed, and sighing as she went about her domestic affairs, she discovered in one of her closets a soiled pamphlet, "The troubled Conscience." That was her case. She read it with interest, with wonder and astonishment, for she found her case was not peculiar; the feelings of another were the counterpart of her own. The remedy was pointed out, the peace-speaking blood of Jesus. She saw its fitness, she saw its fulness; faith and hope sprung up in her heart; her load of guilt was removed; and with a heart overflowing with gratitude, she fell upon her knees, and returned thanks to God "for his unspeakable gift."

Of her spiritual exercises she had never spoken to her husband; she knew not how he would regard her if she became a Christian, but it was her duty to speak to him upon the subject. Upon a Sabbath evening, after his return from meeting, she told him in tender tones what the Lord had done for her soul, and bowed before the Lord by the side of her dear companion, and prayed most earnestly for his conversion. That prayer was an arrow to his soul. The Spirit of God reached his heart, and after some days of intense agony, he too was brought into the light and liberty of the gospel, rejoicing in God, with his wife, whom God had made the instrument of his salvation. Not long afterwards, they both were received by baptism into the fellowship of the church. A Grateful Pastor.

THE LOST BANK-NOTE.

Mr. A—— was an irreligious man, nearly sixty years of age. He had long neglected the house of God, and indulged in the use of profane language. One day he lost a bank-note in his barn. He sought for it several times, but did not find it. At length he said to himself, "That note is in the barn, and *I will search for it till I find it.*" Accordingly he went to the barn, and carefully moved straw and hay, hour after hour, till he found the note.

He had told me, two months before, that he knew that his soul was not right with God, and he intended to live a better life, and seek salvation. His anxiety increased. A few weeks after he lost the note, he sat by the fire musing on the state of his soul, when he turned to his wife and asked, "What must one do to become a Christian?" "You must seek for it," she replied, "as you sought for the bank-note." She said no more. It was "a word fitly spoken." He tried to follow the direction, and through the grace and mercy of Christ, he found the "pearl of great price," and rejoiced in hope of the glory of God.

There is a treasure for you, reader, precious beyond the power of words or figures to express. There is salvation and heaven for you, and eternal glory, if you will seek it with all your heart, believing that it can be found, and resolved to find it. If you have not sought it thus, you have disparaged it, treating it as if it were not worth such earnest regard. P. O.

INFLUENCE OF A WIFE.

Among the early settlers in L——, Greene county, New York, on the Catskill mountains, religion hardly had a name. But there were two females who met weekly for prayer. The Lord heard their cry: a small church was gathered, which was soon visited with a revival of religion, and several of the most respectable families were brought into its communion.

Among those added to the church was Mrs. T. P——, who earnestly sought the blessing of God on her unconverted husband and children; but he became decidedly opposed to all religion, and persecuted his wife in various ways. She was not permitted to pray with her children in the house, but used daily to retire to the barn, and there worship that Saviour whose birthplace was a manger. She was decided in every Christian duty, but yielded, as far as she could conscientiously, to the wishes of her husband.

Mr. P—— was a man of high spirit. He became excessively fond of company, and used to spend his Saturdays at a public-house, where he indulged in drinking freely, and by his associates was called "Old Head."

In the early part of May, more than forty years since, one Saturday evening Mr. P—— returned from his associates, and found his pious wife, who had commended her family to God for the night, engaged in reading.

"What book have you there?" said he.

"I have the Connecticut Evangelical Magazine."

"Where did you get it?"

"It was left for me by my friend B——, who called to see me this afternoon."

"This Mr. B—— has determined to ruin the peace and happiness of my family. You shall not read the book. Put it up, and go to your rest."

Mrs. P—— replied, "I will lay by the book because my husband requires it, though it is a great sacrifice, as I am much interested in it. The blessed Bible teaches me submission to the will of my husband."

They retired to rest—the bosom of the one full of holy peace and anxious solicitude for her wandering husband; the bosom of the other full of dark and fiend-like passions, cursing God, and persecuting his people.

Soon Mr. P—— arose, saying, "I cannot sleep with one so religious and saintlike as you are." She proposed to retire to another room, but this he would not allow. The night was spent in silent but ardent prayer by Mrs. P——, and in anxious tossings and bitter revilings by her husband.

In the morning, the children as usual were assembled in the barn, and commended to God by the pious, heart-broken mother, and in due time were all neatly clad for the house of God, when Mrs. P—— gently asked her husband if he would not accompany them. With an oath he replied, "No; I do not believe in the stuff taught there for religion." With deep solicitude she bent her steps to the sanctuary, where, with his people, she could cast her burden on that Arm pledged to sustain her.

Mr. P—— was now left alone, and to the most bitter reflections. The amiable, decided, and conscientious deportment of his wife; her patient sufferings from his irascible temper; her firmness in every religious duty, shone with such lustre, that the contrast led him to see that there was a difference between the righteous and the wicked here, and must be hereafter. For a moment, he thought he would follow his wife to the house of God; and then, with his razor in his hand, he was about to take his own life; but God was near, and he put away the instrument of death.

When the time of the afternoon service arrived, his wife again invited him to accompany her; but his spirit was unyielding, and he promptly said he would not. After she had gone, however, he determined that for once he would go.

He went, with a heart rankling with hatred to God and his people; but he soon became awed at the presence of Jehovah in his sanctuary. His soul was deeply agitated until the close of the last prayer, when, with wonder and astonishment, he beheld by faith "the Lamb of God, who taketh away the sin of the world." His proud heart was humbled; God was exalted; his people loved; and to use his own words, every spear of grass seemed to praise its Maker.

He returned home, begged his wife's forgiveness, acknowledged his sin against God and her, and expressed his hope of pardon through the merits of the Lord Jesus Christ.

The grateful joy of Mrs. P—— cannot be described. Her persecuting husband was now a man of prayer; the unnatural father was now the pious and devoted leader of his household at the throne of grace.

On sitting down at his first meal, his reflections were most bitter. "From deep poverty," said he, "I have been raised to a comfortable living; God has provided for me; but I have been rebellious against him." He asked God's blessing, and forgiveness for past ingratitude. At evening he called his family around him, confessed his sins to his children, prayed for and with them; and for more than thirty years was a consistent, devoted Christian, and a deacon of the church at L——

H. H.

THE AURORA BOREALIS.

But few that saw it will ever forget the Aurora, or Northern Light, which occurred in the winter of 1836–7. It was pronounced at the time the most brilliant and general that had been seen by any living man. It was not confined, as it usually is, to the northern section of the heavens. The whole horizon was illumined by arches of fiery hue, from which columns and sheaves of light, of the most variegated and beautiful colors, shot up towards the zenith, forming there a fiery coronet of the most transcendent beauty. The agitation of these columns and sheaves was sometimes very great. Of a sudden these agitations would cease, and the light would die away, and the heavens would resume their wonted appearance; but in a moment these columns would shoot up again in increased

size, and with greater splendor, giving an appearance of brilliancy and grandeur to the heavens which called forth the loud acclamations of the admiring beholders. For some weeks previous the earth had been covered with a deep snow, which a cold frost had made to sparkle with a peculiar brilliancy; and such was the effect upon it of the Aurora, that streets, fields, and houses looked as if they were covered with blood. This remarkable phenomenon only disappeared from the sky as the morning light began to dawn.

Not long afterwards I observed, on Sabbath evening, and on the evening of the weekly service, in a corner of my lecture-room, a female who was a stranger to me, and obviously, to the place. Her attention was marked; her attendance became regular. Weeks passed away without my knowing who she was. I received a request to visit a family where was a woman anxious about her soul. As I entered the door I was met by the stranger I had seen in the lecture-room. I was favorably impressed by her subdued and respectful manner, her great frankness and candor, and her deep solicitude to know the way to be saved. Taking my seat by her side, and after hearing her account of her feelings, I asked her if she understood the plan of salvation through Jesus Christ. Her reply was, "I am afraid I do not."

"Then, madam," said I, "will you permit me to explain it to you in a brief and simple manner?"

"That," said she, "is the very thing I want you to do."

"Well, then," said I, addressing her personally, and applying every word to herself, "you are a sinner in heart and in life. God is angry with you every day. Every sin you have ever committed deserves eternal banishment from God. So that you deserve to die as often as you have sinned. From the guilt and punishment of sin you cannot relieve yourself—nor can man or angel relieve you—nor can baptism or the Lord's supper, or any other rite, relieve you. And such is the nature of your sin, and of the justice and government of God, that you cannot be saved unless law and justice are satisfied for the many sins you have committed."

I stopped a moment to see the effect of all this upon her mind. Looking at me with a tearful eye, she replied in a subdued tone, "I feel all this in my soul. My fear of the anger of God which my sins have kindled, is so great that I cannot sleep or eat. My tears flow day and night."

"But," said I, "there is a way of escape from the guilt and the punishment of sin. You are a sinner; and Jesus Christ has died for sinners. He bore the sins of all who ever have, or ever will believe upon him, in his own body on the tree. The law requires us to be righteous, in order to enter heaven; and Christ Jesus is the end of the law for righteousness to every one that believes upon him. If you feel yourself to be a sinner, you have nothing to do but to believe in the Lord Jesus Christ in order to be saved. If you repent of sin, and believe in the Lord Jesus Christ—if you believe what Jesus teaches, if you do as he commands—if now, without a moment's delay, you can trust your soul and its concerns in the hands of Jesus Christ, without waiting until you are either better or worse, he will certainly save you; for he says, "Come unto me, all ye that labor and are heavy-laden, and I will give you rest."

With her bright and beaming eye fixed upon me, she drank in every word that I uttered; and when I concluded, she promptly replied, "This is just the way that suits my case." "Are you willing now," said I, "to believe in Christ; to cast yourself upon the merits of his atonement; to take him to be your Saviour from all sin?" "Yes," said she, with the eagerness of a drowning man catching hold of the boat sent out to his rescue, "yes, I take him now to be my Saviour; I cast myself now upon the merits of his atonement."

I prayed with her. When we arose from our knees her whole expression was changed, and a new song was put into her mouth. I felt there was a new trophy to redeeming grace and love before me.

I now felt greatly desirous to know something about her history, the leading incidents of which she gave me with great frankness. She was born and educated a Roman-catholic. Though well educated, she was on the subject of religion extremely ignorant. Although now in mid-life, and the mother of children, all the attention she ever gave to her soul was to go to mass and to confession; and even that she had given up for years, convinced of their utter worthlessness. And up to the evening of the Aurora Borealis she never had a conviction of her sinfulness. With thousands of others she gazed upon the brilliant heavens, and the apparently crimsoned earth. The thought of the final conflagration, and of her utter unfitness to meet that dreadful scene, seized her mind, and she retired to her room deeply impressed with the greatness of God, and her own sinfulness and ingratitude. Then was made the first of those impressions which resulted in her conversion.

Her husband was a Frenchman, of Protestant parentage, but utterly regardless of religion. When he returned home, on the evening of the day of my visit, she told him of my conversation with her, and its effects upon her mind and heart. She read to him from the Bible, and prayed with him. With his consent she erected the family altar. Her fidelity to him, and her deep anxiety for his salvation, created some restiveness, and he refused to hear her. In the deepest distress she sought my advice. I told her to increase her supplications for him in private, but to do nothing that would fret his mind, as that would be to defeat her great object. She retired, resolved to follow my advice.

Some weeks had passed away without my knowing any thing of what was going on in this little family. On a Sabbath evening, after a day of peculiar solemnity in the house of the Lord, and when with a dejected spirit I was thinking that I had spent my strength for naught, she appeared in my study with her husband. She narrated her conversation and prayers with him, and he frankly confessed his opposition of heart to her change of mind, and especially to her conduct towards him in pressing religion upon him on all occasions. "But," said he, "her prayers and tears have broke my heart."

"I told John," said she, "that if you would tell him what you told me, he would love God too, and that he would feel better in his mind and heart. I have strove to tell him all, but he does not understand me well enough, and I wish you to tell him about Jesus Christ." After hearing with intense interest their narratives as to each other's conduct, I spread out before John the plan of salvation, essentially as I had done a few weeks previous before his wife. When I got through, I asked him, "How does this plan appear to you?" His reply was, "It is the very one for me; I can now and cordially embrace it." I prayed with them, and when we rose from our knees John seemed a changed man. Before he left my study he felt that he could rejoice in Christ as his Saviour.

Not long after, they professed their faith in Christ, and although for years beyond the bounds of my ministry, I believe they lived to adorn that profession;

and their conversion may be traced up as a means, under God, to the aurora borealis.

How plainly this narrative teaches the following truths:

The means of God for impressing the minds of sinners, and leading them to himself for pardon and salvation, are exhaustless.

A clear understanding of the plan of salvation through a Saviour, of its freeness and fulness, of its sovereign efficacy when truly relied on, is the only sure way of securing peace to the anxious sinner.

How important that the believing wife should labor for the salvation of the unbelieving husband; and the believing husband for that of the unbelieving wife!

A word to the reader of this narrative. Are you a careless sinner? If the aurora so impressed the mind of this woman, what will be your impressions when the elements shall melt with fervent heat, when the earth with all that it contains shall be consumed? Are you an anxious sinner? Then Jesus died for sinners; and he died for you, because you are a sinner. To be saved, you have only to believe upon him. Are you a Christian? Then rise from the perusal of this narrative with the resolution to labor for the conversion of some soul, as this woman labored for the conversion of her husband, and yours may not be a starless crown. N. M.

RETURN OF THE PRODIGAL.

F—— was the son of a devoted New England minister, and the child of many prayers. His mind was carefully stored with religious knowledge, and disciplined in the best schools of his native city. Evil companionships, however, early led him astray from the paths of virtue. A vicious habit of novel-reading alienated him from the open fountains of wisdom, and drew him away from parental influence and restraint.

At length his restless and adventurous spirit sought a sphere of unchecked indulgence, and he went to the Pacific coast. There he found his associates among the thoughtless sons of fortune, and gave himself up to the life of a homeless adventurer. Prosperity and adversity served alike to harden his heart. Early convictions were stifled. The house of God was neglected.

But there were bands in his wickedness stronger than those of Satan. The anxious and aching hearts of his parents were turned to God. Unceasing, believing prayer ascended in his behalf. His father especially, cherished the unwavering conviction that his wayward son, after running the prodigal's career of vice and folly, would trace the prodigal's steps of penitence and salvation. Year after year he clung to the divine promises, and pleaded them earnestly at the mercy-seat. He felt that he could not be denied.

At length the hearts of father, mother, and friends were gladdened by the intelligence that the lost was found, that the prodigal had returned. He had visited a remote South American port, and on his return voyage he was the only cabin-passenger. The captain had depended on him to furnish a supply of cards, novels, and other sources of time-killing, soul-destroying amusements; and he in turn, knowing the disposition of the captain, had looked to him for an adequate supply. The few means of diversion were soon exhausted, and after being ten days at sea, the young man found nothing to do but think. His past life came up in review before him, and conscience revived. Early teachings whispered around him. An injured father's persevering faith and a weeping mother's counsels haunted his solitary berth. The emptiness of worldly pleasures and the vanity of earthly plans led him to reflect on the surer joys and riches of the Christian. He turned to the word of God and read his condemnation. His guilt rose mountain-high, as the Holy Spirit unfolded the immaculate law. He fell upon his knees and cried for pardon.

By one of those providences which call forth the adoration of the devout, there were in the cabin of this ship copies of "Nelson's Cause and Cure of Infidelity," "Baxter's Call to the Unconverted," "James' Anxious Inquirer," and "Abbott's Young Christian"—the first to dispel his sceptical doubts, the second to fasten the arrow of conviction in his heart, the third to instruct his inquiring soul, and the last to present encouragements and allurements to the Christian life. He read them all prayerfully. Before the vessel landed at San Francisco, the great question was settled, we hope, for ever. He found peace in believing, and entered at once on the new life of Christian discipleship. He made his way immediately to the sanctuary, engaged in Sabbath-school instruction, sought the company of ministers and godly men, abandoning his former companions in sin, or visiting them only to labor for their salvation; and his letters to his parents breathed the spirit of penitence and consecration, coupled with the most touching expressions of gratitude and affection. The "fatted calf" would be a small testimony of the joy that filled the house long saddened by the wandering prodigal, but now gladdened by his return.

Christian parents, and especially those whose sons are far away from home and from God, will find encouragement to their faith in this narrative. There are few cases apparently more hopeless of reformation and conversion than the one before us. Pride kept him from coming home; an evil conscience restrained him from places and companionships likely to benefit him: only a vigorous faith could anticipate the possibility of a change. Yet grace triumphed; God's truth was vindicated; everlasting promises had their fulfilment; the prodigal returned. Trust that grace; cling to those promises: *your* prodigal son may yet be saved.

What an illustration of the power of prayer! God alone knows how earnestly and constantly that father wrestled for that wayward boy; and how patiently and calmly he expected, nay, relied on his conversion. And in proportion to the darkness of external signs, was the fervency of his petitions. All those prayers were registered on high. In God's time, always the best time, the answer descended in that lone cabin on the broad Pacific. The providence of God arranged the circumstances and the means which the Holy Spirit blessed in bringing to himself the New England prodigal. "Praying breath" was never "spent in vain."

The value of Bibles and good books on shipboard finds in this narrative an admirable illustration, for the thousandth time. It is not known, nor is it of any account, by whose agency the precious volumes of truth found their way to the cabin of this ship; they were in the right place at the right time. And they were blessed of God in doing a work which parental instruction and example, pastoral fidelity, and providential discipline had failed to do. O that every vessel on every sea were thus supplied with preachers for the cabin and the forecastle. Many a wayward youth, many a weather-beaten tar, might find the blessed gospel their chart on life's ocean.

There are many sons of praying parents who are running a career of folly like that of F——. Does the eye of one of them rest on this page? Does it suggest a lesson for you? Is a prodigal life a happy life? Are there not memories of other and happier days obtruding on the hours of gayety and folly, and tainting them all? Does not a mother's voice or a father's prayer sometimes steal into the soul in the silent hour, in tones of tender expostulation? Does not the wonted hour of family worship, when the old family Bible revealed its treasures, and the hymn of praise rose from the domestic group—say, does not this scene sometimes throw its shadow across your spirit, and woo you to the paths of piety and peace? Where is the Bible your fond mother placed in your trunk when you left the paternal roof? Unread? Neglected? What have you done with the pious book, the gift of a sister's love? How will you meet these witnesses of Christian fidelity and domestic affection at the bar of God? Is not the same Saviour whom F—— found on the silent sea ready to receive you? Is not the same Spirit that breathed into the heart of F—— hovering over your soul, and whispering of guilt, and pardon, and hope? And will you not, like him, say, with a broken and penitent heart, "I will arise and go to my Father, and say unto him, Father, I have sinned against heaven, and before thee, and am no more worthy to be called thy son." Then will be heard on earth and in heaven the words of grateful exultation, "This my son was dead, and is alive again: he was lost, and is found." R. S. C.

A YOUNG CHOIR LEADER.

In one of the eastern towns of Vermont, lived a family by the name of B——, consisting of grandparents, parents, five sons, and four daughters. In the fall of 1816, and the following winter, a pleasing work of grace was there enjoyed, under the ministry of Rev. N. B. Dodge, afterwards a missionary to the Osage Indians. The second son of Mr. B——, a youth of seventeen years, was leader of the choir at most of the meetings, and under the sermon one evening, was deeply affected. His praying mother had for some days observed a change in him, but hardly dared speak to him on the subject of his soul, lest she should weaken his impressions, yet she pleaded earnestly for him at the throne of grace. Under the sermon referred to, he sat between two rude young men, and as they were on their way home, they began to ridicule him for being frightened, saying he was under conviction, and if he was caught they might all expect to be, unless they kept away from such meetings. He assured them that there was no ground for their fears, and thus silenced their remarks, but was far from silencing the reproofs of his own conscience. If he had before felt the gentle drawings of the Holy Spirit, and heard his inviting voice to turn and live, he now felt as if the thunderings of Sinai were gathered over him, and ready to overwhelm him in endless misery.

In this state of mind he reached home, and found his mother awaiting his return in prayerful anxiety. O how that mother's heart yearned over her son; and how that devoted heart must have bled, when he, refusing to hear a word from her lips, rushed from her presence to his own room, in the horrors of despair. But he could not sleep, so deep were the agonies of his soul. He arose from his bed, lighted his lamp, and on his table discovered a tract portraying the danger of grieving the Holy Spirit. His despair was increased almost to horror, and he felt that there was nothing before him but tempests of endless wrath. He spent the night almost in agony. His godly mother and grandparents tried to speak comfortably to him, but every allusion to Christ seemed like a barbed arrow to his soul. They proposed to pray with him, but he turned his despairing eyes upon his mother, and said, "O mother, if you love my soul, do not talk to me, do not pray for me; I have so long withstood your counsel and your prayers, that now God cannot have mercy on me; more especially as I have this night denied the Holy Ghost," alluding to his reply to his jeering companions.

He continued in this state of mind about three weeks, when he walked out into a newly cleared piece of land, and on passing a ledge of shelving rocks something seemed to whisper within him, "This is a beautiful place in which to pray." Without stopping to reflect, he dropped upon his knees and attempted to pray, but the heavens over him seemed as brass. Long he remained on his knees, hardly daring to speak the sacred name of God, and with his despairing eyes upturned, he groaned in the agony of his soul, but the Comforter did not come. He arose and walked on a few yards, but seemed almost irresistibly drawn back to those shelving rocks. He returned, and again dropped upon his knees, resolved never to rise until he either received evidence of divine forgiveness and acceptance, or of divine rejection. But he had not given utterance to a word before it seemed to him that all nature was filled with the unspeakable glories of heaven. He could not give utterance to a single desire on his own behalf, for the full emotions of his heart burst forth in words of praise to God and the Lamb, for this wonderful display of his infinitely glorious grace. He was unwilling to leave the place, and lingered long; indeed, until his parents became alarmed and sought him, finding him still on his knees offering up his thanks to Him who had purchased him with his own precious blood.

Unperceived, his father approached him, and said, "My son, excuse me for interrupting you, for the family are all alarmed about you; are you not willing to go with me to the house? And let me ask you, have you found the Saviour?" His reply was, "All things seem changed; my distress is all gone, and every thing seems to be covered with a glory which I never before beheld." His father wept for joy, although he was not then a professor himself, but soon after hopefully gave his heart to Christ. That father, weeping, led his emaciated and enfeebled son home. But the scene of joy in that house I will pass over in silence, for pen cannot describe it. Suffice it to say, that on the first Sabbath of the following January, he was received into the church. He afterwards became a minister of the gospel, and with what success God blessed his labors the last great day will reveal. In his pastoral work he forgot not the value of religious tracts, and to this auxiliary he attributed much of his success in winning souls to Christ. B.

LITTLE JOHNNY AND HIS FATHER.

Some years ago, I became acquainted with a family consisting of the father, mother, and two dear children. The mother was a kind-hearted woman. She had been from early years the subject of conviction, and now for some time a consistent Christian. But the father, from his youth up, had been daring and wicked. Why did such a woman marry such a man? Because, as she said, she loved him, and followed her feelings rather than her judgment and the book of God. 1 Cor. 7:39. He was a member of an Odd Fellows' lodge, and was there very frequently until midnight, and was very popular as a good singer at "free and easy" clubs. This lasted for some years.

Johnny was four years old, and his mother permitted him to go to Sunday-school. There you might see him Sabbath after Sabbath, sitting among the little ones, with an A B C card in his hand. There he learned to repeat hymns and sing, and answer questions put by the teachers. His dear mother attended the same place of worship, and the gospel was indeed food to her soul. But Mr. P——, the father, cared for none of these things; he attended no place of worship. He was "pretty constant" at "his lodge," and generally very late at home, so that he was but little society for his wife. She acutely felt his inattention and unkindness. However, she and "little Johnny" spent the long winter evenings at home, singing, repeating hymns, reading the Bible, and talking about God and heaven.

It was in vain for the wife to remonstrate with Mr. P——. She prudently bore with him as well as she could, and committed her cause to God. She thought, if she could get him under the sound of the gospel, the Lord might change his heart, and thus appear for her. She spoke to him repeatedly, but all to no purpose. But "Johnny" went to Sunday-school; he loved to go, and would remain to the public worship afterwards. The Sunday-school was at some distance, and there was some difficulty in getting him to and from the meeting-house; as he was so young, he could not go alone; his mother did not always like to trust him to the care of other children, and to detain him at home appeared cruel, for he was so happy in his Sunday-school. But "Johnny," in the simplicity of his little heart, removed all this difficulty himself. He asked his father to go with him to meeting. Mr. P——, though a rough man, was very fond of his little son; and though he could say *no*, and that with anger, to grown persons, he could not deny the request of his little child. Hence, after this you might see, up in the gallery, a fine little boy with rosy cheeks, washed clean and neatly dressed; and close by his side a strong, well-built man with a broad forehead, rather bald, listening with attention to the preacher. It is Johnny's father. Henceforward you may see him there as constantly as circumstances will allow. He hears, believes, and is converted. He becomes a Sunday-school teacher. There you may frequently see him teaching Johnny's class. I was at that time a teacher in the same school, and have walked with Mr. P——, in turn with others, five and six miles to teach Sunday-school at out-stations.

I need not say how happy this change made his dear wife. Of course, his place at "free and easy" clubs was abandoned, and in course of time he voluntarily withdrew from the Odd Fellows' fraternity. He lived some years after this a true Christian, and died of consumption, in the faith and hope of the gospel.

Some teachers would say it is of no use to bring such young children to Sunday-school: we want children to *teach*, not to *nurse;* and some Sunday-schools would have excluded "Johnny" as "under age." But he was not too young to speak the name of Jesus, and invite his parent to the house of God. Some teachers are dissatisfied unless they have one of the higher classes. I some time since passed from the Sunday-school to the ministry; but should I return to the Sunday-school and have my choice, I would prefer "little Johnny's" class. These dear little creatures, with their simple, confiding questions about God and heaven, are full of charms for me.

Teachers often need encouragement. Here is encouragement from God. This child comes to the Sunday-school and loves it—goes and draws a man to the house of God whom no one else could bring. He listens to the gospel, believes its truths, repents of sin, and is saved. Out of the mouth of babes and sucklings Jehovah has ordained strength. Psa. 8:2.

R. F.

"MY MOTHER'S PRAYERS."

When I was quite a youth, the Rev. Joel T. Benedict, of blessed memory, related in my hearing the following narrative.

A mother with several children was left a widow. Feeling her responsibility as a parent, she gave diligence to train her household for Christ. That her instructions might be blessed and her children converted, she was unceasing in her supplications at the throne of mercy. She would arise at midnight, and in the chamber where her little ones were sleeping, would kneel and pray for them with wrestling importunity.

Her eldest son becoming restless under religious restraints, abandoned his mother and the home of his childhood. He bent his steps to a seaport, and enlisted as a sailor. He was absent several years, made a number of voyages, and under the influence of wicked companions became profligate.

At length he was induced to visit the place of his nativity. His mother, who had heard nothing of him from the time of his departure, was dead, and the residue of her family scattered. Of her death the sailor felt an interest to learn some particulars, and whether any members of the family were still living, or remained in the vicinity of his birth. But how was he to obtain the desired information? "A man's heart deviseth his way, but the Lord directeth his steps." It was a time of religious revival in the congregation where his mother had been accustomed to worship. He was told of a prayer-meeting in the neighborhood; and knowing that his devout parent used to attend such meetings, he directed his course thither, thinking that he might there meet some of her old acquaintances.

When the sailor arrived at the place of worship, he found the meeting in progress. He entered and took a seat in an obscure corner, intending, at the close of service, to ask for the information he was seeking. The assembly was one of great stillness and solemnity, such as a genuine revival of religion usually produces. The mariner would not have been dismayed at the thunder of the storm upon the heaving ocean, but he could not brave the silent power of the prayer-meeting and religious conference. He could hear nothing, save the voice of one and another relating what God had done for their souls, or the suppressed sigh and stifled sob, which arose from different parts of the congregation. The "still small voice" of the Holy Spirit, who had conducted him thither, was speaking to his conscience. Unable to quench the fire within, or longer conceal his anguish, he exclaimed vehemently, "*My mother's prayers haunt me like a ghost.*"

Those who well remembered the praying mother, and had a slight recollection of the wayward boy, now became deeply interested in the distressed man. Such counsel was imparted as the circumstances and state of his feelings seemed to demand; but he writhed with keen conviction for several weeks. At length he found peace in hopeful reconciliation to God and faith in the Lord Jesus Christ; and in due time became an exemplary and useful member of the same church with which his mother had been connected.

Who can doubt the answer to that mother's prayers? O, Christian mother, cease not to pray for your children.

> "It sha'n't be said that praying breath
> Was ever spent in vain." M. T.

THE YOUNGEST SON.

I knew an aged man, a few years since gone to his rest, a Christian of undoubted piety. He was tall, erect, beautifully symmetrical in his person, and gracefully dignified in all his movements. He was not rich, nor highly educated; he was a plain, honest farmer, whose industry and economy had brought to his possession a hundred and fifty acres of improved land in Northern New York, and the usual appendages of a successful farming business.

He was the father of three cherished sons, all of whom had grown up to manhood. The eldest had engaged in the profession of the law. The second had married and settled upon a small farm in a neighboring township. The youngest was early designated as heir to the paternal homestead, the supporter of his parents in their age and infirmities, and the solace of their hearts as they should descend the vale of years.

More than usual attention and expenditure had been bestowed upon this youngest son, and he had been too much indulged. He early showed a spirit restive under restraint and intolerant of rebuke. His parents finally came to the conclusion, that James did the best to let him have his own way, and to do what they reasonably could to indulge him. But things grew no better, till it was clear that, so far from inclining to consult the wishes of his parents, James seemed to take a sincere pleasure in contravening their most reasonable requirements, and to exhibit an utter disregard of their positive injunctions. Still, his parents dearly loved and gratified him by every means in their power.

Before James was twenty-one, he had wasted hundreds of dollars in amusements and foolish prodigality. At length his arrogance and turbulence increased to an extent which quite exhausted both the resources and patience of his venerable father. The old gentleman finally called the attention of his son to the stern necessities of the case; reminded him of the fact that he was wasting rapidly his little fortune; that much of it had been expended in extricating him from difficulties; that hundreds of dollars had been lavished upon his person, and in gratifying his unreasonable caprices; and that now there must be a reckoning, and this ruining account must be closed.

He spoke of the love which he had always borne him as the Benjamin of his heart, of the sacrifices which he had cheerfully incurred, and of what he would still be willing to hazard, if he could see the slightest indications of his returning to duty and filial propriety; and as the model form of the father earnestly inclined towards the erring boy, the silvery locks flowing gracefully backward, and the mild blue eye sparkling with the burning drops of parental grief, in that powerful eloquence which is the outbursting of parental goodness defied and provoked to desperation, he demanded of his son that he should remain at home, and fulfil the expectation of his father and his mother, long and earnestly cherished.

To this James instantly demurred, and declared that he would be *forced* into no measure, although knowing it to be reasonable.

The old gentleman then composedly and firmly advanced towards the door, and throwing it wide open, said, "My son, there is the door; and there, before you, is the wide world. Go, and forget that you have a father; and I, if possible, will forget that I have a son so wayward and estranged. Go, and never again return to afflict my soul with a recollection of the past!"

James now saw that he was not *required* to remain at home, that he was free to go, and could impose no obligation by remaining, and now a change came over his spirits. He rushed into his father's arms, and for the first time dropped upon the paternal brow the tears of filial penitence, and imploringly asked that he might be permitted to remain, and to obey.

When God requires sinners to do that which in itself is most agreeable, they will not, but perhaps go away and do what otherwise they would not do. But when God says, "Depart," O how bitterly does the soul bewail the folly of resisting his reasonable commands. D.

A CAVILLING SCEPTIC.

Mr. O—— was fifty years of age. He rejected revealed religion, and yet had no settled form or system of infidelity. He would sometimes attend preaching, but it was to return home to cavil. God in great mercy entered his family, and brought his eldest daughter into the kingdom of his Son. He cavilled on, saying, "It is all excitement and delusion."

Soon the Lord appeared again in his household, and his wife and second daughter found peace in believing and joy in the Holy Ghost. And yet he was unmoved. He confessed not that religion was true, or the Bible from God. Months passed. The wife and one daughter being members of my church, I found that a family altar was kept up, and the Bible read in presence of the sceptical husband and father. He *suffered* it, but believed not.

I had a long and faithful conversation with him, but his mind was dark. I gave him "Nelson on Infidelity," and he said he was willing to read it. I saw him not again for some weeks. I presented him as a subject of prayer in our prayer-meeting, while he was reading Nelson. When next I saw him, and took him by the hand, with a smile he said, "I hope I am a changed man. All things seem new to me." Concerning the book he had been reading, he said, "I had not read that work half through, before I found out I was a fool." He added, "Religion is a reality, the Bible is true, and I trust I have found a Saviour."

As soon as light broke in upon his mind, he betook himself to prayer, seeking the Lord until he found a resting-place for his soul. Christ and his own wonderful deliverance were his theme. His heart and eyes overflowed as he talked of the mercy of God and love of Christ, in snatching him from ruin. He bore this testimony to his neighbors and friends. His life was consistent, his end peace. L. S.

A PRAYING SON AND HIS FATHER.

Seth L—— was converted at an early age. After nearly a year, in which he labored under very deep convictions of sin, and fearful apprehensions of the wrath of God, he was enabled with great clearness to see the preciousness and the entire suitableness of Christ's finished work; and coming out of darkness and dread into the fullest confidence in the Saviour, he was even at that early period distinguished as one "full of the Holy Ghost and of faith."

He manifested great anxiety for the souls of his friends, and especially for his father, who was a man of uprightness and a high sense of honor, but wholly destitute of piety. The son wept and prayed over him, and at length he felt that it would be sinful in him to refrain any longer from speaking to his parent. With fear and trembling he introduced the subject to his father one day when they were alone in the fields.

"Seth," replied the father, "I do not feel any need of what you urge upon me. Look at —— and ——; they have got religion, as they call it; but what good has their religion done them? I do not feel that I have ever done any thing to merit the wrath of my Maker. I believe, my son, that you are sincere, and I shall place no obstacles in your way; but you must not again introduce this subject to me; it is not pleasant."

The son left his father in the deepest grief, and retiring to his closet, he poured out his sorrows before God, and set apart a portion of every day for special prayer for his father's conversion.

Seth was, some years after, married to a pious young woman. Time rolled on, his children were growing up to the estate of men and women, and one after another of them were converted, and sat down with him at the communion-table. But his father, who was now a man of nearly fourscore years, was still without God and without hope. Every day, for thirty years, his son had besought the Lord, and often with tears, on his behalf.

One day they were walking together, when the old man thus addressed his son: "Seth, you remember speaking to me about the interests of my soul, a great many years ago. Well, I want to tell you that my sentiments are very greatly changed since then. I feel that I am a great sinner."

The father was brought to enjoy peace in believing, and lived to "bring forth fruit in old age." God is the answerer of prayer. D. I.

A WAYWARD SON.

A pious lady had long and faithfully endeavored to lead her children in the ways of righteousness; but her eldest son gave not heed to her counsels, and with grief she saw him select a companion for life who feared not God, and establish himself in his own home without a family altar. But she followed him with her prayers and entreaties, and he loved and valued her, as his daily visits testified. On one occasion, as he stepped in, the title of a tract which lay upon his mother's table attracted his attention. He wished he could read it. But no, he would not on any account be seen taking it up. Still, he could not leave it; for the Holy Spirit had made use of the title of that tract to arouse him from the deep lethargy in which he had so long been sunk. At last he covered the tract with his hat, drew it unperceived from the table, and left the house.

But what should he then do? He could not well read it at home without the knowledge of his wife, and he was ashamed to read a tract in her presence. As his only resort, he betook himself to the barn, ascended the hayloft, and there devoured its pages. Deep convictions of his sinfulness followed its perusal, and he was led by its teachings to accept of offered mercy through a Saviour's merits. The mother now rejoiced over her son who "was lost, and is found;" and frequently had the happiness of uniting with him around his own family altar in thankful praise to their common Redeemer, and in supplications for his blessing on that Society which scatters so bounteously the leaves of salvation through the land. Anna.

A YOUNGEST SON AND HIS MOTHER.

We were delayed in our journey, and Saturday evening came upon us. As Providence ordered, we were welcomed by a pious father and mother, whose children had all left them and settled in the world, except their youngest son, aged nineteen, who remained as the staff of their old age, and for whose salvation the mother continually offered her agonizing prayer.

He knew his duty, but urged that he should have a more "convenient season."

In family prayer his case was laid at the footstool of sovereign mercy. In the morning, when leaving for public worship, I felt an inexpressible desire to give the young man a tract from a basket with which I was supplied; and the first that appeared was the two-leaved tract, "Do n't put it off." He read aloud the title, and was evidently moved. An arrow had pierced through "the joints of the harness;" and as he afterwards said, his old *refuge* from that moment failed him. He attended meeting, and returned to peruse the tract, every word of which went to his soul. With new interest he looked into his Bible, in which he laid the precious leaf which had proved to him such a messenger of mercy, requesting that it might always remain there. Great was his agony lest he had "put it off" too long; but a reperusal of the tract made him urge his plea the stronger, and while reading those encouraging words, "him that cometh to me I will in no wise cast out," light from on high broke upon his mind. His mother felt that indeed salvation had come to her house, that her son who was dead now began to live. He gave the most decided evidence that he was born of the Spirit. "Do n't put it off," was his faithful admonition to those who were without Christ. When I some time afterwards called on the family, I found the weeping mother bereaved of her son. She showed me the tract, and blessed God that our visit had been instrumental in bringing her child to a saving knowledge of Christ. M. P. G.

A SCEPTICAL FATHER.

A work of divine grace in H—— county, Va., in 1850, was characterized by deep solemnity in the public assembly, and by an unusual spirit of prayer. A daily morning concert was held at six o'clock, and many who were made subjects of special prayer at these seasons, found Christ to be precious.

Among these was a young lady at a boarding-school, who, having experienced a change of heart, became much concerned for the salvation of her aged father, who lived about twenty miles distant. She endeavored to send for him by a special messenger, but did not succeed in procuring one. She then addressed him by letter, informing him what "the Lord had done for her soul," and urging him to come up to the meetings; but fearing that such a communication might offend the sceptical mind of her father, she did not send it. There was one resort, to her covenant God and Redeemer. She not only offered her fervent petitions, but went from one Christian to another, and engaged them to pray for her father at the six o'clock concert. This was on Saturday. On the morrow, many hearts unitedly cried to God, and through that holy day unceasing prayer ascended to the mercy-seat in his behalf. It was a Sabbath full of blessings to that people, and our young friend evidently felt, in common with the people of God, that the place was a Bethel, one of the heavenly places in Christ Jesus.

On Monday morning, we were again convened in the sanctuary; and just as the minister announced his text, "And yet there is room," an aged man, a stranger, entered the church and got the only vacant seat, near the door, the house being crowded. He gave unbroken attention to the discourse, and was much moved; at times the unbidden tear ran down his cheeks. At the conclusion of the service some one remarked, "There is Mr. ——, for whom we have been praying." I looked in the direction indicated, and behold, it was the stranger just alluded to.

I made my way towards him, but before I could reach him he was with his daughter. There she sat, smiling and weeping for joy; and yet, like the incredulous disciples when they heard that "Peter stood at the gate," she could scarcely believe that she saw and heard her own father, while he stood over her, saying to her, "My child, I have been an unfaithful, wicked father to you; I have taught you both by precept and example to neglect religion, and live for the present world; and now I see the folly, the guilt, and the peril of it, and have come here to-day to advise you to seek true religion as your portion for this world and the next."

"My father," said she, "that portion I hope I have found in Jesus, and if you will be a Christian too, dear father, my cup of happiness will overflow."

"I am too great a sinner," he replied; "but you are young, you can be a Christian, and I rejoice in it."

"My father," said she, "you can be a Christian too, the precious blood of Jesus 'cleanses from all sin.'"

The father had been a sceptic, and had lived in the neglect of the public and private means of grace until the last Sabbath morning, when, from a motive unknown to himself, he went to —— church, distant about ten miles, where there was only occasional preaching, and not knowing certainly that there was service there that day. But the Lord directed his steps; for then and there he heard a most faithful sermon from the late Rev. S. T——, who was on a visit to that church. He returned to his home deeply impressed. "The multitude of his thoughts troubled him." He found no rest by day, and sleep forsook his eyelids. In the Bible of his deceased wife he read, to his own conviction and condemnation. And yet he read, and thought, and paced his chamber, and read, and thought again, the livelong night, until the burden of his sins brought the proud, stout-hearted sceptic to his knees. He then thought of his daughter, whose spiritual interests he had neglected, and he resolved to visit her in the morning. He accordingly rode to the school, a distance of nearly twenty miles; and there learning that the family were at church, he hastened on and got there just as the preacher was announcing his text.

Having heard his own statement of God's dealings with him, we were constrained to exclaim, "Surely our Lord is the God who heareth prayer;" and when we told him of the united prayer that had gone up to God in his behalf, he was much moved. He went home that night, saying, "There is no place so solemn as my own chamber;" and many people of God on that night sent up their prayers in his behalf, to Him who is "exalted a Prince and a Saviour," to "give repentance and remission of sins."

On the morrow, he returned again to the church, we trust, a changed man, rejoicing in our redeeming God and Saviour; and we all had great comfort, and rejoiced with him in the love of Christ shed abroad in our hearts.

"Then let us earnest cry,
And never faint in prayer." J. D. M.

AN ELDER AND HIS DAUGHTER.

In one of the counties of Western Virginia, there lived a man who for many years had been an officer of the church, and whose piety no one doubted. While active and earnest in most religious duties, one thing was wanting—he had no family altar. Years had passed without it, till God in mercy visited that circle. The heart of the elder was gladdened by seeing one of his daughters embrace the Saviour. This babe in Christ felt that there was one thing wanting to her growth in piety—she needed the blessings that distil on those that gather around the altar of prayer. She felt too diffident to introduce the subject to her father, who had grown grey in the service of the Lord; but piety prompted an expedient. She had obtained from a colporteur the tract "Do you Pray in your Family?" and one evening as the family had gathered around the fireside, she presented it to her father, and simply asked him to read it. He took it and read it with fixed attention. Every word was an arrow that reached his heart. He finished the tract, paused, remained in thought a moment, and looking at his daughter, burst into tears and said, "Daughter, bring me the Bible. I have neglected my duty too long; henceforth I will pray in my family." He kept his resolution, and every morning and evening witnessed a group of worshippers gathering to the daily sacrifice. From that day a new and brighter light shone into that dwelling. D. B. E.

AN ONLY DAUGHTER.

A fond and affectionate only daughter in a favored part of our country, having her heart touched by the cries of the heathen, and longing to be at work on missionary ground, awaited only the consent of her parents to answer the call of a missionary board. She had been "the pet lamb" of the flock, nurtured by the tenderest care, and cherished by her parents as their constant comfort and solace—the very sunlight of their dwelling, and the expected prop of their declining years. But they had given her to God, and were resolved that no selfish considerations should mingle with his claims when it became necessary to decide the question. They made the subject one of prayerful reflection, made themselves acquainted with the various missionary stations; and when the time approached that the decision must be made, they determined to resign her cheerfully, provided she should not be destined to any part of Africa: they could not feel it a duty to expose so frail and precious a treasure to the dangers and hardships which she must there encounter. The dreaded day arrived. The individual who was to come for the decision was true to the appointment. As these parents entered the room, one said to the other, "We must be firm; if she is to be sent to Africa, we *cannot* consent." During the interview, the necessities and wants of different missions were discussed, and near its close a remark was ventured upon the preference which might be given to that of South Africa. The consent of the parents was given to the departure of their daughter for that field; and the messenger was stepping into the stage, when the mother exclaimed, "We have not once thought of the conditions. The Lord reigns. Africa is no doubt the very spot where he requires her services." In a few months she was in that barbarous region, becoming familiar with the language, having a cluster of children gathered around her eager for instruction, and rewarding her toils by their progress in civilization and morality. Her letters bespoke a most cheerful spirit, and her parents were reconciled to their solitude by her oft-repeated assurances that she was never happier in her life, because never where she could do so much good. M.

THE ONLY SON.

Soon after the Rev. Pliny Fisk and the Rev. Levi Parsons left their mountain homes in Western Massachusetts, near the close of 1819, as the first American missionaries to Palestine, their young friend JONAS KING, from the same neighborhood, was elected professor in Amherst college, and proceeded to Paris to pursue the study of Arabic with the celebrated De Sacy. He there became familiar with an American gentleman, then at the head of one of the first commercial houses in Paris, to whose care his correspondence was addressed.

In February, 1822, the lamented Parsons died, and

the Rev. Mr. Fisk without delay addressed a letter to Mr. King, requesting that he would meet him at Malta, and in the place of Parsons, accompany him as a missionary to Palestine; and fearing delay by waiting the action of the American Board of Missions, he in the same enclosure requested Mr. King's mercantile friend not only to second his invitation, but if possible to raise the sum of $1,500, requisite for his support for three years.

Mr. King, on receiving the letter in the merchant's counting-room, exclaimed, "This is from my friend Fisk; I beg leave to retire to your private office and read it." Oppressed with the weight of the proposition it contained, he spent an hour in prayer for divine direction; and hoping to gain further light as to the path of duty from the indications of Providence, sought the merchant's advice. He returned to the counting-room, and asked with deep solicitude, "What shall I do?" Said his friend, "Go." "But," said he, "what will become of my aged and infirm parents in America?" "I will be a son to them in your stead," replied his friend. "Then," said Mr. King, "I go up to Jerusalem, 'not knowing the things that shall befall me there.'"

"Now," said the merchant, "sit down at this desk, and write to my friends Thomas Waddington of St. Remey, France; Louis Mertens of Brussels; Claude Cromlin of Amsterdam, and John Venning of St. Petersburgh: state to them the circumstances, and that you are willing to go; tell them I will give one-fifth of the $1,500, and leave it to their decision whether they will join me in filling up the amount." By the return of the mails it appeared that God had put it into the hearts of these gentlemen cheerfully to respond to the appeal by enclosing each $300, making the sum required; and Mr. King lost no time in preparing for his departure.

A few months previous to this, Mr. King had established the monthly concert of prayer in his own hired upper chamber in Paris. At the first and second meetings only three were present; at the third, the number was increased to ten; at the fourth, to thirty; and soon after his departure it rose to three hundred, and this concert was continued with interest in that city. A large concourse assembled in the church of the Oratoire to listen to Mr. King's farewell address, and join in commending him to the God of all grace; and he was cheered in a similar manner, on his way, by Christian assemblies at Lyons, Nismes, Montpelier, and Marseilles, where he embarked for Malta, whence he proceeded with Mr. Fisk to Jerusalem; and became the well-known, persecuted, but laborious and successful missionary at Athens.

His friend the merchant, from time to time, wrote to the solitary parents, enclosing some tokens of regard "from their affectionate son:" the next year he returned to America; and early in the spring of 1824 he was at Northampton, about twenty-five miles from the parents, meditating a visit to their humble abode. He applied to the landlord, who furnished him a wagon, with his little son for a driver; and freighted with a bag of groceries which extended the whole length of the wagon, they set off early in the morning; and after encountering snow-drifts and other obstacles by the way, arrived at the cottage about 2 P. M.

Leaving the lad with the wagon in the street, the gentleman knocked, saying as he entered, "It is a chill, uncomfortable day, friends; would you be so kind as to allow a stranger to warm himself a little by your fire?" He was welcomed and seated between the aged couple, in whom he distinctly recognized the features of Jonas, and who in their turn fixed on him a scrutinizing eye. After a short pause he said deliberately,

"I once had a friend, who said to me, 'What shall I do?' Said I, 'Go.' 'But what,' said he, 'will become of my aged and infirm parents in America?' I replied, 'I will be a son to them in your stead.' 'Then,' said he, 'I go up to Jerusalem, 'not knowing the things that shall befall me there.'"

Instantly the aged couple sprang to him, exclaiming, "This is Mr. W——," and almost overwhelmed him with their tears and caresses. "Let us pray," said the father; and they unburdened their hearts at the throne of mercy.

Scarcely were they again seated, when the mother took from the shelf a new quarto Bible, saying, she hoped her friend would not blame her for paying ten dollars for it out of the fifty he had sent her a few months previous. "Our old eyes," she said, "could not well read the small print of the other Bible. I told Mr. King I did not believe we could make any better use of the money, or should ever be the poorer for buying a Bible that we could read; and it is a great comfort to us." Their friend expressed his approbation of the purchase, admired the Bible, and before he returned it to the shelf, slipped into it unperceived a ten-dollar bill; which she afterwards

wrote him had been found on the floor when they were reading the Bible, and which she recognized as from the hand of God, having no knowledge by what means the exact amount expended had thus come again into their hands.

After a brief interchange of confidence and affection, she said to her esteemed guest, "I presume, sir, you have not dined, and must be in need of refreshment. I am very sorry we have not a cup of tea to offer you, but we have some nice ham and fresh eggs, which I will immediately prepare." Her friend remarked, "There is a bag in the wagon, containing several articles from 'your son,' and perhaps there may be tea among them."

The bag, with not a little effort, was transferred from the wagon to the cottage floor, and the mother addressed herself to the task of taking out its contents. Among packages of flour, rice, loaf sugar, coffee, chocolate, raisins, and other articles, each of which she held up with new expressions of delight, as received from one she so much loved, she at length came to a package of four pounds of hyson tea, when she held it out to the father with streaming eyes, saying, "Look here, papa, Jonas is the same dear good boy that he always was; he knew we were out of tea sometimes; he don't forget his poor father and mother." Then opening a package of Turkey figs, "And is this also," said she, "from Jerusalem? Papa, was there ever such a son as Jonas?" By this time all hearts were overflowing. "Let us pray," said the father; and the exploring of the treasures was suspended, while they again united in thanksgiving to God.

It was not long before the little company were seated at a well-furnished table, refreshed by the gifts of the kind "son," mingling their sympathies, and recounting all the way in which they had been led. While thus conversing, the merchant affectionately asked, "Do you never regret the sacrifice you have made in giving up your only son to be a missionary?" The aged father replied,

"'God so loved the world, that he gave his only begotten Son, that whosoever believeth in him should not perish, but have everlasting life;' and shall I withhold my only son from obeying the command of our ascended Saviour, 'Go ye into all the world, and preach the gospel to every creature?'"

All present were deeply affected, a tear standing in the eye even of the young driver: they again bowed in prayer; both the father and the merchant led in turn, commending the little company, the absent son, and a sin-ruined world to the God of missions.

The interview was an hour bright with the beams of the Sun of righteousness amid the dark pilgrimage of life, an oasis in the desert, a season never to be forgotten by any one of the four persons who thus met for the first and the last time on earth.

That young driver, as he afterwards distinctly stated, here first had his mind impressed with the sacredness of the work of foreign missions. He gave his heart to Christ; pursued a thorough course of education; went forth to the heathen, and was no other than HENRY LYMAN, the noble martyr who fell by the side of MUNSON, in 1834, among the bloody Battas of Sumatra.

The aged father, in his will, bequeathed to the merchant, for the purchase of a book in token of his love, the sum of five dollars, which at his death was paid to the widow for the old small-print Bible, which is still possessed as a precious memento. The widow has entered into rest; and the stranger passing a rural graveyard in South Hawley, where the scenery opens in magnificence and beauty, reads on the tombstone of the father his reply just quoted to the question, whether he ever regretted the gift to missions of his ONLY SON.

W. A. H.

DOMESTIC REMINISCENCES.

BUT ONE THING WANTED.

"THERE is but one thing wanted to make us comfortable." So said a young wife to her husband one pleasant spring morning, ere he went to his daily toil. They had been married some months, and had just established themselves in one of the many pleasant villages with which New England abounds. Both were full of hope, the future opened before them rich in promise. A house had been taken in a quiet unpretending part of the town, and for some weeks they had been occupied in planning and getting, and in setting things to rights.

How busy was that young wife during all those bright spring days. She scarcely noticed the rapid and beautiful changes which the God of nature was making all around her, on the hill, in the forest, and over the broad meadow that swept down to the river side but a little distance beyond their dwelling. The frosts had disappeared, the buds had swollen, nay, the green leaves had come out, and the flowers had burst forth, and the sweet warblings of birds floated by as the breeze swept past their open doors, but she gave little heed to them all. Was she not a wife, with a husband dearer to her than herself? And they had a home too of their own, and that home should be made a sanctuary for her husband, whither he could flee from the dust and noise of the world without, and find repose and strength in the smiles and kind words of at least one loving heart. O how many plans were laid and arrangements made within these quiet walls—hardly quiet though, for there was the hurried tread of busy feet, and then two little hands, that rather rebelled against the harsh ways to which they were often subjected, wrought most diligently from morning till night. The bookcase must be placed here, the bureau there, and those pretty engravings must be hung yonder against the wall; and now they must all be changed, to see if another location will not produce a better effect, and give more character to the room.

And now the house is all furnished, and the wife is so happy at the satisfied and complaisant looks with which her husband regards the disposition which she has made of this piece of furniture and that. And how does her heart beat with delight and run over with affection for him as he commends her taste, and speaks of the place she has in his affections; how often he thinks of her when prosecuting his daily toil, and how gladly he welcomes the hours that call him to her side. They are so happy, so essential to each other, all ready to live. Not quite, however, for there was one room, after all, not yet fitted up. This was the parlor, and this is what called forth the words which stand first in our paper from the young housekeeper. Not many days passed before, by the kindness of friends, the parlor was finished, the carpet down, the curtains up, and the sofa inviting to a lounge. The "one thing to make them comfortable" was no longer wanted. The parlor, of course, was not to be used every day; so one evening, after the last touch had been given by those tasteful hands, husband and wife sat together alone, on their sofa, and as they remembered the past and looked hopefully into the future, there was joy in their hearts and exclamations of joy came from their lips. And they did not forget God in their happiness; the youthful pair acknowledged him that evening, and prayed for a Father's blessing to attend them. Rising from their knees, the room was darkened and left. But were they comfortable? We will look upon them again.

Several weeks have elapsed, and during these weeks sad changes have taken place in that new home. Disease has crossed its threshold, and that parlor is the sick-room, it has been used for no other purpose. We will enter it. The shadows have darkened the earth, and the stars are looking from the sky as serenely as though there was no sadness in this world. But there is sadness in that parlor, such as never entered it before. There lies the young wife struggling with pain; you would scarcely know her, so emaciated and thin; the husband is by her side. Through what a fiery ordeal is he passing; how wildly does his heart throb. They are expecting a guest, he may come any moment; they are waiting for death.

The lips of the sick one move, the husband bends over the couch to catch those faint whispers. How much it costs to control himself as he hears, "My husband, we have had a happy home, but we shall have a happier one in heaven; the Saviour is so precious. He is with me. He will be with you. Farewell." And now death has come, he has taken her by the hand, his icy breath has chilled her brow. "The silver cord is loosed, the golden bowl is broken, and the pitcher lies shivered at the fountain." But he did not touch the sweet smile of resignation and joy which the departing spirit in its passage to the skies left on that face; this lingered there till the precious dust was laid away to its rest.

We really need *but one thing* to make us comfortable—that one thing is the religion of the Lord Jesus. Without this, we shall not live well; with it, we shall go safely through the dark valley. F. B. W.

THE FIRST PRAYER IN THE FAMILY.

On the banks of H—— resided an interesting family consisting of father and mother, two sons, and three daughters. It was a beautiful spot; the mansion was spacious and elegant; the grounds around it were ample and tastefully laid out. Every thing without was enchanting, and every thing within was pleasant.

The church in that place was visited with an extensive work of grace, in the progress of which there is reason to believe that not less than two hundred were added to the Lord. After the work had commenced, the two eldest daughters, who had been hopefully converted at a boarding-school a few years before, were much exercised in mind about their parents, especially their father. He was a sedate man, had been brought up in New England, but had given his whole heart to the world. Being in easy circumstances, he had leisure for reflection. His daughters were affected to think that there was no family altar in that house. They conversed and prayed together on the subject.

One evening, as the family were gathered around a cheerful fire, they expressed their feelings, and proposed to their father to set up family prayer. He was taken by surprise, but gave his consent. One of them immediately opened the large Bible and read a chapter, the other led in prayer; it was a solemn time. This was *the first prayer* offered in the family. The effect was great. There was but little sleep in that house that night. The father was powerfully awakened; for several days he was borne down with a sense of his sins; he was at length brought to the feet of Jesus. Salvation came to that house. Several of the family were hopefully brought to a saving knowledge of the truth. Great results were connected with that first prayer in the family. How interesting when children become instruments of good to their parents. Here is encouragement for all to be faithful. We are told that "he which converteth a sinner from the error of his way, shall save a soul from death, and shall hide a multitude of sins."

T.

THE EARNEST INQUIRY.

About thirty years ago, visiting H——, in the wilderness of North-eastern Ohio, in company with the Rev. Luther Humphrey, and examining candidates with a view to organize a church, I was struck with the narrative given of herself by Mrs. M——.

Living about two miles from her father's in Massachusetts, she one day took her little son, five years old, to visit her parents; and a thunder-storm arising, they were obliged to tarry for the night.

"In the evening," she said, "my father, as his custom was, called his family together, read from his large Bible, and commended all to God in prayer. In the morning, the family were also assembled, when he again read the Bible and prayed; and I returned home with my little boy.

"I soon noticed that the little fellow seemed pensive and very sober, and asked him, 'What is the matter?' After a little hesitation, he said, 'Why doesn't pa do as grandpa does?' I said to him, 'Poh, go away to your play.' My little boy looked disappointed at my answer, but ran to his play. He was gone, however, but a short time, before he came running to me, and with more earnestness, again said, 'Ma, ma, why doesn't pa do as grandpa does?' I frowned upon him, and bade him the second time go away to his play. He seemed grieved, but went away. Soon he came running back to me a third time, and still more earnestly cried out, 'Ma, ma, why doesn't pa do as grandpa does?' To pacify him, I asked him, 'How does grandpa do?' 'Why, ma, he gets his great Bible and reads, and then goes to prayer.' 'Well, ask pa when he comes home.'

"My husband was abroad on business, and was not expected home till evening. The boy seemed to wait impatiently for his father to come. When evening came, I said, 'My little boy, it is now time for you to go to bed.' 'No, ma, I must sit up till pa comes.' I soon tried again to influence his little mind to think it best for him to go to bed. But no, he must sit up, contrary to his usage, and see his pa. So he waited till between eight and nine, when his father returned. As soon as he stepped his foot within the door, the little boy ran to meet him, saying, 'Pa, pa, why don't you do as grandpa does?' 'Away, away; what are you up at this time of night for? Off to bed.'

"Nothing more was heard from our little boy until morning. He lay in bed later than usual, even till after we had breakfasted. When he got up, I placed his breakfast before him, and drew him up to the table. But he did not eat any thing. He sat very demure, looking at his food. I said, 'Why don't you eat?' He said nothing, but still sat almost motionless. I soon asked him again, 'Why don't you eat your breakfast?' 'I am waiting to ask a blessing, for I don't see that any body will, if I don't.'

"My feelings were overcome; I could contain myself no longer, and immediately retired into another room, where I might weep and pray undiscovered. I informed my husband. He was deeply affected. Without delay, we sought an interest in the Redeemer. Our own family altar was erected; and soon, as we hope, we found, to our unspeakable joy, HIM of whom Moses in the law and the prophets did write."

The father was elected deacon of the church, in which office he served acceptably to the day of his death. And the little boy, grown into the meridian of life, became an ornament to the Christian name and cause. E. T. W.

A SCENE AT FAMILY WORSHIP.

A group of Christian friends was recently gathered under the hospitable roof of Dr. ——. Among them was Rev. Dr. C——, the brilliant talker, the eloquent preacher, and G. T——, whose life of almost fourscore years, furnishes a record of incidents so remarkable as to have already afforded materials for romance and history. As the circle assembled around the domestic altar, the cheerful old Scotchman requested Dr. C—— to read the third chapter of Proverbs, remarking that he would explain the reason of his request after prayers.

"Last night," he said, "was the anniversary of my arrival in America, after a twelve weeks' voyage from Scotland. *Fifty-seven years ago, this morning*, I opened my chest to examine my luggage, and the first thing I saw was the Bible that my father had packed carefully on the top of my effects. When I looked into the sacred volume, the first chapter that met my eye was the third of Proverbs. I read on, and it seemed as if my father's voice was sounding in my ears, 'My son, forget not my law,' etc. The illusion lasted till the chapter was nearly finished. It *was* my heavenly Father's voice. Here," said the old man, as he drew two small black volumes from his pockets, "here is the old Bible that has been my light and comfort these fifty-seven years." C.

FORTY YEARS' EXPERIENCE OF FAMILY PRAYER.

From the day that myself and wife were installed in our own house as a family, now nearly forty years since, God has had an altar in our dwelling, and upon that altar the morning and evening sacrifice of prayer has been offered. This I have ever considered as an imperative duty and a delightful privilege. Perhaps no religious exercise in which a family can engage conduces more to its peace, its order, or its happiness. Perhaps the head of a family never appears so dignified or so honorable, as when leading the devotions of his household. Perhaps no other service exerts so happy an influence on the temper, affection, and conduct of those to whom he acts as a priest unto God. Aside from the spiritual good to which it directly and powerfully conduces, its bearing upon the temporal welfare of a family should secure its faithful observance. With these sentiments I was early impressed by the precepts, but more by the example of my father, who daily led his family to the throne of grace. And I early decided, that if ever I became the head of a household, I would adopt a practice so reasonable, and fraught, as I believed, with present and lasting blessings.

I was aware of an objection often brought against this service by those whose cares and business are multiform, and thought it quite possible that, in respect to myself, it might sometimes interfere with the plans and purposes of the day. But it has not proved so. And now, at the expiration of nearly forty years, I can aver in all truth, that we have seldom if ever wanted time. Very seldom, indeed, has any circumstance or providence occurred to prevent our assembling morning and evening, "to call upon the name of the Lord." I have known some of my neighbors to be occasionally a little earlier at their business; but never yet have I known the instance, or ever thought it existed, when my worldly interests suffered from attending to the duties of family devotion—*not one instance in nearly forty years.* But the beneficial influence has all been the other way. I do not mean to intimate that God has wrought miracles for us; and yet interpositions have been so unexpected and so kind, anticipated obstacles so remarkably removed, difficulties so smoothed, and our pathway so clearly indicated, that it has seemed sometimes little less than miraculous. The reading of the holy oracles, its precepts, warnings, promises, encouragements, followed by humble, fervent, importunate prayer, has better fitted us for the duties of the day. I firmly believe that the mind has been less disturbed by the crosses and vexations common to us all. .We have felt stronger under the burdens of life, and derived as surance of the divine guidance and blessing—remembering what God has said, " Call upon me in the day of trouble, and I will answer thee; and thou shalt glorify me." Thus prepared, we have in comparative quiet, passed on in the journey of life; our anchor has been cast on safe ground, and if our bark has sometimes rocked, as storms will sometimes blow and waves rise, our anchor has not dragged, nor our vessel been submerged.

In the course of years, sons and daughters were born to us. These events added new incentives to call upon God, and invested the privilege with new and increasing interest. These little dependent beings, who could sustain them—who safely conduct them through the perils and infirmities of childhood? We felt that God alone in his wise providence could do this. And as we had the daily conviction that they were immortal beings, and confided to our care, we felt the need of divine wisdom and instruction to aid us in fulfilling this most important trust. With all our watchfulness, we well knew that we should be unable to direct them safely over the stormy passage of life. We could not be present with them at all times. Often we could not know where they were; nor could we foresee the temptations and trials which would overtake them. These considerations greatly enhanced the value of prayer.

In process of time, these children advanced to manhood and womanhood. In the natural order of things, they left us. Some of them embarked in business. Some were married, and have had children growing up around them. Under these circumstances, we find family prayer as great a privilege now as formerly, perhaps even greater. We have more to pray for, and even greater solicitude on their account. When our children were young, and the cold wintry storm howled around our dwelling, their mother, on the setting in of night, was able to conduct them to their little rooms, and see them quietly and snugly in their beds; each one being able to say, as Cowper so beautifully said of his mother,

> Thy nightly visits to my chamber made,
> That thou might see me safe and warmly laid.

And now, as some of them are men of business and often travelling about, either in the whirling car or in the tossing ship, exposed to varied dangers, why should we not the more frequently and the more fervently commend them to God? Our prayers have indeed been laid up for them, and we trust that God will be faithful to his gracious engagements; we cannot distrust him. Every day brings its desire to kneel down and commend ourselves and them again and again to the God of all our mercies. It is a privilege which I think—yes, I dare aver, that I would not surrender for all the gold which will ever be gathered from the mines of California. What good would all that gold do us, if at the same time we were excluded from the privilege of calling upon our heavenly Father—if we must forego his love and communion? The whole world would make no amends for such a loss.

> Were I possessor of the earth,
> And called the stars my own,
> Without thy graces, and thyself,
> I were a wretch undone.

In praying for blessings upon myself and family, I have always been guarded on one or two points. I have never asked for great temporal prosperity, nor that we might become rich in this world's goods. He that accumulates riches increases responsibility. Wealth is apt to engender pride; it tends to harden the heart. It is better to confine ourselves to asking for a competency. This is desirable. This we may seek for with propriety. Beyond this there is danger. Nor have I sought an exemption from the common calamities of life. We do not wish it. We never so pray. Some trials are best. They are needed. I never yet knew an instance in which mere prosperity ever brought an impenitent man to repentance; so I have seldom known the influx of wealth add to the spiritual prosperity and elevation of the Christian. But as to conformity to God, submission to the divine will, and growth in Christian grace, I know nothing to forbid the largest desires, and the most importunate pleading. For such blessings I have sought, such I have expected, such I have found, and I think *because* I have sought them.

I could add much more of the divine faithfulness, of temporal favors, and of spiritual mercies; but as in reading a portion of Scripture prior to prayer I have studied brevity—and brevity as to prayer itself, not however disregarding circumstances, and especially pertinency—so, in relating my experience, I am brief. My great object is to commend the practice to those who are commencing the family state. No service seems more dutiful, no privilege seems greater, no reward is more sure.

Were I going to live my life over again, I would begin as I began. The very first thing I would do, would be to erect an altar to God. That I did. I have never for a single moment regretted it. But one thing in all truth I can say: if I were to embark on a similar voyage, I would make one grand emendation. I would study to be more faithful in the performance of the duty. I would pray more earnestly, more sincerely, more importunately, more confidingly. And now, for the remainder of my pilgrimage, I hope to do all this; so help me, O God. G.

POOR ZEKE AND HIS PRAYERS.

In a wild, sequestered place, quite away from the bounds of my congregation, there lived a very wicked family—a father, mother, two brothers, and three sisters. None of them attended any meeting. One of the brothers was wanting in common-sense. His name was Ezekiel. As he was not supposed to have mind enough to be put to any work, he used to stroll away, and be gone sometimes several days.

One day, as I was preaching on the pity Jesus has for poor sinners, I observed "poor Zeke" looking me in the face, and every time I said Jesus pitied poor sinners, the tears would start from his eyes. As there was more than usual attention to religion, we had meetings often; and whether it was a lecture, or a prayer-meeting, or an inquiry-meeting, "poor Zeke" was sure to be there.

At length I asked him if he loved Jesus, and he answered, "Yes." "Why do you love Jesus?" said I. "O, 'cause he love poor wicked Zeke so." "Have you been wicked?" "Yes, I *full, full* of wicked." "Do you pray?" said I. "O yes." "What do you say, when you pray?" "I say, O my Jesus, pity poor Zeke. O take all my wicked away."

After a while he went home. His appearance was changed. He had lost his seeming vacancy of look and thought. But he dare not pray in the house, for all were full of fun and noise. So he went to the barn, and there he fell on his knees and uttered his broken prayer to Him who "hath chosen the weak things of this world to confound the mighty." His brother, going into the barn, heard him crying to God so fervently that it alarmed him. He went in and told his father, with an oath, that Zeke was in the barn praying. At this, his father ran to the barn and listened, and found the boy indeed at prayer. He went in and spoke to him; but he "cried so much the more a great deal." "Stop your noise, Zeke," said his angry father; but he kept on. So they took hold of him and got him into the house, in hopes of quieting him.

They asked him where he had been, and how he came to feel so. He told them a very rational story about it. But the more he talked, the more his father scolded. Poor Zeke found he could say no more, and then fell down on his knees again. His father tried to silence him; but his mother loved her poor boy, and begged them to let him pray.

When he had arisen from prayer, his mother said, "It is high time we all prayed. Ezekiel, will you pray for your mother?" "O yes," he said; and down again he went upon his knees, and his mother with him. Not many days after, she too was full of joy at the thought of Jesus' dying pity. By this time, the brother who first heard him pray was sobbing out, "What shall I do?" Poor Zeke said, "Go to Jesus." Then he and his mother prayed for him, and he too found his distress giving way for unspeakable joy. Then there were three to pray for a hardened husband and an unfeeling father. He fought and ridiculed until their three daughters were added to the Lord. This made five who had now joined Ezekiel and embraced his religion.

At last his father saw himself alone. His heart broke; he wept like a child. He went to his son and confessed his sin in opposing him, and asked him to pray for him. His burden was removed; he rejoiced in God. He erected the family altar, and it was a solemn sight to see seven persons who had a few weeks before been profane and careless, now all brought over from the service of Satan to the service of the Lord. And it was a joyful day when poor Zeke, with his father and mother, his brother and sisters, united with God's people, and came together to the communion.

Reflect, that if a poor, ignorant, and foolish child, under God, can do so much good, what a solemn account must they have to render at last, who, having talent, yet often shrink at the cross, and let sinners perish. A Pastor.

A DYING PATRIARCH.

In the spring of 1828, I was invited to take the pastoral charge of the interesting Presbyterian church of W——, in Middle Georgia. That church had been left destitute by the early death of their devoted young pastor, whose premature removal from among us caused many to weep bitterly. There were a goodly number of praying people in that little church; and when I rejected other calls and accepted theirs, I felt as if I was going where the prayers of the pious had drawn me.

Soon after I commenced my labors, I was struck with the venerable, mild, almost heavenly appearance of one of the elders. Whenever he entered the church the preacher could not but be cheered by the thought, If that good man prays for me, I shall have divine aid in delivering God's message to dying men.

The head of this elder was silvered over with gray hairs; he was seventy-two years old. He had been long walking in the path of the heaven-bound pilgrim. Such had been the purity of his life, the amiableness of his spirit, and the ardor and consistency of his piety, that no one could resist the conviction that he was "a good man and a just." His life and deportment constituted one of those living, eloquent arguments which infidelity cannot resist. It seemed as if no preacher acquainted with him could ascend that pulpit and look around upon the congregation without being cheered by the presence, or depressed by the absence of that godly man. We did not know it, but Mr. W—— was fast ripening for heaven. His work was nearly done.

One pleasant evening I received a message requesting me to repair immediately to the house of my venerable friend, a few miles out of the village, as he was very sick. I went, and on entering the room perceived that God was about to call his aged servant home. His mind was clear, serene, and peaceful. His faith was triumphant. But he had something of *special* importance to say to *me*. He left a message of love and admonition for the little church which he was about to leave. This was not all. He partially raised himself up in bed, and cast his eyes around upon the large company present, children and grandchildren, and a sister—the mother of a large family—and her husband, and addressed me in substance as follows: "You see these people. I sent for you to talk to them, and pray for them. I can do no more. My work is done. I have prayed and prayed, and talked and waited, and yet I am about to die and leave them all, with two exceptions—a son and his wife—in their sins. O pray for them, and talk to them, for *I cannot do it*. I leave them with God and with you." He ceased. The solemn message was delivered; his work was done. We all knelt around his bed and prayed for him and for them whose spiritual condition lay with much weight upon the heart of this dying patriarch.

There were two sons and one daughter, all heads of interesting rising families. There were the sister and her husband and their large family, several of the children grown, besides three amiable unmarried daughters. And yet, with the two exceptions mentioned above, all this group of amiable, moral, intelligent, church-going people had, up to this time, succeeded in resisting the prayers and the entreaties of this pious man and his godly wife, who then sat weeping by his dying bed. O what a mystery was before our eyes. God's words and promises are true; and yet, we know not why, this pious aged couple were about to die while their prayers for their children and grandchildren were unanswered. That night the good man slept in Jesus. As I closed his eyes, I could well exclaim, "My father, my father, the chariot of Israel, and the horsemen thereof!" In about six months, Mrs. W—— departed in the same triumphant manner.

I remembered, and endeavored to comply with the dying injunction of my aged friend. I did talk to, and pray with and for his unconverted relatives. And God blessed my efforts, so far as those were concerned who resided in W—— and its vicinity. The counsel and the prayers of the pious departed parents came into remembrance after they were dead.

From night to night I had around me in the inquiry-meeting an interesting group of anxious souls inquiring the way to Zion. And what is remarkable, this religious feeling, this deep anxiety about salvation, was almost, if not entirely, confined to the family connections of the deceased man of God. *They* shared richly in the blessing. The prayers of the parents had ceased, but the answer came at last. It was not long before the sister and her husband, and most, if not all their children, and all the children, with one exception, and several of the grandchildren of Mr. and Mrs. W——, became worthy members of the church. May they all meet in heaven.

Before closing, I would remark, that in the mysterious providence of a faithful God, there may be long delay when there is no denial of the blessing. Let pious parents lead lives of holiness and consistency. Let them pray without ceasing; let them discharge all their parental duties in humble reliance upon God's blessing, never staggering at the promise through unbelief, and ever seeking by a holy example, like Mr. and Mrs. W——, to lead their households to heaven, and they will not, they *cannot* live and labor in vain. God will bless them. N. H.

A MOTHER'S PRAYERS.

My earliest recollections painfully remind me of my father, and the sufferings of a precious mother; but they have long since gone where no disclosures can affect them, and I relate the story of maternal fidelity as an encouragement to mothers in every sphere of life, and especially to comfort those who are exposed to such billows of sorrow as overwhelmed the soul of my dear mother.

My father was an intemperate man, and often very abusive in his family. My mother had but two children, and when she was made miserable by unkind treatment, she would lead my brother and myself to a little spot under a side-hill, near our house, where we were screened from observation by the thick foliage of the trees which surrounded us, and there, kneeling upon a log, with a hand upon each little head, she would lift her tearful eyes to heaven, and commend us to the love and care of our heavenly Father.

Hardships and trials soon brought my mother to the grave, and I was sent to distant relatives, who were kind in providing me temporal comforts, but "no man cared for my soul." As I grew up, I became more and more depraved, and at the age of twenty-one, I was vicious and degraded.

I lived with a farmer, who often sent me to market with the produce of his land, sometimes to distant parts of the state. Once, when going to sell a load of grain, I found myself within twenty miles of the home of my earlier days, and I felt irresistibly impelled to go and take one look of "the cave," as my mother called her little retreat, and see if the dear old log was still there. So, after I had disposed of the grain, I turned my horses from the direct road, stopped for the night, and reached the scene of my childhood at nine o'clock the next morning.

There I found the Bethel, the trees, and the log nearly decayed, but in the very position where I distinctly remembered to have seen it so many years before. I seated myself upon it. The grass looked as if no foot had pressed it since the dear guide of my infant days was laid in her grave. I seemed to feel her warm hand upon my head, and to hear her trembling voice supplicating blessings for *me;* mercies I had despised, privileges I had abused. The anguish I endured, I can never describe. On that spot, for the first time in my life, I felt myself a wretched sinner. I could not tear myself away till I had obtained some relief to my tortured conscience, and it was near sunset before I left the sacred spot. I did not leave it till I had resolved to devote the remainder of my life to God; to leave all and follow him; and by his grace I trust I have been enabled, though imperfectly, to keep that resolution.

My precious mother's prayers were answered, and I, "a miracle of grace," am a monument of the faithfulness of a prayer-hearing God. A Clergyman.

A SISTER'S LOVE.

I was a thoughtless youth, even more regardless of serious things than boys in general. But I had one tie which bound me to home, and restrained me from all outward immoralities; this was a peculiar affection for my sister. Few brothers and sisters, I think, ever love each other as we did. All our thoughts, feelings, and plans were shared together, and neither could enjoy any thing alone. A walk, a ride, a book, or concert, lost half its charm if Anna were away, and she was the first to soothe every rising sorrow.

When I was seventeen, there was a revival of religion in the church to which my father belonged, and Anna and I occasionally attended the evening meetings. I noticed Anna was very silent on our return from these; but as I did not care to say any thing upon the subject, I was content it should be so. Yet there lurked within me an uneasy fear that she was becoming more interested in religious things than I was. I could not bear the idea; it even made me angry to think of my bright, lively Anna's becoming a Christian, for I was certain it would spoil her for me, and destroy our happiness in each other. I became more certain something was weighing on her spirits, for instead of moving merrily about the house, singing snatches of gay songs, her step became slow and thoughtful, and her eye was downcast and often filled with tears. Yet with a cruel selfishness, I refrained from asking what disturbed her; and once, when I saw her eye resting on my face with an expression of intense interest, I turned away from the beseeching glance, and left the room.

The next morning, I found a little note from her on my table. I took it up with a feeling of bitterness in my heart, and crushing it, thrust it into my pocket, determined not to read it, so sure did I feel that it contained something about my soul's salvation. I was then a member of the academy, fitting for college, and I went to the school-room, endeavoring by unusual attention to my books to forget the circumstance altogether. But a sense of my injustice smote me, and in the course of the forenoon I drew forth the note, intending to read it, but determined that it should exert no influence over me. I had even planned a reply to it, in which I should beg her never to let that subject be spoken of between us. And yet my heart was so melted by the contents of that little note, that before it was finished I was forced to bow my head over the desk to conceal my tears. It touched the right chord in my heart. She said she had told no one of the new hope of heaven which was in her heart, because she must first speak of it to *me*, as she had always done of other feelings, and that she could not fully enjoy it without my sympathy. Yes, she was my own trusting, loving Anna still. Becoming a Christian had not made her cold and distant, as I had fancied it would; and when I went home I had a long, frank conversation with her. From that point I date my first religious impressions. To that dear sister's love and prayers I owe my soul's salvation, so far as any human instrumentality is connected with it; and I need not say that she was thenceforth dearer to me than ever. Yet, had she remained silent at this point, and had I learned the state of her feelings from others, a barrier would have been raised between us, which might never have been removed.

Do not fear to speak, young Christian, of your new hopes and desires to your dearest friend; but speak tenderly, naturally, and confidingly, I need not add with humility also; for when was ever a human soul filled with the love of Jesus, that it was not softened and humbled by it, and made "meek and lowly?"

W.

A PRODIGAL'S WELCOME.

Charles was a favorite and only son in a pleasant New England home. Unfortunately, as he entered upon the excitements and pleasures of youth, he caught from infidel companions the poison of scepticism. Wealth and fashion gave to the Puritan piety of the parental heart a repulsive seriousness, and the scornful smile often betrayed the unwilling respect he rendered to the family altar. Remonstrance and tears were in vain. The hue of infidelity darkened daily upon his otherwise fine character, until at length his language assumed a bolder tone, and his disrelish of domestic religion became painfully marked.

One morning after family prayer, he told his father with spirited decision, that if he did not abandon the superstitious custom, he should leave home; he would go to more congenial associations, and find wealth without the annoyance of a faith he entirely rejected. His father with grief assured Charles that he could not demolish the altar of prayer, even if it made a final separation between them; the throne of grace was too precious to desert for a day. The sceptic curled his lip in the pride of perverted reason, and asked for his portion of money. With strange indiscretion in too indulgent parents, it was given, with many tears and strong cries unto the Lord for reclaiming grace.

Charles went to a distant city, commenced business, formed friendships with gay and unprincipled young men, and in a year was a penniless bankrupt. In his destitution, he thought of home; and though pride struggled fiercely with conscience and affection, he arose and started for the place of his birth. Most of the way he was compelled to walk; and on Saturday night, he was within a few miles of his father's house.

He stopped at an inn, and in the morning had not means to pay his bill. The landlord opened his package, and took out a Bible. Charles, weeping, said it was a mother's gift, and begged for the neglected volume. The landlord refused, offering to restore it when redeemed by compensation in some other form. Charles went sadly on his homeward track, lingering in distressful thought by the way, till the sun of that Sabbath was sinking behind the familiar hills. He quickened his pace, and as the full moon rose he reached the threshold of home. By a retired entrance he stole into a silent apartment. He listened, and heard the voice of prayer. Moving forward to the partially open door, he saw the grey-haired father, surrounded by mother and sisters, bowed before the despised altar praying for him. The rustling of Charles' agitated form drew the attention of a sister, who gazed a moment in surprise, and in a wild gush of feeling exclaimed, "Oh, Charles is come." The prayer ceased, and in a moment a network of arms enfolded the prodigal. The mother inquired for the Bible; a frank confession was scarcely uttered, before the exclamation was renewed, "Oh, Charles, we are so glad you have come." Soon all bowed together, and angels smiled over the scene.

And is it so, that God holds an attitude as subduing to every returning sinner? When the interests of two worlds are at stake, how can the prodigal refuse to gather up his rags, and go penitently to his infinite Father? P. C. H.

A HOUSE AND FAMILY LOST.

One dark and stormy night in July, 1830, the family of Mr. John Wilson of New Haven, in the Green Mountains of Vermont, had retired to rest.

The night was cheerless, the wind howled, and the rain pelted; but there had been such things before a hundred times, when they had barred their doors, gone to their rest in quietness, and awoke to their labor in safety and good cheer. And why not now? Alas, the house did not stand on a sure foundation. It was in the midst of a ravine, formed by a branch of the Otter creek. The spot is well known by the name of *Beman's Hollow*—hollow being descriptive of a ravine, closed at one end or both by some nearer approach of the adjacent hills, forming often at the outlet, as here, a cataract.

At night's deadest hour the family were awakened by a crash, and what seemed a moving of the house. And now it seemed afloat, the water gushing in at every open and opening crack. There was no longer any doubt of the dreadful reality: their house had been carried away by the flood, which in so short a time had risen to an unwonted height. And now it was shooting madly through trees and amid rocks, and approaching a fearful cataract. Mr. Wilson and a son plunged into the flood, and with extreme difficulty reached the shore, but not before the wild shrieks of Mrs. Wilson, her sister, and three children, heard even above the tempest's roar, had been stifled by the overpowering billows. The house with its devoted inmates went over the cataract, and scarcely a wreck was found to tell the tale of its destruction.

This narrative, of which the details were contained in almost every journal of that period, suggests serious admonitions. Our Saviour, in the conclusion of the sermon on the mount, says, "Whosoever heareth these sayings of mine and doeth them, I will liken him to a man which built his house upon a rock; and the rain descended, and the floods came, and the winds blew and beat upon that house, and it fell not, for it was founded on a rock. And every one that heareth these sayings of mine and doeth them not, shall be likened unto a foolish man which built his house upon the sand; and the rain descended, and the floods came, and the winds blew and beat upon *that* house, and it fell; and great was the fall of it."

Storms will beat upon you; sickness, bereavement, pecuniary losses, disappointment of worldly plans, are the common lot of men. Can you hope to escape? Some of these, or all together, will beat down the house of your frail body; there is no escaping the storm of death. Like the house that went over the cataract and was dashed in pieces, the house of your frail body must go over the cataract of death and be whelmed beneath its flood.

And there are storms in prospect beyond this life. This world will be burned up; these elements will melt with fervent heat; these heavens will pass away with a great noise. These storms will beat against the house of the undying soul; they will beat against it by the clear intimations they will give of God's wrath about to be manifested against the ungodly. And then the throne of his judgment will be set, and all men will stand before him. Some will be justified freely by his grace, yea, a great multitude; and a great multitude will be condemned, and driven from his presence with an everlasting destruction. This is the storm of which we would forewarn you. All other storms are slight in comparison with this, for they wreck only the body, but this storm will wreck the soul—not the body only, not an earthly house, not the world itself merely, but it will wreck the immortal soul—the soul, the very self, the indestructible principle within us, will be wrecked. As the house in the narrative went over the fearful cataract, bearing all that was dear to the husband and the father to irremediable destruction, so will the soul then be carried over the last fatal cataract. It will plunge into the bottomless pit.

Here then you are. The storms of this world are beating against the house of your decaying body, and fall before them it must. You *must* die. Storms are in prospect—the storms of eternity; and your poor naked soul, houseless, homeless, cheerless, is in danger of being exposed to them FOR EVER. Christ declares that the only foundation on which you can rest, if you will be saved by law, is obedience to that law, not in the letter merely, but in its heart-searching spirit, as he has explained it in the sermon on the mount. But this is absolutely out of the question. You owe ten thousand talents, and have nothing to pay. You cannot safely build your house on such a foundation: down, down, down it will go; like the house on the foundation of sand, over the cataract it will plunge, a dreadful ruin. To Christ, then, you must go for pardon and a new heart; and when the storms of God's wrath shall beat against the wicked, you will be safe. Standing on a foundation which cannot be moved, clothed with a spotless robe, your head adorned with a golden crown, and your hands with a golden harp, you will rejoice with joy unspeakable and full of glory.

"There is a fountain filled with blood,
Drawn from Immanuel's veins,
And sinners plunged beneath that flood,
Lose all their guilty stains."

Remember, there are but two ways by which it is possible for a soul to be saved. One is by keeping the whole law; there must not be one failure from earliest infancy to latest old age. The other is by going to Christ for pardon and a new heart. Will you trust the former for a foundation? Madness. No mere man ever kept the whole law, and no man was ever saved by keeping half the law or any fraction of it. No, you must be saved whole and entire by Christ. There is no sure foundation but Christ. By the law you are utterly ruined, your house is on a foundation of sand; it may be it is already unmoored, is already afloat, is now nearing the fatal cataract, and that you have a few moments only to escape. Be exhorted, then, to make without delay one mighty effort, and plant your feet upon the ROCK. O, the fearfulness of that destruction which awaits the sinner trusting to his sandy foundation! R.

THE LOST FOUND.

On my way from New York to Philadelphia, I witnessed a thrilling scene. The steam-boat for Amboy was crowded with emigrants and their effects on the way to the far West. These passengers are stationed on the forward deck, and there is a plank for their accommodation by which they pass from the dock to the boat, while by another plank the other passengers enter the after-part of the vessel. The wheels had long been in motion, the foaming waters were dashed impetuously to the shore, the boat was tossed to and fro, and seemed impatient to be gone; but her hawsers still held her to the shore. Family after family and load after load arrived and were received on board, and there were parting tears and embraces, as some were about to embark for the great West, while others remained in the great city.

A numerous family of great and small were seen approaching in evident haste; they saw the boat in motion, and thought her about to leave. In vain did the boat's men endeavor to prevent their entering the boat by the after-plank; they dashed on board by the first plank they came to, except one little girl, who was crowded along the wharf and taken to the forward-deck. No sooner were the parents and older children safely on board, than they looked around to see if all were there, and almost instantly the cry was made, "Where is Hannah? Hannah's gone! Hannah, Hannah!" Vain was the attempt to still them. Louder and more earnest was the cry, from father, mother, brothers, and sisters, "Hannah! O Hannah, Hannah, Hannah!" But soon the child was brought, and then as loud and as earnest was the cry, "Hannah is found! Hannah's here, Hannah's here!" Deep was the feeling of that moment. There were tears of joy from the friends of Hannah, and there were tears of sympathy from the passengers around them. There was joy as when the prodigal returned to his father's house. So, sinners, if you will return unto God, there will be joy over you; for there is joy in the presence of the angels of God over one sinner that repenteth. Shall there be joy over you? Luke 15. Shall your heavenly Father say, "The lost is found; the lost one is here?"

Other families came, and were taken on board; and still they continued to come; but when the moment arrived the boat was off, and some were *too late*,

but a minute too late, and they were left. Thus families and friends were separated. In vain they called for the boat to stop; they could only wave their hats, their handkerchiefs, and their hands, and thus bid adieu to their more punctual and successful friends, and then return with disappointed and sorrowful hearts, to their lodgings in the city.

The door of the ark of safety is still open: you are invited to enter; but if you delay, you may apply for admission when it is *too late*, and then you apply in vain. TOO LATE! TOO LATE! O let the words sink into your heart. Awake; be in earnest in seeking the salvation of your soul. Call upon God for mercy; repent of sin; believe in Jesus Christ; yield to the strivings of the Spirit; put your trust in the Triune God, for "salvation is of the Lord." Jonah 2:9.

W. J. M.

A MEMORABLE VISIT.

On a pleasant evening, I called with my companion to spend the evening with the family of a Christian brother, with the view of making a pastoral visit. His children were gone from home; but we were welcomed by the parents, and in the good providence of God, we found there another father and mother, from N——, old acquaintances of ours, both of whom are Zion's friends. During the evening much of our conversation was on the low state of religion, and the reasons why God had to such a degree withdrawn his Holy Spirit. We walked about Zion. We viewed her desolations.

One of the brethren inquired how long things must remain in this way. "Is not the Lord," said he, "on the throne of grace?" "He is," said another, "and that is all our hope." With these words all the company were silent, as if we had heard a voice from heaven—*This is all our hope.*

Another brother broke silence by saying, "Probably we have all a work to do at home. And," said he, "we six of us are parents, and how is it at home? I propose that each one in turn give a history of his own family. Are any of our children professors of religion?"

The pastor began by saying, "At times our children have been thoughtful and tender; yet none of our five children profess to be Christians. They yet give a respectful attention to serious things, but they must be born again. And when I think of the final separation at the judgment-seat of Christ, I am overcome. Can we, who are parents, fix our eyes on the child whom we can consent to see go away to the left hand of the Judge?" As he went on in that strain, his companion wept as if she saw the final separation near.

The next brother gave a similar account of his children. No one of them indulged hope. And he said he feared that if any of them were lost, much of the blame would be chargeable to himself. "But," said he, "when I think of the value of one soul—when I think what it is for that soul to mourn for ever in hell, the thought of sparing one of our children to weep there makes me astonished at my own indifference." And his wife said, "I hope you will all pray for our children; who knows but God will yet have mercy on them." She added a few words, and evidently wished to say something about the final separation, but her sighs and tears expressed what she could not do in words.

The other brother said he must say of their children what the others had said, they were all without God and without hope. He had no reason to think, if they should die as they were, that they could go to heaven; and the thought that God is on the mercy-seat is all my hope for them. We little think what it is to see a child dying in his sins, conscious that we who are parents are chargeable with the neglect of their souls. And his wife added, "Yes, we are willing and even anxious to make our children respectable in the world; and though we may now and then cast a thought beyond the grave for them, we have too much neglected their souls."

The Bible was then brought, and the fifty-first Psalm was read, "Have mercy upon me, O God;" and when the Bible was closed, one of the brethren said he would propose, that we six parents should enter into an engagement to pray for the conversion of our children, until the Lord should hear; "and especially," he said, "let us remember them at the family altar." It was a solemn moment when each for himself and herself covenanted to remember especially the children of these three families. Then all fell on our knees, each with a burden that seemed to call for the deepest prostration; and the brethren, one after the other, prayed and confessed our sins and the sins of our children. One of them, seemingly more burdened than the rest, said, "Come, Lord Jesus, ere my child die."

When we parted that night, each went to his own home, but not to rest. We mourned every family apart, as the mourning of Hadadrimmon in the valley of Megiddon. According to agreement, the next morning we informed our children of the last night's visit, and of the mutual covenant we had entered into for them. Every child dropped his head, and some of them covered their faces. To some the communication seemed welcome; but to all a message from

God. For weeks, however, they all seemed to continue about the same—neither careless nor indulging hope.

One of these brethren saw with pain that his children were remaining stationary, and he feared they would go back. He was led to deep heart-searching. He feared his children would all die in their sins, and that he should sink to hell with them. He thought of the judgment-day; he saw their sins chargeable upon him. The books were opened: his life came up in review; and he was condemned. A horror of great darkness fell upon him. More than once did he cry out in the anguish of his soul, "My God, my Redeemer, why, why hast thou forsaken me?" His sins stood in order before him like an armed troop.

He went to revisit the family where that memorable visit was held. He there found their daughter in deep distress for her soul. She said she had been a great sinner, and asked him to pray for her. He found that for several days her mother, though she had been for near twenty years an amiable professor, was now in deep distress. Her husband said she had been almost in despair for several days, and he was concerned for her. The brother, who himself had come for consolation, forgetting his own pangs, set about pointing them to the blood of Christ. He said we were not required to make atonement; that though we might weep tears of blood, we could give no satisfaction to God's injured law; but Christ had died, the just for the unjust, that he might bring us to God. And when they all went to prayer, the way of salvation through the blood and intercession of our great High-priest, burst upon their minds like the morning spread upon the mountains. This brother went home comforted with the comfort wherewith he endeavored to comfort them.

In our next prayer-meeting, this mother and daughter told us with humility and joy what God had done for them. From this time the work of God was spreading into other families. Meetings were still and solemn. One after another arose to testify how the Lord had appeared in mercy for his soul.

We soon heard from the town of N——, that God had not only converted three of that brother's children for whom we had covenanted to pray, but a great awakening was spreading through all the place; and many of the youth were turning to the Lord.

The first Sabbath in July was a memorable day. With many others, the three families who had entered into mutual engagement to pray for the conversion of our children, saw nine of them, just three from each family, come with us to the Lord's table. S. M.

ONE SIN MAY DESTROY THE SOUL.

It was during a precious season of reviving mercy in N——, that a whole family, consisting of a father and mother and two children, who sat under my ministry, were awakened simultaneously by the Spirit of the Lord. It was a highly respectable as well as amiable family, and soon the mother, with the son and daughter, were rejoicing in hope.

Sabbath after Sabbath the father would stop to walk with me after church, and converse freely and with tears about his soul, and I wondered why he too did not find the Saviour precious, as did the others of his household. At last I was informed by some friend, that he was in the habit of using intoxicating drinks. Upon receiving this intelligence, I went immediately to see him. Soon he came in, and I saw at once by his glassy eyes and his indistinct and incoherent conversation, that he was intoxicated.

Taking him by the arm I led him into his garden, and said to him, with deep emotion, "Sir, you have been drinking; and I now tell you, that if you do not abandon it, you will lose your soul." He replied, "I do not drink any thing stronger than beer, cider, and wine; and Dr. —— says this is not wrong." "I care not," said I, "what Dr. —— says, or any one else; it is clear to me, that unless you abandon them you will lose your soul."

He received it kindly, and leading me to the rear of his lot, he stopped and said, "Sir, on this very spot, eight years ago, I promised my brother that I would not again drink any distilled liquor, and I have kept my promise. I now promise you that I will never drink *any* intoxicating liquor." We returned to the house, when I poured out my heart for him in prayer, and went home.

The day of his pledge was the day of his salvation. When I met him the next Sabbath, he was rejoicing in hope. From that day, now about fifteen years since, he has been a thorough temperance man, and as thorough a Christian. Indeed, I scarcely know a happier man, or a happier family. His expressions of gratitude whenever we meet, are so full and overflowing as almost to be painful.

In this day of increasing intemperance, and when

even those who were once temperance physicians are returning to their alcoholic prescriptions, and moderate drinking is becoming fashionable, I would recommend the Rev. Dr. Nettleton's letter to Dr. Beecher, on the subject of drinking as connected with religion. It is found in his Life, and no man knew better than he the ruinous consequences to convicted sinners, for he was conversant with revivals as very few men now alive have been. L.

A DYING SON.

Several years ago I was called to visit a young man who was on his dying bed, under circumstances peculiarly calculated to touch one's feelings. He was the only son of his mother, and she was a widow. The father, a captain of a whale-ship, had died, leaving his widow, this son, and a daughter in very feeble health, utterly destitute. All the hopes of the mother and the daughter were centred in this young man.

He was about eighteen years of age, and embarked as a sailor on a whaling voyage round Cape Horn. The mother and daughter, sustained by hope, endeavored by means of the needle, during his absence, to obtain a humble subsistence. When about a year out, he was taken sick; but stimulated by the vast responsibilities resting upon him, he persevered in remaining on duty till he was hardly able to lift his hand. He then, with a saddened heart, gave up, still hoping that health would be restored to him. But days and nights came and went, as he lay in his cheerless berth counting the dreary hours, and often weeping in the remembrance of his lost home. All on board the ship were too busy to give the sick man any but the most casual attentions.

Thus several months of weariness and woe passed away. Each week he was growing more wan and wasted, and as the ship rolled upon the billows of the Pacific, he had no strength to shield himself from being violently tossed to and fro in his hard berth. All hopes of recovery seemed now at an end, and the captain meeting a ship which was about to return to the United States, decided to transfer the sick man from his own ship, which was to continue for two years longer, perhaps, its adventurous voyage. It was *possible* that the young man might survive until he reached home. It was *possible* that a mother's care might yet restore him. Mute and exhausted under the dreadful discipline of months of despair, he was passively borne to a berth in the homeward-bound ship. A voyage of five months was yet before him. He was to be tossed upon the tempest-lashed waves of the Cape. The coarse fare of the sailor was all the nutriment which could be furnished for his enfeebled frame, and no nursing could be afforded him, but such as could be offered by the busy hands of a crew collected from all nations.

The months dragged slowly along, and life still lingered, to the surprise of all. At last the hills of his native land were in sight, and the ship dropped anchor in the harbor from which, nearly two years before, buoyant with youth and hope, the young man had departed. He could not raise himself in his berth. Even his sunken and faded eye could not beam with animation, as he heard that his mother and his sister stood by his side. He had come home penniless to die. Even the language of affection could find no utterance from his lips, as in mute despair, he turned his eyes to the still more despairing looks of those he loved.

It was two days, I think, after he had been removed to his mother's room, when I was standing by his bedside. It was as bright and beautiful an afternoon as ever smiled upon this globe. He was lying upon his bed as silent and motionless as if he were dead. His mother, with her head leaning upon her hand, in equal silence, sat by his side. His sister, like a statue congealed by grief, sat by the window looking into those clear blue depths of infinity, into which her agonized spirit doubtless wished to soar and to find rest. Not a word was uttered as I entered the room. A gentle pressure of the hand was the only recognition of my expressions of sympathy. As I stood in silence, looking upon the deep lines which grief had traced upon that youthful brow, the young man languidly raised his eyes, and without the movement of a limb, feebly and slowly articulated, "The—ship—is—sinking!" and his eye was fixed—and he was dead.

My pen can trace this scene of domestic anguish no farther. "Why," perhaps some one may ask, "do you trace it so far? Why relate so sad a story?" When I have murmured at some little trial; when I have felt dejected, and have repined in view of some trifling disappointment, I have often thought of this grief, and felt rebuked. It is well for us to learn a lesson of contentment and gratitude, by contemplating those sorrows which are desolating our globe, and from which *we* have been mercifully protected.

John S. C. Abbott.

ANSWER TO PRAYER LONG DEFERRED.

Half a century past, I was accustomed to frequent places of worship where the houses were situated in a grove, or rather, in the midst of the trees of a dense forest, and far from any human habitation. Although the meeting-houses, as they were then called, were frequently unfurnished—a mere shell without ceiling—yet there was a solemnity in these places of worship which was better adapted to promote devotion, than all the most splendid achievements of architecture. No sombre light let in through painted windows ever affected my mind like the solemn shade and stillness of the natural growth of the forest.

On a certain occasion, when the Lord's supper was about to be solemnized in one of these humble churches, I went early, that I might avoid the conversation and dust of a multitude on the road, and might have an opportunity of solitary meditation under the venerable trees which encompassed the house of prayer. I thought surely that I should be first on the ground; but I was mistaken. I saw an elderly gentleman, who had just secured his horse to a bough of a tree, coming towards the house to meet me; and upon his nearing me, I recognized an old acquaintance, at whose house I had lodged in my journeyings more than once. He had formerly been an elder in a Presbyterian church of some note, but had removed into a neighborhood where there were then scarcely any Presbyterians. Travelling ministers, however, often called upon him and preached in his house, or at some place in his vicinity. As I believed him to be a very pious man, well informed and zealous for the truth, I was pleased to meet with him and hold communion with him.

After some general remarks, we got upon the subject of the efficacy of prayer; and as I was young, and he was aged and experienced, I was glad to throw the burden of the conversation on him, and he was not unwilling to speak on a subject which seemed to lie near his heart. In the course of conversation, he related to me a piece of his own experience. He said that his oldest son, who was a lawyer of some eminence, had as unblemished a moral character as any man in the land; and yet, though respectful to religion, he never had manifested any serious concern about his own salvation. "But," said he, "I have had such nearness to God, and such liberty in prayer for his conversion, that I believe those prayers will be answered in due time, whether I live to see it or not. Indeed," said he, "on one occasion I am persuaded that God gave me an assurance that my prayer in his behalf would be answered."

This, I confess, appeared to me somewhat like enthusiasm, but I made no reply; and soon our conversation was terminated by the gathering of the people. I thought, however, that I would remember this matter, and from time to time make inquiry respecting the person whose conversion was so confidently expected by his father. Soon after this, the old elder was gathered to his fathers, and died in faith and peace. But residing far from his abode, I know not the particular exercises of his mind as he approached the borders of the other world. For some years I forgot the conversation, and made no inquiry; but some person who was acquainted with the family, informed me that after his father's death, this son fell into habits of intemperance; that in fact he became a mere sot, remaining at home and stupefying himself with alcoholic drinks every day. Such a case appeared to me nearly hopeless. I had seldom known a man thus brought under the power of strong drink to recover himself. I now thought that the good old father had been deluded by a lively imagination: and for many years every report respecting the son seemed to render the case more hopeless.

But behold the truth and faithfulness of a prayer-hearing God. See an example of the efficacy of fervent and importunate prayer, though the answer was long deferred. This man, after continuing in intemperate habits until the age of seventy or more, became completely reclaimed; and not only delivered from that vice, but soundly converted to God. He not only gave evidence of a change, but appeared to be eminent in the practice of piety. At this time he was about eighty years of age. How wonderful are the ways of God. His faithfulness never faileth; it reacheth unto the clouds. "Thy faithfulness is unto all generations." "O that men would praise the Lord for his goodness, and for his wonderful works to the children of men." "For the vision is yet for an appointed time; but at the end it shall speak, and not lie: though it tarry, wait for it, because it will surely come, it will not tarry." Hab. 2 : 3.

Let pious parents learn never to give over praying for their unconverted children, however hopeless the case may seem to be, for God will in faithfulness hear their supplications, and answer them sooner or later in one way or another. A. A.

A PRAYING SHOEMAKER.

Not many years since, there was a poor man in the village where I lived, who, with a family of young children and a wife in very feeble health, found it extremely difficult to obtain a livelihood. He was at length compelled to work by the week for a shoe-dealer in the city, four miles from the village, returning to his family every Saturday evening, and leaving home early on Monday morning.

He usually brought home the avails of his week's labor in provisions for the use of his family during the following week; but on one cold and stormy night in the depth of winter, he went towards his humble dwelling with empty hands, but a full heart. His employer had declared himself unable to pay him a penny that night, and the shoemaker, too honest to incur a debt without knowing that he should be able to cancel it, bent his weary steps homeward, trusting that He who hears the ravens when they cry, would fill the mouths of his little family. He knew that he should find a warm house and loving hearts to receive him, but he knew too, that a disappointment awaited them which would make at least *one* heart ache.

When he entered his cottage, cold and wet with the rain, he saw a bright fire, brighter faces, and a table neatly spread for the anticipated repast. The teakettle was sending forth its cloud of steam, all ready for "the cup which cheers, but not inebriates," and a pitcher of milk which had been sent in by a kind neighbor, was waiting for the bread so anxiously expected by the children. The sad father confessed his poverty, and his wife in tears begged him to make *some* effort to procure food for them before the Sabbath. He replied that he had kind friends in the neighborhood, who he knew were both able and willing to aid him, and that he would go to them and ask relief. "But first," said he, "let us ask God to give us our daily bread. Prayer avails with God when we ask for temporal good, as well as when we implore spiritual blessings." The sorrowing group knelt around the family altar, and while the father was entreating fervently for the mercies they so much needed, a gentle knocking at the door was heard. When the prayer was ended the door was opened, and there stood a woman in the "peltings of the storm," who had never been at that door before, though she lived only a short distance from it. She had a napkin in her hand, which contained a large loaf of bread; and half apologizing for offering it, said she had unintentionally made "a larger batch of bread" than usual that day, and though she hardly knew why, she thought it might be acceptable there.

After expressing their sincere gratitude to the woman, the devout shoemaker and his wife gave thanks to God with overflowing hearts. While the little flock were appeasing their hunger with the nice new bread and milk, the father repaired to the house where I was an inmate, and told his artless tale with streaming eyes, and it is unnecessary to say, that he returned to his home that night with a basket heavily laden, and a heart full of gratitude to a prayer-answering God. C. C.

OLD CHAIRS AT INTEREST.

Nobody in all the neighborhood interested me like Mr. ——. I love to think of the dear old gentleman. How pleasant was it to run into his bright little parlor, and sit by his side, hearing him talk, or talking to him; reading to him, or hearing him read; asking questions, or listening to stories of old times, when he was a boy. Though his frame bore the frosts and infirmities of threescore years and ten, they had not chilled his heart; it was still young and fresh, and brimful of kindness. It also held his purse-strings, so that from the little parlor streamed substantial blessings, as well as hearty love; and it happened that I had occasion to know how often they found their way to the humble lodgings of a widow and her daughter.

These two were the relics of a past generation, and they seemed to be almost strangers amidst the new one which had sprung up around them. They had, in a measure, outlived their connections, their property, their early friendships, and the poor make but few new friends. Few cared for them, and they cared for few. The only light which warmed or cheered them was the setting sun of days gone by. But if this warmed them, it could not feed or shelter them, or hinder the embarrassments of poverty, had not the old man's purse come to their aid; and so statedly did he eke out the scanty income of the widow, that I sometimes thought he was likely to make her believe that her last days were her best days. I used often to wonder why he was so thoughtful of her wants: others were not, and what claim had she upon him?

One evening, in speaking of his early struggles, he said, "When Mary and I were married, we were young and foolish, for we had nothing to be married with; but Mary was delicate, and I thought I could take care of her best. I knew I had a stout arm and a brave heart to depend upon. We rented a chamber and went to housekeeping. We got together a little furniture—a table, bedstead, dishes—but our money failed us before we bought the chairs. I told Mary she must turn up the tub, for I could not run in debt. No, no. It was not long before our rich neighbor, Mrs. M——, found us out, and kindly enough she supplied our necessities; half a dozen chairs were added to our stock. They were old ones, to be sure, but answered just as well for us. I shall never forget the new face those chairs put on our snug quarters—they never looked just right before. The tables are turned with Mrs. M—— and me now: she has become a poor widow, but she shall never want while I have any thing, never!" cried the old man, with a beaming face. "I don't forget those old chairs."

Ah, now the secret was out. It was *the interest of the old chairs* which maintained the poor widow. She was living upon an income drawn from the interest and compound interest of a little friendly act done fifty years before, and it sufficed for herself and daughter.

How beautiful is it to see how God blesses the operation of his great moral law, "Love thy neighbor:" and we should oftener see it, could we look into the hidden paths of life, and find that it is not self-interest, not riches, not fame, that binds heart to heart. The simple power of a friendly act can do far more than they. It is these, the friendly acts, the neighborly kindnesses, the Christian sympathy of one towards another, which rob wealth of its power to curse, extract the bitter from the cup of sorrow, and open wells of gladness in desolate homes. We do not always see the golden links shining in the chain of human events; but they are there—O yes, they are there, and happy is he who feels their gentle but irresistible influence.

Do we not sometimes see people blest through channels new and unexpected, in ways and times which they thought not of, and at seasons when the blessing came like an angel unawares? We wonder, for we know not why or wherefore it comes. To us there may seem no natural connection between the spring and the stream, the giver and the gift, the good and our own desert. Could we look farther and deeper, we might possibly find it to be the compound interest of some long-forgotten kindness or affectionate counsel, of some self-denying act or fervent prayer. To us they had as it were ceased to be, but it was only as the seed hidden in the earth, which might spring up hereafter and bear precious fruit.

Are we not our brothers' keepers; and is not this our Christian brotherhood? Shall not he that hath much give to him that hath little? From our abundance shall we not help our neighbor in his extremity? Shall not our ready sympathy lighten the cares and dispel the gloom of our fellow-traveller? Shall not the spiritual wants of our less favored brothers incite us to fresh acts of self-denial, if haply we can send to them the bread of life? Thus in the moral government of the Father of our spirits, is there not preparing a treasury of means, wherein are created interests which may run on through years or a series of years, bringing back blessings when we least expect them, and oftentimes enriching our children and our children's children, in generations to come?

H. C. K.

THE CHRISTMAS-TREE.

It was Christmas eve, and it was a bitter, bitter night. The snow had been falling steadily all day, and towards night the wind had risen, till it was really fearful to hear it moaning and sighing and howling around the house, as it tore up the masses of snow, and flung them against the windows, or threw them into great heaps, like miniature hills and mountains.

Many an old lady, as she sat knitting before her comfortable fire, on hearing a louder, fiercer howl of the wind, exclaimed, "God pity the poor this bitter night!" But *how* does God pity the poor? He does not send down bread and meat and warm clothing from heaven to supply their wants, but he puts it into the hearts of their brethren and sisters of the human family to "visit them in their affliction." Ah, "the *poor* ye have always with you, and when ye will, ye may do them good."

The moaning and howling of the wind passed almost unheeded in the brilliant parlor of Mr. M——, where a group of happy children were assembled around the Christmas-tree, whose top reached to the lofty ceiling, and whose branches, illumined by many gay-colored wax tapers, hung laden with tokens of affection from one member of the family to another.

It would take me a long time to enumerate the beautiful things which were on the Christmas-tree. There were presents for grandmamma and father and mother, made by busy little fingers; there were toys and candies, and baskets and boxes; there were dolls seated among the branches; and hanging from the end of some of the boughs were little purses, with half-dollars in them—presents from grandmamma to each of the children.

After the presents had been distributed, and sufficiently admired, and thanks and kisses had been exchanged, the children engaged in a merry game, in the midst of which little Ellen, who had been running through the folding-doors, came hastily up to her mother, and whispered in her ear,

"Mamma, there is a poor little girl out in the hall by the stove; she seems almost frozen, and when I offered her some of my candy, she thanked me, but said she would rather have a piece of bread. What a strange child, mamma, to like bread better than candy."

"Perhaps, if you had had nothing to eat all day, you would like bread better than candy too, Ellen," said her mother, rising to go and speak to the child, the children all following her into the hall. "Where do you live, my child?" she asked. "In Fisher's lane, ma'am." "Are your parents living?" "Father's been dead a year, ma'am, and mother's lying very sick: she thinks she is going to die." "Did your mother work when she was well?" "Oh yes, ma'am, and I never had to beg a bit, till since mother's been so ill." "And why did you come out, this stormy night?" "Oh, I've had to take care of mother and the little ones all day; and to-night the landlord—he's a very hard man, ma'am—came in and said, if the rent was not paid to-night, he would put us all in the street, for another family wanted the room; and mother said there was no way but for me to come out and try to raise the rent."

"How much do you owe?" asked Mr. M——. "Half a dollar a week we owe, for four weeks, sir." "Have you any wood?" "Only some bits I pick up about the street, sir." "Have you had food to-day?" "Some bits of dry bread, sir; I could not leave mother, to beg food to-day."

A greater contrast could hardly have been presented, than that between the miserably clad, half-frozen, half-starved little beggar-girl, and the group of bright, happy, gaily-dressed children, with their hands full of beautiful gifts; and a tear stood on the poor child's cheek, as she looked into the cheerful, warm parlor, and thought of the cold, dark room at home, and the sick mother, and starving little ones there.

All the time Mrs. M—— was questioning the poor child, little Ellen was pulling at her mother's dress; and in every pause in the conversation, she whispered, "Mamma, may I give her my half-dollar? Do, mamma, let me give her my half-dollar."

The children soon perceived that their father was putting on his great-coat and socks, and tying up his face, as if preparing for an encounter with the storm. Crowding round him, they exclaimed, "Why, papa, dear papa, are you going out this dreadful night?"

Their father said to them, in a low tone, "Do you think we could sleep comfortably to-night, children, or enjoy our warm fire, if we thought a sick woman and her little children were perishing in the street? It will not do to trust this child with money; but I must go with her, and see if her story is true, and their wants must be relieved."

"Then, papa, you will take my half-dollar to help pay the rent, will you not?"

"And mine!" "And mine!" "And mine!" shouted other little voices.

"Yes, children, you shall all have the pleasure and

the *benefit* of *giving*," said their father. And ordering Patrick to take his hand-sled full of wood, and a basket of provisions, Mr. M—— started out with the child, who was now wrapped in a comfortable, warm shawl.

The children were allowed to sit up till their father came home, and much gratified were they to hear that the poor child had told the truth, and that their father had not left the family till they had been made quite comfortable, and Patrick had brought a physician to see the sick woman.

There were at least *two* happy homes in that village on Christmas-day. "Go thou, and do likewise," and you shall receive the blessing of Him who has said, "Inasmuch as ye have done it unto one of the least of these, ye have done it unto me." L. L.

THE LITTLE WORD NO.

Last winter I spent a short time in a pleasant family. They were wealthy, influential, and so far as I could judge, a Christian family. The father had at different times occupied a prominent place in the legislative and judiciary departments of his state. He held office in the church; he had erected and preserved through years of trial that made him prematurely gray, the family altar; and as one who knew him well remarked, it was doubtful if a shadow could be cast upon his character. He was honorable and upright in business, courteous, kind, and forbearing in his intercourse with the world. The mother, an estimable woman, professed herself willing to do and suffer for Christ, hoping to die and reign with him. The only daughter was a mild, lovely girl; but the sons—and here was a mystery.

The eldest, a child of uncommon promise, entered at an early age upon a vicious career of drinking, gambling, and licentiousness, which ended in forgery and crime, until he was cast out of the family circle as one unknown, and after a term in prison, found his home in one of the vilest haunts in a southern city. The second, following in his footsteps, was awaiting in the county jail a trial that might sentence him for years to the state's prison. Children of prayer, of pious teaching and example, the fact was to me inexplicable. I expressed my wonder in the hearing of an old man who had known them from birth. Said he, "I can explain in a few words; it is from the father's want of power to say, 'No.'"

When they were beautiful children, and it needed but a word to guide them, he neglected to say, No. As years rolled on, and he noticed the first steps in the way of wrong-doing, he excused them on the plea of youthful exuberance of spirits. And when they went too far, and he strove to curb them, the boys, by caressing, arguing, or bickering, had their own way, for it grieved him to say, No. In after-years, when their souls were blood-stained with crime, when with all the yearnings of a father's heart he took them again to his home, striving by gentleness to win them to the way of life, he dared not say, No.

Christian parent, learn to pronounce, at proper times, this simple word, No. On it, under God, may depend the welfare and happiness of your children for time and eternity.

Day.

AUNT SALLY'S BIBLE.

"Fanny," said James B——, a fine little fellow of seven, as he wound his arm around his cousin's neck, and drew her ear close to his red lips, "aunt Sally will tell us a story." She had chosen the story of Moses. She commenced with the infantile beauty of the babe bound to the mother by imperishable ties; then depicted the strange decree of the wicked king; the efforts made to save the darling; the preservation of the tiny cradle on the banks of the mighty Nile; the guiding hand that led the princess to the very spot; the workings of her heart, that led to the adoption of the babe, and embalmed her name for all future ages; the providence that chose the mother for the nurse; the power that kept him pure amid the vices of a profligate court, and fitted him to guide the chosen of God; and so on, step by step, till he received, amid the thunders of Sinai, the ten commandments of the living God.

Fanny was silent, now in delight, now with her lip quivering, and her bright eye filled with tears. As aunty finished, she said timidly, "Will you give me *your Bible?*" "Have you no Bibles at home, Fanny?" She hesitated a moment at such a question, and then replied, "Why, yes; papa and mamma have big Bibles to read in, morning and evening, and dear little ones to carry to church, with roses on the covers and shining clasps, besides Eddy's and mine that are full of pictures; but we have no Bible *like yours.*"

There seems to be an error in teaching children the Scriptures. There are fathers and mothers whose home-altar is fragrant with the incense of heaven;

who pray that their children may tread the highway of holiness, and gem the Saviour's brow; who see that the Bible is early placed in the hands of the little one—that his eye daily follows over a portion of sacred truth—that he commits the given number of verses to repeat in a Sunday-school, and feel that their whole duty is performed; and some more indulgent, like Fanny's mamma, procure Bibles richly inlaid with arabesque and gold; but how few are there who, like aunt Sally, study the heart till they know what chord responds with sweetest music to their skilful touch, and then choosing an hour clustering with golden associations, when the waves of passion are at rest, impress, with sweet simplicity and truthful earnestness, on that yielding heart, soft as wax but as enduring as marble, the story of Jesus, of Joseph, Moses, Samuel, and a host of worthies now surrounding the throne of God. Thus taught, they reverence the truths of the Bible, and it becomes to them a storehouse more precious than their richest toys.

Fond father, watching the unfolding charms of your precious child—young mother, nursing a golden blossom of immortality for heaven on thy bosom, go thou and do likewise. Day.

OUR FAMILY-MEETING.

In a secluded spot amid the rough New Hampshire hills stands an old farm-house, the home of our early years. Around that spot cluster many tender recollections; but dearest of them all, is that of our family-meeting.

As often as the shadows of the Sabbath sunset lengthened on the plain, did the voice of an honored parent call us to the meeting. Cheerfully laying aside our books and papers, we gathered in a family circle. Father, mother, child, each was in his place. All was still except the slow ticking of the clock behind the door.

Then began our interview, and each in turn, from the youngest, who, with his mother's help, could just repeat the text, to the eldest, rehearsed some portion of the discourses preached during the day. Afterwards the oft-repeated questions of the catechism were asked, and the familiar answers recited.

The shades of twilight gathered gently, and the hour seemed indeed holy time. Affection ruled in every heart, and each was willing unreservedly to express his feelings. The moment so favorable was improved, and tenderly the father asked each child of his hopes or fears, his interest in the Saviour's love. Then all knelt in prayer.

Years have passed. Those children have been called to leave their home. Yet the influence of those hallowed hours has been with them, and guarded all their youthful steps. Many of them, through the instrumentality, it may be, of these seasons, now rejoice in the hope that they have passed from death to life.

Christian parents, gather your household daily at the family altar before the throne of grace, and O, speak tenderly, earnestly to your little ones, telling them of their relations and obligations to God, of the guilt of their sin and their need of a Saviour, of all the events of life; on these will probably cluster their earliest, latest, fondest memories. W. H. K.

A VISIT TO MY BIRTHPLACE.

Through the kind invitation of the present occupants, I was again visiting that dear old parsonage, and permitted, after an absence of years, to roam through those familiar scenes of childhood.

That great kitchen, how changed! Yet I could see it, as in days of yore, with its huge fireplace, around which clustered so many endeared and venerable forms on Sabbath noons, when they resorted thither to fill their foot-stoves, and perchance share the hospitalities of the minister's family. Their loved faces have long since been laid in the dust, but I seemed to see them still. The old-fashioned dressers had given place to modern conveniences. Paper and paint had renovated its walls. Even the old "social library" case, which from my earliest recollection stood out in bold relief against the ceiling, had been removed. The little shoe-closet, which used to contain such a motley assortment for all ages and sizes, that too was gone; but in imagination I could see them all.

Next came the sitting-room. O, what tender recollections cluster about that room. There we were wont to gather at the morning and evening sacrifice, which daily arose like sweet incense from the family altar. There was the place where our father read and prayed; there the corner where mother sat; and there the cradle's place, which for so many years was never absent—but all were gone. Even the old clock was missing from the corner, and its place looked strange.

The parlor too was no longer the "east-room."

A rich-toned piano sent forth sweet sounds from the place formerly occupied by the chintz-covered sofa. The fireplace no longer displayed the shining brasses, in rubbing which my own hands had so often ached; other figures had taken the place of the old familiar roses upon the carpet, and all was new, and elegant, and strange.

I would gladly have sought the chambers alone, that my thoughts might once more dwell upon the treasured memories of the past. There was the chamber where my brothers slept; there the rooms in which we six sisters lodged, with the door between. How often was that door left open, that our conversation might be carried far into the night, and all our girlish plans of usefulness or amusement discussed. How I wished just once to rearrange all that new furniture, and set the bureau, and bed, and chairs, and desk all as they used to be, and see if it would seem my own old chamber once more.

The spare chamber too, though tasteful and nice, looked less dear to me than would the snow-white counterpane and toilet-cover, the great "easy-chair," and the little gilt looking-glass of former years.

We entered my father's study. There were studied and written the sermons which for more than fifty years were dispensed as pure beaten oil from yonder sanctuary. There many of the sons and daughters of affliction had resorted for advice and consolation; and there many inquiring what they must do to be saved, had been guided to "the Lamb of God, who taketh away the sin of the world." But the old library, with its great mysterious-looking tomes, had disappeared; new volumes in rich bindings had taken the place of that long row of massive folios in their black leather covers. The little desk was gone, and the modern study-table and study-chair were there, instead of the familiar objects of my youthful days.

I would have lingered long amid the tender associations connected with my mother's chamber. There we were all born—eleven of us. There, most of the sickness of the family had been experienced; and there healing mercy had been sought and bestowed. In that corner stood the bed, and there the high "case of drawers;" and there, just beyond, is a door—it opened into a little sanctuary, a sacred retreat—a "holy of holies" it seemed to me. How it recalled the times when mother was missing, and none thought of intruding farther than to see the door was shut. If sickness or trouble came, if death of those near and dear, or if peculiar trials were to be borne, or peculiar blessings sought, how silently we noticed the absence, and then the return, with serenity and cheerfulness and a heavenly unction, from the scenes of that inner temple. And then who of us could not recall the time when we had there bowed the knee *with* her; as on birthdays, eve of expected absence from home, or when guilty of misconduct, we had there been commended to the hearer and answerer of prayer. Were I to choose a boon for my own little ones, rather far would I ask for them *that closet*, with its precious influences, than the possession of the noblest halls of wealth or fame.

God's mercies to that household have been great. The angel of death has never yet been permitted to cross that threshold. Parents and children still live an unbroken band, and though scattered from beneath the paternal roof, he who for half a century occupied that old parsonage, still lives to offer the prayer of faith for his successors in the ministry, and his children and children's children. Selina.

LOG-CABIN MEMORIES.

There is great and lasting power in faithful exhortation. I have a case in my own experience, yet fresh in my memory after a period of forty-three years. I was twelve years old when the occurrence which I am going to describe took place.

My father had removed his family from the state of Vermont into the western wilderness, in what at that time was called, "The Holland Purchase." The settlement consisted of ten or fifteen families, occupying a space five or six miles square. We had no sanctuary and no clergyman; and such was the neglect of sacred things, that it used often to be facetiously remarked by the people, that "Sunday had not yet crossed the Genesee river." After a time a few professed Christians came and settled in the neighborhood. Religious meetings began to be held in the log-cabin of a pious deacon. In these Sabbath assemblies, though destitute of a minister, except at long intervals, the greatest decorum was always observed. Songs of praise were sung, prayers were offered, and the Bible was read. Commonly a sermon was also read from a printed volume. After the service was brought nearly to a close, a certain pious layman sometimes added a fervent exhortation.

One of these lay-sermons my memory retains after so long a period with perfect vividness. It was founded on that parable of the rich man who said to his soul, "Soul, thou hast much goods laid up for many years; eat, drink, and be merry." The speaker gave a touching narrative of what had happened in the place of his former residence. He commenced by describing the town where the occurrence had taken place, and mentioning the name of the man and his physician. This physician, while riding his accustomed rounds, passed the newly erected dwelling of a thrifty farmer. As he looked up he saw the owner of the house upon its roof removing some fragments of shingles, and picking up a few scattered nails that had been left there by the mechanics. The doctor paused, sitting upon his horse, and addressed a friendly salutation to the man upon the roof, and congratulated him on the completion of such a beautiful and commodious dwelling. "Thank you," replied the farmer; "it is a good house, it is all that I want; I have labored hard for many years to pay for my farm, and acquire the means of building this house. I have just attained what I have so long been striving for. Now I mean to take life easy, and enjoy it." "I hope you will live long to enjoy it," replied the physician. "Thank you," rejoined the farmer. Then making their mutual adieus, the doctor rode on his way. He had not gotten out of sight before his attention was arrested by a voice calling after him, "Doctor, doctor, come back; Mr. Winslow has fallen from the house, and we are afraid he is dead." The doctor returned. The man who had just been congratulating himself on having secured a happy life for many years, had gone to render his account to God. That hour his soul had been required of him.

Forty years after this, in travelling through Vermont, I found myself on the outside of a stage-coach, passing through the very township where this event had occurred. The name of the place brought every thing fresh to my memory. While reflecting upon the influence of the narrative on my own mind, and the probability that it had been remembered by every person living that was then present, we suddenly drove up to a country inn where the identical name of the man that so suddenly perished, appeared plainly painted on the sign. The letters were legible, but dim with age. Was that name painted there before the house was finished? Or was it the name of his son? Did *he* die thus unexpectedly? How many may there have been deeply, solemnly, and savingly impressed by that striking providence? How many others that knew the circumstances may have related them as I heard them related? How many may have thus retained the impression for more than forty years? How long may this narrative live now in a printed form? How many colporteurs, and other pious laymen, may be incited by it to treasure up affecting and solemn illustrations of gospel truth, and utter them on suitable occasions to listening, dying men? How many will read this story, and be influenced by it?

Reader, if you are a worldly man, let me beg of you to ponder its import in application to yourself. Most men who have succeeded in the world, or who deem themselves near to success, are precisely in this condition. They are counting on years of enjoyment. Nor do they really rest on any other hopes as a source of happiness. The Psalmist describes them with great truth and accuracy. He calls them "men of the world, who have *their portion* in this life." The folly of such a limiting of your hopes to this world is amazing. It is especially so, when you admit that there is a state of eternal blessedness or eternal misery depending upon the course you pursue in this life. God said to the worldling, "Thou fool, this night thy soul shall be required of thee; then whose shall those things be which thou hast provided?" Here our Saviour leaves the narrative, and makes this faithful application: "So is he that layeth up treasure for himself, and is not rich towards God."

The most solemn and affecting consideration, however, suggested by the narrative, and brought to view in the parable that gave rise to the exhortation referred to, is the sudden and resistless character of the call: "Thy soul shall be required of thee." While you are setting your heart upon your gains, and making earth your portion, God may be saying to you, "Thou fool, *this night* thy soul shall be required of thee." Some fatal disease, or some messenger of death, may be even now commissioned and on its way to require your soul. Unseen hands may be tolling your funeral knell.

Restless worldling, list; in vain
   Shall thy death-knell sadly toll?
Why so busy with thy gain?
   God demandeth back thy soul.

What availeth all thy store?
   Thou art hastening to thy goal:
Death is standing at the door;
   God demandeth back thy soul.

Who shall *then* thy gain possess,
  When the waves of terror roll
O'er thee in thy deep distress?
  God demandeth back thy soul.

Restless worldling, bend thy knee;
  Once again the bell doth toll:
The arm of vengeance lifted see,
  God this night demands thy soul.

P. J.

RELIGION IN SOCIETY.

JOHN AND HIS COUSIN.

WHEN John was seventeen, he was the only one of his father's family who had not professed faith in Christ. There he stood alone, the eldest of four children, surrounded by his family and pious relations, hating religion—as rebellious and stiff-necked as the Israelites of old whom God overthrew in the wilderness. He had no sympathies in common with his relatives; they were zealously pursuing one course, he with equal earnestness another; and he turned from them, and sought intercourse with those like-minded with himself.

At this juncture, Mary M—— his cousin arrived from New England, and spent some months in the family. John hailed the event with delight. She was at the age of sixteen, beautiful in person, interesting in her manners, and as gay as himself. "Now," thought he, "I have one associate, if the religious ones don't get her."

But the fear that she would yield to their influence kept him in a fever of anxiety. At length his fears subsided; he saw that religion was disagreeable to her; that she shrunk from the society of those who, as Christians, made their light shine, evidently preferring his. He now seemed as happy as one out of the ark of safety amid such light could be. He had one friend, one relative with whom there was unison of feeling. They could strengthen each other, and laugh together at the piety of those around them.

He was interrupted in this dream of happiness one evening, as the people began to gather at his father's for a prayer-meeting, by being informed that Mary had knelt for prayers the previous evening. He knew that she often attended meetings with his mother and sisters, but was not aware that she had been affected by them. He was shocked by this intelligence. He sought where to weep alone, and shed bitter tears.

When somewhat composed, he sought Mary and requested a private interview. She designated a room where to meet him. He went there; it looked as desolate as he felt. The seats had been removed to the large kitchen for the meeting. He rested his elbow on the window, and endeavored to calm the feelings of mingled grief and anger that swelled in his bosom.

When she entered he met her, threw his arms around her, and burst into tears.

"Why, John, what is the matter?"

"Oh, Mary, you are going to leave me alone; you are going to be like the rest of them."

Poor Mary, who was but partially awakened, and not prepared for this assault, had no power to resist it. She replied, hesitating, "Perhaps not—I don't know yet—I—I—really don't know, John."

"But why did you kneel for prayers last night?" said he, with the air of an injured person.

"Because I thought I had need of prayers. Come, John," said she, affectionately, "let us seek religion together. We both need it; let us become Christians, and then we shall be happy."

"Happy!" he muttered with a sullen air, turning to the window, where he again wept.

She tried to soothe him, but his countenance was shrouded with gloom till she descended from the eminence she had gained to his level; then sunny smiles shone forth.

"Come, John," said she, tapping him on the shoulder, "cheer up. Don't be frightened. I am not very good yet."

He did "cheer up," and things passed on as usual; but Oh, what occasion had both to "be frightened," thus to quench the Spirit, and say, "Go thy way for this time."

After about three months, it being a new country, religious meetings were held in a grove near by. Mary was at that time residing with her own family, who had removed there, but she had not escaped the influence of John. His anxieties were all awake, lest she should become interested, and he attended the meetings constantly for no purpose but to keep an eye on her. She had yielded to his solicitations, and partially promised to attend a ball with him in an adjoining town on a day previous to the close of the meetings. This ball had been planned for the express purpose of counteracting the influence of the meetings; and many parents' hearts bled as they saw their wayward children turn their backs upon the place where the "still small voice" of the Spirit was whispering, "Turn ye, turn ye, for why will ye die?" and draw off to the place of amusement, thus stepping over the line of separation, and joining the ranks of the enemy.

But it was a time of the right hand of the Most High, and to the raging billows of sin he said, "Hitherto shalt thou come, but no further." There are times when he seems to "rend the heavens and come down;" when the mountains of sin flow down at his presence, as when melting fire burneth—times when he shows in a peculiar manner that he sitteth King in Zion, and this was one of them. By the day appointed, Mary had become too much interested to attend the ball, and John's entreaties were of no avail. Fearing what would follow, he remained also, and before the close of the meetings, saw her kneeling among anxious inquirers, deeply awakened.

Up to this time he had continued indifferent; indeed, he had been so absorbed in watching Mary, that he seemed not to have heard any thing. When he perceived her among the anxious, he pushed his way to her. "Mary, Mary, why are you here? Come away; come with me," taking her by the arm. "Leave me, John; leave me," she cried with streaming tears; "would you drag me down to hell with you?"

He left her without speaking. This sentence, accompanied by the Holy Spirit, was an arrow from the quiver of the Almighty. The facts, that he was seeking to drag her down there; that he was himself rushing headlong to its mouth; that he was rashly snapping asunder every friendly cord that love had thrown around him to check his mad career, now became living realities. His sins became a burden too heavy to be borne; his agony was intense. Hell seemed opening under his feet, and he descending into its fiery billows. He attempted to leave the place; but before proceeding far, his groans and cries for mercy burst forth. The young men, his companions in sin, fled at his cry; but others of a different spirit soon found him, and intelligence was conveyed to his friends. Oh, what a time was that! Christians wrestled like Jacob, and had power with God; especially those of the large circle of his kindred who had an interest at the throne of grace. Prayer rose like a cloud of incense, and the Spirit who reveals Jesus to the soul descended to melt the stony heart.

Soon, Mary was "happy in pardoning mercy;" and ere long the groans of John were exchanged for songs of salvation. Both adorned their profession, especially John. From that day he lived like "a new creature in Christ Jesus." The same zeal manifest in his blindness, now distinguished him as a Christian. He soon commenced preparation for the ministry, and for more than thirty years was a faithful herald of the cross on the walls of Zion.

Orpha.

A RIDE AND A STORY.

About midnight, in the month of May, 1828, I was called by the watch at the old "Eagle," in Richmond, Va., and told that the stage would soon be ready. In a few minutes I found myself in a crowded stage on our way to Fredericksburg. When the morning came, I discovered that my fellow-travellers were five well-dressed men, and a well-dressed, matronly colored woman, who had under her charge two white children. They called her "mamma," and such was her good character, that she was trusted with these children on a journey of about one hundred and forty miles. She and they were going to see some relatives in Spottsylvania. Soon after breakfasting, conversation became quite lively among a portion of the passengers. The exhaustless theme of politics received some notice. Then we heard of what had recently occurred in the city. Lastly, religion was introduced.

The most voluble of the company gave us his views quite flippantly. He was quite opposed to religion. It made hypocrites. It was an enemy to innocent amusements. It made men mean. It was neither good for black people or white people.

At first he was listened to by several of the company with apparent respect. But soon most of us paid no attention. Not so "mamma." She was all attention. Her manner was very respectful and dignified. At length the infidel noticed her, and by something he said, invited her to give her opinion. With much modesty she said, "All you have stated may be true, but it surprises me very much. I live down on Roanoke, and religion produces very different effects there. Mr. G——, one of my master's neighbors, is very wealthy, and has been a very passionate man. He had a servant named Tom, who was one of the worst men in the neighborhood. Tom would lie, and steal, and run away, and fight.

"Some months ago, Tom went out on one of his rovings, and on Lord's day came to a meeting, and heard the gospel preached. The minister preached beautifully about the love of Jesus to poor sinners, and told the people that if the worst man in the congregation would forsake his sins, and cry to Jesus for mercy, he would be forgiven. Tom heard this, and began to weep. As soon as the meeting was over, Tom started for home, but he was in great distress.

The next day he went to work, but said little. He continued so some days. At length one of the servants heard him praying alone. In a month or two Tom began to put his trust in Jesus, and then he was so happy he wished that every body should be religious. So he talked to the servants, and had prayers in his cabin at night. Some of the servants mocked him, and said he was only after some mischief; but all confessed he was very much changed; for he showed no bad temper, even when they told him he was mad.

"At length Mr. G—— heard how Tom was carrying on, and he too thought Tom was laying some plot to make a disturbance. So he came and told Tom he must quit singing and praying in the quarters. Tom said, 'Master, I have been a very bad man, and a very bad servant, but I hope God has forgiven me. I now intend to quit all my bad practices, and prove to you that I am a better man. I will serve you faithfully; but, master, I feel as if I must praise God, and tell my fellow-servants what the Lord has done for me.' 'Then,' said the master, 'I will whip you.' So he tied him up and whipped him severely. As soon as he let him down, Tom fell on his knees and prayed for his master, for himself, and for all the family. The master left him on his knees, but he went to the house very unhappy. He began to think and read the Bible, and pray too. So it was, Mr. G—— was soon converted himself. And last month Mr. G—— and Tom both joined the Baptist church; and when they were going to be baptized, Mr. G—— went and took Tom by the hand, and they both walked down to the water together, and now they are good friends. Tom don't lie and steal and quarrel any more; and his master has prayers, and brings all the servants in to prayers every night, and the change there is beautiful."

"Mamma" closed her story. One or two of the passengers gave a significant look at each other. I kept silence, feeling that it was best to let the truth work its own way, and our infidel made some remark, after a short pause, on another subject, but gave us no more of his religious opinions. We reached Fredericksburg in the afternoon, and I have never met any of the company since. Doubtless many of them have gone to eternity, and I am left to tell the story. It may suggest, that,

1. There is a time to speak, and a time to keep silence. A word fitly spoken, how good is it. "Mamma" was the best preacher in that stage. She alone had a good opportunity to say any thing pertinently, and without exciting angry words. She did not obtrude, but she bore an humble, modest testimony, and gave a reason of the hope that was in her, with meekness and fear.

2. True religion produces the same effects on the heart and character in every age. It has lost none of its power to renew the depraved, and save them from sin.

3. The doctrine that impressed poor Tom's mind, is still the melting, subduing doctrine of Scripture. Let it be preached. R.

DEBATE WITH A ROMISH BISHOP.

Western steam-boats furnish a miniature picture of the world. You will often meet men of many nations and tongues, of every trade and profession, and of every creed. A single day will sometimes give one a specimen of gambling, drinking, fighting, swearing, praying, and preaching. The good and evil are strangely commingled.

A year or two since, I took passage in one of these boats from St. Louis to Louisville, at a low stage of water in the Ohio. As we were about to leave, I noticed a passenger with unusual garb and appearance, who was attended to the wharf by several ecclesiastics. When we reached a little town on the Mississippi, the stranger with the long coat made his way to the Jesuit college there located; and our captain, an Irish Roman-catholic, made an extra landing in front of the college to receive him again on board. The long-coated professors accompanied him to the shore, and kissed him reverently as they parted from him. Every thing betokened the presence of a distinguished member of the so-called "order of Jesus," and so it proved.

Among the passengers were two gentlemen having the aspect of Protestant clergymen. They were observed to deposit tracts and little books in places of convenient access to the passengers and crew. One of them devoted himself to the comfort and instruction of a dying cholera subject on the lower deck. They mingled familiarly with the crowded company of the cabin, but with a dignity that indicated the remembrance of their sacred calling.

When ascending the Ohio the steamer grounded, and lay helpless for an entire day. While in this condition, the papal emissary was seen with groups around him, with winning words insinuating the dogmas of his church into the minds of his hearers; now expatiating on the glories of St. Peter's, then explaining away the worship of the Virgin, and adroitly preparing them for the service that was to follow. At nightfall, after supper, a jovial lawyer from the mouth of the Ohio announced to the passengers that we were honored with the presence of one of the most venerable and distinguished of the Roman-catholic bishops in this country, who had consented to address us in reference to the tenets of his church. A crowd gathered around the ladies' saloon, and the bishop, who seemed to be an amiable and intelligent man, commenced his harangue, first "saying a little prayer." He spoke kindly of his "separated brethren," as well he might, with almost none but the captain of the boat committed to his system, and expressed the charitable hope that they would all be brought to the faith of Rome. The burden of his discourse was a skilful exaltation of tradition above the Bible, of "the church" above the Redeemer. Faithful to the instincts of his communion, he made an adroit onset upon the only true basis of a spiritual religion. The prestige of a live bishop seemed to give weight to his influence with a company not overstocked with biblical knowledge. It seemed to be an hour of peril to the cause of evangelical truth.

As the service was about to close, one of the gentlemen to whom I alluded, and who gave fixed attention to the bishop's address, arose, and in a calm but firm manner expressed the interest he had taken in the statements of his venerable friend. "But," said he, "all must be aware that quite different sentiments are entertained by Bible Christians as to the topics here discussed; and if God gives me the strength, I will endeavor, to-morrow night, to exhibit their views of the matters which have now occupied our attention." The tone of the speaker indicated more than his words.

The company dispersed, some to resume their gambling occupations, some to the bar-room, some to renew their oaths and imprecations, some to discuss the merits of the debate thus opened, some to their berths. The noisy lawyer, strengthened in his vices by anti-scriptural doctrine, renewed his cups. Standing within a few feet of the state-room of the bishop, his voice was heard till a late hour by the unwilling multitude of would-be sleepers, in ridicule of the truth he found in some Protestant tracts, and in obscene and vulgar jokes. Iniquity seemed to have found new license, and profanity new terms of blasphemy. It was a miserable night for us all.

On the next evening the company of passengers gathered as by a common impulse, to listen to the promised reply to the bishop. Mr. ——, apparently thinking that there might be an aspect of obtrusiveness in a voluntary engagement in the debate, expressed his readiness to forego the opportunity of speaking, if any one of his hearers desired it. Thus securing his position, he announced the hymn, " Come, Holy Spirit, heavenly Dove," which was sung by the assembly with solemnity. He then invited his friend from Boston to pray; and the rich unction and happy adaptation of that warm-hearted puritan prayer, contrasted with the formal, lifeless prayer "said" by the bishop, half finished the debate.

Mr. —— disclaimed all love of controversy, and avowed his purpose to deal with principles lying at the foundation of human obligations and hopes. He entered on the discussion less to refute the errors of the bishop, than to save the souls of his hearers. He then gave a rapid sketch of the doctrines and history of the primitive church; the rise and influence of popery; the efforts of the reformers, and the triumphs of the truth in the sixteenth century, and demonstrated the substantial unity of the evangelical churches. Having thus cleared the way, he planted himself on the impregnable ground of D'Aubigné and of Protestantism: *the word of God only*, excluding tradition; *the grace of Christ only*, striking at the roots of a religion of works; *the work of the Holy Spirit only*, as distinguished from a religion of external rites; and unfolded with earnestness the great themes that cluster around the cross. The application of these fundamental principles to the church of Rome, and to the dogmas of the bishop, was left to each hearer; but the least intelligent mind could perceive, that if such were the teachings of Scripture—if "the just shall live by faith"—then the whole superstructure of papal superstition rests on error, and must fall at last. Without the aspect of controversy, and with direct bearings on the spiritual state of those addressed, every leading position of the bishop was underminded, and evangelical truth fully vindicated. It only remained to dissect the seven pretended sacraments of the Papal church, which the bishop had proclaimed and defended; in doing which, Mr. —— indulged in the wit and sarcasm which alone some of them deserved. He closed with an appeal to the conscience, tender and solemn.

The bishop, with less of discretion than might have been expected from an aged prelate, attempted to recover his ground, by asserting the friendliness of the Papal church to the Bible, denying that it was a prohibited book in the Papal states; also denying the existence of "indulgences;" assailing the credibility of D'Aubigné as a historian, etc. The issue being thus joined, Mr. —— replied firmly, and brought home to the bishop's own diocese the allegations which had been general and indefinite. It was a triumph of the truth. The "smooth stones" from Siloah's brook reached their mark, and another giant measured his length on the plain.

I spent another day on the boat, and had abundant opportunities of observing the influence of the discussion. The only oath I subsequently heard was from the pilot at the wheel, whose duties had kept him from the cabin. I saw no more gambling. Many of the passengers sought friendly intercourse with the Protestant preacher. And when he and his travelling companion left the boat, to keep holy time—leaving the bishop to pursue his journey on the Sabbath—many thanks were tendered for the timely and effective refutation of Papal error sought to be imposed on a crowd of American Protestants.

I add but a word to this incomplete sketch of a steam-boat debate.

1. The only weapon needed in the conflict with the man of sin, is "the sword of the Spirit."

2. Providential occasions for controversy with errorists will bring with them providential aids.

3. It is best so to conduct polemical discussions that the spirit of a true faith may win confidence for its doctrines, and so that souls may be saved, even if the argument be lost.

4. There is little danger from the Romish church in this country, if its bishops will consent to discuss its principles in the newspapers and in steam-boat cabins. The system will not bear ventilation.

5. "By their fruits ye shall know them." The moral tendencies of the Papal and evangelical systems, as seen in the unchecked vice of a western steamer after an evening's discourse by a distinguished prelate, and in the quiet and order produced by an exhibition of gospel truths by an unknown Protestant, were so palpably demonstrated as to leave no doubt which system can trace its origin to the great Source of wisdom and purity. Heber.

THE CONFESSION OF A DEIST.

In 1848, I became acquainted with an intelligent Deist, by visiting him in affliction. From several conversations, I learned somewhat of his history. His father lived and died a Deist; and the son, from his youth up, had read all he could to fortify his mind in Deism. He was conversant with the greatest infidel authors; he had been a diligent attendant on lectures by celebrated advocates of Deism, and thus had become a proficient in deistical views and arguments. In addition to this, he was a clear-headed man with a metaphysical cast of mind. He knew well how to argue on the subject of infidelity. No man could converse with him without being convinced of this. He could easily detect and point out the weak side of an argument brought against his views. He was cool in reasoning, and considerate in his replies.

One day I found him at his work, but in a thoughtful mood of mind. After the usual salutations, he commenced the conversation thus: I give it as nearly as possible in his own words.

"Mr. F——, I have been thinking of you, and of myself. I consider you must be a happy man: your religion must make you happy. I have buried two dear children, and I have buried them as worms. I believe I shall never see them again, for they will rot and perish as worms: there is something very gloomy in this. But you believe in a resurrection—that you will see your children in another world. This must make you happy. I wish I could believe the Bible as you do."

To this I replied, that I had enjoyed the soul-inspiring thought, under the loss of one dear child I had been called to lay in the cold tomb, whose image frequently rose up before me, that I had buried her in sure and certain hope of a joyful resurrection, and through grace I expected again to meet her in heaven.

He also informed me that he was reading and laboring and praying to God to convince him of the divine inspiration of the Bible. He was very much concerned about the education of his children who were then living, and was sending them to Christian schools. Such was the man, such his circumstances, and such his confession.

To the thoughtful mind this honest and unasked-for confession will suggest serious reflections. We invite attention to five.

1. *What a difference between the tendency of Deism and Christianity.* The one debases the mind, the other ennobles it. If I look upon my children "as worms" and nothing more, which are to live a short time, and in the grave perish for ever, will not the tendency in my mind be to treat them as such? But if I regard my children as immortal beings, living that they may be prepared to die, dying that they may live for ever, in happiness or woe, will not the thought of such an existence ennoble my mind; and shall not I train them accordingly? Does not the one view assimilate them to the beast? Does not the other, to angels? The one to earth, the other to heaven?

2. *There is no sure foundation for the faith of man to*

rest upon apart from divine revelation. The man who throws this overboard has no anchor. His mind, however intelligent, then becomes the sport of every wind, subject to doubts and difficulties on every hand. Such was the case of the Deist whose confession we have given. This thought has frequently occurred to me while in conversation with infidels, and in reading their productions. They unsettle every thing, but settle nothing. To them mystery and doubt surround every thing. The state of their minds is epitomized in these grand questions: "But who knows?" "How do I know?" It is all uncertain. The work of demolition is theirs: to pull down, not to build up; to uproot Christianity, and establish nothing in its stead. Some of the purest minds the world ever saw have felt this, and acknowledged the necessity of a divine revelation.

3. *The danger of moral poison.* The effects of poison on the mind are as fatal as on the body, and more lasting. This man felt the truth of this, and labored to extricate himself from the moral poison which he had imbibed; but alas, he could not. Let young and old avoid moral poison as they would opium; what the one is to the body, the other is to the soul. It may please, but in the end it will destroy. Not that error is more powerful than truth; but many, especially of the young, read a work or two on the side of infidelity, find it congenial to their own feelings, and then never consider the Bible and its own internal testimony, or the other evidences that it is from God. An acquaintance of mine visited six infidels, and when they began to accuse and misquote the Scriptures, he asked them to point out the passages, but not one of

them had a Bible to refer to. If the facts could be gathered, no doubt we should find this to be the general rule—what Deists know of the Bible is through the works of its bitterest enemies.

If authors, editors, and publishers would vend less of this moral poison, and say less about their patriotism, they would be more truly patriotic. These infidel sentiments in their various forms and channels are the great danger of the age. Oh, do not tamper with this poison; you may get it into your soul, but never get it out again.

4. *How cruel is infidelity.* Here is a kind father burying two dear children. How painful the parting. How sad the bereavement. But Christianity, like an angel of mercy from the world of bliss, steps forward and tenderly whispers, "Weep not." "They sleep in Jesus." "Not dead, but gone before." "Through grace you shall meet them in glory, and never part again." Oh, what a cup of consolation this to the bereaved parent, as he casts the last sad glance at his dear ones in the cold grave! But infidelity with a hand hard, cold, and cruel as death, steps up and dashes this cup of consolation from his lips: says it is all fabrication—a lie. They shall never rise again, but shall sink into annihilation, and "rot as worms." Oh, infidelity, how cruel art thou to the bereaved parent; dashing the last drop of consolation from his bereaved and sorrowing heart.

5. *What a boon to man is the gospel of Christ*—its enemies being judges. "It makes you happy," says this honest-hearted Deist. Yes, the gospel of Christ lays a glorious foundation for the happiness of man in time and through eternity—a foundation firm as the

"everlasting hills," yea, as the throne of God itself—a foundation built upon the principles of eternal right, fixed by the immutable counsel and purpose of God, cemented by the blood of his Son, revealed to us in the Bible, imparted to us by the Holy Spirit in conversion, and in heaven we shall enjoy its full fruition.

Are you an infidel? Read the other side of the question, and pray God to guide you. For what will infidelity profit in the day of affliction, and in the hour of death?

Are you unconverted, yet a believer in the Bible? Let me entreat you at once to seek salvation through the blood of Christ, and "flee from the wrath to come."

Are you a Christian? Be grateful unto Him who called you out of darkness into the marvellous light of the gospel. "How much owest thou unto thy Lord?" R. F.

COULD NOT FIND CHRIST.

The late Judge Niles of Vermont, who in the early part of his life was a preacher and a missionary to the new settlements, related in substance the following narrative:

"I was preaching in the western part of Pennsylvania, which was then chiefly a wilderness. I called one day on a man who lived in the forest, far from neighbors and Christian society. I asked him if he thought himself a Christian. He said no, and proceeded to give me his religious experience.

"'I removed to these parts,' he said, 'many years

since, from the vicinity of Philadelphia. On one of my visits to my former home, I found a great attention to religion in all that region. Whitefield had been preaching there, and almost every body was engaged in the subject. I heard of this one and that of my acquaintance who had *found Christ*, and multitudes were spoken of who had found Christ. At length one addressed me, and asked if I had found Christ. I said no, but I should like to find him. He gave me a Bible, and said if I would read that, I should find Christ. I read my Bible a great deal while there, and on my way home, and after I reached home, but did n't find Christ.

"'I then built an arbor a small distance from my house, and went there every day, and read my Bible, and prayed; and every time I came out from my arbor I looked up through the trees, expecting to see Christ coming down; but I did n't see him, and I looked around, but could n't find him. And this I did so long without finding Christ, that I grew discouraged, and began to think I was so great a sinner that Christ would not show himself to *me*, and that I should not find him, though so many others had. I said, I will go once more to my arbor and pray, and if I do not find Christ then, I will not go again.

"'I went and prayed, and when I came out I looked up through the trees to see if Christ was there; and again I could n't find him. But as I looked, the leaves of the trees, and the branches, and the openings between them, looked as they never looked before—all beautiful and glorious. I looked around me, and every thing appeared just so, and I wondered I could n't find Christ. I was sure Christ was there, and that if any one who was a real Christian were there with me, he would certainly see Christ; but I am so wicked and vile, I said, Christ will not show himself to me. Again I looked up and around me; every thing appeared lovely and beautiful, but still I could n't find Christ. And then I said, I know Christ is here, and if there were any real Christians here they would see him, and that is enough for such a vile and wicked sinner as I—to live where Christ is, and where Christians would see him if they were here. So I have lived ever since. I have not yet found Christ, and I am not a Christian, but I love to live here and go to that arbor and pray, because I know Christ is there, though I cannot see him. It is delightful to live so near to Christ.'

"And," said the judge, "if there ever was a Christian, I believe that man was one, though he thought he could not find Christ."

Once God appeared to man in human form—to Abraham, to Moses, and other patriarchs. In later ages, before Christ, he manifested himself by visible signs. See Hebrews 1:1. Christ showed himself after his resurrection to his disciples in miraculous ways, and once, after his ascension, to Paul on his way to Damascus, Acts 9:26; and to the apostle John, Rev. 1:13. But we do not know that, since the age of the apostles, Christ has ever appeared in human form, or manifested himself by miracle. Nor should we expect him to do so until his second coming "in power and great glory."

Yet there are some now who will tell you they have seen Christ in a vision, or they have seen a bright light in which he was, or they have heard an audible voice from him; and they look on this as evidence of true conversion. We should not undervalue such persons for relating things which seem to them real, for in many cases it is probable persons have been truly converted in connection with such imaginings. But we should understand their nature, and not suppose we cannot find Christ unless we can see him with our bodily eye. All that is necessary is, to see him with the eye of faith—"Christ *in* you, the hope of glory," not before the bodily eye. The man in the anecdote we have related saw Christ by the eye of faith, but much did he suffer from misunderstanding the language about "finding Christ."

Such language is useful; it contains precious truth; let us strive to get hold of the kernel, let us hold on to that and throw the husk away. It is related of the Rev. Dr. Nettleton, that when he was preaching in the state of ——, where revivals of religion attended him, he took an early walk one morning, and passing a family of much pretension, he called. The lady of the house came to the door. "Good-morning, madam," said he; "does Jesus Christ live here?" The lady, thrown off her guard, replied, "No, sir; he does not." "Ah," said he, "then I was mistaken; I thought he might. Good-morning, madam," and walked immediately on. This put the lady on a course of thinking which resulted in her conversion. She pulled off the husk and got at the kernel.

I pray that you may "find Christ," and that "Jesus Christ may live in your house." R.

A PRAYING WOMAN AND AN UNGODLY YOUNG MAN.

A few years ago, there lived a poor woman in an obscure village at the West. She supported herself by severe labor, yet always found time to pray, and attend upon public ordinances. Her heart was full of love and zeal in the Redeemer's cause. She seemed always to enjoy his presence and support, so that all who saw her took knowledge of her that she had been with Jesus.

In the same village, there lived a young man of an honest and ardent character, but entirely destitute of the sanctifying grace of God. He had been brought up by a pious relative, and was intelligent on religious subjects, but his *heart* had not received the gospel. He was fond of finding fault with professors of religion, and once remarked to a friend, that he believed the only Christian in that village was Mrs. H——, the poor woman to whom we have referred.

He did not then know that Mrs. H—— was praying for him without ceasing. He did not know that she had called others together to pray for his conversion, and that with a strong faith she laid hold on the promises of God in his behalf.

But soon he felt the effects of these prayers, for it seemed as if a sword had pierced his heart, so that he could not keep silence. In his anguish he wrote to Mrs. H——, and entreated her to pray for him. God only knows with what thankfulness and joy she received his letter. She did continue to pray, and He on whom she called heard and answered. The young man at length embraced the gospel with a fervent heart, and began to sing of the glory and sovereignty of God.

Nor was he a half-way Christian. A voice seemed ringing in his ear, "Woe is unto me, if I preach not the gospel." He obeyed that voice, and when he stood in the pulpit, the love that was in his heart flashed from his eyes, and trembled on his lips, so that those who heard him wondered that the flame should so burn within him, and he remain unconsumed.

He was indeed in labors abundant, and God blessed him by making him the means of great good among the people where his lot was cast, till, at the age of thirty-five, he was called up to receive his crown.

"He looked always wearied when he was here," said his weeping wife; "we ought to be willing to have him rest." The rest of heaven. He caught a glimpse of it, as he breathed his last. When one who stood near him asked if all was peace; raising his hand, and looking upward with a dying effort, he answered, "Peace, and joy in the Holy Ghost."

S. A.

THE THIRTY YEARS' PRAYER.

At the weekly prayer-meeting in ——, an aged wealthy and influential man entered, who during a long life had been seemingly indifferent to his spiritual welfare; and to the surprise of all present, he rose, under deep emotion, and asked the prayers of God's people for his own conversion. The next week he was again among them, apparently a penitent at the foot of the cross.

As the intelligence of his hopeful conversion spread

next day in the congregation, it reached an infirm and aged Christian who had for years been confined to his house, and was daily waiting his summons to depart. On hearing it, he insisted on being carried to see the wealthy man, and would intrust his message to no one. After a long interview, he returned home rejoicing.

The cause of the infirm man's interest in this visit was perhaps known only to himself and his venerable pastor. Thirty years ago, as he was burning coal on the mountain-side, two of his neighbors visited his little shantee, found him engaged in reading his Bible and in prayer, and joined him in his devotions. Ere they separated, they agreed to meet again the next week on the mountain to pray, as did the Saviour; and from week to week they met in this quiet retreat, which proved indeed a Bethel. One evening they spoke of their wealthy neighbor, mourning that he was living for this world only, when he was so much needed in the church of Christ; and they at last entered into a written, secret covenant with each other before God, not to cease praying for his conversion until he should be brought in or die, or they should all be called to their final account.

Years of prayer passed on, during which their faith failed not: one of the suppliants was at length called home; then another; and the old coal-burner, though left alone, yet persevered. Thirty years had passed when the above news reached him; his visit was made, and he came out of the house of his wealthy neighbor saying, "Now, Lord, lettest thou thy servant depart in peace; for mine eyes have seen thy salvation." E. T. C.

AN ANGRY CONTROVERSY SETTLED.

In the year 1831, in one of the southern states, there existed a legal controversy between two neighbors, who had up to this time been intimate friends, and soon it engendered a bitter personal animosity between them, and alienated their respective friends. Their families belonged to the same congregation, and their wives were members of the same church, and were held in high esteem for their intelligence and piety. Considering the family relations of the parties, it is not surprising that the church and the community should be seriously agitated by this quarrel; and that it proved a source of annoyance and grief not only to Christians, but to all their right-minded neighbors.

They were men of strong nerve, of great physical power, and distinguished in a high degree by what the world calls courage. Urged on by pride, ambition, or revenge, the contest waxed hotter and hotter, so that all acquainted with the circumstances were in constant fear of a bloody, if not a deadly rencontre.

One of the parties had prepared and intended to file a bill in chancery within the next ten days, which he knew would greatly irritate his antagonist, and provoke him to a personal assault, when the case would probably have been settled by the death of one or both of them. On all public occasions they carried deadly weapons.

In this state of things the Lord poured out his Spirit upon that community; hundreds of minds became impressed with religious truth, and it is believed many souls were truly converted to God. The third

Sabbath in June is a day to be held in everlasting remembrance by that congregation. On that day more than one hundred and fifty persons presented themselves as inquirers after the way of salvation, some of whom then and there sought and found hope in Christ. These two litigants were present, and were smitten and wounded by the sword of the Spirit. "The strong men" bowed themselves, and at the close of the services went away overwhelmed with a sense of their guilt and ruin, though entirely ignorant of the state of each other's minds.

On the morrow they again repaired to the house of the Lord; and previous to the commencement of public worship, the two belligerents providentially met face to face, while walking in a beautiful grove near the church. Mr. —— first spoke, and said, "Captain ——, I have a proposition to submit to you." The "captain," supposing he had reference to the suit that was to be tried in a few days, replied with as much coldness and hauteur in his manner as he could command, "I am ready to hear you, sir; what is it?" Mr. ——, unable any longer to restrain his feelings, answered with the deepest emotion, "It is, sir, that we cast behind us our follies and sins, and live together from this day as neighbors and Christians."

The captain was subdued and unmanned; in a moment they were locked in each other's arms, weeping like little children, and vieing with each other in making acknowledgments and concessions. They were friends. The pious rejoiced, and were greatly encouraged in the work of the Lord, and the impenitent received a most impressive illustration of the power and value of the Christian religion, and many more sought and found in it the "pearl of great price." The lawsuit was settled without a trial, the loaded pistols were uncharged and put away; and henceforth they lived as neighbors on terms of amity.

J. D. M.

KEEP TRYING.

In one of the large towns in Eastern Virginia, there lived a gentleman with an interesting family, much respected by his neighbors and friends, but he was inclined to be sceptical on the subject of the Christian religion. He was a man of mind, and of more than ordinary intelligence. A lingering disease at last brought him down to his bed, and his Christian friends became exceedingly solicitous in reference to his salvation. Various attempts were made to approach him on that subject; but he met every advance with a cold repulse that disheartened his friends, and paralyzed their efforts.

Among others that felt deeply for him, and prayed earnestly for his conversion, was an interesting Christian lady who lived next door to his residence. She was often in his room, and made frequent efforts to draw him out in conversation upon the subject of religion, but was unsuccessful. He seemed unhappy, but he preserved outward cheerfulness, and kept up the impression that his scepticism was unshaken by the hand of disease and the near approach of death.

He was very fond of reading, and constantly kept by him some book that served to beguile his weary hours. When he grew so feeble that he could not read, he called into requisition the services of one of his little daughters, who sat by his bedside and read for him by the hour. His kind friend, the good lady at the next door, was still anxious to approach him on the subject of religion, but without success. One day she entered his room and found him asleep. A new idea struck her. She returned and got a tract containing a solemn appeal to a sinner in prospect of death, which she carried into his room, laid it on his pillow, and retired as softly as an angel, without waking the sleeping man. She went to her home and prayed that some good might come of it.

By and by he awoke, and, apparently by chance, laid his hand on the little book. Without attempting to examine it himself, he called for his little daughter, who was in an adjoining room, to come and read for him. She flew to his bedside and commenced reading it to her afflicted father. She had not proceeded far before his eyes filled with tears, his chin trembled, and his bosom began to heave with emotion. The voice of the little girl trembled as she saw the effect upon her father, but she continued reading. He asked her to pause for a moment, and tried to regain his self-possession; and after a few moments told her to read on. She did so. But presently his feelings became too strong for concealment. Tears gushed from his eyes, and he gave way to violent weeping. The child read on, as she was able; for she too was sobbing as though her little heart would break.

The conviction came home with tremendous power to the man's heart, that he was a sinner, condemned by God's holy law, and exposed to hell. He began to pray. The Holy Spirit applied divine truth to his

heart and conscience; and directly he sent for his friend at the next door, and for other pious persons, to pray for him and instruct him in the way of salvation. He confessed his sins, and tried to give his heart to God. The minister was sent for, and he was taught more fully the way of life. Before that man died, his friends had the happiness to believe that he was savingly converted by faith in the Son of God. Here is another example of the good accomplished by prayerful, persevering Christian endeavors. Never tire. "Try, try again." When all else had failed, this effort succeeded. J. E. E.

THE STONE ROLLED AWAY.

In 1842, an unusual seriousness prevailed in one of our New England colleges; meetings for prayer were held in different rooms, and there was less rudeness and levity in the halls and about the college grounds.

In one of the prayer-meetings held by the pious students of the Senior class, it was determined to make a direct personal appeal to each of their unconverted class-mates. It fell to my lot to converse with one who had been a master-spirit among the ungodly, who ridiculed every thing serious, and in fact made a mock of all religion. The duty was declined, as I felt that I was altogether inadequate to the task. I was diffident, slow of speech, and could not think of approaching one whose tongue was ever ready with biting sarcasm and brutal infidel wit. But my brethren would not excuse me. With a trembling heart I consented, though with little faith as to any good result flowing from the interview.

At the close of the meeting I retired to my room, and falling on my knees, prayed for courage and arguments. I determined to go at once to the room of the irreligious student: on approaching his door, my fear returned and almost drove me away, but summoning resolution, I knocked, and entered. Once in I would gladly have been out again, but suddenly the thought arose, this is but a man, and he has a soul of unspeakable value: you have associated with him for nearly four years, and have never introduced the subject of personal religion; soon you are to separate, do not lose this opportunity of doing him good.

With a silent prayer, the object of my visit was introduced. "I am come, Mr. V——, to confess to you my unfaithfulness, to make known to you my interest in your spiritual welfare, and to urge you to give immediate attention to the concerns of the soul." Imagine my surprise when the individual from whom I expected only abuse, took me by the hand, and with a voice broken by deep emotion, exclaimed, "Mr. W——, I am glad to see you. I have been a great sinner—will you pray for me?" Both sobbed aloud. What had God wrought? "The stone was rolled away"—"Saul was among the prophets." That interview of an hour was a precious one. I discovered that V—— had been serious for some time; in fact, that he was studying his Bible when I sought admittance, and had been wishing that some one of his pious class-mates would speak to him on religion, though his heart was too proud to allow him to seek an interview. For the remainder of his college life, V—— was a changed man.

Pious young men in literary institutions are prone to excuse themselves from religious effort among their companions, from fear of ridicule; these fears are often groundless; the approach of a warm Christian heart is seldom repulsed.

The path of duty may be difficult and trying, but difficulties and trials vanish as one advances. God opens doors, disarms prejudices, and softens hearts.

O that the pious students throughout our land might be faithful to their divine Master, waiting not for the completion of their studies before they seek the salvation of men, but with zeal and love marking their whole course of study with efforts for the conversion of those with whom they are so intimately associated.

F. B. W.

BRANDS PLUCKED FROM THE FIRE.

In the spring of 1847, I was travelling with a brother clergyman, on our way to an ecclesiastical meeting in P——, Va. Having to pass through the county of A——, we purposed going by the village at the court-house, and to call on friends there; but being engaged in conversation, we passed a cross-road leading to the court-house, and did not discover our mistake until we had gone several miles, when it was too late to return. While we reproached ourselves for our inattention, the Lord was guiding us.

We had not proceeded far, when we perceived a house on fire about half a mile distant. The younger of the two put his horse into a gallop, and soon came up to the fire. It was a log-house, and the roof was in a blaze in three places. On entering the house, he was met at the threshold by the piteous cry of an old man, who was lying on a trundle-bed in one corner, entirely crippled with rheumatism, and as helpless as an infant. "Oh, sir," cried he, "for mercy's sake, take me out, or I shall be burned up alive!" He became a little more calm when assured that he was not in immediate danger, and that he would be taken care of in time. In the loft above was found his aged wife, terror-stricken, who had been trying in vain to extinguish the fire with a little tin bucket half full of water, and a small gourd.

As soon as the young minister found an axe, he went heartily to work; and after knocking off a large portion of the roof, succeeded in extinguishing the fire, and had the pleasure of assuring the old couple that the danger was over, and all was safe. They expressed their gratitude with flowing tears and many exclamations of thanks. The minister told them to give thanks to God, whose providence alone had saved them––that they intended to have taken another road, but had been led this way.

"Wonderful mercy!" said the old man; and trembling and turning pale at the thought, he added, "Oh, had you gone by the court-house, we by this time should have been burned to ashes. What a mercy, what a mercy!" he continued to repeat; and said, "Oh, how wicked I have been! I have never believed in a providence. I laughed at it, and hated the thought that God took *any* notice of us; but now I feel there is a Providence. Yes, there is a Providence that sent you here to save us from the fire."

He then inquired who we were, and where from; and when told that we were ministers of the gospel, and that one of us lived twenty-five miles, and the other one hundred miles distant, he was deeply affected, and said, "How strange it is! I have always hated ministers, and would not permit them to cross my door-sill; and now God has sent two of them to save such an old vile, crippled creature as I am from death!" He began to confess the sins of his past life, and particularly expressed regret that he had so long opposed his wife, who, he said, always wanted to be a Christian. He had been a soldier in Wayne's army; and there, he said, he had learned to drink liquor, to scoff at religion, and to make Tom Paine's book his bible; and "now," said he, "I begin to feel the guilt of it all; it comes upon me like a mountain load."

They were told that their sins had kindled the more dreadful fire of perdition, from which no human arm could save; and they were both urged to flee from the wrath to come, and lay hold on the hand that was nailed to the cross.

A tract entitled, "The Conversion of John Price," was then read to them. It contains a brief notice of the downward course of an habitual drinker and gamester, and of his wonderful reformation and conversion to God. One of the most touching passages in the tract is that in which he asks his little daughter to read the Bible to him. She read the fifty-first and one hundred and third Psalms. The father was much affected, and wept, and said, "Surely, God made her choose those two psalms."

The old couple, both in tears, listened to the reading, and when it was completed he said, "Surely, God made you choose that tract for us—every word of it comes home to my heart; and now will you be kind enough to read to us the same chapters of the Bible that the little girl read to her father?" The request was gladly complied with, and the fifty-first Psalm was read, "Have mercy upon me, O God," etc. It was read very distinctly and slowly. There he lay upon his bed, a man of large frame, with a finely developed head, a high and full forehead, a large blue eye, and expanded chest, but with his arms and legs so contracted by rheumatism, that for sixteen years he had been unable to move himself without aid; and as the reading proceeded, his broad chest began to heave with emotion, and the tears ran down his cheeks in a stream. On hearing the fourth verse, "Against thee, thee only have I sinned," he cried out, "O yes, that is the worst of it; it is all against God—all against God. Have mercy upon me, O God!" He became more composed as the reading was continued; and when it was finished he said, in a low, subdued tone, "That is God's word, and seems made on purpose for me."

His aged wife, who was filled with wonder and delight at what she had both seen and heard, asked that the other Psalm might be read. The hundred and third Psalm was accordingly read, "Bless the Lord, O my soul," etc. The old lady was greatly agitated; she walked up and down the room exclaiming, "'Bless the Lord, O my soul!' bless the Lord; he has saved us this day from fire, and will save us from our sins; he forgiveth all our iniquities! Bless the Lord that I have lived to see this day. My old man will now let me read and sing and pray: he will let ministers come to our house; and we will both seek and serve the Lord together." After much such talk, we kneeled and prayed—the first prayer, as the old man said, that was ever made in that house.

We bade them farewell, not expecting to meet them again until the judgment-day. The old couple lived about three years after this event, and we are credibly informed that they lived in a manner to illustrate and magnify the wondrous grace of God to the chief of sinners, and then died both in the same year, fully fourscore years of age, in the faith and lively hopes of the gospel of Christ.

J. D. M.

A HAPPY MISTAKE.

The heart of Miss Y——, who was afflicted with deafness, had been deeply moved to a sense of the danger of the unconverted. Receiving a call from a young lady, an impenitent friend of hers, and acting according to her quickened sense of duty and her yearnings for the safety of her friend, she urged her to yield herself to God, and accept the great atonement. Miss E—— listened politely for a time; but the subject was irksome to her, and seeing a piano in the room, she thought to change the conversation by saying abruptly to Miss Y——, "Will you play for me?" Miss Y——, from her defective hearing, supposed her friend had asked her to *pray* for her, as Miss E—— made the request soon after having been asked to pray for herself. With glad surprise Miss Y—— knelt beside her, but had scarcely begun a prayer before a conviction of her mistake flashed across her mind. Instantly there followed the thought, "*This is from God;*" and recovering from her embarrassment, she pleaded for the descent of the Spirit upon the heart of her friend.

At the close of her prayer, Miss E—— seemed in much distress of mind, and soon after left the house. The next morning, before nine o'clock, Miss Y—— discovered Miss E—— approaching the gate. It was a bleak, chilly morning early in March, and the snow was still quite deep. Miss E—— entered with a heart so burdened with a sense of sin as not to allow her to say any thing except, "Oh, I am *so unhappy!*" Then followed an interview of the deepest interest. Her distress continued two or three days, and then she trusted in a forgiving Saviour. From that hour, Miss Y——'s affliction has seemed to her to possess more of the brightness of a blessing, and she rejoices in the dealings of that infinite wisdom which "doeth all things well." C.

AN AGED SINNER.

Mrs. F—— had started on an errand of mercy, when she met an aged female groping her way. She was a wretched-looking object, bent with age, and clothed with tattered garments. Mrs. F—— had passed her, but conscience whispered that she might be losing an opportunity of doing good and relieving suffering, and she retraced her steps.

"My friend," she said to her kindly, "you seem very aged and infirm." "If I see the seventeenth of next month, I shall be ninety-two." "That is a great age," said Mrs. F——. "And is your soul at peace with God?" "Who asks about my soul?" she exclaimed. "You are the first person that ever spoke to me about it. I cannot see you well, for I am so blind, but go with me and talk." Mrs. F—— determined not to defer the opportunity, and accompanied the old woman to her miserable home. She found her the inmate of a low, wretched family, who boarded her for the rent of the hovel they occupied, which belonged to her son in an adjacent city. From the family the old woman suffered the most unkind treatment. So long had the voice of kindness been a stranger to her ear, that she was deeply affected by it, and seemed not only willing but anxious to hear, while Mrs. F—— talked to her of Jesus, and his love for ruined man. She had wonderfully retained her mind for one of her years, and was not so ignorant as she was hardened in vice, for in childhood she had been instructed in her Bible, and its blessed precepts were not wholly forgotten. What encouragement to parents to sow the seed.

Mrs. F——, upon inquiry, learned much of her history. A wayward youth and ungovernable temper, that had driven husband and children from her; a life of infamy for twenty-five years, followed by wretchedness and poverty; discarded by the respectable friends and family to whom she belonged, and disowned by her son, she was reaping the bitter wages of sin when met by our good Samaritan Mrs. F——, whose first efforts were to relieve her bodily wants, while she did not neglect her still greater spiritual need.

Daily did Mrs. F—— visit the aged sinner, reading and praying with her, though the family who professed to take care of her often insulted Mrs. F—— with coarse language, and even interrupted her while she knelt to pray; but she heeded them not, for she was engaged about a great work, under God, "saving a soul from death." Christian friends, too, remonstrated with her upon expending so much effort upon such a hopeless case, and the impropriety of visiting so bad a character. She only replied, "The more wicked she is, the more faith and effort she requires." Amidst all the discouragements in her labor of love, she persevered, until God saw fit to bless her by sending the Holy Spirit to enlighten her darkened mind, and break the bondage of sin which had so long bound her. The work seemed a very gradual one, but not the less sure. She was permitted to live long enough to manifest the wonder-working power of God.

A year from the day Mrs. F—— first met her, she was called to stand by her death-bed, and hear her rejoice in the love of Jesus. Her last words were, "I am a great, great sinner, but Jesus is a great, great Saviour; glory be to his name." What a reward for a short year of prayer and effort was this! Fellow-Christian, go thou and do likewise; be not discouraged. Remember, "with God all things are possible."

H.

ANSWER TO UNITED PRAYER.

On the 20th of October, 1799, twenty-four persons joined a church in New England, of whom four youth were intimate friends. One of them married a worthy young man, and another a virtuous young woman, and the other two had each a father, none of whom were pious; and they agreed on a concert of prayer for each other, and for their relatives.

They knew what they wanted; it was the life of the soul for which their united and earnest cries continued to ascend. But it was not in a day, or a week, or a month, or a year, that they obtained what they greatly longed for. To cheer them when almost ready to faint, a letter from one of the four announced to two at a distance, that his wife was rejoicing in hope of the glory of God. This news called forth joyful thanksgivings. Some few years passed on, and the young man that had been the subject of these united intercessions gave signs of spiritual life, which again thrilled their hearts with holy gratitude and joy.

But the case of the two aged fathers was more trying. Increasing hardness made faith stagger; and often did the fear arise that their day was past. About twelve years thus rolled on; one was more than fifty, and the other more than sixty years of age. Suddenly, at length a friend wrote to the son at a distance, that his aged father had apparently awaked from the long slumber of a state of sin, and given evidence of conversion. This was as "life from the dead;" this was a rebuke to unbelief. More earnestly did the friends ply the throne of grace; and what was their joy, when about twenty years from the time that the concert commenced, the other aged father, more than threescore and ten, was baptized into the name of the Father, and of the Son, and of the Holy Ghost.

Will not young Christians go and do likewise, with only this word of exhortation, Have more faith in God; pray more in the Spirit, and hope more confidently in the promise that it shall be done for you, if you ask any thing according to his will.

E. Y.

A DEAF HEARER.

Mr. B—— was not born deaf, yet he did not hear; he afterwards became deaf, and then he heard. How is this? In all the years of his outward hearing, his life was deeply estranged from God, and no heavenly voice penetrated his heart to unstop its utter deafness. The precepts, "Hear, ye deaf," and "Ephphatha, Be opened," were unheeded. He had ears to hear, but did not hear. But when deprived of his natural hearing, the Holy Spirit removed the deafness of his heart, and he had ever-listening ears to hear what God the Lord would say. By embracing the Christian faith, he received a new life, new hearing, new understanding, and long and worthily maintained the Christian course.

He was still deaf to the recitals of Christian experience from others, but felt its blessed power in himself, and disclosed it to their joyful edification. He never heard a sermon, or a prayer, or a hymn of praise, during his religious life; but the sanctuary, and the social meetings of Christians, were often to him as the open gate of heaven. He could hear no sound of his own voice; and when he spoke, he feared that no one would understand his broken speech; yet he audibly and with great delight read the holy Scriptures, conducted the stated family worship, and intelligently and earnestly addressed his brethren upon the great things of the kingdom of God. He often complained of great barrenness of soul, and what he termed an empty-head religion, in distinction from a living and glorious devotion of the heart; while you would have judged him to be unusually deep, spiritual, and abounding in the Christian exercises. He keenly felt his deprivation, and especially in its obstruction to Christian intercourse, yet he bore it with submission, and expected to pass all his remaining days upon the earth shut up in this profound silence.

But, deaf and faithful Christian, be cheered. Rejoice that the ear of your heart has been opened to hearken to the word of the Lord. Rejoice that the blessed Bible is still your constant and divine preacher. Rejoice that the Spirit of God unfolds to you glories that the mere external ear of man hath never heard. Rejoice that you are yet to share in the finished beatitude, where the ears of the deaf shall be for ever unstopped, and the tongue of the stammerer shall sing the new and everlasting song. C. B. D.

A SCEPTICAL CAPTAIN.

In 1845, when passing from Buffalo to Detroit, I was led into an interesting conversation with the captain of the steam-boat. He had been long engaged in navigating the lakes, and related many valuable incidents of the early commerce of those inland seas. A casual remark indicated that his views of religion were sceptical. This led to a protracted discussion, lasting most of the night, and ending in the promise that he would carefully read a copy of Nelson's incomparable work, the "Cause and Cure of Infidelity." In a very courteous manner he declined receiving payment for my passage, and expressed much gratitude for the interest taken in his spiritual well-being.

Five years afterwards, I took a steamer at Sandusky on the route eastward. At a crowded breakfast-table, when seated in an unusual position in conversation with a travelling companion, a gentleman at my right hand interposed a remark which recalled at once the intelligence respecting lake navigation received from the infidel captain. I turned inquiringly, and exclaimed, "This must be captain ——." "Yes," said he, for the first time observing my features; "and you are the man who gave me *the books.*"

Our surprise and gratification were mutual. The remainder of the trip to Buffalo was spent in conversation about the one theme of salvation. He seemed to have been placed again providentially within my reach. For two years or more he had not been upon the lake till this excursion; and I had crossed it but once during the intervening five years. Had his seat at table been elsewhere than the one he chose, or had the conversation taken another drift, we should not have recognized each other, and the opportunity would have been lost. As it was, I endeavored to make the most of it. I learned that he had abandoned his infidelity, but was still resting in some speculative errors from which I sought to dislodge his mind, leading him to the atoning almighty Saviour as his only resource. As we entered Buffalo harbor, I again placed in his hands appropriate books, which he received with many thanks, and the remark, "Sir, I will read any thing you give me." Our next meeting will be at the judgment-bar, in all human probability. May it be at the right hand of the Judge.

There is a providence choosing our changes, directing our courses, and appointing our opportunities of usefulness. Happy the man who closely eyes it, and implicitly follows its indications.

Christian travellers are specially bound to seek the spiritual good of captains and crews of the craft on which they sail. Their occupation leads them away from the sanctuary and the means of grace, and they are peculiarly liable to be neglected and lost, but for friendly interposition.

A careful selection of religious books and tracts should as much form a part of the luggage of a Christian traveller as his dressing-case. They are always useful—often indispensable. He who would reap bountifully, must sow bountifully, and beside all waters. Let every Christian be supplied with the seed, and the providence of God will provide the opportunity of sowing it where it will take root and bear fruit unto eternal life. Heber.

AN INQUIRING JEW.

Among the passengers from Detroit to Buffalo in a steamer on lake Erie, was a lady who, in a casual remark on some subject of religious interest, attracted the attention of one or two clergymen, and they immediately entered into conversation with her. Some of the important points of Christian belief—the sinner's responsibility, God's power and willingness to save—were discussed, when the lady observed a stranger advancing towards her party, and listening with much apparent interest to their conversation on gospel themes. All nations and tribes were spoken of as belonging to one family, through Jesus the elder Brother. The Jews in particular were mentioned as being objects of hope and desire to the church, cast off now by their unbelief, yet destined to a final and complete restoration.

The stranger's countenance brightened, and bending forward he eagerly exclaimed, "I am a Jew; and our nation think not so lightly of your Jesus as you suppose; we consider him a good man."

"If he is no more than a man," said the lady, "he cannot be good, for he 'made himself equal with God.'

There is no middle ground; he is either the long-promised Messiah, or a vile impostor."

"What shall we Jews believe?" said the stranger. "If we credit the Old Testament, and listen to the rabbies, we are taught that all will be well."

"But do you read your old Testament?" said the lady. "That is by no means silent with regard to our Saviour. 'They shall look unto Him whom they have pierced,' is but one among very many passages pointing to him."

"But we who are so deeply immersed in business," said the stranger, "have no time to study these things for ourselves. We follow the example, and receive the faith of our fathers."

"But," said the lady, "if your Bible is what it professes to be, is it not worthy of your time, attention, and heart? Should not its laws govern you, its promises attract, and its threatenings terrify you? Let me ask you, if you would consider it wise, in your common affairs, to sacrifice the greater interest to the less? Is it more wise to overlook eternal things in the less important or trifling pursuits of this short life?"

"Ah," said the Jew, "I know not what to think. My teachers tell me one thing, and you tell me another."

The lady thought a moment, and said earnestly, "I will tell you what to do, read your own Bible attentively, studiously, and pray God to lead you in the right way, to show you what is truth. Make it the grand business of your life to find out whether Jesus is your Saviour or no."

The stranger looked as if struck with a new idea,

and the lady thought there was some hope for him, as it was so evident that his heart was not entirely callous. It made her deeply serious to reflect that she had never before seen this poor Jew, and that very soon they would part to meet no more, until it should be before the tribunal of that Messiah who on the day of triumph will bear about him the scars of his conflict and death. M. A. H.

MR. BINGHAM AND HIS NEIGHBOR.

More than twenty years ago, Mr. Bingham of C——, in the state of Vermont, then an old man—now, I trust, in heaven—gave me the following narrative:

"When I first came to this town in my youth, Mr. L—— came with me, and we pitched our tents here in the wilderness, not far from each other. Here we lived and labored, side by side, for many years.

"Soon after our settlement in C——, it was my happy lot to be led to embrace the Saviour. But my neighbor L—— remained as he was, unreconciled to God, without hope, and even manifesting a marked opposition to spiritual religion, till he removed about three miles from me, when I had fewer opportunities to see him and converse with him; and at length had almost ceased to think of him, with solicitude for his salvation.

"One evening, during a season of the outpouring of the Spirit, as I was casting my thoughts over the town, before the hour of family prayer, the case of this former neighbor came to mind, and deeply interested my feelings. After prayer I retired, but sleep departed from my eyes; my mind was too active, and my emotions too powerful to sleep. An apprehension of the lost condition of my friend, and of his exposure to death and the judgment, with a sense of my neglect of opportunities to warn him of his danger, pressed so heavily upon me, that I could not rest in bed. I retired into a grove, where I walked and meditated and prayed, till I felt an inexpressible desire to see him, and once more converse with him on the things which concerned his 'everlasting peace.'

"It was a beautiful night. The autumnal air was soft and balmy. The moon shone with peculiar brightness. All nature seemed to be resting in silence. I saddled my horse, and rode slowly towards the residence of my friend, which I reached about two o'clock. Under impressions which it would be in vain to attempt to describe, I knocked at his door, and requested a short interview. I related to him, as well as I could, the object and occasion of my untimely visit; and no sooner did I begin to speak, than the tears began to flow from his eyes—eyes which had probably never before wept for sin, or looked up for pardon and salvation. Apparently under the deepest conviction of sin, and with a full apprehension of the danger of his case, he besought me to pray with him, and for him.

"The result was a marked and happy change—a subsequent consecration of himself to the service of God—a life, for a few years, of habitual obedience to the divine will, a triumphant faith in the hour of death, and an assured hope of a blessed immortality."

J. B.

A DIFFICULTY OVERCOME.

It is a delightful thought, that all who have been given to Christ shall come to him: not of themselves, not always in paths of their own selection, not always with open eyes, and knowing whither they go. Still, though astray, averse, and blind, they all come to the Shepherd of their souls.

A teacher in one of our cities called upon his pastor. It was evening, and the clergyman was just about leaving the house to attend a meeting. The teacher soon made known his errand. "I have come, sir, to ask you to visit my school and pray with the pupils. The Holy Spirit is evidently there; many of the older scholars are asking me what they shall do. I am not a Christian myself. I know not what to say to them. Will you not come over to guide these inquiring souls to the Saviour?"

"No, sir," said the pastor; "yours is a public school. No pastor of any one congregation can lawfully take the charge of its religious instructions. I cannot go."

"What shall be done, then?" inquired the teacher. "Mr. P——," said the pastor, "God has at length brought you where you cannot excuse yourself from duty. All your life you have been evading responsibility; now it has come upon you, and you cannot escape from it. These children are in your hands. You, and you alone are to guide them to Christ. No pastor in the city can enter that school. God has drawn you into a strait place. You must not decline the work to which he so manifestly calls you."

"I cannot do what you recommend. I am not a

Christian." "Mr. P——, your duty is plain. You can trust in Christ for mercy, and he can and will help you. Promise me that you will begin to-morrow to pray with these pupils, and try to guide them to Christ."

The teacher was standing, his hand in the hand of his pastor, his face pale, his whole frame quaking with emotion. "You must not contend against God," said the pastor. "I will try," stammered the trembling man, and left the house.

The next day witnessed a new scene in that school, teacher and pupils praying and weeping together. The evening of the second day saw the teacher walking his room in great agitation, till at a late hour he suddenly turned to his sweet and anxious wife, and said, "Mary, let us try to pray." The family altar was established. A few weeks passed, and the teacher was at the table of Christ, thanking God that that visit to the pastor had been the journey of a blind soul led on its way to the gates of life. C.

A FOOL ANSWERED.

During the month of November, 1843, I was travelling in one of the night-trains from Albany to Utica. The weather being very cold, the passengers gathered as closely as possible around the stove. Among the number thus brought into juxtaposition were a clergyman and an atheist; and as the latter was very loquacious, he soon engaged the minister in a controversy touching the relative merits of their respective systems. They soon became much excited, and thus continued to dispute, to the great annoyance of all present, until long after midnight, although often requested to desist, and though it had been especially urged upon the clergyman that he "was casting pearls before swine."

In answer to an inquiry of the reverend gentleman, as to what would be man's condition after death, the atheist replied, "Man is like a *pig;* when he dies, that is the end of him." As the minister was about to reply, a red-faced Irish woman at the end of the car sprang up, the natural redness of her face glowing more intensely with feeling and the light of the lamp falling directly upon it, and addressing the clergyman in a voice peculiarly startling and humorous from its impassioned tones and the richness of its brogue, exclaimed, "*Arrah, now, will ye not let the baste alone; has he not said he's a* PIG? *and the more you pull his leg, the louder he'll squale!*" The effect upon all was electric; the clergyman was humbled, and apologized for his thoughtlessness and folly. But upon the atheist it was perfectly stunning; he had been "answered according to his folly," and confounded with his own argument by an illiterate Irish woman. God had evidently used the "foolish to confound the wise;" and while he remained in the car he was literally speechless, and he seized the first opportunity and left, although he had paid his passage through to Utica.

S. D.

TAKING THE RIGHT GROUND.

One Saturday noon, when school was dismissed, a number of us stopped a little while, to devise ways and means of passing the afternoon most pleasantly. I was then, I think, about nine years of age. We could not fix upon any plan; so we separated, agreeing to meet after dinner, at E—— H——'s, and take up the subject again.

I received permission to spend the afternoon with E——, or to go where the boys went, provided they "kept out of mischief." I found the boys, some five or six in number, assembled there when I arrived. One of them was earnestly urging them to go to the I—— orchard, for apples. There was a tree, he said, of excellent apples, at a great distance from the house, and so near to the woods that we could get just as many as we wanted, without being seen.

I saw at once that I could not be one of the party, for I was not brought up to steal apples or any thing else. As I did not wish to be left alone, I was very desirous that the plan should not be adopted. I accordingly brought forward several objections—the distance of the orchard from us, the probability that we should not succeed, the shame that would follow detection in the attempt, and the fact that none of our parents would be willing to have us go upon such an expedition.

My objections were plausibly answered by the proposer of the plan, and I began to fear that I should be left in a minority, when R—— A—— joined us. When he had learned the state of the case, he said the expedition was not to be thought of, FOR IT WAS WRONG. It would displease God. Disguise it as we would, it was stealing, and God's law said, "Thou shalt not steal."

His remarks settled the question. The plan was

given up. We concluded to go and play in a large new-mown meadow.

I have related this incident to show how important it is to take the right ground in opposing that which is wrong. R—— took the right ground. He planted himself on the everlasting rule of right. I have observed that when young persons are asked to do what their consciences will not approve, they often assign various reasons for declining, instead of boldly stating the true and chief reason, namely, *that it is wrong.* Never be afraid or ashamed to avow your adherence to the rule of right. If a thing is not right, say you will not do it, *because it is not right,* and do not think it needful to add any other reason.

Perhaps you would like to know how we spent the afternoon. We went and played in the meadow. By and by a dark cloud rose in the west. A laborer, passing through the meadow, told us there would be a thunder-shower, and advised us to go home in season. But we were so much interested in our play that we did not heed his advice.

The cloud rose higher, and the thunder began to roll. Then we looked up and saw that the rain was so near that we could not get to a house before it would reach us. There was a ledge of rocks on one side of the meadow, and one of the rocks projected so far as to form a shelter. We ran thither, and thus secured ourselves from the rain.

The lightning grew sharper, and the thunder louder, and we became very much alarmed. I prayed mentally, and wished very much to kneel down and pray aloud, but was ashamed to do so.

A bright flash, which seemed to cover us all in its

blaze, was accompanied with the loudest peal of thunder I ever heard. A large chestnut-tree, which stood a few rods distant in the meadow, was split in two, from the top to the bottom, by the bolt.

"Let us pray," said R——, taking off his hat and kneeling on the rock. Most of us followed his example. He prayed that our lives might be spared, and our souls saved. Our lives were spared. The cloud passed over, the sun came out, and all nature seemed freshened into new life.

It was too wet to play in the meadow. Indeed, we did not feel like playing. We all felt solemn. We went home and told our friends what we had seen.

Would you believe it, some days afterwards, when they had got fully over their fright, some of the boys told about R——'s praying, and tried to make sport of it. R—— told them that they did not laugh at prayer when the lightning was so near them, and that they would not laugh at prayer when they came to die.

How often will those laugh in the sunshine, who tremble in the storm!

What became of R——? He was long a minister of Jesus Christ. His object was to glorify God on earth, and to go and dwell with him in heaven.

J. A.

AN IMPORTANT INTERVIEW.

Before going out last evening, I asked my heavenly Father to furnish me, if it might please him, with an opportunity of saying or doing something for my

Saviour's cause; and I thought I saw his hand in the following circumstance.

On my way home, in the vicinity of a toy-shop, I observed a genteel-looking youth of about eighteen stoop down and pick up something, to which, as I passed, he called my attention. It was a number of little painted leaden dishes, which some child had evidently just purchased and dropped on the snow. As the youth spread the dishes on his hand for my inspection, I remarked that the loss of the toys might then be filling the bosom of the little loser with poignant sorrow, perhaps as keen as an owner of great wealth would experience at the loss of valuable property. I added, that although losses were painful, and generally hard to make up, many might, nevertheless, be retrieved. Health might be lost, but skill and temperance might restore the treasure; riches might take wings and leave their possessor bankrupt, but industry and frugality might recall them; reputation might be blasted, and yet, by a course of unwearied integrity, a good name—more precious than rubies—might be regained; but there is one loss that is irretrievable: "know you what it is?" He hesitated, and upon my repeating the question, acknowledged his ignorance. I told him it was the soul, the precious, immortal soul of man, which, once lost, is lost for ever.

By this time we had reached a corner where our ways separated. Laying my hand gently on his shoulder, and fixing my eyes upon his, which the glare of the lamp showed me were beaming with awakened interest and intelligent expression, I solemnly and affectionately besought him to "flee from the wrath to come," by repentance towards God, and faith in the Lord Jesus Christ. He listened most attentively to the few cogent reasons I adduced, and thanked me heartily for my interest in the eternal welfare of a total stranger. As we bade each other good-night, I repeated my remark, "Remember, *the soul once lost, is lost for ever.* Will you not at once attend to this mightiest of all concerns?" "I will, I will, sir," he emphatically rejoined; and we parted, in all probability not again to meet until, with "the dead, small and great," we stand before "the great white throne."

My mind was deeply affected with this incident, and my heart went out towards that young man. I thought of his frank and prepossessing countenance, of his ignorance and neglect of the great salvation; of the multitudinous perils to which he is exposed in this great city, where vice never wearies in weaving her nets for giddy youth; of the time when I too was a wild and thoughtless young man, spurning the restraints of religion, and turning a deaf ear to the gracious calls of long-forbearing mercy; of the inestimable value of the soul; and of its costly redemption—its free and full salvation through a divine and crucified Redeemer.

Upon reaching my dwelling I retired to my closet, and with a melting heart and "strong cries," besought the Triune God to call this precious youth "out of darkness into his marvellous light"—to translate him into the kingdom of his dear Son, and by the power of his grace change the rebel to a loyal subject and loving child.

And should we not, my readers, ask ourselves, if there are not many other young persons, of both sexes, to whom we ought to "run" and "speak?" Zech. 2:4. Let us not loiter, for

"Death steals on man with noiseless tread;
No place, no prayer delivers him;
From midst of life, unfinished plan,
With sudden hand it severs him;
And ready, or not ready—no delay;
Forth to his Judge's bar he must away."

"Whatsoever thy hand findeth to do, do it with thy might." Eccl. 9:10. "In due season we shall reap, if we faint not." Gal. 6:9. "They that turn many to righteousness shall shine as the stars for ever and ever." Dan. 12:3. H. S.

HAPPY EFFECTS OF DECISION.

Not long since, there came to our city an unassuming young man, whose delicate health had prevented him from entering the ministry, and made it advisable that he should commence business as a merchant's clerk. Entering an establishment here, he found himself the room-mate of the head clerk, a moralist, and proud of his virtues, and of a second clerk, kind, but gay and thoughtless. And now came the first struggle of duty. Should he retire without reading the Scriptures and prayer? Conscience told him his duty, but his fears answered, "Give me any cross but that."

After two months of disquiet and remorse, days of ceaseless unrest and nights of sleepless trouble, he drew forth his mother's Bible from his trunk, and endeavored to extract consolation from it; but alas, he saw that those who would find rest must take the yoke; and every passage seemed addressed to him, summoning him to take up the cross, however great the sacrifice. He resolved to obey. That night, however, his companions entered the room unusually gay, and amid laughing and trifling and varied conversation, there seemed no place to introduce devotional exercises. He anxiously awaited the favorable moment, but it came not; and when sleep succeeded to silence, he had failed of duty, and was again in distress. The night was spent in penitent confession and secret resolutions for the next evening. These resolutions he determined nothing should thwart.

As the trio were again brought together in their room for retirement, he saw the time had come. With trepidation and trembling, he said to the eldest clerk, "Henry, we have been room-mates for a long time, and have never prayed together. Let us neglect this duty no longer. I have done wrong in delaying as I have." The moralist was struck dumb with amazement. The other clerk was silent also. He opened that dear Bible of his mother, read, kneeled by his chair, and then was verified the promise, "It shall come to pass, that before they call, I will answer; and while they are yet speaking, I will hear." Night after night the three clerks bent the knee in prayer. The moralist acknowledged a power he knew nothing of. Conviction ensued, and he is now rejoicing in the hope which maketh not ashamed, and ascribes his first impressions to that prayer of the trembling junior clerk.

How heavy the cross when it is a cross in anticipation; how light the cross when it is the cross remembered. How insignificant the consequences when anticipation measures them by her fears; how immense the consequences when the reality arrives. E. T. C.

HELP ONE ANOTHER.

A traveller who was crossing the Alps, was overtaken by a snow-storm at the top of a high mountain. The cold became intense. The air was thick with sleet, and the piercing wind seemed to penetrate his bones. Still the traveller, for a time, struggled on. But at last his limbs were benumbed, a heavy drowsiness began to creep over him, his feet almost refused to move, and he lay down on the snow to give way to that fatal sleep which is the last stage of extreme cold, and from which he would certainly never have waked again in this world.

Just at that moment, he saw another poor traveller coming along the road. The unhappy man seemed to be, if possible, even in a worse condition than himself, for he, too, could scarcely move; all his powers were frozen, and all appeared to be just on the point to die.

When he saw this poor man, the traveller who was just going to lie down to sleep, made a great effort. He roused himself up, and he crawled, for he was scarcely able to walk, to his dying fellow-sufferer.

He took his hands into his own and tried to warm them. He chafed his temples; he rubbed his feet; he applied friction to his body. And all the time he spoke cheering words into his ear and tried to comfort him.

As he did thus, the dying man began to revive, his powers were restored, and he felt able to go forward. But this was not all; for his kind benefactor too was recovered by the efforts which he had made to save his friend. The exertion of rubbing made the blood

circulate again in his own body. He grew warm by trying to warm the other. His drowsiness went off, he no longer wished to sleep, his limbs returned again to their proper force, and the two travellers went on their way together, happy, and congratulating one another on their escape.

Soon the snow-storm passed away; the mountain was crossed, and they reached their home in safety.

If, dear reader, you feel your heart cold towards God, and your soul almost ready to perish, try to do something which may help another soul to life and make his heart glad; and you will often find it the best way to warm and restore and gladden your own.

THE YOUNG LADY'S FIRST GIFT.

Not far from forty years ago, Miss H——, in a New England city, heard one Sabbath, for the first time, a missionary sermon. She had distinguished family connections; her personal character already gave promise of great superiority, and more than all, she was an ardent Christian. With a glowing heart, she listened to the story of the wants and woes of the heathen. Her attention was especially called to the Sandwich Island mission, and she shed many tears of pity in thinking of the misery of those who had never heard of *her* Saviour. "What can *I* do?" was the question she asked herself.

On returning home, she said eagerly to her astonished father, "Father, I want *all* my money." "All your money to-day—what can you want it for?" "I must give it to that good man who preached this morning, that the poor Sandwich Islanders may have the gospel." It amounted to sixteen dollars, and she cast the whole into the "Lord's treasury."

The interest felt for the new mission spread throughout the town. By and by the church was repaired, and the old pulpit was sent to the Sandwich Islands, for the new house of worship erected there.

Years rolled on. The young lady entered upon the arduous duties of a pastor's wife, and had become a mother, yet she still found time to labor and pray for "the nations sitting in darkness;" and though in early womanhood her warm heart and liberal hands became cold in death, "God still had respect unto her and her offering."

One of her sons, after some years' absence attending to his profession in a remote part of the land, found it necessary, owing to the declining state of his health, to take a voyage. He embarked for the Sandwich Islands. He arrived in safety, and found himself not among heathen, but was immediately surrounded by Christian friends. He was hospitably entertained; his wants and sicknesses were cared for, and in due time he was enabled to go up to the house of God, when almost the first object that met his eyes was the "old pulpit," beneath whose droppings his sainted mother had felt the first springing up of missionary fervor. Yes, there was the pulpit, and there was her son, both witnesses that God is faithful.

How little that young lady thought, so many years before, when she placed her sixteen dollars in the contribution-box, that she was thus providing for the future comfort and entertainment of her own child.

But God saw it all; and every gift, wish, effort, tear, prayer which we bestow upon his cause, are "bread" cast upon the great waters of his truth and benevolence, and shall surely return unto us after "many days."

M. A. H.

THE OLD PARASOL.

In one of the churches in the village of M——, the Sabbath had arrived for presenting the claim of missions in our own country; and according to the usual custom, in each pew was placed a slip of blank paper. The eye of a young lady, as she entered her pew, rested on the paper; she knew its purport, and a cloud gathered over her usually sunny face. It was not that she did not love the object for which that little paper asked a subscription; of the varied calls to promote her Master's kingdom none was dearer to her heart, and she was a cheerful giver. But now, if she gave, there must be a sacrifice, and for her, a great self-denial.

She had heretofore given a dollar annually, besides her efforts in the Sewing Society. Small this may seem to those who give their fifties, but it was not small for her. Her mother, unhappily, thought much of making an appearance in the world, and often reproved her young daughter for what she deemed her unnecessary liberality. Her father, at her request, had granted her a stated though limited allowance, for his income was small. Unexpected calls upon her purse had left her with only one dollar. She had designed with that, and a small addition her mother had promised, to purchase a parasol, and had considered she must withhold her mite until the next year, hoping then to double it.

But the sight of that silent little pleader which she had never returned blank, caused her some misgivings, and a struggle commenced in her heart, that did not lessen as she listened to the destitution in our western states—how thousands must perish for the bread of life, unless the church awoke to her duty and sent forth laborers, for "the harvest truly was plenteous, but the laborers few."

The young lady cast one look at her old parasol, as it stood in the corner of the pew, for it was old-fashioned, and much the worse for wear. She thought of the appearance it would make beside the richly dressed city cousins who were soon to visit her; how it would excite their mirth and ridicule, if not their compassion for her poverty. And then she might incur the displeasure of her mother, if she appropriated her money to any other purpose than to buy a new one.

All these thoughts passed rapidly through the mind of the young follower of Jesus. Then came that saying of his, "He that taketh not his cross, and followeth me, is not worthy of me." It was a slight cross, she felt, for her to bear, and taking the little paper, she wrote on it with her pencil, "C—— H——, one dollar." The cloud passed from her brow, and when the service was ended, she took her old parasol and walked home with a light heart, blessing God for an opportunity of making any sacrifice for his glory.

A few days passed, and a letter came for her from an absent brother, containing an unexpected gift of *fifty dollars*. Taking it to her mother, she said, "See, mother, how God has returned my dollar, and with such interest; but I shall carry my old parasol this summer, for it seems like an old friend who has done me good." If all the professed followers of Jesus would make some sacrifice, forego some anticipated gratification for his cause, how would the treasury of the Lord be increased. You may not receive your dollar back with interest here, but you will have what is worth more, the sweet consciousness of your Saviour's approval.

USEFUL WOMEN.

Two sisters who had sought to be useful in the city of New York, were providentially removed to a village not far distant, and as a means of doing good as they had opportunity, provided themselves with religious tracts. After circulating them for a long time, with apparently no good result, they became interested on behalf of a young lady who was well known in the circles of worldly fashion. They made her a subject of special prayer; and when about to visit her on one occasion, bowed before the Lord in secret, asking divine direction and a blessing. They selected the tract, "Don't put it off," and when they presented it, they prayed with her. They returned home, and in secret asked the Lord to bless the tract they had given. He heard their supplication; and from the time that she read that tract, the young lady was deeply convinced of sin. She felt the terrors of the law, and was heavily burdened during several months, before she realized that Christ was her peace; yet she was much concerned for others, and anxiously sought, by reading to them the tract the Lord had blessed to her, and by conversation, to be the means of bringing them to Christ. At length she became a happy Christian, testifying the grace of God wherever she had opportunity; and from that time was more assiduously employed in efforts to do good.

One of the persons to whom she read the tract during the season of her anxiety, soon indulged hope, and joined her in the service of her blessed Master. A young married woman, to whom she endeavored to communicate religious truth, repelled it, saying that her child so fully engaged her attention that she had no time to think of religion. The young lady recollected the excuses she herself had made and what others had done for her salvation, and retiring to her closet, laid the tract that had been made useful to her before the Lord, and besought him that he would in like manner bless it to that young woman. She then went and gave it to her, with the request that she would immediately read it, and then returned to her closet again to pray that it might be blessed. Presently she was called from her knees to receive a message from Mrs. ——, requesting that she would return to her immediately. She did so, and found her kneeling on the floor, crying to God for mercy. Her conviction of sin was abiding; it increased in depth; and after a while this woman also was enabled to see that the chastisement of her peace was upon Christ, and that with his stripes she was healed.

This young married woman has also been blessed in efforts to do good. She lately made a visit to the parents of her husband, and in the evening related what the Lord had done for her soul, and read the tract that had been the means of her awakening. Her mother heard with much attention, and the admonition, "Don't put it off," came home to her with power. She wept, and from that evening regarded herself as a sinner, ready to perish; the fixed purpose of her soul appeared to be, "I 'll go to Jesus."

> "I can but perish, if I go;
> I am resolved to try;
> For if I stay away, I know
> I must for ever die."

Here were four persons who had reason to praise God for one copy of a tract of four pages; for though they subsequently read other tracts and Bunyan's "Come and Welcome," and derived much instruction and comfort from their perusal, "Don't put it off," in connection with prayerful personal effort, appeared to have been the means of their awakening. There were other persons in the neighborhood who appeared to be concerned for their spiritual state, and as God employs the influence that individuals exert upon one another as a means of carrying on his work, who can tell whereunto this may grow? O.

TAKE CARE OF THAT OX.

Travelling, not long since, through one of the western states, I stopped at a very neat public-house and called for dinner. While it was preparing, I had a few words of conversation with the landlord, who kept a temperance house, and gave me a brief history of it.

Some years ago, he informed me, though a professor of religion, he had sold an immense quantity of liquor, and his house was noted far and near as a resort for respectable tipplers. Travellers loaded him with their favors. His conscience often troubled him, but he was accustomed to appease its clamors by the argument, that "if he did n't sell, somebody else would."

One day a venerable Christian neighbor, who had often kindly spoken to him on the subject, left at the house, while he was absent, a tract called "The Ox Sermon." Picking it up on his return, and glancing over it, he was filled with resentment that his old neighbor should be constantly meddling with what did not concern him. Yet he read the tract, and was forced secretly to admit the truth it contained, and the inference it drew. This conviction only made him more angry with the old gentleman; and meeting him that afternoon, he went so far as to tell him that his grey hairs alone saved him from the chastisement his impudence deserved.

That night, as usual, he gathered his family together for evening prayers. While he was praying, that ox seemed to stand directly by his side. He retired to rest, but sleep departed from his eyes. Once he arose and went away by himself to pray, but there too stood the furious ox close by his side, while a long row of decanters appeared in front. He turned round with his face the other way, but still there was the ox, and there were the decanters as before, plain as noonday. The next day the ox accompanied him wherever he went. Retiring early that night, he determined to sleep it off. But there the ox stood, close by his bed, rather more fierce and desperate than before. He slept not a moment all night. Next day he determined to drive off these strange misgivings; and proceeding to the city, purchased fifty dollars' worth of choice liquors, decanters, etc., resolved to enlarge his business and overcome his fears. But he was more miserable that night than ever before. The ox still haunted him, and a voice seemed to ring in his ear, "TAKE CARE OF THAT OX." He passed several restless nights and gloomy days. At last he could endure the ox no longer. One morning just before day, having spent a horrible night, he made a solemn promise that, if he lived till morning, he would wind up his iniquitous business.

As soon as it was light enough, he began to pour

the contents of his decanters back into the barrels. This being completed, he rolled the barrels down into the road, and began to knock in the heads with an axe. His family were dreadfully alarmed, and fearing he was insane, dared not approach him. At length one of his hired men, having more courage than the others, cautiously approached and inquired what he was doing. As soon as the family were convinced of his sanity, they assisted him in his work of destruction, and in an hour his choice wine, brandy, sherry, gin, and whiskey were all running in the gutter. The bar was torn down, and though his customers nearly all forsook him, his conscience was at rest, and he saw the ferocious ox no more. P. B. D.

AN EXCITING SCENE.

A great "experience meeting" was to be held one evening in —— church, where the speakers were, as usual, to be reformed drunkards. An estimable woman, whom I will call Alice, was induced to attend. When the meeting was somewhat advanced, a late member of Congress arose, with apparent sadness and hesitation:

"Though I had consented, at your urgent solicitation, to address this assembly to-night," he said, "yet I have felt so great a reluctance to doing so, that it has been with the utmost difficulty I could drag myself forward. As to relating my experience, that I do not think I can venture upon. The past I dare not recall. I could wish that the memory of ten years of my life were blotted out." He paused a moment, much affected, and then added in a firmer voice, "Something must be said of my own case, or I shall fail to make the impression on your minds that I wish to produce.

"Your speaker once stood among the respected members of the bar. Nay, more than that, he occupied a seat in Congress for two congressional periods. And more than that," he continued, his voice sinking into a tone expressive of deep emotion, "he once had a tenderly loved wife and two sweet children. But all these honors, all these blessings, have departed from him. He was unworthy to retain them; his constituents threw him off because he had debased himself and disgraced them. And more than all, she who had loved him devotedly, the mother of his two babes, was forced to abandon him, and seek an asylum in her father's house. And why? Could I become so changed in a few short years? What power was there so to debase me that my fellow-beings spurned, and even the wife of my bosom turned away, heart-stricken, from me? Alas, my friends, it was a mad indulgence in intoxicating drinks. But for this, I were an honorable and useful representative in the halls of legislation, and blessed with a home, and with wife and children.

"But I have not told you all. After my wife separated from me, I sank rapidly. A state of sobriety brought too many terrible thoughts; I drank more deeply, and was rarely, if ever, free from the bewildering effects of partial intoxication. At last, I became so abandoned that my wife, urged by her friends no doubt, filed an application for a divorce, and as cause could be readily shown why it should be grant-

ed, a separation was legally declared ; and to complete my disgrace, at the congressional canvass I was left off the ticket, as unfit to represent the district.

"When I heard of this new movement, the great temperance cause, at first I sneered, then wondered, listened at last, and finally threw myself upon the great wave that was rolling onward, in hope of being carried by it far out of the reach of danger. I did not hope with a vain hope. It did for me all and more than I could have desired. It set me once more upon my feet, once more made a man of me. A year of sobriety, earnest devotion to my profession, and fervent prayer to Him who alone gives strength in every good resolution, has restored to me much that I have lost; but not all, not the richest treasure that I have proved myself unworthy to retain—not my wife and children. Between myself and these the law has laid its stern impassable interdictions. I have no longer a wife, no longer children, though my heart goes towards these dearly beloved ones with the tenderest yearnings. Pictures of our early days of wedded love are ever lingering in my imagination. I dream of the sweet fireside circle; I see ever before me the placid face of my Alice, as her eyes looked into my own with intelligent confidence; the music of her voice is ever sounding in my ears."

Here the speaker's emotion overcame him; his utterance became choked, and he stood silent, with bowed head and trembling limbs. The dense mass of people were hushed into an oppressive stillness, that was broken here and there by half-stifled sobs.

At this moment there was a movement in the crowd. A single female figure, before whom every one appeared instinctively to give way, was seen passing up the aisle. This was not observed by the speaker until she had come nearly in front of the platform on which he stood. Then the movement caught his ear, and his eyes that instant fell on Alice, who, by the kindness of those near her, was conducted to his side. The whole audience, thrilled with the scene, were upon their feet, and bending forward, when the speaker extended his arms, and Alice threw herself upon his bosom.

An aged minister then came forward, and gently separated them. "No, no," said the reformed congressman, "you cannot take her away from me."

"Heaven forbid that I should," replied the minister; "but by your own confession she is not your wife."

"No, she is not," returned the speaker mournfully.

"But is ready to take her vows again," modestly said Alice, in a low tone, smiling through her tears.

Before that large assembly, all standing, and with few dry eyes, the marriage ceremony was again performed, that gave the speaker and Alice to each other. As the minister, an aged man with thin white locks, completed the marriage rite, he laid his hands upon the heads of the two he had joined in holy bonds, and lifting up his streaming eyes, said, in a solemn voice, "What God has joined together, let not RUM put asunder." "Amen" was cried by the whole assembly, as with a single voice. J. S. B.

THE PERIL AND THE VOW.

On a pleasant summer day two young men were off the coast of Cape Cod in a small boat, fishing. Interested in their pastime, they did not see the rising cloud, nor heed the white crests increasing around them, till a wild wave, dashing against their frail bark, aroused them to their danger. It was too late to gain the shore, and driven before the gale, that blew off the land, they were at the mercy of the billows. It was a fearful hour for the youth, who had neglected their souls, and were unprepared to leave the stormy sea for eternity's ocean.

It was proposed by one, that they promise God, if spared to reach the coast, to serve him the remainder of life. His companion refused to make a vow, but felt that he had too long perilled his soul. The distressed young man who desired the mutual pledge, kneeled on the bottom of the boat, and promised the Lord, if he would save him from the waves he would live for his glory.

God protected that tossing skiff, till, outriding the surges and the storm, it was laid upon a beach many miles from its pleasant moorings a few hours before.

The rescued youth hastened to the embrace of friends. But the heart upon which the vows of God rested, after a brief performance of religious duties, returned to old habits of sin with a lawless indulgence, as if to recover the time lost in the transient regard to religion.

The companion became thoughtful, attended all the means of grace, and sought earnestly the salvation of his soul. He was soon a devout, believing disciple, and continued to honor Christ.

In these two experiences we have a suggestive exhibition of the human heart, and God's saving grace. The terrified sinner who was in haste to conciliate God with a vow of repentance, like thousands on a dying bed, who mistake the remorse and promises of the dire emergency for a work of salvation, went again to his sins. His friend was truly *awakened* by the Holy Spirit, and feeling *his guilt*, sought with his whole heart the pardoning mercy of God.

What an eventful scene was that upon the deep! What a widely different thing, is a promise extorted by danger, and a sense of vileness in the sight of a holy God.

And if that reckless covenant-breaker perish, how

will he, amid the howlings of an eternal storm, remember the billows of the angry sea, and amid the shoreless waves of despair, exclaim with anguish, "Thy vows are upon me, O God." P. C. H.

CLAIMS OF OUR COUNTRY.

A few years since, a gentleman in Kentucky gave the following account of scenes which he witnessed among the mountains of that state.

"After spending a few weeks in B—— and M—— counties, I went into the mountains. It is enough to make one's heart sick to see the moral condition of those mountain counties. There are probably some fifteen or twenty adjoining counties without an educated minister of any denomination, and whiskey drinking with all its accompaniments seems to be the order of the day. In B—— they have the only meeting-house I saw for some sixty miles. I found two ladies in B—— who seemed to feel deeply for the desolations of Zion; one of them had tried to sustain a Sabbath-school. She could get forty children to attend, but could prevail upon no one to act as teacher. I believe it to be a very promising missionary field. If a few devoted young men could be found, of the right stamp, who would be willing to spend their lives for the benefit of those poor mountaineers, they would be richly rewarded for it in the moral and religious improvement which, under God, they might effect.

"An aged man told me that in his neighborhood they had preaching but once a month, and but few good books. 'In the part of the country where I was brought up,' said he, 'they supplied the people with Bibles, but they do not do it here.' I asked him if the families were not generally supplied with a Bible: his answer was, '*Not half of them.*' Learning from him that most of his neighbors could read, I asked him if he thought they would read good books. He said, 'Yes.' I then gave him twelve volumes of our best practical works, and thus I have established a circulating library in that destitute neighborhood. May the Lord use them as instruments in his hands of the conversion of many souls.

"At every turn one beholds marks of moral degradation, and darkness that may almost be felt. When I think of their condition, my heart sinks within me, and I am ready to exclaim, How long, O Lord, how long ere thou wilt make this wilderness to bud and blossom as the rose, and these high places of wickedness to become vocal with the praises of our God?

"Oh that I had the voice of an angel, that I might proclaim, upon every mountain and from every valley, a crucified Saviour, and tell the story of the cross to those who sit in darkness and in the region of the shadow of death. But I feel that I may have my wish more than realized: I may speak to them through the voices of hundreds who have long since gone to join the *angelic host*, who speak in accents of heavenly wisdom and power from on high. In all these fifteen or twenty counties, we have not one colporteur to scatter the leaves of the tree of life. O can you not send us some two or three devoted, self-denying men, who will be willing to live upon the coarsest fare, and labor year after year for these perishing souls?

The books circulated must be almost wholly granted, and every family should be visited at least as often as once a year, and I firmly believe this field might produce a most abundant harvest. On my journey out and back I scattered about ten dollars' worth of books and tracts, mostly by gift; but all I can do for them at present is to recommend them to the notice and sympathies of our Christian friends, and offer up my most fervent prayers to the Lord of the harvest, that he will send forth laborers into his vineyard; for the harvest truly is great, but the laborers are few.

"I have if possible a more necessitous field to cultivate, and Oh who is equal to the responsible task of enlightening and guiding the deluded votaries of the man of sin, and leading them out of the labyrinths of error and superstition in which they have been enveloped by an infidel and designing priesthood?"

RELIGION IN THE CHURCH.

AN IMPRESSIVE SERMON.

NEARLY half a century ago, when I was a small boy, I lived in the neighborhood of the Staffordshire coal-mines in England. One morning considerable excitement was created by a statement, that on the preceding night a man wandering among the old worn-out coal-pits was lost; and being unable to grope his way longer in the dark, he stood still and cried at the top of his voice, "*Lost! lost! lost!*" At length a poor man, a collier, was awoke out of sleep by the sound, and rising from his bed, proceeded with a lantern to the spot, where he found the lost man standing on the very edge of a deep precipice. Had he, instead of standing still and crying out as he did, taken another step, he would have fallen in, and probably been dashed to pieces. Much public interest was felt in this great deliverance.

It was at that time my privilege to attend the ministry of a venerable servant of Jesus Christ, who displayed surprising ingenuity in the selection of subjects for his sermons; and if any thing remarkable occurred during the week, it would be generally used on the following Sabbath by way of instruction or admonition. On the morning of the Lord's day after the occurrence at the coal-pits, instead of putting on his spectacles to read his text, as usual, he laid them beside his open Bible, looked with intense interest over the whole church, and as the tears streamed down his cheeks, exclaimed in tones which even now seem to ring in my ears, "*Lost!* LOST! LOST! Yes, my dear hearers, this is your condition—*lost!*" Then did he go on to illustrate the depravity and folly of man in departing from God, forsaking the narrow path of righteousness and duty, and wandering among the bogs and pits of a corrupted world, in search of enjoyment—ever disappointed, and yet eagerly pursuing what had always eluded the grasp of man. Clearly did he show the danger of sinners thus straying from heaven, and in millions of cases falling into eternal perdition before they were aware of their real state; and in contrast, the safety of the man who becomes acquainted with his real character and prospects, and cries out in self-despair, "Lost! lost!" "Happy, happy man!" exclaimed he; "God is appearing for your deliverance."

Then with solemn dignity, as he put on his spectacles, he said, "Brethren, I bring to you a glorious message from heaven; will you hear it? 'The Son of man is come to save that which was lost.'" Matt. 18:11. He showed this message of mercy to be adapted to the circumstances of sinners lost to all right feeling and happiness, to the divine glory and usefulness among men, to heaven and to God. While he presented with graphic power the transgressor against God standing on the very brink of the bottomless abyss, we seemed to hear the voice of infinite mercy saying to divine justice, "Deliver him from going down to the pit; I have found a ransom." The infinite dignity of the Son of Jehovah, his boundless love in becoming incarnate to die in the stead of the sinner, and the inconceivable and eternal blessings he bestows on the returning penitent, were beautifully presented to our view. Nor with less clearness did he prove the ability and willingness of Christ to save sinners; showing the price, even that of his own blood, paid for their redemption, and the fact that he is still engaged in the heavenly world in interceding "for the transgressors." Every one seemed to feel that Jesus is still able and willing to save the vilest sinners; but that if his salvation be rejected, there remains no hope for the rebel—*no hope!* J. B.

A USEFUL SERMON.

In the summer of ——, a church in one of our Atlantic cities was in a very languid condition. The attendance on public worship was large; but meetings for social devotion were thinly attended, and the services were heavy and spiritless. The little life of the church seemed to be concentrated in a few who continued to walk by faith, though nearly dispirited, while the great majority were cold and worldly. The pastor had for months been oppressed at heart by the unpromising state of things, and at times had felt that he must retire from a field where severe labor had been productive of so little fruit.

After earnest prayer for divine direction, he called together six of the more prayerful and active brethren, stated to them his feelings, and proposed that they should hold weekly a private meeting for conference and prayer, with special reference to a revival of piety in the church. The proposition was cordially received, and the whole seven, upon their knees, gave themselves to the work. It was then agreed to invite two more to join them at the next meeting. They came; and two were added at every successive meeting. In this way the number slowly increased through a period of four months. The meetings were held in private dwellings; few, except those personally invited, knew of their existence. The pastor was encouraged, especially as he found the weekly prayer-meeting more fully attended, and better sustained in its devotional services. Towards the close of the year, those private meetings were marked with a peculiar tenderness and the spirit of wrestling prayer.

On Saturday morning, December 30, the pastor rose at a very early hour, and commenced the preparation of a discourse for Sabbath evening, from the words, "Boast not thyself of to-morrow, for thou knowest not what a day may bring forth." As it was to be the last day of the year, he wished to make a solemn appeal to the unconverted upon the danger of presuming on the future. Scarcely had he written the introduction, when he was called to visit an estimable young man, a friend of his earlier years, who was regarded as near his end. It was not yet daylight; but he hastened to the chamber of the sufferer, and passed two hours with him, endeavoring to direct his attention to the Saviour whom he specially needed. There he heard from the lips of the dying words of apparent contrition and agonizing desire, which made upon his mind an ineffaceable impression. He returned to his sermon with a practical commentary upon his text which was better than any reasoning of his own. As yet, however, he knew not the purpose of God in thus burdening his mind with a painful fact. In a few hours, he learned that the young man was dead.

The next morning, he preached from the words of Christ to the cured lunatic, "Go home to thy friends, and tell them how great things the Lord hath done for thee;" showing the obligation of the Christian to labor for the spiritual good of his kindred. After service, he was summoned to a scene of unutterable sorrow. A young lady of his congregation, without any apparent cause, had terminated her own life. How dreadful was that place! There was anguish indeed. His burden before was nearly insupportable. There his heart was crushed. What did God mean by this?

In the evening, with such emotions as he had never previously known, he preached the sermon prepared under a mountain pressure. The house was densely filled; an unusual solemnity pervaded the congregation, but it was not known that in all the crowd there was a single anxious inquirer. The discourse was one of the simplest in both method and style, but somehow it secured unwonted attention. While the preacher was describing and illustrating the uncertainty of life, a lady, overcome by the strength of her emotions, was borne insensible from the house. A silence, unbroken by an audible breath, reigned, and paleness came over many a face. At the close of the service, a minister present said to the pastor, "You will hear from that sermon."

The next day, the first Monday in the year, the church, according to its custom, met for special prayer. The lecture-room was filled; there was a general melting down before God; prayer was offered with many tears. In the evening, more came than could find admittance. It was then evident that the Holy Spirit was acting with power upon the minds of the unconverted. Meetings were multiplied, and constantly thronged. There was excitement, but it was deep, still, and effective. Every sermon, every exhortation seemed to have unusual power, and do unwonted execution. The revival spread to other congregations, and large accessions were made to the churches. The number added to that one church during the year, by profession, was one hundred and seventy-seven, and in five years from the commencement of the revival, five hundred and two.

The pastor did hear from that sermon, and often to his amazement. He had the pleasure of welcoming into the church more than *one hundred* who referred to that discourse as the means of their awakening and conversion. Several others, who professed their faith elsewhere, made the same reference. The hand of God was perceptible in the whole matter. To him belongs the glory. S.

THE YOUNG PASTOR'S TEMPTATION.

Many years ago, in the commencement of his ministry, a young pastor entered his pulpit with more than usual trembling. He had endeavored carefully and prayerfully to prepare himself for the solemn services; he had selected his text from one of the most interesting portions of the evangelical prophet, in which the *richness* and the *freeness* of the provisions of the gospel are foretold, in the glowing language of him "whose hallowed lips were touched with fire." The herald of mercy anticipated for his own soul "a feast of fat things," and a joyful season in preaching Christ, the bread of life, to his perishing fellow-sinners.

It was a beautiful morning in midsummer; the grove in which the temple of God was situated, was melodious with the songs of birds, which dwelt in safety there; the zephyrs that played through the courts of the Lord, came perfumed with the fragrance of meadow and field; the hush and quietness of the Sabbath morn were over all; nature itself seemed subdued, and a holy awe and calm serenity to impress every pious heart.

A large and solemn congregation waited upon the ministry of the youthful pastor. The service commenced, and with the anthems of praise and the offered prayer his confidence increased, his fears subsided, and with calm assurance he rose and announced his text: "When the poor and needy seek water, and there is none, and their tongue faileth for thirst, I the Lord will hear them, I the God of Israel will not forsake them. I will open rivers in high places, and fountains in the midst of the valleys: I will make the wilderness a pool of water, and the dry land springs of water." Isa. 41 : 17, 18. On reading these words, he cast his eyes over the congregation, when in a distant part of the house he noticed the intelligent countenance of a gentleman from the city of B——n, whose position in society and cultivated mind he knew were such as would qualify him to notice and appreciate the deficiencies of the speaker.

Impressed with this thought, Satan, always ready

for our halting, took advantage of his weakness, and "the fear of man," which "bringeth a snare," took possession of his mind. He commenced his sermon with hesitancy, and although he used every effort to overcome his embarrassment, it was some time before he could rise superior to the depressing influence of fear. It was a barren season. Dissatisfied with himself as he came down from the pulpit, he felt ashamed to look his brethren in the face as they clustered around him, lest he should discover in their looks the failure of his sermon. He was tempted to make a resolution never to attempt to preach again, but from this temptation he was mercifully delivered. The solemn duties of his office pressed upon him, and through grace he was led more humbly to preach the gospel, "not with excellency of speech," nor "with enticing words of man's wisdom, but in demonstration of the Spirit and of power:" his desire now was, not to please man, but "by manifestation of the truth, to commend himself to every man's conscience in the sight of God."

It was not many weeks before God was pleased to pour out his Holy Spirit upon the church and congregation; believers were quickened, their graces were revived, and sinners were converted. A revival was enjoyed which extended to several of the neighboring churches, and in the course of a few months it was the privilege of the young pastor to welcome fifty-eight precious souls to the communion of the church. Among the first converts received was Mrs. T——, the mother of several children; in giving the relation of the dealings of God with her, she stated in substance as follows:

"I was not accustomed to attend the house of God, but on a certain Sabbath last summer, I was induced to come to this place, hoping to meet a friend that I greatly desired to see. I had no wish nor expectation to be profited by the religious services, but as soon as I entered the house I felt that God was in the place; and when the pastor named the text, 'When the poor and needy seek water,' etc., my attention was arrested by those beautiful words; and as the minister proceeded in his discourse, my interest increased, for I felt that every word was addressed to me, and that the speaker knew and was describing my case: I became very uneasy; my sins began to rise as thick clouds before me, and to weigh heavily on my soul; I saw I was in a perishing condition. Oh, what will become of my poor soul? was now my earnest cry. With downcast eyes and a heavy heart I returned to my home, but not to enjoy comfort and peace: with tears and cries, for weeks I sought the mercy of God. I was almost in despair, till at length I was enabled to exercise faith and to look to Calvary, and to yield myself to Him who died for our sins, and rose again for our justification. Then did I find that when the poor and needy truly seek water, and turn away from the broken cisterns of this world, the gracious Lord will hear their cry, and 'open to them rivers in high places, and fountains in the midst of the valleys;' for to my thirsting soul the river of life has come, and with joy have I drawn water from the wells of salvation. I praise God for having led my feet to the house of God on that blessed day, when so precious a sermon was preached, which proved to be a word in season, and the power of God to my salvation."

Then did the minister bow his head and weep, while he lifted his heart to God in prayer that he might never distrust him again, but that "his strength might be made perfect in weakness," and that ever after he might preach the gospel with an eye single to God's glory.

"Sow in the morn thy seed;
At eve hold not thy hand;
To doubt and fear give thou no heed,
Broadcast it o'er the land.

Thou canst not toil in vain;
Cold, heat, and moist, and dry,
Shall foster and mature the grain
For garners in the sky." Davies.

NEAR THE CROSS.

A venerated father says, "I once entered a colored congregation of four or five hundred, whom one of their own number was fervently addressing. He paused, that I might take his place; but beckoning him to proceed, he went on nearly in the following words:

"'Well, my Christian friends, I was a-goin' to say, you all know, that so long as de little chicken keeps near its mother, it finds something to eat; but when he tink he know better, and stray away from his mother, he not only find nothing to eat, but de *hawk* do come and pick him up. Just so it is with us, my dear friends; so long as we keep near de foot of de cross of our Lord Jesus Christ, so long we are safe, and we do find spiritual nourishment for our souls; but when we tink we know better, and we stray away, not only we do find no spiritual food for our souls, but *Satan* do come and pick us up.'

"Thus the speaker continued to occupy the attention of his audience, in a strain of natural eloquence well suited to their comprehension. For myself, I was so truly surprised, delighted, and edified, that fearing to detract from the good effect already so evidently produced, it was with extreme reluctance that I assented to follow, even in a few words, a discourse so truly admirable."

A pastor states that he was once placed in very similar circumstances. "I did not hear the text," he says, "but I soon found that the preacher's subject was the sickness and prayer of Hezekiah: 'And Hezekiah turned his face towards the wall, and prayed unto the Lord.' 'And why towards the wall, my Christian friends? First, perhaps it was to turn away from wife, children, and friends, so as to be more alone with God; or, secondly, perhaps the windows of the king's apartment looked towards mount Zion, and like Daniel in captivity praying towards Jerusalem, so now did Hezekiah turn towards that holy temple, where the bleeding lamb and smoking sacrifice spoke to him of a Saviour yet to come, an atonement yet to be made for his sins and the sins of the world.'

"From this, the preacher went on, in a most interesting and simple manner, to touch upon the great truths of the New Testament, as shadowed forth by the whole ceremonial law, and revealed more clearly in the prophets. Evidently taught by the Spirit, this man, despised no doubt by many of the great of this world, had, in the diligent study of his Bible, found that 'to Jesus Christ give all the prophets witness' that he alone is the Alpha and Omega of the inspired word, its beginning and its ending."

It struck me, that these fragments of the discourses of these humble preachers were most appropriate to our times; for what numbers do we see who, leaving the simple story of "Jesus Christ and him crucified," seek out for themselves many inventions, philosophies falsely so called, spirit-rappings, mysticisms, and transcendentalisms. Broken cisterns, miserable comforters are these all.

Again, how many, wise in their own eyes, neglect the Bible as the inspired word of God; and groping thus, blind leaders of the blind, fail to discover its highest glory, its sublime unity—Christ and his salvation being the glorious connecting link, reconciling every part, and filling the whole with life and light and peace.

H.

THE MISSION OF A TEAR.

Maternal affection and confidence in God prompted the mother of Moses to hide him by the river's brink. The providence of God directed the daughter of the king to select the proper time and place to perform her ablutions, that she might become the protectress of the helpless infant. When the ark of bulrushes was discovered and brought to the princess, and she had opened it, "she saw the child, and behold, the babe wept." The tears and plaintive cry of the child excited compassion in the bosom of the high-born maiden, and she became the foster-mother of the future deliverer and lawgiver of God's chosen people. Upon what a slight incident, to human view, did the destiny of Moses turn. Who can calculate the influence of the tears of that child upon the world, in all time and throughout eternity?

A faithful and devoted teacher had a large class of young ladies committed to her care, in the Sabbath-school connected with one of the churches in the city of Philadelphia. For a long time, Sabbath after Sabbath, she earnestly labored with them, seeking to instil into their minds the saving truths of God's word. The class were, for the most part, respectful and attentive, and evidently much attached to their teacher; but her instructions and her earnest entreaties seemed to make no lasting impression on their minds. They were thoughtless, inconsiderate young people, in love with the pleasures of the world, and charmed with the scenes of gayety by which they were surrounded. As they advanced in years, they manifested less interest in the exercises of the class, and were at times disposed to turn away from the warm and affectionate pleadings of their faithful friend and teacher.

By degrees her heart became discouraged; she felt that her labors were in vain, and that perhaps the instructions of some other person might be more appreciated by the class, and result in their conversion to God. On one occasion, when the class had been more inattentive than usual to the instruction imparted, Miss S—— resolved that at the close of the session, she would give up her class-book to the superintendent, and request him to appoint another teacher in her place. As she came to this conclusion, sorrow filled her heart, and tears dimmed her eyes: it was no small sacrifice she was about to make; she loved her class, the affections of her heart were entwined around her pupils, and the thought that these ties must now be sundered, filled her with distress.

As was her usual practice, she addressed a few words to each one of the young ladies before dismissing them. She had nearly gone through the class, when, as she was speaking to one on the duty to yield her heart to God, and no longer resist the invitations of the gospel, she saw with gratitude and joy the quivering lip, and a tear glistening in the eye. The influence of that tear was electrical; hope at once sprang up in the heart of the desponding teacher, and silently her heart was lifted to God in prayer that he would deepen the impression which had been made. The exercises closed with a deeper seriousness upon the minds of all, than had ever been noticed before; and nothing was said about resigning the class.

When next they came together, it was evident that the Spirit of God was moving on the hearts of several of the members of that class, and the teacher labored with new zeal, animated by the remembrance of the tear she had seen in the eye of her pupil.

In a few weeks, she in whose eye the pearl-drop shone, stood before the church to give a reason of the hope she cherished that she was a child of God. She began her relation by referring to the impressions made upon her mind on that Sabbath, when her beloved teacher addressed her so tenderly and solemnly on the duty of serving God. It proved to be a "word in season." Led by the Spirit of God, she earnestly sought the pardon of her sins through the atoning sacrifice of the Crucified, and God, in his rich mercy, had spoken peace to her troubled soul, and filled her with joy unspeakable.

The conversion of this dear young lady, and her consecration to God in baptism, were the means of the awakening of many others, and the commencement of a gracious work in the church; and in the course of a few months, thirteen of that Bible-class were hopefully converted and added to the church, several of whom became faithful and devoted Sabbath-school teachers.

It was a scene that angels beheld with joy, when these happy converts clustered around their teacher, and related how deeply they felt what she had said to them on that ever-memorable Sabbath; and the teacher told them how discouraged she had been, that she had meditated giving up the class, and was only prevented from doing so by the tear which sparkled in the eye of one of them. And now, what has God wrought! How blessed was the mission of that tear, how mighty its influence; who can comprehend its results?

Laborers for Christ, "be not weary in well-doing; for in due season ye shall reap, if ye faint not."

"Let those who sow in sadness, wait
Till the fair harvest come;
They shall confess their sheaves are great,
And shout the blessings home." Davies.

"YE MUST BE BORN AGAIN"

Solemnly pondering what and how to preach the next Sabbath to the precious souls recently taken under my charge, my hostess, the good wife of the deacon, ventured into my study, saying, "Mrs. C—— has come up, this morning, to inquire about the new birth. I have talked with her as well as I knew how, and now wish you would." What a message! the first of the kind I had ever received; and deep awe came over my spirit at the vast responsibility thus devolving upon me. My own heart had called for anxious searching whether I had known what it was to be born again; but I must now instruct and counsel another as to this wonderful work of the Spirit in the human soul.

Oppressed with the scantiness of my knowledge and experience for this great duty, I approached the inquirer, after serious thought respecting her immortal interests. I learned from her that God and Christ appeared to her as they never had before, so glorious were they, so worthy of her love; and that objects around her wore a new aspect, reflecting the glory of their Creator, while a sweet serenity and peace settled upon her spirit. "And now, sir, what does this mean; and what am I to think of myself?" was her inquiry. My business was to instruct, not to decide whether she was now a subject of regeneration, but to guide her by the light of revealed truth, that with her Bible and prayer she might learn, under the Holy Spirit's teaching, whether she had true submission to God, repentance, and faith in the Saviour. Following on to know the Lord, she gained fuller views of divine truth, with the comfort of humble hope, professed her faith, and exemplified the Christian character.

Who and what brought that woman to me that

morning to be taught? Ere she left her threshold, God had already taught her what infinitely surpassed my power to impart. His "still small voice" had spoken in her heart; a glimpse of his moral beauty had shone upon her soul, and she was filled with surprise and wonder. "The wind bloweth where it listeth." How few mothers on that morning left the care of a large family, to ask their pastor why God appeared so glorious. He gave her her errand, and in teaching her, taught me how great was my work; and he summoned me forthwith to visit my people, and diligently feed the flock committed to my charge. I found that, to encourage me, in faintness, weakness, and fear, the Lord had gone before me. A blessed work of the Spirit ensued, the subjects of which, every one, as once said the father of Samuel J. Mills, "will remember it *long after the judgment-day*." J. L.

"I AM LIKE THAT LEAF."

In the village of H——, a laborious pastor was standing in his place on a beautiful Sabbath of October, and with aching heart was delivering his message to a people that *seemed* indifferent to all his utterances. Behind the pulpit was a window, through which could be seen a tree whose foliage had been changed by autumnal frost. A young man in a remote pew, while gazing listlessly in the direction of the pulpit, saw a leaf separate from a twig of the tree, and with slow vibrations descend to the ground. Instantly, he said, as if the leaf had a tongue and spoke to him, the reflection arose, "*I am like that leaf.* My hold on life is just so slender. I may soon be detached and fall like that sere leaf. Then where shall I be?" One consideration started another, and thought piled on thought, until his mind was stirred to its lowest depths, and he was in an agony of solicitude respecting his prospects for eternity. God's still small voice in the leaf spoke louder to him than thunder.

But this case stood not alone in that Sabbath assembly. Christ had his eye and his heart upon another precious soul of that company to whom the anxious pastor thought he was preaching with little effect. There was another preacher and another sermon there, in a form which the minister knew not of. At the close of the service, while the choir was singing,

"Almighty God, thy grace impart,
Fix deep conviction in each heart,"

another young man, who was looking up at the singers, observed that a pious lady, as she sung those lines, unaffectedly raised her eyes heavenward, as if uttering an earnest prayer. "Perhaps she is praying for me," was instantly his reflection, "and yet I have never prayed for myself. Wretch that I am, to live so prayerless and mindless of God and the future. What can I expect from the hand of a righteous God but everlasting destruction?"

The train of thought thus started by God's sermon in the leaf, was pursued under the direction of God's Spirit in the heart, and he too that very morning became intensely anxious to know what he should do to be saved.

In the evening, both of these young men were found at the prayer-meeting, and there they expressed a desire to be prayed for, and to be guided into the way of life. The effect of such a development upon the meeting was electric. The pastor himself and most of his church were taken by surprise. The impenitent were startled and awed. It was a time of confessions, tears, and prevailing prayers. A revival of great power ensued, and the fruits thereof were eminently gracious.

Though God thus manifested his own sovereignty in these instances, by so choosing means as, in the words of Elihu to Job, to hide pride from man, and that no flesh should glory in his presence, he so exercised that sovereignty as to honor his own appointment that he will be inquired of by the house of Israel to do these things for them. It subsequently became known that a few members of the church had quietly met for some time on Saturday evenings, in a private house, to implore the influence of the reviving Spirit. The young men, too, were in God's place for improvement, the sanctuary. God, we have seen, heard and answered, but in his own way, and blessed were the results.

How seldom, perhaps never, does a revival occur, where earnest prayer in one portion of the church or another, in one family or another, is not the necessary antecedent. And how seldom does a revival commence just in the line of human expectations. The sovereignty of God, while it is a sovereignty of grace, is always exerted in his own divine order in answer to prayer. And the practical lesson to be learned by Christians is, to give ourselves more and more unto prayer, and to be willing that God should answer as he sees best. "Trust in him at all times, ye people;

pour out your heart before him." "Lo, all these things worketh God oftentimes with man, to bring back his soul from the pit." The fall of a leaf, the upward lifting of an earnest eye, the twitter even of a bird, may be used by the Spirit of God to bring back a soul to himself, when prayer is made for that soul with fervor and faith. Then the reflection, "*I am like that leaf*," may be the soul's first step in its return to God. H. T. C.

"HE WAS BESIDE HIMSELF."

God had graciously visited the village of H——, in New Jersey, with a refreshing from on high, and the whole community were more or less influenced. Religion was the theme of conversation in every circle; groups of men gathered at the corners of the streets and in the places of business, and talked of the presence of the Spirit of God. Many found a "place to pray" who had been unaccustomed to bend the knee, and many a dwelling became a "house of prayer," from whose altars the incense of praise daily ascended. The social meetings were thronged, and the voice of mourning blended with the songs of the converts happy in their new-born hopes. Every hour brought intelligence of new cases of awakening, and of fresh accessions to the ranks of those professing to have found Jesus precious to their souls. It was truly a pentecostal season, and the Lord added daily to his church. Zion's cords in that beautiful village were lengthened, and her stakes strengthened.

As might be supposed, the revival with its wonderful scenes, and the surprising changes which were wrought, occasioned great talk and excitement in the surrounding country and neighboring villages. Some thought the people in H—— were all "beside themselves," and that it would be an act of kindness on the part of their more rational neighbors to step in and interpose their argument and authority to bring them back to a right mind. Of this way of thinking was I. M. E——, an inhabitant of a village six miles distant. He had at one time resided in H——, the scene of this "wildfire excitement," as it was called, and he had many particular friends who were among the number of the "deluded ones." Moved with compassion for their miserable condition, he determined to make one effort to save them from ruin, and for this purpose he hastened to the village to reason with them on the folly of their conduct.

He could not ask a more cordial welcome than his friends gave him, and before he could introduce the purpose of his visit, he was affectionately addressed upon the subject of religion, and tenderly and earnestly entreated to become a Christian, and yield his heart to God. He was taken by surprise, and in vain sought to turn the conversation to other subjects, or to defend himself. He could say nothing—he could neither command words nor arguments. A guilty conscience condemned him. He turned away, and sought one and another of his former associates; but the same scenes again occurred; all talked to him of Jesus and of the joys of religion, and gave him the same affectionate invitation, "Come thou with us, and we will do thee good."

Excited, he turned away and left them, disappointed in the purpose of his visit: failing to convince his friends of the foolishness of their course, he was self-convicted of the folly of his own; he was vexed with himself and angry with his friends. He reached home in the evening, "being exceedingly mad" against those whom he had visited. At an early hour he retired to his chamber to seek repose, and while every thing around him was still, and he was alone with God, conscience awoke from a profound slumber, and her voice was heard pronouncing fearful woes against the sinner; the Spirit of God came upon the trembling culprit in the might of his power, and as he felt the barbed arrows of conviction in his soul, his eyes were opened to his lost condition. Before him was the pit of despair, and he about to drop into the awful gulf. Overwhelmed with anguish, as he felt himself about to be cast into hell, he began to call upon God, but in tones so loud and so earnest that the neighbors heard him, and were alarmed at his cries of distress. The family, who came running in, were struck with affright when they saw his countenance of despair, and heard his agonizing prayers. In imploring tones he called on them to pray for him; but they had never learned to pray for themselves, and could not now pray for him; they stood pale and trembling as in the very presence of God.

A messenger was dispatched in all haste for some young Christian men, who were urged to come and see Mr. E——, for "he was beside himself," wanting some one to pray for him. Gladly they hastened to his chamber, and found him almost in agony, surrounded by his pale and affrighted, yet prayerless friends. The visitors soon learned from the lips of the awakened sinner what was the true state of the case; he had looked into the prison of despair, and his sins were pressing him down like mountain weights. They prayed for him and with him; they pointed out the way of salvation through the peace-speaking blood of Jesus, directing his mind away from himself to "Christ, and him crucified," and together sung praises at the hour of midnight. Blessed be the name of our merciful God, long before the rising of the sun, the "day-star" of hope arose in the heart of the penitent, and the bright beams of the "morning star" streamed into his soul—the storm was over and gone, and with "anthems of rapture" he was enabled to

"Praise and bless redeeming love."

The next morning, while the report of his being crazy was rapidly spreading, he was, in the happiness of his soul, permitted to tell to all around that he was "not mad," but had "come to himself," and was now in his "right mind, sitting at the feet of Jesus."

Years since, he emigrated to the far West, where he lived an honored and useful member of the church of Christ.

Davies.

THE UNWELCOME SNOW-STORM.

Those who have read Dr. Tyler's memoir of the Rev. Dr. Nettleton, will recollect the wonderful revival of religion which took place in 1820, in Nassau, about nine miles east of Albany, N. Y. To show the sovereignty of divine grace, I state the following facts relative to the origin of that revival.

In February of 1820, the writer, then living at Saratoga Springs, a young man looking forward to the ministry, went to Malta, ten miles from the Springs, to enjoy the further luxury of being with his friend Dr. Nettleton, then engaged in a precious revival in that region.

We spent a happy day at the house of Mr. P——, who had been a Universalist, but was then a humble convert; and while there I was much interested in the serious appearance and conversation of Mrs. C——, an intelligent relative of Mr. P—— from Nassau, though she seemed not to have deep convictions of sin.

This lady appeared to be anxious to converse with Dr. Nettleton upon the subject of her salvation. She had heard him preach several times, but he had not said a word to her. He evidently avoided doing what Mrs. C—— expected and desired him to do. I discovered this, and asked him why he did not talk with the lady. His reply was, "O, she is expecting it so much." That night there was to be a prayer-meeting at the house of Mr. P——, where many of the young converts and many anxious sinners were expected to attend. A little before night Dr. Nettleton proposed to me to ride with him to a Mr. D——'s, about a mile distant. After we had spent a short time with Mr. D—— and his family, Dr. Nettleton said to me, "I shall not return with you to Mr. P——'s to-night. Do you go back and conduct the meeting as well as you can. I give it up to you. Go." It was in vain that I entreated him to return and take charge of the meeting. He positively declined, and I left him with a trembling heart. The people would expect Dr. Nettleton to be there, and how great would be their disappointment. What should I do?

However, just at night the heavens gathered blackness, the wind blew violently, and the result was one of the most furious snow-storms that I ever witnessed. Not a soul came to the meeting. We were all sadly disappointed, though I felt relieved of a great responsibility.

Supper being ended, and finding no one present except the family, I conversed with Mrs. C—— as to her prospects for eternity. I soon found that she was self-righteous, trusting in her daily prayers and her amiable, irreproachable life. I endeavored to show her that her prayers were dead, her heart unrenewed, and her precious soul under the condemnation of God's holy law. The smile which had been playing upon her lips instantly passed away; she raised and fixed her eyes upon me, and sat in silence. New thoughts were passing in her mind. She saw that she was lost. She burst into tears, arose, and went to her room, and did not return for some time.

There was sitting in the room Miss J——, a daughter of Mr. P——, who had passed thus far through the revival without sharing its benefits. I immediately turned to her, and began to talk with her about her soul. She listened very attentively a few minutes, became agitated, burst into tears, and left the room. After a while both of these ladies returned to the sitting-room bathed in tears, and writhing under the deepest convictions. I pointed them to the blessed Redeemer; we prayed with and for them again and again, and in this way we spent a great part of the night—a night never to be forgotten. At length morning came, but no light dawned upon those benighted souls. To them, all seemed as dark as Egypt. We prayed for them, and wept over them; but God alone could relieve them.

Perhaps about eleven o'clock I said to Mrs. C——, "Will not your heart yet yield to God?" Putting her hand to her breast, and fixing her streaming eyes upon me, she exclaimed, "My heart will kill me."

Soon after this, the storm without having passed away, I stepped into a sleigh and rode over to Mr. D——'s to inform Dr. Nettleton of what God was doing. In relating the solemn transactions of the night and the morning, I mentioned to Dr. Nettleton the striking expression of Mrs. C——, "My heart will kill me." Instantly he replied, "That woman is near the kingdom of heaven. I will go back with you."

We returned, and as we entered the house Mrs. C—— and Miss P—— both came rushing from their room with countenances beaming with holy, heavenly joy. The moral storm was over. All was calm. Mrs. C—— ran to Dr. Nettleton, seized his hand, and stood for some moments overwhelmed with emotion. As she stood weeping for joy, Dr. Nettleton asked her, "Have you submitted your heart to God?" Her answer was spontaneous and singular: "O yes, sir—but no thanks to you." Dr. Nettleton was almost convulsed with laughter, which was *very* unusual with him.

That afternoon Mrs. C——, while her heart was almost bursting with joy, wrote a letter to one of her friends in Nassau, which she read to me. That simple letter, giving an account of her own convictions of sin and hopeful conversion, was the means, in God's hands, of awakening several impenitent sinners.

When Mrs. C—— returned to Nassau, she found some deep seriousness, and immediately wrote to Dr. Nettleton, begging him to repair to the place as soon as possible. He went, and the glorious results are well known to all who are acquainted with the life and labors of that extraordinary man.

"Behold how great a matter a little fire kindleth!" How mysterious are the ways of the Almighty. If Dr. Nettleton had returned with the writer to Mr. P——'s on that night, or if that storm had not come, and that house had been filled with people, would those personal conversations have taken place?

N. H.

A GRATEFUL CONVERT.

A new church had been erected in a destitute part of an eastern city, a faithful pastor had commenced his labors, the Spirit of God had descended, and among those brought to Christ was an infidel, from a large circle of friends, over whom he was exerting a deadly influence. Being called to spend some months at the West, he wrote to his pastor in the fulness of his overflowing heart. God grant that such events as are here referred to, may be witnessed in every part of our land.

"I feel," he says, "the same anxiety for the prosperity of our little band, the same prayer for them is daily offered, and they are as often in my thoughts as ever. My hope is now in God, and my heart goes forth to them who worship him. The world grows smaller in my esteem; I find that I love a different object from what I formerly did, and 'my brethren' come in for a good share of that love. I rejoice to hear that others are enlisting under the banner of our Lord. The tidings of additions at the last communion bring tears of gratitude. Is it so, indeed, that our mutual friend ——, who has done so much for our enterprise, has been blessed himself, and that my son C—— also has come out on the Lord's side—that both have entered into a holy covenant to be the Lord's? Truly this is great cause of joy.

"How changed! Ridiculed as was the builder of that house by me, the motives questioned, and vain and foolish declarations as to the whole enterprise coming from my lips; yet in this short space of time the majority of my family, father, mother, and son, are members of that church, and myself rejoicing 'with joy unspeakable,' that God directed my steps there to see that edifice given to his cause. Truly I can say, 'God's ways are not our ways.' He has turned folly, ridicule, and blasphemy into praise for redeeming love. He has enlightened a poor deluded soul to see the pit from whence he was digged, and has turned 'darkness into marvellous light.'

"Well may my old acquaintances reproach me for the change. 'Help me, O Lord my God; O save me according to thy mercy, that they may know that this is thy hand, that thou, Lord, hast done it.' I am still striving to *live* that I may be prepared to *die*. I am still 'a miracle of grace,' and a happy man, as my flowing tears of gratitude testify. Will you say to our little band, that they are remembered, and that my prayer is, that many more may be added to them 'of such as shall be saved.' May we all 'grow in grace, and in the knowledge of our Lord Jesus Christ.'

Ask my brethren to be faithful to their covenant vows; to 'speak often one to another,' and let the world know that they are on the Lord's side, and love each other. Then will the Holy Spirit dwell with us, and we shall prosper." W. A.

SQUIRE D—— AND THE TEACHER.

Travelling in a mountainous region at night-fall of a tempestuous day, and having lost my road, I was directed for a lodging to "Squire D——'s, who keeps the ferry." After supper, I had a pleasant talk with the father of Squire D——, on whose head the snows of eighty winters had fallen, and soon the family were gathered around us, engaged in delightful converse. I had heard of the high-handed wickedness of a neighborhood not far off, with which my host was well acquainted, where, when a young man who had wandered to a city was to be hung for murder, his father and other relatives celebrated the day with a fine supper and a dance: no school could be kept, for the boys had whipped off every teacher who came among them; and meetings were frequently held in mockery of religious worship.

"Yes, yes," said the squire, with just enough of the Welsh accent to betray his origin, "and our neighborhood here was just as bad ten years ago; we were all alike; no church, no preacher, no Sunday-school, no day-school. One evening a minister and a young lady stopped at my house for the night; I thought them very inquisitive people. They asked if we had any preaching. No. Any schools? No; we have had several teachers, but no one will stay more than a quarter with us. The young lady said she would come and take a school among us, if we would employ her. After some further conversation, I told her I would see what could be done and write her the result. Next morning they left for the minister's home at M——, some fifty miles distant.

"In a short time I had a school made up and board engaged for the new teacher, and wrote her to that effect. She came, and commenced her school at the time appointed. But soon there was complaint that the new teacher read the Bible and prayed in her school. And her troubles did not stop here. The man at whose house she boarded insisted that she should leave, because she prayed, sung hymns, and would keep talking about religion all the time. Miss H—— then set out to look up another home for herself; she applied to most of her employers, but met with the same reply from all: 'We cannot receive you, unless you leave off praying and singing.'

"When she applied to me, I objected on the same grounds. Finally, I told her if she would come on my own terms, I would take her into my family. She inquired what those terms were. 'Why,' said I, 'you shall have such a room to yourself; there you are to stay from the time you return from school until you start to go back, only when you come to your meals; you must not sing hymns; you may pray as much as you please, but mind you don't let us hear you at it; and remember, the first time you infringe this contract, you leave the premises. To all this she agreed, with as much meekness as if my terms had been reasonable and right. That evening she took up her abode under my roof; and little did I think what a blessing God was sending me in that frail, delicate girl.

"The children all loved the new teacher very much. So one day she told them to ask their parents' permission, and if they were agreed, she would teach them on Sunday too. This proposal pleased us all. If she taught on Sunday, that was so much clear gain to us. And to school the children went every Sunday with clean clothes and clean faces.

"I soon observed that my children took to staying in the teacher's room much of their time. At length, one Sunday morning, they came down with some tracts; I looked over them, and found they were on the subject of religion. Ah, said I, my lady, I've caught you now. I called her down, told her she had violated her contract, and must be off. The poor girl began to weep; I felt ashamed. 'Dear sir,' said she, 'will you read these tracts? If you do, and still continue in your present mind, I will leave your house immediately.'

"Here was a pretty fix; the children were all crying, and begging me not to send Miss H—— away; and the books, Oh, they could not part with the books. I was mightily perplexed; at last I gave in. Said I, 'Miss H——, you may go back to your room; I will consider the matter.' I shall never forget the smile that passed over her face as she thanked me and went back to her room. Thanked me, indeed! I deserved a sound beating instead of thanks. Well, I set to work, read one of the tracts, felt self-condemned; read it again, felt dreadfully troubled. Then I read them all, and felt that I was a great sinner. I said

nothing more to Miss H—— about leaving my house. Each day my convictions became deeper. At last, I could bear it no longer. Thought I, this wont do; I must talk with Miss H——. So I invited her to come and sit with us in the family room. She cheerfully complied. I asked her a great many questions about the doctrines of the Bible, not meaning to let her know any thing about my concern. But all would not do; my distress continued, or rather my agony, for I thought I was the greatest sinner on earth.

"At last, I sent one evening for Miss H—— to come down, and I told her my troubles; for my proud heart was well-nigh broken. Said I, 'Miss H——, I feel so and so ever since I read those tracts of yours;'

and I related all that was passing in my mind; and said I, 'do you think there is any mercy or hope for such a poor miserable sinner?' The tears began to run down her cheeks; then she laughed; then she caught me by both hands, and looking up into my face, she said, 'Oh, my dear friend, I am *so* glad.' 'Why,' said I, 'are you glad because I am in trouble?' 'Oh, my dear sir,' says she, 'this is the Spirit of God operating on your heart.' All at once a great light seemed to shine into my mind. All that I had been learning for so many weeks seemed now just as plain as A B C. Said I, 'Come, Miss H——, kneel down then, and pray for me;' and she did pray for me, and I do bless God for his wonderful mercy to such a poor hardened sinner. I believe that God did change my heart just while that very prayer was going up. All at once it just came; I loved my Bible and I loved to pray, and I could not bear the company that I used to take so much delight in.

"On the next Sabbath, Miss H—— asked me to go along with her and the children to school—which was, and had been a Sunday-school, though we never suspected it—and here came a trial. If I go, they will say I am getting religious; if I stay, it will be a sin, for I know I *ought* to go; and then it will grieve Miss H——. These last considerations were the strongest; so I went. The room was crowded with children, all waiting for their teacher; I thought they all looked happy. After a little while, Miss H—— took the Bible, and coming to me, she said, 'Mr. D——, will you read and pray with us this morning?' I was startled; my very heart trembled. Said I, 'Oh, no; not now.' Then she read a chapter and prayed herself. Oh, how I felt, to think that I was ashamed to pray before those children! Ah, thought I, this will never do; I will come here and pray next Sunday. That night I read and prayed with my family; and the next Sabbath I opened the school with prayer.

"The news spread soon all through the settlement. D—— has got religion, and is praying in the Sunday-school! D—— going to school on Sunday, and praying! very strange news this. Very soon the people began to drop in to our Sunday-school; every Sunday a regular increase. Then Miss H—— said to me, 'You had better read us a sermon at the Sunday-school, after the other exercises are over.' She selected the sermons, and I read them. Our meetings grew very solemn. Presently we sent word to a good man at B—— to send us a minister; he did so. The minister came and preached for us. The little school-house could not contain one-half the people who crowded to hear him. We held our meetings in the open air, under the trees.

"Ah, that was a wonderful time; the cry of the anxious sinner went up from every hearth-stone and roof-tree. The Spirit of God was moving mightily upon the hearts of the people, and many were born into the kingdom every day. All this brought a great change in our settlement. Instead of the dance, and the gaming-table, and the foolish song, we had meetings for prayer and praise; and the tavern and still-house were exchanged for the temple of God.

"The Sabbath became a day of holy rest among a people who used to spend it in revelry or idleness. Houses of worship were built, where our population flocked every Sabbath to hear the preached word from the living minister; and in the course of two or three years, hundreds professed faith in Christ, and joined the church. We have had a flourishing church here ever since. Ah," said the good man, in his peculiar emphatic way, "see what God hath wrought for us."

How often have I reproached myself, when I contrasted the heroic conduct of this devoted female with my own man-fearing spirit! She has gone to her reward; her memory will be cherished for a few more years in the hearts of those to whom her humble efforts were of such immense value, and then pass away and be forgotten. But her *influence* will pass on, an ever-increasing current, down the long tracts of time, and throughout the endless ages of eternity.

J. C.

"VOYAGE OF THE DUFF"—STRIKING PROVIDENCE.

Who has not heard or read of the ship Duff, and of her missionary voyages, and of her pious and excellent captain, James Wilson? At six in the morning, August 10, 1796, she sailed from London for the Southern Pacific ocean. The missionary flag, three doves bearing olive-branches in their bills, was raised to her masthead, her sails were given to the favoring breezes, and to the music of a hundred voices singing the hymn,

> "Jesus, at thy command we launch into the deep,"

she turned her bow to the billows, to convey the beloved men with whom she was freighted to the pagan islands to which they were destined. These men, Cover, Eyre, Jefferson, and Lewis, with twenty-five others, formed the first company sent out by the London Missionary Society for the recovery of the heathen world to Christ. Amid peculiar trials and many divine interpositions she pursued her voyage: she doubled the stormy cape in safety—she visited Otaheite, the Marquesas, and other islands—she landed her missionaries on the islands selected for the commencement of the work of missions; and after a three years' voyage, whose narrative forms some of the most delightful chapters in the history of modern missions, she returned home to England, to make another at a subsequent period.

The narrative of this voyage was soon published in London, dedicated to the king. It excited extraordinary attention among all classes in England, by the revelations which it made of the awful degradation of the islanders of the Pacific. The book was republished in America, and although there were no tract societies to print it, nor colporteurs to scatter it over the land, it obtained, for that day, a wide circulation.

At that time there was a village rising amid the woods of Western Pennsylvania, composed mainly of Presbyterian emigrants from Scotland and Ireland, a people whose influence in shaping the institutions of our country has been great indeed. In this village there was neither church nor settled pastor, nor stated means of grace. It was occasionally visited by a missionary, whose visits were long anticipated with pleasure, and remembered with gratitude. By some kind providence a copy of the narrative of the voyage of the ship Duff was conveyed to this village. A good new book was then regarded, when there were so few in circulation, as a great acquisition to a family, and even to a village. The volume went from house to house, until it was read by nearly every family in the settlement. In one of these Scotch families was a young boy, on whose mind its perusal made a very deep impression, and who, although not then pious, made the resolve that if ever he should become pious, he would go as a missionary to the heathen.

Soon afterwards this town was visited by a missionary, whose preaching was greatly blessed. A delightful revival accompanied his labors, and some conversions occurred in every family, without an exception, in which the little volume had been read. The young boy to whom I have alluded was among the first subjects of the good work; and faithful to his resolve, he commenced a course of preparation for the work of the ministry, and of a missionary. Circumstances which he could not control, just as he was concluding his studies, gave an entire change to his subsequent life, but without in any degree calling off his mind and affection from the heathen world.

It was to him a day of joy when his first son was born. Remembering the vows which he once made, but which he was prevented from fulfilling, he dedicated that infant son to God, and to the work of missions. That son was hopefully converted in his youth; and when prepared for the work of the ministry, devoted himself to God as a missionary. He went to India, where his feeble health permitted him to remain only a few years; but in those years he laid the foundation of missionary operations in Northern India, which from their commencement have been remarkably successful. Seeking health at a sanatarium among the

Himalayas, he laid a tract upon the table. It was read by an officer and a physician attached to the English army, and was blessed to the conversion of each. How wonderful are the ways of God! These men, unimpressed by Christian ordinances at home—thrown amid circumstances only calculated to wean them from God—abroad, at the very ends of the earth, and at the farthest possible remove from gospel institutions, are brought to embrace the gospel by a Tract! Surely, "there is no restraint to the Lord to save by many, or by few."

This father had a second son born to him, whom, like the first, he consecrated to God and to the work of missions. Early in life he was made a subject of saving grace, and devoted himself to the ministry. The heathen world opened before him; and although endowed with talent and acquisition which would have made him the ornament of any pulpit in our land, he selected down-trodden, perilous Africa as the field of his labors. The fact that so many missionaries found in Africa an early grave, seemed only to strengthen his resolution to go there. And he was induced to yield his preference only by his brethren, who wished him to enter the wide field just then providentially opened in China by the success of the British arms. No more able or promising missionary has the church of God sent to that country. There, for a few years, he labored with untiring zeal, respected and beloved by all with whom he had to do. And when the centre of many high hopes and expectations—when best qualified to discharge his duties—when exerting a wide influence at home and abroad, and in the zealous pursuit of his one great object, the conversion of China to God, the Christian world was called to mourn his death by the hands of cruel pirates. Long will the winds that sweep over the Chinese seas be regarded as singing his requiem. And although his grave is amid the pearls and corals of the ocean, many a voice will be heard rising from it through coming generations calling upon the sons of the church to devote themselves to the salvation of China.

It is not for me to say, nor for man to know, all the influence of that one book in preparing the way for that revival of religion—in preparing the mind of that young man to receive the impress of the Holy Spirit—in inspiring that faith which led the father to consecrate his infant boys to the work of the ministry, and of missions—in laying the foundations of influence in India and China, which will continue increasingly for ever. Yet the narrative teaches us,

1. The real value of a good book. What would be the blessing to the church of the ministry of such men as Baxter, Doddridge, Whitefield, continued in its vigor for a thousand years. And a good book, more eloquently than they, and to far more people, may preach for that number of years twice told! Well may any man exclaim, O for grace and strength to write a good book or tract!

2. It teaches the importance of circulating good books. A boy found an old volume of poetry, covered with dust, on the sill of a window in his father's house. Its perusal led him to attempt poetry, and he became one of the greatest of English poets. We know not what we are doing when we secure a serious perusal for a good book. We may be putting springs

in motion that will never cease acting for good. Perhaps the "Voyage of the Duff" was sent to that little Pennsylvania village by some pious man. If so, and had he never done any thing else, would he have lived in vain? If that missionary had never done any thing else than lay that tract upon the table of the hotel upon the side of the Himalayas, would he have lived in vain?

3. It teaches us what fruits we may expect from parental fidelity. None can tell how many holy ministers, devoted missionaries, or self-denying members of the church we owe, under God, to parental consecration from the hour of their birth. Let every parent that reads this article consecrate anew their children to God; and although they may not become lights on high to guide the movements of the church, they may become centres of influence in the circles in which they are to move; and if they can do no more, they may lay a tract upon a table. N. M.

NOAH'S CARPENTERS.

It was a late hour at night. The city of N—— with its many turrets and spires was sleeping under the shadow of those rocky sentinels which have guarded the plain since the flood. The waves of the ocean fell gently and soothingly on the beach. The moon waded through the fleecy autumn clouds, now playing with the waters and lighting up the scene, and then concealing her glory as if to make its revelations more prized. It was a night for pious thought and conversation.

Two persons were leaving the city and passing along the water-side to a beautiful villa, where one was a resident and the other a guest. The taller and elder of the two was actively engaged in a work of benevolence, in the blessings of which the people of N—— and the students of —— college mutually shared. The work was "too heavy" for him, and he had invited his young friend, an impenitent lad, of whom we will speak as Henry, to aid him. Together they had spent many a weary day in supplying the Christian laborers who coöperated with them, with the choicest means of usefulness, as they crowded the depository of truth. Exhausted by their toils, they were now returning for a night's repose. Hitherto not a word had been addressed to the obliging lad about his soul. The fitting occasion seemed to have arrived. A quaint, but fitting manner was chosen.

"Henry," asked the elder of the younger, "do you know what became of *Noah's carpenters?*"

"Noah's carpenters!" exclaimed Henry; "I didn't know that Noah had any carpenters."

"Certainly he must have had help in building one of the largest and best-proportioned ships ever put on the stocks. There must have been many ship-carpenters at work for a long time, to have constructed such a vessel in such an age. What became of them, think you, when all the fountains of the great deep were broken up, and the windows of heaven were opened?"

"What do you mean by such a queer question?" Henry replied.

"No matter what, just now. Please answer the inquiry. And you may also tell me, if you will, what *you* would have done in that dreadful hour, when the storm came in its fury, and Noah's prophecies were all fulfilled, and all but the family of the preacher of righteousness were ready to be ingulfed in those black waters?"

"I don't know," said Henry, in a half-thoughtful, half-trifling manner; "but I think I should have got on the rudder."

"That is human nature exactly, Henry. It would 'climb up some other way,' rather than enter the fold by the only door. It would 'get on the rudder,' in its pride and short-sightedness, rather than go into the ark of safety. It would *save itself* by hanging on, at the hazard of being swept into the gulf of despair, instead of *being saved* by the provision of infinite love.

"But I'll tell you plainly what I mean, Henry, by Noah's carpenters. You have kindly and generously given me your aid, day after day, in building an ark in N——, by which many, I trust, will be saved. I feel grateful for your help. But I greatly fear, that while others will be rejoicing in the fruits of our labors, you will be swept away in the storm of wrath which will by and by beat on the heads of those who enter not the ark Christ Jesus. No human device will avail for you. 'Getting on the rudder' will not answer; you must be in Christ, or you are lost. Remember Noah's carpenters, and flee to the ark without delay."

We reached the house and parted. The winter came. The lad was placed at a boarding-school in ——. He visited his home during the winter vacation, and presented himself to the church for admission to its communion. He then stated that the conversation detailed above had never passed from his memory.

Though Noah's carpenters were all drowned, there are a great many of the same stock now alive—those who contribute to promote the spiritual good of others, and aid in the up-building of the Redeemer's kingdom, but personally neglect the great salvation.

Sabbath-school children who gather in the poor, or contribute their money to send libraries or tracts and books to the West, or to aid the work of missions, and yet remain unconverted, are like Noah's carpenters.

Teachers in Bible-classes and Sabbath-schools who point their pupils to the Lamb of God, but do not lead the way, are like guide-boards that tell the road, but are not travellers on it; or like Noah's carpenters, who built an ark, and were overwhelmed in the waters that bore it aloft in safety.

Christless parents who instruct their children and servants, as *every* parent should, in the great doctrines of the gospel, yet fail to illustrate these doctrines in their lives, and seek not a personal interest in the blood of Christ, are like Noah's carpenters, and must expect their doom.

Printers, folders, sewers, and binders engaged in making Bibles and religious books, booksellers and hawkers, and publishers of religious newspapers, who are doing much to increase the knowledge of the gospel and to save souls, but so many of whom are careless about their own salvation, will have the mortification of knowing, that while their toils have been instrumental of spiritual good to thousands, they were only like the pack-mules that carried a load to market without tasting it; or like Noah's carpenters, who built a ship they never sailed.

Wealthy and liberal, but unconverted men who help to build churches and sustain the institutions of the gospel, but who "will not come unto Christ, that they may have life," are hewing the timbers and driving the nails of the ark they are too proud or too careless to enter. Perhaps they think they will be safe on the "rudder;" but they may find too late, that when they would ride they must swim—that when they would float they must sink, with all their good deeds, unmixed with faith, as a millstone about their necks.

Moralists who attend church and support the ministry, but who do not *receive* into their hearts the gospel they thus sustain, are like Noah's carpenters.

Professed ministers of the gospel who preach the truth without practising it, who commend the love of Christ without experiencing it, who guide the wandering to the fold of Christ without entering it themselves—are they not like Noah's carpenters? If Paul might indulge the apprehension lest, when he had "preached to others," he should himself "be a castaway," may not those of us who follow at a sad distance from Paul in the Christian race, well see to it that we are not left to buffet the waves of an overwhelmed world, when some of those we have led into the ark are borne triumphantly above the billows in which we are ingulfed?

Perhaps the Christian reader will be encouraged by this narrative to speak a word in season to some of these ark-builders. They are numerous. Their kindness should be acknowledged. "These things ought they to have done." The danger is, that *the great thing* will be "left undone." "Run, speak to that young man." Tell him that the storm of wrath will come. Tell him that "getting on the rudder" of the ark, and all other human devices for salvation, are vain refuges of lies. Tell him that the ark is open; that it is safe; that it waits for him. The dove and the olive-branch are in this ark. The bow of mercy spans the heavens above it. Peace and hope and salvation are there. But, if scorned or neglected, when once the door is shut, they only that are "in the ark" will "remain alive." Who can abide that storm? Who can buffet those waves? Who will survive that deluge? Heber.

MY FIRST INQUIRY MEETING.

One man soweth, and another reapeth. The town in which it was my privilege to commence my ministerial labors, had enjoyed much valuable preaching. The people regularly attended public worship, but no additions had for a long time been made to the church, which now consisted of only about twenty-five members. In some families, as many as five or six sons and daughters, from sixteen to twenty-six, were living at home, all in an unconverted state, and the father and mother, in several cases, were in the same condition.

I had held the usual meetings on the Sabbath, and on Thursday evening what was called a conference-meeting was held in one part of the town, at the house of Dr. M——. The parable of the prodigal son was read, and remarks and prayers offered by myself and others. In the course of the meeting, several appeared considerably affected.

"I perceive," said I, "that a number present are awakened to a view of their condition as unpardoned sinners. I am well aware, that persons who are inquiring what they shall do to be saved, may be greatly benefited by personal conversation with Christians. For such a purpose, it is proposed that such persons remain on their seats when the meeting shall be closed, and interviews will be had with them."

Eight stayed where they were. They were respectfully approached and conversed with, to their benefit, and to that of those who undertook to direct their inquiring minds. The results were so profitable, that the practice continued through the winter, and the next summer that church consisted of about four times as many members as when the work began. Several of the young men who then made a profession, became useful ministers in different states of the Union. We had then never heard of such meetings; but the voice of Providence seemed to direct us to a course which, with various modifications, has been blessed in other places. W. D.

THE UNWELCOME SHOWER.

In the year 1842, I was invited to assist a ministering brother on a communion occasion, at a country church in the county of ——, Georgia. As the house of worship could not contain the vast multitudes assembling on such occasions, the people had prepared an extensive bush-arbor, with temporary pulpit and seats for the accommodation of preachers and hearers.

The congregation was very large, and the services commenced under favorable auspices. I selected the text, "God is love," 1 John 4:8, and after the introductory remarks, had proceeded in my discourse about ten or fifteen minutes, when the heavens, which had been for a few moments gathering blackness, poured out upon us torrents of rain. The services, in which the people were beginning to take a very lively interest, were almost instantaneously closed, and the people rushed for the church and for the bodies of large trees and into carriages, and wherever they could find shelter. All was confusion. The sermon could not be preached, neither could the Lord's supper be celebrated.

After an hour, or an hour and a half, the rain abating, the people manifested the deepest anxiety to hear the discourse so suddenly interrupted. They even went to work to beat the dripping boughs of the wet arbor, to see if the place could be made comfortable, so that the congregation and the preachers could reassemble and go through with the service. But this was impossible, the seats were too wet; we could not proceed. I endeavored, however, to satisfy the people in some measure, by promising to return, if the Lord should permit, at some future day, and preach that sermon.

A year rolled around, and the people of that congregation resolved that they would build tents and a substantial framed and shingled arbor, so that they could hold regular camp-meetings, and be uninterrupted in case of rain. This was in the year 1843, a year memorable for revivals of religion in portions of Georgia and Florida.

In October of that year, the first camp-meeting was held at Thyatira. There a large congregation and several ministers assembled from different and distant counties, to give themselves up to the uninterrupted, delightful service of God for several days together. There, under the new and rain-proof arbor, which cost about $500, I redeemed my pledge in reference to the broken sermon; and there I heard other brethren preach in the demonstration of the Spirit, and with power. There I witnessed the glorious displays of the power of sovereign grace in the conversion of sinners, and in the quickening of God's people. There, at that meeting, after having prayed and agonized for years and years for my son, my first-born, I had the happiness to see that son—then in college, and now in the ministry—slain by the law and made alive in Jesus Christ, as we fondly hope. There I saw scores and scores of stout-hearted young men and young women cut down by the arrows of conviction, and there made to rejoice in hope of pardoning mercy. It was a season never to be forgotten by those who were present.

Eight additional camp-meetings have been held since that time upon that consecrated spot, the last of which has just closed; and never has there been one at which ministers and Christians have labored and prayed in vain. Every time we have assembled in that native forest, and worshipped under that waterproof arbor, erected, as the people say, and as I believe, in consequence of that unwelcome shower, God has met us by his Spirit and poured out showers of melting mercy and renewing grace upon the people. As there is joy in heaven over every repenting sinner, angels must make annual visits to that favored spot. How wonderful, how mysterious are the ways of the

Almighty. How many will look back in eternity from the heights of glory to that place in the wild woods of Georgia, as the place of their second birth, as God's house and the gate of heaven to their souls.

N. H.

THE HAYMOW.

My first settlement in the ministry was in a valley in one of the middle states, beautiful beyond description. A broad and winding river enters it at the north, between two high rocky peaks, which bear the evidence of being torn from each other's embrace by some dread concussion of nature; and after a course of fifteen miles, takes its exit at the south, and through a gap probably made in the same way. On either side of this river the bottom-lands are exceedingly rich. As you leave the river, these lands gradually undulate, until, at the distance of about two miles, they rise into mountains on the east and west, which seem built of heaven to guard the quiet vale from all disturbing intrusions. As the traveller reaches the brow of the eastern mountain, a scene of surpassing loveliness spreads itself beneath him; and he feels that if peace has not utterly forsaken our world, its residence must be there. The valley seems as if expressly made for the home of the Indian; and for moons beyond the power of his arithmetic to calculate, the red man fished in that river, and planted his corn in that rich bottom, and sought his game upon the mountains. And before he could be compelled to yield it, he made the white man feel the power of his anger in many a dreadful surprise.

But sin, and in its very worst forms, found an entrance into this beautiful spot. Early in the history of the settlement a church was collected there, which continued a feeble existence until 18—, when I became its pastor. Young, ardent, and without experience, I here commenced my ministry in a community proverbial both for its intelligence and its disregard of religion, amid external opposition, and with a church small, and rent by internal discords. A more unpromising field none could desire.

I entered on my duties with zeal, and was diligent in their performance. I prepared my sermons with care, and thought them conclusive; but few heard them, and none seemed convinced by them. I felt deeply myself, but my hearers semed unmoved. Months thus passed away without, to my knowledge, a religious impression being made on any mind; and feeling that I labored in vain, and spent my strength for naught, I was about giving up in despair. My preaching seemed more to excite the opposition of the wicked, than the prayers of the pious.

There was among my people a man in mid-life, a German by birth, and a remarkably simple-hearted, pure-minded Christian. Whoever was absent, he was always present at the place of prayer. One evening early in December, as I was about retiring to rest, I heard a knock at my door, and my German friend was introduced, his countenance full of emotion. On taking his seat, his first words were these: "My dear pastor, I have come to tell you that the Lord is about to revive his work here." Surprised at his appearance and language, and at the lateness of his visit, I asked him, "Why do you think so?" He replied as follows: "About eight o'clock this evening, I went up to my haymow to give hay to my cattle; and while there the Spirit of God came upon me, and has kept me there praying until now. I feel that God is about to revive his work, and I could not go in to my family until I told you." The entire simplicity and earnestness of the good man convinced me that God had vouchsafed to visit his servant. After some conversation we parted, mutually agreeing to pray and labor for a revival of religion, and to engage as many as we could to do the same.

Every meeting for religious services was now to me one of intense interest. A few days convinced me that the spirit of prayer was on the increase. Meetings for prayer were numerously attended. The church on the Sabbath became more full and solemn. And a few weeks after that evening of wrestling with God on the haymow, found me in the midst of the first revival of my ministry, and one of the most precious I ever witnessed.

Permit me to narrate a few incidents which occurred during the progress of this revival, and which illustrate some great truths that should not be forgotten.

Among the first that expressed seriousness, was a fashionable and well-educated young lady, belonging to one of our richest families. She was the pride of a mother whose ambition it was to have her shine in elegant society. Miss E—— expressed a hope in Christ. In a few days she was sent to spend the winter in one of our principal cities, with some gay friends, who were directed to take her to all the fashionable amusements. She yielded to the temptation;

and when she returned in the spring seemed farther from the kingdom of heaven than ever. Another refreshing was soon enjoyed, when the former feelings of this young lady returned; she became hopefully pious—and in a few months the wife of a godly minister. And her large family, perhaps influenced by her example, followed her into the fold of Christ.

There was in the place a young man, a profane, but yet an industrious mechanic. Like Nicodemus, he came to me by night to know what he should do to be saved. His feelings seemed of the most pungent character, and his visits were often repeated. He thought he understood and could joyfully embrace the plan of salvation through Jesus Christ. Yielding to the influence of one wicked companion, in a few weeks he forsook the house of prayer and the people of God. As long as I knew him afterwards he was among the most obdurate men I ever knew. He ripened for ruin; and not long ago, with one stroke, as the woodman removes the saplings out of his way, God cut him down. It is a fearful thing to quench the Spirit!

Mr. C—— was a pleasant, moral, and interesting man. Under the prayers and conversations of a pious mother, he grew up a friend to the institutions of religion. His mind became deeply interested. But a more convenient season was always an excuse for the putting aside of present duty. In the midst of the revival, when some of the sturdy cedars of Lebanon were bowing, his aged mother, and with tears, besought him to make God his portion. "Mother," said he, "you are dependent upon me for a subsistence, and so are my motherless children. To provide for you all is my pleasure and my duty. I am now engaged in a very profitable work among the mountains, and when I have made enough to support you all comfortably, in connection with my own industry, I promise you I will attend to religion. But you must excuse me now." And with a solemn warning against the folly of such reasoning from the lips of his aged mother, he hastened to his business among the mountains. On the evening of the third day from his departure, he was brought back to that mother, and was laid at her feet a mutilated corpse. Before he could escape its track, a log of timber rolling down a steep precipice, caught him, and rolling over, almost ground him to powder. And as we laid him down in the grave, I heard that mother exclaim, in the bitterness of her sorrow, "Would to God I had died for thee, my son, my son!" O, the folly of boasting of to-morrow, as we know not what a day may bring forth.

Some of our pious people undertook the circulation of religious tracts. The tract, "The Way to be Saved," was selected for the purpose of placing in the hands of our people a plain and simple guide to the Saviour of sinners. One of these was placed in the shop of a mechanic who was noted for his profanity and vulgarity. Blotting out the word "saved" in the title of the tract, he wrote in its place "damned;" so that the title thus amended, read, "the way to be damned." Now tearing it nearly in two, he flung it into the street. It was soon picked up by a young woman deeply serious, and who, although shocked by its title, carried it home. She read it with care; she pasted the torn leaves together, and read it again and again. She went as directed, and found peace and joy in believing. And in a conversation with her about her hope, she drew from her bosom this mutilated tract, saying, "This is the little book that told me the way to the cross." If yet alive, I have no doubt she preserves it among her choicest treasures. Thus it is that God often makes the wrath of man to praise him.

Many instances like these occurred during that revival, which the time would fail me to enumerate. But even these emphatically teach us,

1. That when faithfully and prayerfully discharging duty, ministers must not be unduly discouraged by unpropitious external circumstances. If they go forth weeping, bearing precious seed, they will return again with rejoicing, bringing their sheaves with them.

2. They teach us the power of prayer. It moves the hand that moves the world. That revival with its consequent blessings, I have ever traced, under God, to that prayer on the haymow. The prayer that God inspires, he will answer.

3. They teach us the awful guilt of parents who sacrifice the souls of their children at the shrines of worldly ambition. And alas, how many such parents there are!

4. They utter warning notes in the ears of those who quench the strivings of the Spirit, or who postpone the duty of submission to God *now* to an uncertain future.

5. They teach us, that even pearls cast before swine, may not be in vain. Through the wickedness of the wicked, God is ever accomplishing his purposes of love. How invincible the combined agencies

of mercy, when even one mutilated tract becomes the instrument of life from the dead to a human soul.

Years have passed away since this revival occurred. Some of its subjects have already entered on their reward. That simple-hearted, pious German has gone up to his Saviour. But the influences of that prayer on the haymow will live for ever. Good men never die. They rest from their labors, but their works do follow. May our churches never want members like him who wrestled and prevailed with God on the haymow. N. M.

INFLUENCE OF TWO YOUNG LADIES.

There had been no revival in the church of A——, for a long time. Professed Christians were cold; their services formal and spiritless; few, if any, were alive to duty. Difficulties multiplied. Heart-burnings and worldly conformity endangered even the existence of the church. The Spirit of God had withdrawn, apparently for ever. Alas, thus is it when the love of many waxes cold.

While things were in this state in A——, the Lord was blessing a small church in a neighboring town. In his providence, two gay and worldly young ladies of A—— passed a few days in the immediate vicinity of this work of grace. They found themselves unexpectedly in the society of those who were enjoying the presence of the Spirit of God. At first their hearts rose in opposition to the work, especially to its power over them. They were, however, both soon led to feel their own deep sinfulness, their entire dependence on the Holy Spirit to renew and sanctify them, and to discover the way of salvation through the Redeemer of men. Great was the change they experienced. They found Christ infinitely, absolutely precious, and determined to live for his glory.

When they returned to A——, the change soon became apparent, and produced, as is usual in such cases, much and varied excitement and remark. In their pastor they found a true, sympathizing friend and guide, but they were much tried by the exertions of their former gay companions to lead them back to the world. How artful were the plans adopted for this end—how persevering the efforts! Scenes of temptation and gayety were multiplied, urgent and repeated invitations given them. Flattery was resorted to—jests and raillery, sometimes scorn, and even abusive epithets, oaths, and reproaches, were employed.

These temptations led them more frequently and importunately to the mercy-seat, and gave them clearer views of the desperate depravity of the sinner's heart. They were aroused to exertion, and determined, with the help of God, to labor for the salvation of souls. They prayed, they entreated, they warned, they invited one and another to be reconciled to God. Many around them began to think of eternal things, and not unfrequently they led several of their friends and companions to the house of prayer.

Their labors were not in vain. God has said, "When they call upon me, I will answer." His Spirit was evidently working upon the hearts of multitudes. Members of the church previously at variance, began to weep and to seek reconciliation. The love of Christ constrained them to be at peace. The men of the world beheld this change, and trembled. They no longer pointed the finger of scorn. Some were brought to inquire earnestly, "What shall we do to be saved?" Even the gay and profane, as well as the cold formalist, were troubled, and joined in this inquiry. Things now wore a solemn aspect in the once careless and mirthful society of A——. The hall of revelry was deserted; vain amusements, and even opposition ceased. They who had been first in scenes of pleasure, were heard confessing their sins and imploring the mercy of God. Numbers yielded their hearts to Christ and rejoiced with exceeding joy. They were heard recounting the story of the cross, and entreating their companions to believe and be saved. How still and solemn was the house of God! The word of truth fell with power on hearts unused to any susceptibility of religious emotions. In the social district meetings, sobs and tears were mingled with rejoicings, and with the convert's prayer. This was the Lord's doing, marvellous to all. Thus was he pleased to strengthen and bless the feeble instrumentality of these two youthful converts.

The spirit of discord which had torn asunder an ancient church was brought to an end. Christians again loved each other, and prayed, wept, and conversed together, confessing the presence and power of the Spirit of God.

Multitudes also, who were dead in trespasses and sins, were made alive unto God. Sinful habits and amusements were abandoned, while prayer and praise were heard in almost every family. Many now sang "redeeming love;" and joy, new joy was felt in heaven—the angels' joy over repenting sinners.

The church was no longer a reproach. That was a Sabbath long to be remembered when, in an aisle side by side with those two young ladies, there united with the church of A—— one hundred and forty-nine persons, young and old, in whose conversion it might be truly said they had abundant reason to rejoice. "They that turn many to righteousness shall shine as the stars for ever and ever." Dan. 12:3. Long ere this they have gone, as we suppose, to their rest above; but from generation to generation such a work of grace is worthy to be held by Zion in delightful remembrance. God is faithful. He notices and rewards the faithfulness of his children.

FORTY YEARS of subsequent prosperity, benevolence, and Christian action in that church, are the highest testimonial that this work was of God. In the weakness of man was manifested divine power. The full happiness and glory of this work of grace, in which two young female converts thus labored, can only be reckoned up when its aggregate richness shall be unfolded and enjoyed in the world to come. A work this worth living for—*dying* for, a thousand, nay, ten thousand times. S. H.

SKETCH OF A REVIVAL.

In the autumn of 1854, a few Christians in S—— who felt the desolations of Zion, and could plead the promises of God, gathered around their pastor to sustain him in the faithful preaching of the gospel. They pledged to him their fervent prayers and cheerful activity, in the fearless exhibition of the truth. Then the tearful eye of faith was lifted to Him, "with whom is the residue of the Spirit."

There were cases of the most pungent conviction, while the surface of society apparently remained calm and unmoved. When indications of anxiety appeared among the impenitent, the troubled sinner was made the subject of prayer and effort till led to the cross of Christ. Soon the subduing breath of the Almighty began to fall upon the public assembly.

With the tokens of God's presence to encourage faith, the brethren who loved the souls of men went forth to visit every dwelling within the bounds of the congregation. They returned with kindled zeal, and additional evidence that the Lord is often working when a small remnant only expect his appearing. Days of fasting and prayer followed, and verily God filled his temple, while his backslidden people wept in the dust before him. The meetings were still and solemn. One evening after the sermon, a number of young persons rose and desired the prayers of the saints; and in a brief period, they were rejoicing in hope.

The godly women, with appropriate tracts, entered the homes of the poor, and ministered to the wants of soul and body. Each week brought new manifestations of divine grace.

At length there seemed a pause in the gracious movement, and as with an index-finger, God directed the attention of his people to bitter alienations of feeling of long standing between them and a sister church, and also between them and a former pastor. The Lord hath gone out before them, and words could not convey a full impression of the intense and joyful excitement, when, in the great assembly, the tears of reconciliation fell like rain, and the extended hand was the signal of a rapturous reunion. After the rush of Christian sympathy had passed, the manifestations of sovereign grace were renewed with augmented power, until more than sixty cherished the hope of pardon.

Never before did we witness so palpably the Spirit attending the use of means. The impenitent were invited to the pastor's study, and to remain for prayer and personal conversation, at the close of public service. Others were visited at home, and emphatically "pulled out of the fire," by the earnest and believing efforts of the people of God. Not a few who paused in the house of God till Christians could reach them, were smitten down, and hopefully made the surrender of the soul to Christ.

We recollect a stranger, a young lady, who, lingering, was addressed with the question, "Will you give yourself penitently to Christ *now?*" She hesitated, suppressed her emotion, trembled, then said, weeping, "I fear, if I do not to-night, I never shall." She sunk on her knees, and we believe, into the arms of Christ.

One Sabbath morning, the pastor was summoned to the house of a man who had opposed the work of God. And Oh, the anguish, as a sense of merited condemnation rolled down upon the soul. "I am lost; God will never accept me," were some of the expressions of remorse, and conviction of sin.

To encourage God's people, we notice a few impressive facts illustrated in this revival.

1. God *hears prayer*, not according to *numbers*, but the measure of faith. In this way he comes when *apparently* the whole church is asleep.

2. That instead of waiting till difficulties are healed, for a season of refreshing, the *unusual* presence of the Holy Ghost, in answer to supplication, effectually secures this glorious result.

3. That while the Spirit works with humble believing Christians, he, like the wind, bloweth where he listeth. He subdues hearts which seemed most unlikely to yield, and sometimes leaves to their rebellion the most hopeful ones.

4. That God will bless appropriate effort for the conversion of men. This he has promised. How criminal, then, the worldliness and infidelity of those upon whom are the vows of God. How great the guilt and peril of the self-hardened sinner, for whom so much is done by Jehovah. P. C. H.

THE ELDERS' PRAYER-MEETING.

A young minister in an inland village in the state of New York was made happy in the addition of thirty-five converts to his flock. That day in which, for the first time, at the table of our Lord, they solemnly commemorated his death, was an occasion for melting of hearts, and the Saviour's broken body was seen by many in an applying faith. Some can never forget that day: with the new disciple of gray hairs, were those of tender years—a strange garland of

God's grace, the fresh opening buds, and the almost withering flowers.

What was singular, this gathering of new-born spirits was entirely from the *outskirts* of the pastor's field. Those who came farthest to hear the word, embraced the truth: the villagers under the very sound of the sanctuary, and in the centre of all this outpouring of divine love, were alarmingly indifferent. The dew of saving mercy had descended upon the surrounding mountains and the lower part of the valley, completely encircling with a halo of glory that part where stood the village with its church; but while all around were thus refreshed with God's dew, that little group of dwellings, like Gideon's fleece, was very dry. The meetings for prayer in the outskirts were well attended by all classes, but in the village, all except a few church-members, stood aloof. The pastor saw and felt it.

One Sabbath morning, entering the sanctuary with a heavy heart, he requested one of the elders to inform the consistory in a private way, that the pastor wished to see them. The elders met their minister at his house. He reminded them what great things God had done in the outskirts of the congregation; but that the central part seemed entirely passed by, and Satan kept possession like a strong man armed. He spoke of his love to the interesting young men running fast their career of danger; nor did he think it could be true of his elders, that "no man cared for their souls." He unbosomed his deep solicitude, lest the harvest should be ended, and they not saved. He mentioned his closet-wrestlings with God, day upon day, and week upon week, to send his saving power among them, and his faith that God would do it. He then reminded them of their high responsibilities to God and his church, as fathers in Israel; and he implored them to see how it stood in their hearts, and to beseech God to take away every hinderance, and to quicken them with renewed life.

A solemn silence followed; and with swelling hearts, as a suitable prayer, they sung the hymn,

"Come, Holy Spirit, heavenly Dove,
With all thy quickening powers,
Kindle a flame of sacred love
In these cold hearts of ours."

The pastor knelt with his beloved elders, and in prayer commended them to God, imploring him of his mercy to give them such direction and strength as should make them efficient in the church of his Son; and before rising from their knees, each one of the four elders prayed also.

Their prayers were remarkably short—the burden being sincere confession of remissness, and supplication for pardon and grace; after which they closed with earnest entreaty that God's mercy might not be kept from the village. One of them in a few words addressed his brethren, in which he expressed himself as grieved at his own omissions of duty; he spoke of the new sense he entertained of his responsibility, of his hopes that God would forgive his remissness, and also his belief that the Saviour was about to be manifested among them. Each elder followed in a similar strain of contrition and hope.

The pastor reviewed what they had done, and spoke of it as a scene over which the angels of God might rejoice. He reminded them that this was in effect a solemn covenant, and that they were now about to resume their duties in the church under a fuller sense of their obligations.

That Lord's-day evening the minister preached with much of God's presence. The fathers in the church were found having more of the spirit and the gift of prayer. And still the secret of the Lord was with them that feared him; for no one knew what had taken place, but every one said that things seemed unusually solemn. That very evening sinners were found troubled at heart, and Christians were returning to their first love. The pastor and elders had borne with them from their little meeting an increased portion of the Holy Spirit. The world knew it not—"for the kingdom of God came not with observation." The pastor almost felt the words verified, "It shall come to pass, that before they call, I will answer; and while they are yet speaking, I will hear." Isa. 65:24. The village was now the scene of God's mercy. The young were its trophies, and among them some of the very wildest young men in the place. Men looked on and wondered, the work seemed so great, and yet all was so quiet and so solemn. Oh, it was the Saviour's powerful love, and that in answer to his people's prayers.

Upon communion-day, twenty new disciples took their places at that holy feast of remembrance. And some months afterwards others were gathered into the church; so that more than thirty souls dated at that season God's gracious work upon them.

Now look at some of the facts here presented.

1. The minister *felt* deeply for souls.

2. The officers in the church caught his spirit;

they awoke to new views of duty; they repented their remissness; they prayed God for help, and in that help resolved to labor for the church.

3. God answered their prayers.

Growing out of these facts are some weighty reflections.

1. The pastor may best in privacy stir up his officers when remiss. Heb. 10 : 24.

2. Prayer is power. Psalm 106 : 23; James 5 : 16.

3. God will answer prayer. Psalm 99 : 6; Matt. 21 : 22.

4. The church must go to God to prepare her for the blessing. Isaiah 58 : 9.

And now, brethren, lay and clergy, "all these things happened unto them for examples; and they are written for our admonition." What is it the church needs, but such a visitation through all her assemblies? then would she be a mighty host, and glorious her song of praise, and heavenly her spirit, and liberal her resources for the various claims of new testament benevolence, overflowing the banks of "the river, the streams whereof shall make glad the city of our God." S. L.

THE WICKED NINE.

In the town of W——, Mass., a powerful work of grace was several years ago enjoyed. Old and young, rich and poor, the moral and the profligate, were subjects of its power. As is often the case in seasons of revival, the hostility of the wicked was aroused, and their vituperations poured upon the praying people of

God. At the commencement of the work, *nine* young men banded together to oppose the work of grace. They formed a sort of an association, having certain rules adopted by general consent, to be strictly regarded. They pledged themselves to attend every meeting, but for the purpose of "making light" of religion, and in whatever way they could to wound the feelings of Christians.

Evening after evening this band were seen to enter the meetings to execute their design. But the people of God, whose hearts were now truly broken and contrite, had faith in the sovereign grace of Christ, and earnest were their cryings at the mercy-seat. They set apart some precious moments in which to offer special prayer for the conversion of "the wicked nine."

One evening after the usual exercises, a few devoted Christians repaired to the study of their pastor to pray for the subjects of this narrative. While earnestly pleading with God in their behalf, a rap was heard at the door. The pastor hastened thither, and on opening the door, a young man grasped his hand, with the inquiry, "What must I do to be saved?" He was the *ringleader* of the "nine." In deep anguish of spirit, he was now seeking Christ. Suffice it to say, that he was ushered into the study, to the surprise of all; and left it, as we could not but hope, a child of God.

On the following day he started on a mission to his old comrades in sin, not ashamed to tell them the story of his conversion. The first house at which he called was the residence of one of the wildest of the "nine," and he had a praying mother. As he entered abruptly, that anxious mother exclaimed, "I pray you, don't come here, for I believe Henry is *serious*." "And I hope I have given my heart to God," he replied, to the astonishment of the woman, "and am come to invite Henry to go with me to our pastor's study." What blessed moments were these to that pious mother. Scarcely could she believe what she heard. Oh, the worth of prayer.

But the work did not stop here; for "praying breath" is not "spent in vain." That whole church were not so intensely moved in behalf of that band of youth for naught. The work went on with wonderful energy until *the whole nine* were numbered among the happy converts. And our feeble language cannot describe the feelings awakened in that community, when the tidings went abroad that *the last one of the nine was converted*. What a lesson to the Christian upon the triumph of grace and the power of prayer.

A Pastor.

INCENTIVE TO CHRISTIAN LABOR.

"*The distracted meeting*" was the name given by a wicked and profane man to a series of religious meetings in a village not far from his residence. He lived midway between the Green mountains of Vermont and lake Champlain. In the midst of beautiful scenery and of religious privileges, he had grown up to mature life a bold blasphemer. God was not in his thoughts nor on his lips, save as his holy name was associated with profanity. He was a man whom Christians shunned. Good men felt that the less they had to do with him the better.

But God was moving in the hearts of his children. The Spirit was shedding down his influences, "reproving of sin, of righteousness, and of judgment." The place of prayer was a "Bochim." After solemn deliberation, the church resolved to district the whole town, giving to certain members, male and female, a distinct field of labor. Every family was to be visited, and every accessible individual to be conversed with on the subject of personal religion. Among these members was a plain man, who had mingled but little with the world, and who, like Moses, was "slow of speech, and of a slow tongue." Strange to say, it fell to him, in the providence of God, to visit the neighborhood where this reviler dwelt.

His heart almost died within him at thought of it. What could he do with such a man? Every advance of his would be met with ridicule. All his arguments would be turned to his own discomfiture. But the pressure of duty could not be resisted. Conscience told the disciple he ought to go. After much prayer, with humble reliance on God for aid, one morning he went forth for the dreaded interview. With trembling he approached his neighbor's dwelling, stood at the door and rapped for admittance. He was informed that the person he sought was in a forest near by, to procure fuel. At once his fears and doubts returned in full force and strength. It was suggested to him that he had done his duty—he had visited the house, and the man was not there; what more remained for him to do? Surely it was not for him, on that cold and wintry day, to go further, and to such a place. He yielded for a moment, and turned his face homeward. No, said conscience, sadly but sternly, this will not do; you should go further. You should see the man.

Arrested in his homeward course, he retraced his steps, passed along the wood-road, and entered the forest. Soon the object of his search appeared. After the usual salutations were exchanged, he in broken language made known his mission, spoke of the religious meeting in progress, and urged his neighbor to attend. "What," replied the reviler, "do you wish me to go to yon *distracted meeting?*" "Yes," said the other, giving no heed to the sneering tone and scornful words; "we are getting great good from these meetings, and we are anxious to have you share with us. We have felt for you, we have prayed for you, and as a friend I have come to you this morning, to urge you to seek the salvation of your soul."

The cross once taken up, timidity vanished. Faithfully and earnestly was this man warned of his danger, and entreated to flee to the cross. At first he seemed to be taken by surprise, then to be rousing himself to his old work of opposition. Soon, however, he turned away from his faithful friend, evidently to hide his emotion. At last, completely overcome, he approached his visitor, his eyes swimming with tears, saying, "Mr. B——, I have been wondering why some of you Christians did not come to see me. I have been expecting you. I am glad you have come. I thank you for it. I will go immediately home, and attend the meeting this afternoon."

He was true to his word, and from that day was a constant attendant upon all the means of grace. He became a Christian man, united with the church, and labored with his might to build up that blessed kingdom against which he had so long bitterly contended.

This simple narrative furnishes an instructive lesson to Christians who shrink from duty from fear of opposition. God is able to disarm prejudice, remove hate, and open the heart. If any one will trust in him, however timid he may be, God will go before him, preparing his way, giving him strength and putting words into his mouth. Difficulties, real or imaginary, will vanish, and he will probably be surprised at the results of his labor, undertaken in great weakness and distrust.

Impenitent men are often expecting the children of the Most High to converse with them, and wonder they do not do it. Let us never miss an opportunity of doing good in this way. A "word fitly spoken" may be instrumental of arresting attention, and lead ultimately to the conversion of a soul. Let no one wonder why we do not speak to them on the subject of religion. F. B. W.

A DELIGHTFUL DISCOVERY.

The Rev. Mr. —— preaching in his native town, in Western Massachusetts, from the text, "Cast thy bread upon the waters, and thou shalt find it after many days," stated that when he was a child, he had one day been absent from home, and on his return, his pious mother said to him, "There has been a strange occurrence this afternoon. A slip of paper has been found on the desk, with these words, 'The Master has come, and calleth for thee.'" The call came with power, as if direct from heaven to his heart. He had no rest until he found it in Christ. He engaged in business for a time, but his Master's call grew louder and louder, until he left all to prepare to preach the gospel. Soon after he commenced preaching, in travelling through the western valley, he was suddenly called to address a waiting congregation. Trembling with anxiety, it flashed upon his mind to speak from that text, "The Master is come, and calleth for *thee*." He did so; he was unusually assisted, and the truth was attended with a power that the Holy Ghost alone can give. There followed a glorious revival of religion.

A lady who heard that statement says, "What do you think were my feelings, when I recollected very distinctly to have placed that slip of paper on the desk, expecting the praying mother would baptize it with her tears and prayers?" S.

A PLEASANT SURPRISE.

When I settled over the only Presbyterian church in —— county, East Tennessee, I extended my labors to the destitute in various parts of the county, taking a few Bibles in my saddle-bags. On one occasion, after I had parted with the last Bible, a lad came to me and very modestly asked for one. I promised one to him, and on my next visit supplied him with the precious book. I learned that he was an orphan boy, and was bound apprentice to an infidel; but twelve or fifteen years had since gone by, and the boy and the circumstances had passed from my memory.

A few months ago, my wife accompanied me to a

Baptist church, where we listened to a fluent, warm-hearted discourse presenting a clear view of the way of salvation by Christ, near the close of which the preacher especially urged the young to the diligent reading of the Scriptures.

"When I was a small boy," said he, "I was taken and bound apprentice to a man who was an unbeliever in religion, and would not furnish his family with the Bible. I went one day to preaching, at such a place. The congregation was so large that neither the house nor the barn would contain them, and the congregation moved into the orchard. I felt the force of the sermon, my conscience was awakened. After the sermon the preacher was giving Bibles to a few poor people who had none. I thought then was my time to get one. I went up and made my request. There was none left for me, but the minister promised to furnish me with one, which he did in a short time. I took it home, and for fear it would be taken from me, hid it in the barn in a pile of straw, and every time I went to the barn by myself I would, in my feeble manner, read a portion of it. That book proved to be the means of my conversion. I had the name of the minister who gave it to me written in it, with my own. I have that Bible yet, and have been preaching out of it for many years."

You may imagine my surprise when he read my name as the giver of that Bible. After he had dismissed the assembly, I need not tell you of the pleasant greeting we had. This young brother is now one of our most successful preachers, and an ardent friend to all the benevolent institutions of this age.

N. H.

A YOUNG MISSIONARY.

It was many years ago, wrote a minister in 1848, when I was young in the ministry, that two little boys, both under twelve years of age, came among us. They were orphan boys, having neither father nor mother. How it happened that they came to our village I never knew. They came from Boston, and I understood that their father was a sailor. Two of my people, young farmers, took them in and gave them a home. The youngest was a fair, curly-headed little fellow, with a countenance as bright as a smile. He declared himself to be a Unitarian, though not ten years old, and stoutly did he stand to it. They came into the Sabbath-school, and the warm hearts of the teachers, then young converts, yearned over them. After being with us a while, the orphans met me on the steps of the church one Sabbath morning, as I was going in, and handed me a little paper. The purport of the contents was, "Thomas and George F—— have lost their grandmother, the only friend they had in the world, and they wish prayers in their behalf." I read the note just as it was written. It affected the congregation; and when we came to spread out the case of these young orphans before the mercy-seat, there was the stillness of the grave, save that now and then the audible sobbings of the people were heard from every part of the house. I knew that my people were praying fervently for the boys.

In less than six months from that time, these boys were both hopefully converted, and both members of my church. Then at once the little white-headed boy became a tract distributer. I never heard any thing more about his Unitarianism.

After a few years I removed from that part of the country, and knew little of my first dear charge. Many changes have since come over me, but nothing more pleasant than the scenes through which I then passed.

About three years ago, at a meeting of the American Board at Brooklyn, a young man came to me and introduced himself as a young missionary, soon to go to the East. It was my little curly-haired boy, George. The young farmer had reared him—sent him to college, and to the seminary at Andover, and he was now girding up his loins to enter upon the work of life. His errand was to ask me to go back to the old church where he first found Christ, and there preach at his ordination for the missionary work. I could hardly refrain from tears. In a moment the past rose up before me, and I seemed to see the little orphan as he used to go into his Sabbath-class, with his little Bible under his arm. Blessings on the young farmer who has reared up a missionary of the cross. What a noble use to which to put his property. My young friend is now far away on the shores of India, preaching Christ to the heathen. I may never see him again, but I think of him as we do upon children that are taken from us in early life—they are always children. But if he is faithful, he will one day become an angel of light, and stand up more beautiful than when I first saw him in the budding of his being. Blessings on his head. May it wear a crown eternal. God can take the orphan and carry him safely and kindly, and make him a great blessing to men. Since that time, I have never looked upon a Sabbath-school but it seemed to me that I could see among their bright eyes some who would yet become missionaries of the cross.

PRAYER ANSWERED AFTER DEATH.

Many years since, some young men belonging to the Senior class in —— college, resolved to unite in earnest prayer for a young and thoughtless class-mate. In a few months commencement came, and the class and the praying band were scattered. But the soul of that godless young man was felt as a burden on the heart of one of his pious class-mates, and though alone, he continued his supplications. Then, in his far western home, he found one like-minded with himself, and he persuaded the stranger to join him in his petition for his former companion.

A few years passed away, and the two class-mates met again upon their native soil. The careless youth was still careless, and was then engaged in the study of law in a neighboring city. The other one, it was manifest, had come back to his early home to die. An incurable disease was wearing out his life. Still, his desire for his friend's salvation was as fresh and strong as ever. It seemed to grow more intense as life waned. It mingled in all his thoughts; every person whom he saw, whom he knew as a praying person, he besought, saying, "Oh, pray for that young man!" and to the last hour he continued his own intercessions.

His early companion, for whom his heart had so

yearned, stood at his grave, and saw it close upon him with no other emotion than that of regret for a friend of his youthful days. The prayer of the dead was yet unanswered. But ere the grass grew over that grave the Spirit of God was poured out upon the church in which they in their boyhood had worshipped, and one of the first converts was the young man so long and so earnestly prayed for. He then devoted himself to God in the ministry of his Son, and his hand has recorded these facts, that it may add another illustration to the truths, that the Lord's ear is not heavy that he cannot hear, that he is "not slack concerning his promises," and that the "effectual fervent prayer of the righteous man availeth much."

M. B. G.

KINDNESS TO A PASTOR.

A great discovery was made by a New England pastor several years since. He had been absent for some weeks, for the purpose of recruiting his strength, and had just returned with renewed vigor to the scene of his labors. He had been but a few hours in his house when he bethought himself of his favorite place of prayer and labor—his study. He ascended the staircase with great quietness and composure of mind, little imagining what a surprise was at hand. He walked peacefully and thoughtfully through the spacious upper hall towards the pleasant room he was seeking. He opened the study door with the same calmess of spirit which had marked the history of five and twenty years. He shut the door, and as yet nothing remarkable had occurred, and all was well. The stove door stood open, and it occurred to him to kindle a little fire, as it was somewhat chilly, and it was done. Up to this point the worthy pastor was utterly ignorant that any thing important awaited him. He was a man of a well-balanced mind, of a uniformly peaceful and unruffled temper, and strove to keep himself in a proper position for whatever might occur. He had had his sorrows, and meekly did he sustain himself under them; and such scenes of prosperity as now and then gladdened him, were not suffered to intoxicate and unman him.

But such a scene as was soon to open before him had had no parallel in the whole previous history of his life. There had been striking events in his history. His ministry had been one of success, yet often had he known the bitter cup. He had loved the people of his charge, and up to the startling event soon to be related, was eminently devoted to their highest welfare. He had entered the study that day in a state of mind as kind and tender towards them as he had ever been conscious of experiencing.

The fire in his stove had begun to crackle most cheerfully. He had closed the stove door, so that all might be safe. He had placed the tongs he had used back again in their proper location. A little ashes and dust, which had fallen while making the fire, were swept away with a neat little brush, and the brush itself was hung again upon the peg where it belonged.

When all this had been done, and the worthy man had taken a step or two towards the centre study-table, his eye fell upon the objects crowding that table, and all but crushing it to the floor. And such objects! Did he dream? Where was he? He could hardly believe his eyes. And he ventured near and tried his hands. There was no mistake. The senses could not be imposed upon. All scepticism fled, and there came over the astonished man the sensation of the existence in his study of *seventy-five valuable and elegantly bound volumes*, with a label in modest capitals, "A Present by the People to their Pastor."

That is what I call a great discovery. The good man thought so too. It greatly moved him, and it moves me to state, in divers particulars, some of the practical bearings of such discoveries.

1. In them is discovered the genuine kindness of a people to their pastor. Pew-taxes, or subscriptions for his support, do not show it. They are business transactions merely, and have no necessary connection with the warmth and fervor of real and heartfelt kindness.

2. Herein is a delicate and eloquent hint to the pastor to bring "beaten oil" into the sanctuary. Those valuable volumes--they are full of the deep thoughts of thinking men. They will help the pastor to think. And they will make him think, that the best return he can make for his people's kindness, is earnestly to endeavor to bring out for his people thoughts as near in value and worth to those found in the books sent him as possible—and even better, if he can.

3. Such an offering is a very comforting intimation to the pastor, that he is desired not to take wing and leave his people just at present. If one good massive, valuable volume fairly says, "stay longer," I think fifty of them would come very nearly into the neighborhood of saying, "We should be glad to have you grow grey and lay your bones among us."

4. Such a discovery might be made by hosts of pastors in the land without any thing like a dreadful pecuniary bankruptcy on the part of their benevolent people. A discovery even a seventy-fifth part as great as that above recorded, would accomplish two important ends, not to speak of more: first, it would fill a painful gap in the pastor's library; and secondly, it would tell him, as straws do, which way the wind was blowing. H.

A SEAMSTRESS AND A POOR MINISTER.

A Christian minister was settled, near the close of the last century, in a small parish on the mountains in western Massachusetts. With a family of five sons and five daughters, and with the expenses of severe and protracted sickness, he was obliged, for years, to anticipate the whole amount of his support before it became due. His good and generous parishioners, always awake to his interests, did much, by gifts and donations and prompt payments, "to strengthen his hands and encourage his heart." Still, prospects were dark, and a small extra expense, such as the purchase of a new suit of clothes, was met with delay and with difficulty. At one time he met such a marked providence, that he could not but say, "This is the finger of God."

A young lady from a distance, poor indeed, but noble in heart—one who lived by her needle—called on the pastor, and after mutual expressions of civility, said the young seamstress with modesty and some embarrassment, "Sir, shall I measure you for a coat?"

After doing this, she added, "Shall I measure you, sir, for a vest?" After a little delay, she then added, as if her benevolence was expanding beyond her first intention, "I think I will take measure, sir, for a suit entire." Having done this, and no question being asked, or pledges given, the young lady retired, and soon returned to her distant home, near the borders of Canada. After many months, a neat suit of clothes, of the finest texture, spun and prepared almost wholly by her own fair hands, arrived. It was at a time when ingenious mothers and daughters could produce a fabric not unbecoming the Sabbath or the pulpit. American factories had not yet risen up, and foreign broadcloths were at their highest prices. The gift was timely, and in itself valuable.

And God, who had thus supplied the wants of one of his poor ministers, took care of the young maiden who stretched forth her hand for his relief. She had become an orphan by the death of an excellent Christian father, but in the providence of God she formed a connection by marriage which introduced her to wealth, and became the mother of a family of high respectability. One of her sons graduated with honor at a New England university. How true it is, that "charity is twice blessed; it blesses him that gives, and him that takes."

This record is made, as one among testimonials without number, that God is true in his promises to his ministers and to the friends of ministers.

T. M. C.

THE NEGLECT OF RELIGION.

CONVICTIONS STIFLED.

MANY years ago I had the pleasure of spending some time in two places in the state of New York, in which powerful revivals of religion were in progress by the blessing of God upon the labors of Rev. Dr. Nettleton.

In the course of the first revival in the town of ——, a gentleman of my acquaintance became deeply anxious for his soul. He wept, he mourned, he sighed, and no doubt prayed for days and days together. But he was proud and obstinate—he would not submit to God.

One day his pious, amiable wife, whose anxieties about her husband were almost beyond control, came into his room, and finding him still lingering in his wretched condition, and solemnly fearing that he would grieve away the Holy Spirit, and turn back to the world, she fell upon her knees in his presence, and fervently prayed for him. The husband's state of mind after that prayer may be conjectured, but not easily described. He literally *writhed* in mental anguish.

Dr. Nettleton was the wisest man that I ever saw in tracing out the operations of the human mind when under the influences of the divine Spirit. He seemed to possess almost intuitive knowledge of this subject. When he saw a sinner long lingering under conviction he judged that there was a special cause, and he was pretty sure to detect that cause.

One day, after my friend Lambert, for so I will call him, had been struggling with and stifling his convictions for some time, Dr. Nettleton called to see him once more. He talked with him, pointed him to the Saviour, and perhaps prayed with him. But there Lambert lingered still, a miserable, disconsolate, lost sinner. No light, no hope. What could be the matter? Dr. Nettleton smelt ardent spirits. That was enough. He immediately intimated to Lambert that he was drinking with a view to drive away his convictions; and I believe the latter did not deny the charge. Dr. Nettleton solemnly warned the wretched man, and left him. What was the result? The Spirit of God left my friend, and the unclean spirit who had gone out returned to his old habitation, accompanied by seven other spirits more wicked than himself; and the last state of that man was worse than the first.

Perhaps ten months passed away, when a blast and a mildew rested upon all that pertained to this miserable man. Nothing prospered in his hands. His business, though formerly flourishing, was in ruins; and he was compelled to leave the beautiful house in which he lived. This was not the worst—he was given up of God. He was undone, to all appearance, for time and for eternity. His lovely wife and his interesting children were disconsolate and broken-hearted.

Go with me now through yonder street of the town at night, and what do we see? There lies poor wretched, ruined Lambert, a drunkard in the ditch! O God, what is man when left of thy Spirit? Let a veil, for the present, cover the sequel.

Reader, if the Spirit of God strive with you, as you value salvation, grieve him not away.

N. H.

THE PLEASURE RIDE.

In a powerful revival of religion in a town in Connecticut, some years since, there was an interesting young lady whose mind became deeply affected with the subject of religion. She felt that she was a poor lost, ruined sinner, in infinite danger of dying without hope. She wept, she prayed, she threw herself among the anxious, she visited the house of God, and, I believe, conversed with the preacher about her sad condition.

Could she give up the pleasure of the world at that early, interesting period of life? It seemed hard. Conscience admonished, the Spirit wooed, the world allured, the devil tempted. What an awful conflict! She hesitated, she lingered, she prayed and struggled and resolved, and still clung to her idols.

A thoughtless young man, no doubt sent by the adversary of souls, came and said, "Will you take a pleasure ride?" O, what a question to be put to one in her state of mind! How could *she* find pleasure in the society of young companions, while that fearful pressure was upon her soul, and that hell in her bosom? Might not the Spirit be grieved away and leave her for ever? It was a tremendous thought. But—will the reader believe it?—she *did* go and take that ride. It was a fatal one.

About two days had elapsed; and now let us go

and see that same young lady. She does not notice us as we enter the room; but she lies upon the bed, crying out in horrible anguish of spirit, "I have sold my soul. I have sold my soul! I have grieved the Spirit. I am lost!" Oh, it was a dreadful sight. Her voice of wailing seems even now to be sounding in my ear. We left the house, but her mournful voice followed us: "I have sold my birthright for a mess of pottage. I am lost—I am lost!"

Reader, as you value salvation, rush not into vain company when the Holy Spirit is striving with you. At such a time, one pleasure ride, or one pleasure party, may cost you the loss of heaven. "Grieve not the Spirit." N. H.

THE FATAL RIDE.

Miss G. S—— resided in a village in one of the southern states, and at the time to which this narrative refers, was about fifteen years old. She was surrounded by worldly and fashionable friends, who admired her, and who allured her into their circles of gayety. A pious lady in the village established a Bible-class for young females, and Miss S—— was solicited to join it. Without much hesitation she consented; and took her seat regularly every Sabbath with her young companions, to receive lessons from the word of God. These instructions were such as she had not enjoyed at home, and they engaged her attention, and seemed gradually to fasten upon her a serious impression. She at length acknowledged her solicitude on the subject of religion; she said that she needed a new heart, and hoped the Lord would give her one. Her deportment was changed. She ceased to take pleasure in gay society, and chose that of her teacher and other pious friends. She appeared to be "not far from the kingdom of God;" and her instructress was fondly looking for her full consecration of herself to the Redeemer, and public profession of his name.

The winter with its fashionable parties and entertainments now approached, and the pleasures of the season excited and absorbed the young people of the village, and excluded every serious thought. Sleighing parties and balls were the subjects of conversation, and created high enthusiasm. Miss S—— watched these movements of gayety, and seemed to take a deeper and deeper interest in them, and to be less in earnest about the salvation of her soul. Her worldly companions perceived this, and ventured to propose that she should accompany them on one of their parties of pleasure. The day appointed was the Sabbath. The proposition at first shocked her. The thought of desecrating those holy hours, which she had for a long time been accustomed to spend in the Bible-class and at the sanctuary, brought a faithful remonstrance from her own conscience. But the temptation was perseveringly urged, and it at length prevailed.

She went on the Sabbath sleigh-ride, while the other members of the Bible-class assembled as usual in their little school-room. The instructress looked around anxiously for G. S——. She was absent. The painful discovery was made that she had gone on a pleasure excursion. The heart of the pious teacher was filled with distress. After being exposed for hours to the wintry air, Miss S—— returned to her home unhappy. Remorse took possession of her mind, but led not to repentance. Alienated from her religious duties and her pious companions by a sense of guilt, she returned to the world, and to the paths of folly.

A ball was to be given in a neighboring town; the time was fixed, the company selected, and extensive preparations were made. Miss S—— was to be at the ball. The materials for her ball-dress were purchased. But a "slight cold," which she had taken during her Sabbath sleighing excursion, grew worse. The ball night came; the gay company assembled—but Miss S—— was not there. She was not in this world! That night her soul had been required of her. The ball-dress had become a shroud. At the hour of the dance and festivity, in which G—— S—— was to have borne her part, she was summoned away to the scenes of the eternal world. The summons found her confessedly unprepared. She had declined choosing the "good part," and she was now to die in bitter regrets, and without hope.

AN EASTERN STUDENT.

Many years since, two young men were fellow-students at an eastern college. In an outpouring of the Spirit, one of the two became convicted, and urged the other to join him in asking permission from the tutor to attend an evening inquiring-meeting. His friend had no wish to go; but he obtained permission for both, and again entreated his companion to accompany him. Overcome by this persevering importunity, his friend at length agreed to "walk down town with him." They went together to the place of the meeting. At the door they paused, and looked in, still debating the question of entering. At length, the one who had been so reluctant yielded, and passed in. But lo, the other also changed his mind, turned, and went his way. The one who entered was found by the Spirit of God, and made a rejoicing convert. The other went back to the world.

At the close of their college course, they separated. He who was converted became an able and faithful minister of Christ at the west. After many years, revisiting the place of his education, as he was riding to preach in the very place and church in which he was converted, he heard some one calling him. On turning, he met a sight that filled him with grief. Before him stood the friend of his early days, the student who urged him to attend the inquiring-meeting. But alas, how changed! That bright and splendid intellect was a wreck; the fires of genius and intelligence had been quenched in the drunkard's bowl. "Why, ——, you are a drunkard," was the first exclamation of his sorrowing friend. "I know it," he answered mournfully. "But why do n't you reform?" "I have tried, but it is of no use." "Then you are ruined, both body and soul." "I know it," was the reply. He then went on to give his history since they had separated. "You recollect," he said, "the time of that inquiring-meeting. From that time I date my fall. From the instant that I made my decision not to enter that meeting, my heart became steeled. My serious impressions vanished, and I ran the way of my passions without control. I have thus gone on, till I am what you see; nothing now has any power to restrain me."

After further discourse, they again separated. He who had thus stifled his convictions, soon ran his race, and descended to a dishonored grave, and we fear, to a miserable eternity. The other was still honored with the privilege of cultivating the blooming field which his labors aided to recover from the wilderness.

D. E.

GRIEVING THE SPIRIT OF GOD.

As, in the providence of God, I have been brought into contact with thousands of persons who have told me with much candor the history of their own minds, and conversed freely in reference to the all-important subject of their own salvation, I have thought it to be my duty to record some of the facts I have met, for the benefit and warning of others. That there is a turning-point in the history of every soul that lives under the light of the gospel, no one doubts who believes in the renewing and sanctifying agency of the Spirit; but too many take it for granted that this point is not reached till the close of life, and neglect or resist the strivings of the Spirit till he gives them up to hardness of heart and blindness of mind, perhaps many years before their earthly existence has terminated.

The first case I shall mention is that of a woman about thirty years of age, with whom I conversed in the presence of her mother. I inquired if she was a member of any church. She answered, "No." I asked if she had not at some time felt concern for her salvation. "Yes," she said, "I think but few have been more anxious on the subject than I was once." I asked at what period of her life this occurred, when she gave me the following account of God's dealings with her. "When I was about fifteen years old, I felt that I was a great sinner in the sight of God. Often my distress was so great that I could not sleep; and for three years I seldom had peace a week at a time. I knew that the Holy Spirit was striving with me, and that I ought to yield my heart to his influence; but I thought it would cut off my pleasures in the midst of youth. I tried to banish the thoughts of eternity; but they would still return and interrupt my pleasure. I tried reading novels and romances; they gave me relief for a while, but my distress returned. At last I went to the ballroom, and I have never since had such feelings as before." "And have you no fears," said I, "that you have grieved away the Spirit of God for ever?" "Yes," she replied, "I have no doubt of that, and that I shall be lost." I proceeded to describe the state and misery of the lost, and appealed to her, by the prayers of her mother, and the tears which were then falling from her sunken eyes; by the danger of an eternal separation from pious friends; by the glories of heaven, and the agonies of the Son of God, now to make her peace with him and be saved. "All this," she calmly replied, "has been tried upon me before. Nothing that you or any other man can say on that subject, can move me now. My doom is fixed."

Another case was that of Mr. B——, who was

over seventy years old, and living an ungodly life. I approached him with kindness, and at length he conversed freely. I spoke of the goodness of God to him in his advanced years, and asked if he hoped he had an interest in Christ. He replied, "No." I asked if he received the Bible as the word of God. He answered, "Yes." I said, "The Bible teaches that a man must be born again before he can enter the kingdom of God; do you think you have experienced that change?" "No," said he, "I never have." I saw that he was intelligent, and inquired if no "still small voice" had ever whispered to him, "Son, give me thy heart?" "Yes," said he, "often. I used to feel; but for many years I have not felt as I did when I was young. I then had some very serious times." I asked at what period he had felt most deeply the importance of religion. He replied, "When I was seventeen I began to feel deeply at times, and this continued for two or three years; but I determined to put it off till I should be settled in life. After I was married, I reflected that the time had come when I had promised to attend to religion; but I had bought this farm, and I thought it would not suit me to become religious till it was paid for, as some time would have to be devoted to attend church, and also some expense. I then resolved to put it off ten years; but when the ten years came round, I thought no more about it. I often try to think, but I cannot keep my mind on the subject one moment." I urged him by all the terrors of dying an enemy of God, to set about the work of repentance. "It is too late," said he; "I believe my doom is sealed; and it is just that it should be so, for the Spirit strove long with me, but I refused." I then turned to his children, young men and young women who were around him, and entreated them not to put off the subject of religion, or grieve the Spirit of God, in their youthful days. The old man added, "Mind *that.* If I had attended to it then, it would have been well with me to-day; but now it is too late."

On conversing with a man in middle life, he informed me that his father was a devoted Christian, that he was faithfully instructed, and his mind was early impressed with the importance of religion. In his youth, there was a period of six months in which he was in distress, day and night; and a voice within seemed to be continually saying, "Forsake your sins, and come unto me, and I will give you peace." "But," he added, "I did not wish to be a Christian then; I thought it would ruin my pleasures. I visited a part of the country where dancing and balls were frequent; in a little time my serious thoughts were gone, and I have never had any since." I asked if he did not fear that God had given him up. "Yes," said he, "I am afraid he has. I go to church, and read the Bible, and try to feel, but I cannot." I strove to arouse his fears; but it was in vain. I afterwards learned that he was pursuing his worldly business on the Sabbath.

It is not for me to pronounce that God had said of all these persons, they are "joined to their idols, let them alone;" "Woe to them when I depart from them;" but the state of all such is unspeakably alarming. If such is your case; if you have wilfully dashed the cup of salvation from your lips, when God by his Spirit was wooing you to himself; if you have persisted in saying, "Go thy way for this time, let me alone that I may have the pleasures of this life," and have quenched the Spirit by resorting to amusements, the novel, the ballroom, or the theatre, God may have given you what you desired; but what have you now of all these pleasures? Can you look back upon them with an approving conscience? Will they bring you consolation in a dying hour? No. You have, even now in your own soul, if you would make the confession, the gnawings of the worm that never dies, the burning of the fire that is never quenched. You will have no excuse when you stand before the throne of the eternal Judge. He will say, "I called, but you refused; I stretched out my hand to you, but you did not regard it."

But to the dying sinner with whom the Spirit of God is now striving, let me say, it is the most momentous period of your existence. It is perhaps the turning point between heaven and hell—the songs of angels, or the wailings of the finally lost. O seize the present moment, while the voice of the Spirit is whispering in your ear, "Now is the accepted time." Beware of stifling that voice. Multitudes have told me the dreadful tale, "I went to scenes of amusement, or turned to the exciting romance, and I have felt no anxiety since."

O awakened sinner, while the Spirit strives, it is the seed-time of eternal life, the embryo of a happy immortality. Sit not down to count the loss of sinful pleasures; receive the Saviour into your heart, and you will have pleasures lasting as eternity—pleasures that leave no sting behind—pleasures that will sustain the soul when on your dying pillow, when the last trump shall sound, and the congregated world stand before God.

J. C.

RELIGION DEFERRED.

In the early part of my life, writes a lady in 1846, I was attending a boarding-school for young ladies. The school was flourishing, and we were a peculiarly united and happy company. We enjoyed much in the society of each other, and in the instructions of our loved teachers.

In the early part of the term the school was visited by the precious influences of the Holy Spirit. Some of our number were hopefully converted to God; and many others were deeply impressed with the necessity of attending immediately to the concerns of the soul, one of whom was Maria B——. Her natural temperament was rather gay and lively, but her disposition very amiable, and she readily won the affections of all who became acquainted with her.

Our principal labored with us all faithfully. She strove to impress upon those of us who were professors of religion, the duty of seeking earnestly the salvation of our dear companions. She reminded us not only of our duty to converse with them, and pray for them and with them, but that we ought constantly to exhibit our principles and *live* religion before them.

But after a season this special religious interest died away, and among those who were left unconverted was Maria. Her health was always delicate, and towards the close of the term it began considerably to decline. She appeared uniformly gentle and amiable, and with a spirit somewhat subdued. I often thought I ought, in some way, manifest the desire which I still felt for the salvation of her soul, and resolved repeatedly that I would entreat her to consecrate herself to the service of God, and become a sincere friend and follower of the Saviour. But as no very favorable opportunity occurred for a long time, I continually delayed what I felt to be an important duty.

She was frequently absent from the table on account of ill health; and on one such occasion I obtained permission to carry her some light food, and sit with her while the family were at tea. When I entered the room I found her alone, and very sad. She appeared grateful for my attention, and it seemed to me a favorable opportunity to direct her thoughts to the Saviour, and to dwell upon the realities of eternity. But I felt reluctant to commence the conversation, and allowed the time to pass by without saying one word on the subject which was weighing so heavily upon my heart. After tea was over, some gay young ladies came in, and I withdrew. A few days after this she left us, and returned to her parents, sick. We frequently heard that she still remained feeble, but we heard nothing of the state of her mind.

The close of the term was rapidly approaching; and with it the excitement of the coming examination, sorrow that we must so soon be separated, and joy at our anticipated meeting with our beloved families and friends. Soon we were all scattered, and I returned to my home far away from all my school-fellows. I occasionally heard from one and another of them with much interest, but nothing from Maria; until at length a paper was sent me, and in the list of deaths was the name of Maria B——. My pen would vainly attempt to describe my feelings on seeing it. A remembrance of my unfaithfulness came over me with crushing weight. She had gone into eternity, and all further opportunity to beseech her to come to a merciful Saviour was gone for ever. I might have besought her once, but now it was too late.

I eagerly examined the few words which were said of her, to catch, if possible, some ray of hope that she had, in her last days, made her peace with God; but I only found a notice of the sweetness of her disposition and of the general loveliness of her character, while nothing was said of a change of heart, of repentance for sin, of faith in the Lord Jesus Christ, or of hope of salvation through the efficacy of his atoning blood. I took the paper and retired to my chamber, to weep and pray over my neglect of duty, to seek forgiveness from God, and implore his assistance to enable me in future to obey, without hesitation, the voice of conscience and of his word.

For a long time the day of judgment was vividly before me. The mild eye of Maria seemed resting upon me, with a look unutterably expressive—a look which pierced my heart with anguish; for it seemed to say, "You saw my danger, but you warned me not. You knew the way of life, but you directed me not to walk in it. You had experienced the love of the Saviour, but you invited me not to come to him. Now it is for ever too late." The record of my unfaithfulness was in the book of God, and my sin was continually before me. I did not attempt to relieve my overburdened heart by expressing its anguish to any one, but to my God. I felt that through his mercy he might forgive me, and grant me grace to be more faithful. That he would do so, for the Redeemer's sake, was my earnest prayer.

Oh, if we lived with eternity constantly in view—

if we felt at all times the infinite value of the soul, we could not be so negligent and unfaithful as we are prone to be, but should work while it is day; knowing that "the night cometh, when no man can work."

Serena.

THE CRITICAL MOMENT.

It was a time of awakening in N——. Serious thoughts were taking possession of a number of minds. Among those who were in some degree impressed by divine truth, was our young friend H—— W——. She attended the stated meetings, and sought the advice of her pastor. Her whole deportment showed that she felt she was not safe in her present condition. It was hoped that she would soon come to such a view of her own evil heart, and of the love of Christ, that she would be led to yield to him in cordial submission, and devote to him the remainder of her days.

But among her acquaintance was one who feared not God. O—— Y—— was a young man who showed her marked attentions, and exerted much influence over her mind. He disliked the humbling doctrines of the Cross, to which H—— W—— was accustomed to listen. They were unacceptable to his proud, unrenewed heart, and steadfastly he set himself to oppose them. He began to rally her on her seriousness, to laugh at her as he saw her countenance sobered by those unwonted thoughts which were struggling for a place within her bosom. He derided the meetings which she attended, and sported at those who were seeking to serve God in truth.

As he saw that those meetings and the words there

heard had influence on her mind, he determined to draw her away from them, hoping that thus he might bring her back to her former state. He therefore appointed to visit her on the evening of the meeting for prayer in which she felt deeply interested, and assured her, that if she should attend the meeting, he should regard it as a marked token of personal disrespect.

Here was a trial. Here was the critical time, perhaps the turning-point of her religious history. On the one hand stood the service of God, on the other the service of the world; on the one hand the favor of God, on the other the favor of the world; on the one hand conscience, on the other her own inclinations; on the one hand the Spirit of grace, on the other the voice of the tempter.

And what was the decision? She chose to risk the eternal interests of her immortal soul, rather than lose a few hours of empty enjoyment. She chose to meet the frown of God, rather than that of a poor weak worm of the dust like herself. The next day her seriousness seemed to have vanished, she appeared as light and gay as ever; though it could be seen that she was ill at ease. She felt that she had taken a step which she could not retrace.

If, dear reader, you feel that you are in the wrong way, then let nothing upon earth, nothing of all its joys, its pleasures, its friendships, call you away from *now* seeking the salvation of your soul. And above all, see to it that you never occupy the place of him who thus drew away one who was beginning to turn her steps heavenward. May it not be feared that, in a terrible sense, he has murdered her soul; that while he was pleading friendship, he was the worst enemy which she had, or could have, since he thus led her to eternal ruin? Who would stand in his place? Who would lead an undying soul to perdition? W.

"I CANNOT GIVE UP THE WORLD YET."

The despairing death of a young man in my congregation, was followed by a deep seriousness among his companions. There appeared to be genuine contrition for sin, and in none more decidedly than in a young lady who was the pride of the youthful circle. She was the daughter of a prosperous merchant, surrounded by the attractions of wealth and the gay company and pleasures it brings; but a pious mother had sought to lead her to the Saviour. She had often been serious, and was now more decidedly so than ever. Before, she had grieved the Spirit; now, she wished to become a Christian. Her Bible was read; she prayed in secret, and came to her pastor and freely unburdened her soul. Her convictions of sin were pungent; her views of the way of salvation apparently clear and correct. With childlike simplicity she besought me to counsel her and pray for her.

I believed she was near the kingdom of heaven, and expected the Saviour would very soon appear precious to her. But upon a closer examination I found an obstacle of fearful magnitude. She did not understand her own heart. She thought she was willing to give her affections to Christ, resigning every idol, but she had not looked closely. The world and her old associates still had a power over her, though she knew it not. She would be a Christian, yet like the wife of Lot, looked back with a wishful eye to what she had left. Seeing the fearful peril of her soul, and the importance of a speedy decision, I showed her the danger of continuing in her present state, and urged her to surrender her heart to God.

After an interval of a few days I sought her residence, and found her much as before. She frankly revealed to me the exercises of her mind. "In the silence of my chamber, away from the world, where I can seriously weigh the all-important subject, I think I feel willing to give up all. I can there feel that I am a great sinner, that Christ is just such a Saviour as I need, and that the world is false; but the moment a companion comes in I am changed, and feel unwilling to renounce all. I want to break away from these; but how can I?" I again represented her danger, and told her that if she did not become a Christian now, she probably never would. As the Spirit had often striven with her, he might now take his departure, never to return. I trembled for an immortal soul, over whose conversion angels desired to rejoice. She soon made a choice—but alas, she chose the world. When I again approached her on the subject, she said, "I find I cannot give up the world yet." She had too many sacrifices to make.

Years have since passed. She has been no more conscious of a Saviour standing at the door of her heart and asking to come in; no Spirit's whisperings have been breathed in her ear; no tear of penitence has moistened her cheek. She acknowledges she has no feeling—no desire to be a Christian at present. She drowns all thoughts of death and the judgment in the cup of pleasure.

There is a crisis in the life of every impenitent sinner, a season when the Spirit comes to him for the last time—when he must choose between the pleasures of the world and the service of God. You may not know when you pass that crisis. With eagerness you may be pursuing the world, deferring for a convenient season the one thing needful, while God has written your name among those of whom he says, "Ephraim is joined to idols: let him alone." O cherish the strivings of the Spirit, before it is for ever too late. Cast in your lot with the people of God. Go with your wicked heart—all that you value on earth; carry them to Calvary, and resolve that if you perish, it shall be there, pleading for mercy. W.

A NOVEL-READER.

I believe I was about fifteen: the precise time has vanished from my memory, but never can the circumstances of that day be forgotten. It was a pleasant Sabbath morning, and I went to the house of prayer with my friends, with no unusual interest in religious things. But something in the prayer fixed my attention, and prepared me to listen to the sermon. My interest deepened. I began to feel as I had rarely felt before, that the truths spoken had a solemn bearing upon my own destiny. The voice of God spoke in my soul of wasted hours and talents, and of the coming eternity with all its tremendous realities. It was not the earthquake, nor the fire, but the still small voice. I was neither terror-stricken nor overwhelmed; but it seemed to me as if an angel spoke, setting my sins before me, and inviting me to turn and live. For a moment the rebellious passions were stilled, the way of holiness seemed a blessed way, and my heart *almost* said, "I will arise, and go to my Father."

Never before had I felt it my immediate duty to turn unto God. Often, from my early childhood, had I had fearful forebodings of a coming judgment; but until this time no voice had ever said to me, "Now is the accepted time." I knew that these feelings could be easily dissipated, but that by earnest prayer and diligent study of God's word, they might be deepened and strengthened, and I *almost* resolved that I would give no rest to my spirit until I found it in peace with God. *Almost!* alas, it was only an *almost*. What came between me and my God? Am I not giving the history of many, when I say it was the fascinations of a novel? I had been reading one the previous day, and had left it with an earnest desire to know the close. I had indulged myself in novel-reading until it had become a passion, until almost every thing else was forgotten for its pleasures. And now, as the sermon closed, the thought of that story rose before me. Shall I read it? was the mental question. I knew that if on my return home I turned to its pages, every religious impression would be obliterated; and during all the closing prayer, during all my walk home, the struggle was going on—and the novel conquered. The voice of the Spirit was silenced.

Blessed be God, it was not for ever. Five years after, after months, I might almost say *years*, of conflict and darkness—darkness that might be felt, and which at times shut out every earthly enjoyment, and made me exclaim in the bitterness of my spirit, "Would I had never been born," I found, I humbly hope, peace under the shadow of the cross. But those lost years—what would I not give, what sacrifice would I not make, could I redeem them. But they are gone, with their opportunities of doing and getting good—lost to me for ever. It was in some sense a forming period of my character. How different should I now be—how much more could I now do for God and my fellow-beings—how much more might I now be conformed to the likeness of my Lord, had these years been passed under his training—employed in his service. I can never look back without a pang upon that Sabbath, upon that deliberate rejection of the offers of mercy.

Is not this history substantially that of multitudes? Have not thousands sold their birthright for the pleasures of novel-reading? Are there not thousands more, who have entered the church of Christ shorn of their best years and their noblest energies, through the same seductive influence?

Christian parents, you love the souls of your children; your daily prayer is, that they may be early consecrated to the service of their Saviour; guard them then against making fiction the food of their minds. Do not let them form a habit which may bind them as with chains of adamant for ever, and which, if its power is ever broken, will surely prove a clog in their progress heavenward. God's grace is all-powerful, but he works by means. He appeals to the conscience and the heart, and whatever blunts the sensibilities or lowers the standard of duty, must lessen the probability of their conversion. This, novel-reading does. He whose mind has been excited by the high-wrought scenes of fiction, or who has loved to dwell on scenes of imaginary distress, will be but slightly moved by the simple story of the love and death of Jesus. God's voice, speaking from Sinai, proclaiming his immutable law and its terrible penalties, will be as unheeded as the voice of love speaking from Calvary; for conscience too is deadened. The standard by which the confirmed novel-reader measures his moral character, is generally *at best* only the low standard of a worldly morality, from which all reference to our relations to God is excluded. How then, if his life has been such as the world will not condemn, can he be convinced of sin, of righteousness, and of judgment? Like Felix, he may tremble for a moment, but having no true sense of the majesty of holiness, or the requirements of God, it will be only for a moment.

But even if it be not so, and there are certainly many exceptions—even if the example and instructions of pious parents, and the light of God's truth shining continually on his path, have kept his heart tender and his conscience alive, novel-reading throws yet another obstacle in the way of his conversion. If not of a temper naturally very active and practical, he has probably lived in a land of shadows and dreams. He has mourned over sorrows he has not been called to alleviate, and has admired achievements which he has not thought of imitating, and so has formed the habit of indulging emotion which was not to terminate in action. He has dreamed of glorious things to be done, he has formed magnificent plans, but the dream and the plan were all. But the religion of

Christ from its very commencement requires action. "*Strive* to enter in;" "Deny thyself, and take up thy cross, and follow me," are the words of our Lord. We cannot enter into the kingdom of heaven by mere emotion. We must act as well as feel. We must not only see our sins, but strive against them. Now, though the novel-reader may see his sinfulness, may have some longings after the joys of holiness and usefulness, and may form some resolutions for good, the probability is that sighs and tears and resolutions will be all. He sees the good and approves it, but has lost the moral stamina which would enable him to struggle against the current of temptation.

And even if he is brought at last into the church of Christ, how rarely is he an active laborer in the great work to which God has called us. He sees how much there is to be done, he envies those who with cheerful and earnest spirit are engaged in it, he makes some weak and faithless efforts to conquer his easily-besetting sins, and to combat evil around him, but he accomplishes little. The strength of his will is broken, the power of patient action gone, and he will achieve little of worth for himself or the world.

R.

THE FROLIC IN PLANTING-TIME.

Upon a bleak winter day, I was travelling through one of the sparsely inhabited counties of Western Kentucky. A wretched log-cabin near the roadside attracted my attention. It stood in a small field of cleared land, surrounded for miles by the unbroken forest. There was sufficient tillable ground, if industriously cultivated, to yield a subsistence for a small family. But it was easy to perceive that the plough and hoe had not during the summer disturbed that soil. A rank growth of weeds, deadened by the frost, covered the ground. I reined in my horse, and repeated to myself the words of Solomon, "I went by the field of the slothful, and lo, it was all grown over with thorns, and nettles had covered the face thereof."

There was no window in the hut, the space between two of the logs having been left unchinked in order to admit the light. The roof was dilapidated, the mud chimney was leaning out from its perpendicular, threatening soon to fall, the fences that enclosed the field were partially prostrated, all giving evidence of wretched poverty.

Impelled by a desire to know something of the habits of a family living in such apparent misery, I alighted and entered the hovel. It was a filthy place. In one corner, on what seemed a pile of rags, lay a miserable looking man—the husband and father—evidently sick unto death, and that sickness produced, as might at a glance be seen, by intemperance. A pale, sickly looking wife, and four ragged, dirty children composed the household.

Their history is soon told. He had neglected his little farm, spent his time in carousing and drunkenness, depending on his rifle to provide food in winter. Dissipation had produced disease. Death was at his bedside waiting the appointed moment, and his wife and little ones were suffering for food. After some conversation, in which these facts were elicited, I asked why he had not raised corn and potatoes in his clearing.

"Ah," said he, with western frankness, and with the honesty of a dying man, "I was on a frolic all planting-time."

Alas, thought I, a striking emblem is this scene of the conduct and condition of multitudes, in relation to their spiritual interests. How many "frolic away their planting-time," without making any provision for the drear winter of eternity. Many, many when they gaze upon death, wail with streaming eyes and bursting hearts, "The harvest is passed, the summer is ended, and I am not saved."

If any reader is living far from God, let me say, It is now your planting-time, and as you sow so shall you reap. God, in the dispensation of his grace, now furnishes you every facility for securing your soul's eternal welfare. The Bible, your neglected Bible, is the infallible guide in the way of life. Sabbaths, your profaned Sabbaths, regularly interrupt the current of your worldly employments, to remind you of eternal verities. The house of God, by you unvisited, or visited unprofitably, opens its door to urge and encourage you in the path to heaven. Over the mercy-seat, erected in your unfrequented closet, the ear of Jehovah listens for your unoffered prayers. The affectionate entreaties and importunate prayers of pious kindred and friends, by you disregarded, are uttered to win and wean your hearts from earth. Conscience, your stifled and seared conscience, approves the claims and commands of God, and urges you to obedience. The cross, the despised cross, planted in your path, appeals to your grateful love by reminding you of the price paid for your redemption. The Holy Spirit, the grieved and insulted

Spirit, still whispers an assurance of welcome to Jesus.

These are obstructions to your ruin, and facilities for your salvation. You may wisely use them, and live for ever. You may thoughtlessly neglect them, frolic away your planting-time, and be for ever lost!

Are you young? Youth is the planting-time. If it pass away and leave you unconverted, the probability is that you will be lost; for mark and ponder this truth—few, comparatively very few, are regenerated after the spring of youth is gone.

Are you of mature age? The best portion of your planting-time is over. The probabilities of your salvation are greatly lessened with every passing year. Is not eternal life worth one instantaneous, earnest, agonizing effort? Make that effort.

Are you in old age, and impenitent? Alas, there is for you but a bare possibility of gaining heaven. There have been a very few instances of conversion in old age; yours will be another, if you now cast yourself upon the mercy and merits of the Redeemer.

How fearful the guilt, how insane the folly, how tremendous and irreparable the ruin of the man who, careless of his soul's interests, frolics away his planting-time! J. L. B.

TOO LATE.

I had not seen my aged father in nineteen long years. On a beautiful morning in May, 1847, I bade farewell to my family, and started upon a journey of some twelve hundred miles, with a view, after attending the Assembly in Richmond, Va., to pay one visit more to my only surviving parent before he should be called hence. But when I had arrived within one and a half days' travel of my father's residence, I heard of his death. I went and dropped a tear over his fresh grave, upon the banks of a beautiful lake, but him I saw not; I was too late. He died in peace.

I left my friends in New Hampshire, and proceeded to the city of Troy, New York, where I formerly preached, and where for eleven months I lived in a continued revival of religion. I was anxious to see dear friends whom I had not seen in nineteen or twenty years. But I was too late. I found several dear friends, but I was anxious to see Mrs. B——, and Mrs. McC——, who, when I was sick nigh unto death, had been, with several others, like ministering angels. They had recently died. Mrs. McC—— was buried just before I arrived.

I went to Saratoga Springs, where I formerly resided, and there met with several dear friends. But I was too late. There was one, deacon T——, a moral jewel in the church, whom I was particularly anxious to see. He died a little before my arrival, while absent from home.

I had left at home a dear friend, Mr. J. C——, extremely ill. I had long loved and prayed for that friend; but he was not pious. In point of morality, amiableness of disposition, usefulness in life, scientific and literary acquirements, and general knowledge, he had few if any equals in the southern country. But he had been poisoned by bad books and sceptical associates in early life. For years I had been laboring, apparently in vain, for his salvation. I left him, so far as I could judge, upon his death-bed, and yet in all the cheerless darkness of unbelief. Letters came, saying he had hopefully renounced all dependence upon his pure morality, and embraced the Saviour. My feelings were indescribable. I relinquished all idea of visiting the falls or other places, and started for home, hoping to see and to speak with my friend once more before his death. In one week, though I rested on the Sabbath, I passed from the Springs in New York to A——, in Georgia. But notwithstanding this speed, I was *too late.* My friend was gone—his amiable and pious lady is a widow, and his children are fatherless.

I once had an acquaintance in early life, who passed through the revival in which I indulged a hope, an open scoffer. Not long after the close of that precious season, A. S—— was seized with consumption. He gradually failed, till he at length became satisfied that his end was near. He was horror-stricken at the thought of dying. To think of meeting God was more than he could bear. He entreated every body around him to pray for him. But it seemed to be *too late.* The spirit of prayer was gone—no one could pray. In deep anguish of mind, he cried out in despair, "God is determined to show me no mercy," and died. How many thousands there are who, like my friend A. S——, and like the foolish virgins, apply for salvation *too late.*

Said a wretched, dying nobleman, "Oh, if the righteous Judge would try me once more—if he would reprieve and spare me a little longer, in what a spirit would I spend the remainder of my days! Every means of grace, every opportunity of spiritual improvement, should be dearer to me than thousands of gold and silver. But alas, why do I amuse myself with fond imaginings? The best resolutions are now insignificant, because they are *too late*." He continued, "I see a sad, horrible night approaching, bringing with it the blackness of darkness for ever."

Reader, are you unconverted? take warning. Many fail of salvation, because they seek *too late*. May it not be so with you. N. H.

A SECRET DRUNKARD.

At the commencement of my ministry, I found a family in the congregation which interested my feelings very much. It consisted of a husband, a wife, and two or three beautiful children. The man was a mechanic, industrious and prudent. His wife was mild, pleasant, and kind; and had chosen the good part which can never be taken away.

Soon after my settlement, and while making a call upon the family, the wife begged me to take an early opportunity of conversing with her husband. "His mind," said she, "is much troubled on the subject of religion." This was good news to me. My heart, I trust, was somewhat alive to the value of souls, and I received the intelligence with gratitude and delight. It was not long before the wished-for opportunity was found. Our conversation was tender and solemn, and we closed it with earnest prayer to God that his salvation might be magnified in bringing a sinner to the knowledge of the truth. My feelings were deeply moved, and I looked for help to the convincing and converting Spirit of God. The case appeared hopeful. So far as I could judge, the man's views of himself as an offender against God were correct, and he was anxious to be led in the way of life. He seemed to see that nothing short of the blood of Christ could wash away his sins.

My heart was lifted up in gratitude to God. It seemed as if I were to be made the happy instrument of leading a lost sheep to the fold of the Redeemer. I thought of our feeble church. I thought, too, of the wife. The conversion of her husband, so far as we could judge, was all that was necessary to fill her cup of blessing. I saw him again and again. We conversed on the subject of salvation at length. All things appeared ready. He was like a man whose foot was on the very threshold of the kingdom of heaven.

Still, though his seriousness continued, he made no progress. Often did his wife entreat me with tears not to forget her husband. There was a heavy burden on her heart. He would often spend hours of the night in reading the Scriptures and prayer. At length I began to feel discouraged. I could see no advance. My heart whispered that perhaps the instruction I gave him was not explicit enough, or was not evangelical enough. This filled me with agitation, and sent me often to my knees. But after a while the mystery was explained. This anxious sinner was found to be a secret follower of strong drink. Even his poor wife, I believe, was ignorant of the habit he was forming. This intelligence was astounding to every one. What could I do now? Must I hold my peace, and leave my neighbor, my friend, and my parishioner to perish? I was younger by several years than he, and I knew not what to say.

After seeking wisdom from above, the path of duty seemed plain. I felt that I must go and tell him all, whether he would hear or forbear. This I did without delay. In as tender and serious a way as was in my power, I said, "My dear sir, you know what it is that keeps you from the Saviour. God knows it too. I know it. We have often talked and prayed together, and I have been hoping to see you come over on the Lord's side. But there is one thing which you must give up, or lose your soul." I trembled while I uttered these words. My prayer went up to God that his Spirit would give success. I tried to be faithful: how else could I act, or do? One sin might destroy the soul.

His countenance fell as I expostulated with him. He was sullenly silent. He seemed to be sorry that the thing was known. In vain did I plead with him to rise, and in the help of God break the fetters that bound him. From that day he went rapidly down. The sequel is sad, but short. Bad became worse, until his beautiful house went into other hands, his family was broken up, his children scattered, and he, a poor forsaken man, was taken in by his aged parents, to be to them a living sorrow.

But the end soon came, and came in a way to make the ears of every one that hears it to tingle. One Sabbath, in cold weather, the venerable father went to church, leaving no one at home but his feeble wife and this wretched son. In the mean time he found access to some liquor in the cellar, came up, and fell in the fire. The affrighted mother could not pull him out. Before assistance could be obtained, he was literally almost roasted alive. He breathed for a few hours, but never spoke.

To me this was teaching "terrible things in righteousness." Truly, thought I, God is known by the judgments which he executeth. When his hand is lifted up men will not see, but they shall see. It gave me a fearful impression of the evil of sin indulged and cleaved to when the Spirit is striving.

Who knows how many such cases the light of eternity may reveal? It is a fearful thing to grieve the Spirit of God. If, when the mind is agitated, relief is sought anywhere but in the Saviour and the Bible, the effect may prove fatal. To have recourse to unnatural stimulus, may cost the sinner his salvation.

Let me lift up the voice of warning. Sin must be relinquished—every sin, secret as well as open, though dear as a right hand or a right eye, or the joys of pardon can never be felt. His name is called Jesus, because he saveth his people from their sins.

Pastor.

STORY OF REAL LIFE.

There is an interesting class of the community for whom many a heart beats with solicitude and apprehension. I mean the bright, ardent, and unsuspecting youth just leaving the security of a loved home, the eye of a watchful parent, and the sweet influence of a sister, to be thrown at once into all the perils of a merchant's clerk, a mechanic's apprentice, or a college life, with no just idea of the dangers which beset their paths; or if they are in any measure aware of them, without the moral courage to resist them. I would like to specify many of these dangers, but shall now speak only of one, the cheap and poisonous books scattered throughout the land. The poison is so hidden, so mingled with what is alluring to the young, that ruin is effected before the victims are aware of any peril. I speak of those noxious books which pollute the heart, and plunge the simple and unsuspicious into vice and infidelity. I once saw a living victim of this pernicious reading, and such a story may yet be told of many a young man lost and ruined in our cities.

One Sunday evening, an old servant came in entreating me to go "into the kitchen and see a wild-looking man who asked permission to warm his feet." Upon my entrance he looked up, but instantly turned from me one of the finest faces I had ever seen. As I drew near, I wondered not that his feet were cold, for the relics of a tattered pair of boots hardly hanging together over the shreds that had once been stockings, covered but a small part of his red and bruised insteps; he wore the remains of an old military dress which had been given him; still, there was something almost majestic in his appearance, for his head was a model for an artist, his eyes full and soft, his features all fine—it was a noble specimen of "nature's workmanship" in ruins. At first he seemed morose and unwilling to be teased by questions; but he had probably been unused to words of kindness, for when I proposed something to make him comfortable, he seemed melted and subdued, and manifested that kind of confidence which one feels among friends. The

wickedness of wasting life so recklessly was represented to him, till at last, with a look of indescribable woe, and with shuddering emotion, he exclaimed, "Must I disclose to you what no one on earth besides myself knows? It was revealed to me by an unearthly voice years ago, that I must die the fifteenth of next July. I am the victim of infidel books. I have destroyed my own soul, and I *must* die then, and go into eternal misery."

At that moment my father entered from church, and hearing his last words repeated with a dreadful emphasis, he said, "Why, you should have heard the sermon to which I have been listening; then you would have learned that it is never too late to repent." "Oh," exclaimed the poor vagrant, "*you* know nothing about it; there *is* no repentance for me." He discovered much ingenuity in answering every argument with appropriate texts of Scripture, until at last, as if to escape from the annoyance, he abruptly said, "I will now disclose the revelation of which I spoke." He then related a dream, in which his soul was doomed to hell; and here he was so overcome with apparent horror, that we begged him to say no more of his dream, but to explain the cause of his misery. He then told us the name and residence of his parents, and spoke with great emotion of the piety and tenderness of his mother, whom he had not seen for eight years; nor had she had the slightest tidings from him during that time.

When very young, books were his delight, and he had access to the foolish tales which vitiate the taste of children. This excited a thirst for novels, which being ill chosen and of a demoralizing character, led him on to other works of infidel writers. His watchful mother discovered his love for this dangerous reading, and aided by his father's authority forbade the indulgence; but as he found means to elude parental care, his father resolved to place him in the store of a pious man, whose eye would be constantly upon him. However, he eluded even his vigilance, and found access to the books; but being detected, he could not endure the restraint, and resolved to escape from it. After some difficulty, he secreted himself in a vessel bound to the Mediterranean, and escaped the detection of his master. From that time he had been a homeless wanderer in foreign lands. The details of his wanderings were thrillingly interesting, but his narrative was broken again by the most touching reference to his "dear mother," or by the terrific tones in which he would cry out, "Oh, those books—those wicked books! Oh, that Tom Paine knew my misery; my soul is lost, lost for ever!" We saw that there was but too much reason to regard his case as hopeless as he considered it, and believing his mother's care more essential than any thing to his well-being, we entreated him to go to her at once. Now and then he would promise to go; then again, with a convulsive shudder, he would start as from a distressing dream, and in a piteous tone repeat, "No, no, I *cannot* see her;" and when urged to follow the example of the prodigal, he would still say, "No, no; the prodigal did not oppose his mother—did not go contrary to the wishes or without the knowledge of his parents; his misery, his guilt was not like mine—those books, those horrid books!"

Could any of those young men, just entering the world, realize the perfect wretchedness of this poor ruined being, they would as soon touch a viper as a questionable book. A fondness for reading has no doubt secured many a youth from ruin, but books must be well chosen; and parents who expose their children to the influence of immoral and corrupt sentiments, no matter under what guise, or whose example, may have their lives made miserable by such a son.

E. M. C.

A NEGLECTED FAMILY.

S. R——, in the year 18—, commenced his profession in a large southern city, under very disadvantageous circumstances. He was poor; and the wants of his young family pressing hard upon him, in the strength of an indomitable spirit he determined to be rich. He prosecuted his business with industry and perseverance. He allowed no opportunity to pass unimproved, in the promotion of his grand aim. He labored day and night. He toiled all the week; and instead of refreshing his exhausted frame, and composing his excited spirit with the holy rest and privileges of the Sabbath, at least one-half of that precious day was generally occupied by him in attention to his worldly affairs, and the other half in sinful recreation.

Success in the accumulation of wealth rewarded his incessant toil. Dollar was added to dollar, and house to house, until he contemplated his possessions with the exultation of one who seemed to say, "See what I have accomplished!". In his devotion to his gains, his family enjoyed little of his society; and having the means, his children were sent from home to be educated. Thus a stranger to his household, he exercised therein but little influence for good. His children were not restrained from dissipation and licentiousness by his occasional notice of their irregularities, while their fond mother supplied them secretly with the means of self-destruction.

This individual, of course, rarely attended a place of worship, though he always rented a pew for his family, if they chose to occupy it. The minister of the church on one occasion reminded him of his frequent absence from his place, and kindly invited and urged him to attend regularly. His reply showed that he was offended. He felt that his duty was discharged by the punctual payment of the pew rent; and he expressed the hope, that "he should not be annoyed by any farther importunity upon a subject for which he alone was responsible."

In conversation with pious friends, he showed great depth of feeling, and often appeared willing to admit many truths of the gospel. But he was effectually hardened in his opposition to God, by the conviction that among men he was honest, and in his profession had been successful. Of this he boasted, and upon this he rested. He repelled, as a personal insult, the idea that it was the deep depravity of his elated heart which refused submission to the will of God, and excluded from his bosom all sense of the need of a Saviour.

With so great wealth, with such a family, and in such a state of heart, what could he be but a miserable man? And to dissipate the anxiety of his mind, he devoted himself more and more to his earthly gains. When he reflected on the dissolute character of his sons—that they were incompetent to assist him in his business, and could never take his place in his establishment, he felt that they were unworthy of his regard and friendship; and turning from them in disgust and indignation, he lavished upon strangers the kindness and affection which, had he been faithful to his children, might have won them from the paths of the destroyer.

His increasing business at length required frequent visits to Europe. There he saw much to engage his attention, and in the companionship of the gay and licentious, his affections were almost entirely estranged from his family.

Upon one occasion he left his home for Europe, purposing to take passage in a particular steamer; but delaying a few hours to attend to some unimportant affair, he reached the wharf in time to see the stately vessel depart without him. The next packet that sailed was the ill-fated ——. In her he embarked, and shared the melancholy end of her lamented company. In this, however, to the world at large, there appeared nothing peculiar. He was lost—all on board were lost, when the gallant ship found her resting-place beneath the ocean's stormy wave. But to the friends who knew his character, and had remarked his career, there was visible the hand of Providence rebuking ingratitude towards God, and "turning the way of the wicked upside down." The announcement of the probable fate of the vessel filled them with painful concern for one whom on many accounts they esteemed, and their grief was assuaged only by the reflection that, in death as in life, he, and all men, are in the hands of a just and merciful God.

His family were otherwise affected. While other bereaved persons were slow to realize their affliction, and for years cherished the undying, yet delusive hope that their absent loved ones were safe, and would, or at least might return, this family found no difficulty in believing at once the bad tidings, and seemed to be under no apprehension that either the vessel or the husband and father and proprietor would ever be heard of again. And while others "refused to be comforted," in the confidence of better news, this family, with indecent haste, assumed the habiliments of sorrow, as it were to invite the sympathy and consolation of their acquaintance. As soon as legal authority was obtained, the estate was divided. And the sons, from long-continued habits of idleness and intemperance, being incompetent to conduct the large and lucrative establishment, it passed into the hands of strangers on easy terms. From this time a melancholy scene was presented. The widow, sons, and daughters, feeling themselves suddenly emancipated from what they regarded domestic tyranny, gave way to the fatal imagination of enjoying an inexhaustible fortune. Very soon were they surrounded with mercenary and designing *friends*, who contrived to absorb their income, as it was eked out to them in protracted payments. In a few years they were nearly all reduced to poverty; and in peculiar wretchedness, were "holden with the cords of their sins." A long time has elapsed since these events; yet their family and personal history form no exception to the experience of the patriarch, "Who hath hardened himself against God, and prospered?"

How painful the reflection to a parent who, in the midst of the toil and anxiety of accumulating wealth, anticipates the rejoicing of his rebellious children at his sudden decease. Yet thus it must be to the man who, in his service and worship of mammon, neglects God and Christ, his household, and his own soul. Parents, beware lest you commit this capital error. Remember, God is not mocked; "for what a man soweth, that shall he also reap." Whatever be your lawful calling, while you are diligent therein, seek not first the gold that perisheth, but "seek first," for yourselves and your dear children, "the kingdom of God and his righteousness," and his word is pledged to add unto you all else that may be needful. Though you accumulate all wealth, and bequeath much substance to your families, you leave them poor indeed, if they inherit not from you the memory and the blessing of a Christian parent. Look around you in the world, and be suitably impressed with the emphatic affirmation which God's providence is ever giving to his own momentous declaration, "The curse of the Lord is in the house of the wicked; but he blesseth the habitation of the just." C.

A FATHER'S PRAYER.

Sad indeed may be the consequences of a want of resignation to the will of God. A few years since, a pastor was called to visit a family where a son, the only child, was supposed to be past recovery, with sudden illness. The parents were living "without God, and without hope." As the pastor entered the room, the father said to him, "Pray that my child may *live*, but do not pray that I may be resigned to the will of God, should he take him. I cannot—no, never; he is my only son. Pray that he may live." Aware of the responsibility resting upon him, the pastor offered a prayer in accordance with the truth of God's word and promises to the humble believer, in holy resignation to his sovereign will. Favorable symptoms soon appeared, and the child recovered. That son had an uncommon intellect, was prepossessing in his person, and received all the advantages money could purchase, but was an unwearied source of trial and vexation to his family and the neighborhood. He became a reckless infidel, a victim of the most degrading vices, a "by-word" and a "reproach." I have seen the grey-haired father in the street wringing his hands, and mourning aloud the disobedience and ingratitude of his child; and at last he became deranged—dying with a bleeding, broken-heart, his life sacrificed by the treatment received at the hands of that "only son." C.

A SINNER OF FOURSCORE.

I was about to take my leave, for a season, of a friend and benefactor, who was nearly fourscore years of age. The conversation, as we drew near the place where I was to take the steam-boat, took a religious turn, though I did not succeed in rendering it as personal as was desirable. The boat was in sight as we reached the wharf. "I hope," said I, "that I shall see you again in the spring."

"It is not likely," said he, "that I shall be living in the spring."

"Have you no hope that you are a Christian?" said I, perhaps too abruptly, but not without emotion.

The tears rolled down his cheeks, and with some hesitation he said, "No, I don't know that I have any."

For a moment I was too much affected by this painful confession to be able to speak.

"Don't you think," said he, wiping the tears from his cheek with the back of his toil-hardened hand, "that there are some who seek for religion all their days, and never find it?"

I knew that he referred to himself. During his whole life, he had been thoughtful, and more or less interested on the subject of religion. I suspected that he thought it was not altogether owing to himself that he was not a Christian. "Have you ever sought for religion as earnestly as you have sought for property?"

"No, I do not know as I have."

"Can you expect to gain eternal life and glory with less earnestness of effort than it cost you to gain your farm?"

He shook his head. The boat was at the wharf. I bade him farewell, and was borne away. I watched him standing on the wharf, and my heart ached for the aged sinner, so near to death's door, and yet not willing to seek with the earnestness which is necessary in order to find.

I am afraid there are many who have an experience similar to that of this aged sinner. They should remember, that those who seek FIRST the kingdom of God, enter therein, and that the kingdom of heaven suffereth violence, and the violent take it by force. They should remember the command of Christ, "*Strive to enter in at the strait gate.*" I.

"THE LAST CALL."

Amelia H—— was an orphan. In early childhood her father and mother died, and she was left penniless and without a home. But Providence cared for her.

She became the member of a pious family, where she enjoyed all the advantages of a religious education. She respected religion, and often desired to be a Christian. She frequently became anxious for the salvation of her soul, but as often her interest abated. It was not until she was seventeen years of age that she received "the last call."

A revival of religion was in progress, and many of the old and young were born again. Amelia, among the rest, was deeply anxious for herself. She attended the prayer-meeting, meeting of inquiry, and seemed to use the various means of grace with earnestness, yet without coming to Christ. In the midst of this interest she proceeded to fulfil an engagement of some months standing, to visit relatives in an adjoining state. Her friends advised her to the contrary, setting before her the danger of losing so favorable an opportunity to seek the salvation of her soul. But she thought that she should continue to cherish her serious impressions, and when she returned would improve the time to that end.

She went; was absent several weeks. There she mingled in worldly scenes, and lost her religious interest. She returned—but, to die. Scarcely had she reached home when a violent fever prostrated her, and she was brought to hear the painful tidings, "You must die." The reader can imagine her reflections and despair. Pointing to the above-named period, when she appeared to be almost a Christian, and when the Spirit of God was striving with her, she said, "It will do no good to seek now; that was *the last call.*" Fully persuaded that she then grieved away the Spirit for ever, she refused to use the means of salvation, and yielded to despair. For three days she lay tossing from side to side, frequently replying to the counsels of Christian friends, "*That was the last call*," and finally sunk to the grave, hurried thither by mental agony, rather than by bodily suffering. There was not a moment after disease attacked her, when she felt that there was hope. She could not endure the voice of prayer at her bedside, nor listen to the reading of the sweetest promises in the Bible. In this dreadful state she expired, an example of the danger of trifling with the Spirit, and a warning to all who now hear "the still small voice."

Phocion.

ONE THING WANTING.

The morning sun which ushered in the first day of 1852, shone not on a lovelier circle than the one where dwelt Helen Sutton. Neither was the wish for "a happy New-year" more cordially or affectionately expressed, than by her. She devoted herself to the interests and happiness of that group, and was their delight and joy. Being the eldest child, and having at this time advanced to womanhood, she had much influence over its different members. Indeed, she was a striking example of an obedient and dutiful child; ever ready to fulfil the wishes of her parents, and to honor them in all her ways. They have been heard to remark, that they had never known her go contrary to their expressed desires, or treat them with want of respect or affection. What a blessing to a household is such a child! It is a perpetual sunshine, which will banish clouds and darkness from the abode.

But these parents were Christians; and notwithstanding their hearts *safely trusted* in this daughter, they knew she lacked one thing to make her valued services acceptable in the sight of God, and their spirits yearned over her.

When a child, her amiable disposition, united with her correct and praiseworthy deportment, blinded her eyes to the necessity of the renewal of her heart by the Holy Spirit. But at last, her parents had the happiness of seeing her mourning over the discovered guilt of her inward life, and inquiring the way of access to Him who can wash away sin. She *had* looked upon herself as whole, and without need of a physician; but she now saw and felt that she had a stubborn will, that must be bowed to God's will, and a vile heart, that must be cleansed by atoning blood, or she must be miserable for ever. She conversed freely with her parents, her Sabbath-school teacher, and other Christian friends, and they began to hope she was "not far from the kingdom of God."

One day she was sitting alone with her mother, when the danger of delaying to yield herself to God was so strongly impressed on her mind, that she retired to her chamber with the expressed determination not to leave it with an unsubdued heart. Hour after hour passed, and still she remained in her room. At length her footsteps were heard upon the stairs. Her anxious mother scarcely dared raise her eyes to her child, but when she did, she met the sweet smile of other days. "My dear Helen," she asked, "have you found the peace and joy of pardoned sin?" She replied, "Oh no, mother; I have tried to repent of my sins, and exercise faith in the Redeemer, but I cannot, and I have concluded to give up all such efforts, and enjoy myself again as well as I can."

In vain did that mother point her to the dangerous state of one who had spurned the Saviour, and resisted the Holy Spirit. In vain did her Sabbath-school teacher, and other pious friends, urge her to renewed application to Him, who never sends the earnest pleader empty away. She had decided on her course, and as if to shield herself more surely from Christian admonition, her kindness and attention to her parents and other friends was redoubled and untiring.

This occurred many months before the New-year's morning of 1852, and these parents were still hoping and praying that God would yet bless their lovely, darling daughter with the joys of his salvation, though she discovered no disposition to seek it.

Weeks rolled away, and spring began to robe the earth in its beauty. Who admired the opening season, or gathered more of its earliest blossoms than Helen? But she drooped a little, and fell sick—not a sickness to alarm her friends, or disturb her prospects of health and happiness. Medicine was administered. It did not produce the expected result. She was restless, and her mother bathed her temples, and soothed her to repose. As she found herself yielding to these influences, she impressed one kiss on her mother's cheek, and fell asleep. But alas, it was a sleep from which she never awoke! Nothing could arouse her to consciousness, and she slept her life away. Without a word, or a struggle, she entered that world for which she had before deliberately concluded she would not *then* prepare.

Anna.

THE PRICE OF A SOUL.

Some years since, the writer sat in the midst of a weeping congregation, collected in a church in one of the eastern counties of Pennsylvania. It was the middle of the week, but the Spirit of God was abroad upon the hearts of the people, and they came willingly to the sanctuary of God. It was solemn without the walls of the old church, for an ancient forest waved around it, and hard by the dust of our fathers was sleeping; and solemn within, for God's Spirit brooded over the vast assembly. A young and earnest servant of Christ was addressing them on the value of the soul, and well do I remember how the hearts of all were thrilled, and how their tears started, at the narration of the following sad tale.

"A few years ago," said he, "there was living in one of our large cities, a young lady who was the only child of wealthy and worldly parents. She was fond of the gay pleasures of the city, and plunged into them with all the enthusiasm of youth. Her gayety, youth, and wealth, were sure passports to the highest circles of fashion, and there she lived as though there were no higher world.

"While thus living in pleasure, she was asked one evening by a female friend to accompany her to the weekly prayer-meeting in a church of the city. There the Spirit of God met her, and awakened in her the consciousness of sin, and bowed down her heart in anguish at the thought of her guilt. Her heaviness of spirit was soon discovered at home, and her parents were in consternation, lest their beautiful daughter should leave the circles of pleasure for the service of God. They besought her and commanded her to return to the gay world. They surrounded her with her fashionable friends. But there was a power above theirs at work, and she was still stricken in heart. At last those parents actually bribed her to attend a large party of pleasure, by the gift of the richest dress that could be purchased in the city. She reluctantly consented—went to the festival, and returned without one trace of her religious emotions.

"But the joy of her miserable parents was short. In another week their daughter was at the point of death, and the skilful physicians they summoned, in their alarm, could only tell them that there was no hope.

"When this opinion was made known to the dying girl, she lay for a few minutes in perfect silence. Her soul seemed to be surveying the past, and looking into the awful future. Then rousing herself, she ordered a servant to bring that dress and hang it upon the post of her bed. She next sent for her father and mother. In a few minutes they stood weeping at her side. She looked upon each of them for a time, and then lifting up her hand, and pointing to the dress, said to each of them distinctly, and with the terrible calmness of despair, 'Father, mother, there is the price of my soul.'"

O what a disastrous exchange was that. A precious soul, with all its hopes and aspirations, its immortal powers, and high endowments, for a dress! How infatuated those guilty parents. How full of fearful danger is the strife against the Holy Ghost.

Reader, what is the price for which *thou* art parting with thy soul? M. B. G.

A MEMBER OF A CHOIR.

"Mary is dying, and wishes to see you immediately," said one of my parishioners, as I entered his dwelling one delightful May morning. The earth was beautiful with returning life, and the air vocal with the sweet melody of birds.

There was nothing that looked like death in the world without, for the winter was over and gone, and nature was crowding the spring with preparations for a glad and glorious summer. Yet death had come to our little hamlet, and was claiming one of my flock, whom I was unwilling to spare. Mary, whose sweet voice so often had thrilled me in the songs of the sanctuary, the light and the life of that pleasant home embosomed among the green hills, was about to leave us, never to return.

Hastily summoned to her bedside, I followed the weeping father to the room where his darling child was struggling with disease. Alas, it was too true. I saw at once that the golden bowl was breaking, and that the silver cord would soon be loosed. O what a change had come over that young and beautiful form during a few sad days. I scarcely knew her, so worn and haggard. But the eye had not lost its brightness, nor the voice its sweetness, though the bloom had fled from the cheek, and the ruddy lip was swollen and rough.

In a tone that startled every one in the room, she exclaimed, "Oh, Mr. B——, I am dying; and what will become of my soul?" I took her cold and clammy hand, and pointed her to Jesus the Saviour of sinners—in words few and simple, opened to her the way of salvation. She heard me with fixed attention, throwing her whole soul into her searching gaze. "Oh," said she in reply, "these things and the eternal world are so dark to me."

I prayed with her, commending her to the grace and mercy of God, and soon she sunk into unconsciousness, and I saw her no more. But those words will long be remembered. I thought of them as I stood by her coffin, in which the sinking and decaying body contrasted strangely with the bright and fragrant May flowers which her companions had plucked from the fields and the woods for her burial; and when the earth fell heavily upon that coffin in the deep, damp grave, these dying words rung in my ear, "These things and the eternal world are so dark to me."

Mary was the child of pious parents, and was instructed in the truth, but her heart was wild and wayward, and she put far from her all serious things. She intended to be a Christian *some time*, but death came suddenly, and she found herself all unprepared. Thick darkness gathered around her soul, and sh seemed plunging into an eternal night. How awful, when light is most needed, to be in the midst of gloom so thick and dark.

The fearfulness of such a condition is self-imposed. The Lord Jesus "hath brought life and immortality to light." Through faith in him, the mists that hang about the grave are broken, and eternity glows with the light of blessedness and love. The humble believer may instinctively shrink from dying, dark films may creep over his eyeballs, but his inner vision will be unclouded, so that he will grasp with certainty the things eternal of the kingdom of God.

My dear friend, art thou without Christ in this dying world? O come to him now, lest darkness steal over thy soul when thou shalt die, and the hopes of this life perish in the despair of a wretched eternity.

Saco.

A GAY YOUNG MAN.

A few years ago, I was called to visit a gay and thoughtless young man, then on his sick and dying-bed, and trembling in view of death and eternity.

Favored as he had been with the instructions and prayers of a godly mother, and with the consistent and eminently pious life of his brothers, yet, whatever he may have felt, he had never before manifested any concern about his spiritual interests. But now, "distress and anguish" had come upon him; "a fearful looking for of judgment" filled his thoughts, and with sad moans and cries and bitter tears, he lamented his dreaded doom.

He was told of the infinite sufficiency of Christ's atonement for all the wants and woes of perishing sinners; of his perfect willingness to receive even the most guilty, the very "chief of sinners," of the "dying thief," etc., to all which he listened; but, interrupting the speaker, he said,

"It is of no use to offer the gospel to *me;* it is too late now. I do not doubt that some might embrace the gospel on a death-bed and be saved, but I cannot; for I passed the turning-point in the wrong direction two years ago. You remember the revival at O——, two years ago this summer; you know I was there, and it was the most solemn place I ever was in; every one seemed to be interested in religion, and then I felt that the time had come for me.

"The text on Sabbath morning was, 'I, if I be lifted up, will draw all men unto me;' and Oh, I felt that powerful drawing, and determined that day to seek the Lord. At the close of the service, an invitation was given to all who were concerned on the subject of religion, to remain for the purpose of receiving instruction, and for prayer. I resolved to accept the invitation, and arose and walked towards the pulpit, when I saw an old companion gazing and smiling at me. I could not bear his taunts, and turned into a cross aisle and went out of the house.

"Then I broke asunder the cords of Christ's love, and preferred this world to Christ and heaven. I have never felt those drawings since, and believe that my turning-point was then and there, when I stood hesitating in that aisle. I took the broad road; I chose death; and now, Oh, now I have got it; I begin to feel it; the darkness of the pit enshrouds my soul; the fires of perdition are burning me up: O God, O God!"

I tried to pray with him, but so great was the terror of his mind, that his outcry of despair repeatedly drowned my voice. In a few hours the fever settled on his brain, and the poor young man left this world in a raving delirium.

Dear reader, are you unreconciled to God? O, take the solemn warning and reproof that this case presents. "Wisdom crieth aloud, saying, Turn ye at my reproof." How often, when listening to the preaching of the gospel, have you felt the divine drawings? As often have you turned into the "broad way." Beware, beware; you too may pass the turning-point in the wrong direction, and if you do, all will be lost for eternity. J. D. M.

THE AGONY OF DESPAIR.

Not long since, in one of our northern cities, when the influences of the Holy Spirit had been descending on many, a father called on me and stated that his son was in great distress, and anxious to see me.

I immediately accompanied the father, and on entering the young man's chamber, found him lying upon the bed, with his face turned from the door, engaged in audible prayer. He did not at first observe us, and continued his entreaties that God would have mercy upon him.

The father spoke to him, and directed his attention towards me, and on taking his hand I asked him if he was sick. He replied, "Oh sir, my body is well enough, but my soul is sick. I am in the greatest distress on account of my sins, and am unable to obtain any relief. I fear that I have committed the unpardonable sin."

I asked him what he had done that caused him such sorrow. "I have," he replied, "opposed the revival, and made sport of the young converts, and tried to keep my companions away from the inquiry-meeting; and I feel as though God would never forgive me." As he uttered these last words his eyes filled with tears, and he appeared to be in deep anguish.

I said to him, "My young friend, it is not surprising that such reflections distress you, but still God may have mercy upon you." "Ah, there is no mercy, no mercy for me. I have sinned against such light and such privileges, and so long resisted the strivings of the Spirit, that"—here his emotions overcame him, and he was unable to proceed. I referred him to the thief on the cross whom the Saviour pardoned, and dwelt upon the freeness and fulness of the atonement. I recited those precious passages of Scripture wherein the weary and heavy-laden are invited to come to Christ, and all are urged to partake of the water of life. But nothing that I could say seemed to move the mountain-weight that was crushing his soul. I asked him if I should pray with him. "Oh yes," he replied, "do pray; pray earnestly that I may not eternally perish.' I did so; and while pleading for divine mercy, his suppressed groans indicated his deep distress, and the struggles of his spirit to be released from the pangs of remorse.

On leaving him I promised, at his earnest solicitation, to call the next day. With an anxious heart I again visited him, and found that his distress had rather increased than diminished, and he seemed very feverish and much debilitated. He had passed a sleepless night, and been most of the time pleading with God for mercy. He had no inclination to take either medicine or food, for his mind was absorbed by one overwhelming thought, the awful danger to which his soul was exposed. I endeavored to soothe him, and again prayed with him.

The following day he seemed almost in despair, and his fever raged with violence. The intensity of his feelings was evidently consuming his very vitals. He tossed from side to side, and pleaded with me to pray for him. Again I complied with his entreaties, and I used every argument to persuade him to put his trust in the Saviour, and endeavor to compose his mind.

While addressing him, I could not but think of the hundreds and thousands of impenitent sinners whom, instead of laboring to *soothe*, we in vain strive to *arouse*—whom the most solemn appeals from the pulpit, and the most awful warnings of God's providence, fail to move. Could some of them have stood by the bedside of this despairing youth—could they have witnessed his agony, and heard his cries, and seen the power of irreligion to blast his hopes, they would have felt that it was no light matter to despise the Saviour, and treat with contempt the strivings of the Spirit.

The next day the young man seemed more composed, but before night such was the violence of his fever that reason was dethroned. He did not recognize me when I entered the room. His emaciated form and wildly glaring eye and flushed countenance, all told the sad tale, that he held his death-summons in his hand; and indeed, before the week closed, his spirit had taken its everlasting flight.

Reader, did you ever make sport of a companion for being interested in the welfare of his soul, or regard with contempt the means which God has provided and appointed for the salvation of man? If you have, then remember the death-bed scene, the cries and tears and groans of this young man. If you are resolved to neglect religion yourself, I beseech you not to throw obstacles in the way of others who seem inclined to turn their faces towards heaven. Spare your own soul the anguish of feeling that you have dragged others with you down to the gates of death. R. W. C.

A MOURNFUL RETROSPECT.

During a season of special religious interest in one of our New England colleges, the youth who had consecrated themselves to the service of Christ were roused to renewed zeal and fidelity. Groups of praying students were often assembled to give thanks for the renewing mercy of God so abundantly bestowed upon them, and to entreat that none of their unconverted associates might be passed over in this gracious visitation.

As Edward L——, a youth of devoted Christian character, was passing through the hall, on his way from the evening prayer-meeting to his room, Harry H—— joined him, and seizing the arm of his classmate, abruptly addressed him: "L——, do you believe the Bible?" "I do," was the brief decided response.

"It cannot be," said H——, "or you would have warned me of my guilt and danger; you would have labored to pluck me as a brand from the burning. For months we have met almost hourly, you a professor of religion, I an acknowledged unbeliever, yet you have never spoken a word to me on my spiritual interests. If there is any truth in the doctrines you hold, if the book which you call the inspired word of God contains any thing worthy of belief, you have grossly neglected your duty, you have sinned fearfully against my soul. I will trouble myself no more about these matters. My prospect for a long life is as good as any one's; I will enjoy it while I may, and the future, if there be a future, must care for itself. A month ago I might have been a Christian; but that is past, and now it will never be."

The last words were uttered in a low, solemn tone, and the speaker withdrew his arm, and retired to his own apartment. His ready, sarcastic wit had deterred more than one, anxious for his welfare, from speaking to him on personal piety, and now he dared the vengeance of God. Having graduated with honor, he passed through a course of professional study; all his future seemed bright; but on the very opening of a brilliant career, the heavy hand of disease was laid upon him, and in the strength and beauty of early manhood, he sunk beneath its power. His aged and pious parents sorrowed over their gifted only son as those without hope, for he had scorned the mercy proffered to his youth, and on a dying-bed he had none to sustain him.

Edward L—— became a devoted and successful preacher of the gospel; but though many years elapsed since he parted from his class-mate, he never recalled that evening's conversation without a thrill of horror.

E. H.

A CIDER-DRINKER.

In the early settlement of Pennsylvania, three men of the same name came from Connecticut, and settled in a row along a mill-stream. They all commenced alike in the woods by putting up their log-cabins and felling the trees, clearing the land, and tilling the soil as fast as they obtained an opening for culture, and seemed to have an equally fair prospect of comfort and usefulness in the future.

One of them was a member of a Congregational church, and lived to see all his ten children professors of religion.

Another was a Methodist, and had the confidence and respect of the community for his intelligence, piety, and stability of character. He too lived to see all his children professors of religion, and one son a preacher of the everlasting gospel.

The third was "*not so.*" Like the survivor of the deluge, he "began to be a husbandman," and planted an orchard and drank the cider, "and was drunken." He had no children. The little fatherless boy that he obtained from a distance, ran away from him as from a monster of brutality, when twelve or thirteen years of age; and that boy and his twin-brother afterwards proclaimed the gospel in the Methodist connection. More than once this man fell into the stream near which he lived, by the influence of his "good old cider," as it was termed. On one occasion two of his boon companions took him out of the creek, when his life was nearly wasted by strangling. So great was their alarm at this revolting spectacle, that they immediately quitted a practice so destructive and unbecoming a man. But Mr. —— continued cider-drinking. And while his neighbors of his name supported their numerous families genteelly, and supported society also, and had put up comfortable framed dwellings, his cider-drinking habits constrained him to remain in his log-house, though it was sinking beneath its own weight by decay. After a long time, however, he began to build, but on a plan so large and ill-adapted to the size of his family and the length of his purse, that he "was not able to finish." Luke 14 : 30.

His habit gained so rapidly upon him that he could not finish his house, though he finished his work of suicide. Delirium tremens seized him at times. Finally, his end was as public as awful. He had gone to a camp-meeting on a neighbor's field. There he was seized with the delirium tremens, and ran away in a paroxysm of insanity, shouting and crying, and alarming his acquaintances. He hastened through the standing corn, and slunk away through all the rooms of a neighbor's capacious house, to one most retired and secluded; and there begging the neighbors who had followed him, to keep the devils off, and slapping himself violently with both his hands, crying out with the most acute pain, "The bees are stinging me to death," he died of mortification, an awful warning against intemperance, which the by-standers can never forget; no, never, never.

Resist the beginnings of intemperance. Venture not on the first drop. One man I knew to fall on his face in the dusty road, and strangle with the dust. Another, not thought to be intemperate, six months after he commenced tavern-keeping, died of *mania a potu*, leaving a wife and five or six children in poverty and want. O beware of the intoxicating cup.

D. C.

A YOUNG NOVEL-READER.

Charles F—— was an orphan boy. When but eleven years old, he was taken by his guardian to a clergyman in a New England village, to be fitted for college. He was a boy of uncommon talents; his manners were winning and gentle, his voice was sweet, his disposition generous; and he early manifested a contempt of danger and a power of endurance rarely to be seen in a child.

But he was a novel-reader. He had read all the Waverly novels, and many of Marryatt's, before he was eleven years old, and their effect was apparent. He had no taste for other reading, and no taste for study. The life of an adventurer was the only life he seemed to desire. It was in vain that the clergyman sought to divert his mind into a better channel; and in vain that his wife, with a mother's kindness and affection, labored for his good. He was mild and lovely; but he had chosen his path in life, his plans were matured, and nothing could deter him from his purpose. He remained three years, and all the family became greatly attached to him. They loved him for his amiable qualities, and because he was an orphan. Perhaps, too, they loved him more on account of their fears for him.

Alas, those fears were soon realized. One morning he was missing. Hours passed, and he did not return. Days passed, and then they heard of him by the seacoast; and then, that he had become a sailor.

Many were the lamentations over the poor child who had so early made himself a wanderer and an outcast. His name could not be mentioned without calling forth sighs from the members of the family he had left; and often, in the long winter evenings, as they sat around the cheerful fire, they talked of poor Charles, and wondered upon what part of the wild ocean he was then tossing.

Once they heard from him, that he wished himself back among them; and again, that he had become reckless and bad; his gentle manners had quite forsaken him; he was no longer the thoughtful, romantic boy, but was fast growing up to be a bold, abandoned man. Novels had accomplished their work.

Five years passed away, and one summer morning, as the family were sitting together in their pleasant parlor, a low and feeble knock was heard. On opening the door, a young man entered, and sunk into the first chair that presented itself. One glance was sufficient to show that he was in the last stage of consumption; the next, and they recognized Charles F——. "My poor boy," exclaimed the mother, throwing her arms about his neck, and bursting into tears. All wept except the prodigal himself, and he only compressed his lips and became more pale.

At length one said to him, "You can't think how we mourned for you, Charles, when you went away."

"It was the worst day's work I ever did," was his reply, in a subdued voice.

But Oh, the fearful change that five short years had wrought in him. He had grown prematurely old. Scarcely a trace remained of the once beautiful boy, except in his large dark eyes. His countenance expressed unspeakable woe and despair. He knew that he must soon die, and felt that he was not prepared. "It is too late," he said. "I have tried in vain to fix my mind on serious things. I have been very wicked; it is too late." "Oh no," they answered; "it is never too late while life lasts; the merits of Christ are all-sufficient; cast yourself on him." He shook his head mournfully, and again replied, "It is too late for *me*."

In this state of mind he went to reside with a physician, and once more left his early home, never to return. They had put into his hands the "Pastor's Sketches," by the late Rev. Dr. Spencer, referring him particularly to the story of "The Young Irishman," and he promised to read it. No more could be done for him now, except to commend him to God, with whom "all things are possible."

A few days afterwards, as the family were sitting at dinner and talking about the unhappy boy, the book was returned. A note came with it from a member of the physician's family with whom he had been placed. He had requested that it might be sent to the clergyman, with his "kind regards." And he was dead. He had been left alone for a few moments, when he burst a bloodvessel, and died suddenly. No one knew to whom his last thoughts were given, or what had become of the undying soul. "He died, and made no sign."

So sunk into the grave, in his nineteenth year, one who, but for the corrupting influence of bad books, might have lived a long and happy life, an ornament to his country, and a blessing to all around him. And I wish that all who print, circulate, or read such ruinous writings, could but look upon that orphan's grave, and hear his history. S.

THE LAST REBUKE.

In 1831, there were nine powder-mills on the banks of the pleasant stream which flowed through the village of S——. In one of them worked a young man named Luman C——. He had enjoyed a common-school education, and his religious training had not been wholly neglected. In his new employment, exposed to recklessness, profaneness, and intemperance—too common vices with those engaged in pursuits of unusual danger—he soon became corrupted, and practised these evil habits, and in the end he was a proselyte to Universalism, which was advocated with extraordinary zeal by several of his companions. His profanity increased with the growth of his zeal. He boarded with a plain, pious woman, who had noticed, not without pain, the downward career of the young man. One Sabbath she kindly said to him, "Come, Luman, come to meeting with me to-day." His reply startled the good woman: "I 'd sooner go to hell."

Near these powder-mills was a grist-mill, tended by a pious miller known as "Deacon F——." One day young C——, seeing some children playing on the bank of the stream near the grist-mill, commenced talking in a tone so depraved and with words so profane, that the children ceased their play and looked at him in terror. The miller gently remonstrated, saying, "Such language is dreadful at any time, but before children it is shocking; if you have no regard for their morals, take care lest God bring you to judgment for this thing."

"See here, deacon F——, I want none of your

preaching. You take care of yourself, and I 'll take care of myself. When I want your services I 'll tell you." Thus enraged, young C—— returned to the powder-mill.

This was about mid-day. A few moments afterwards a dead, dull sound went rumbling up the stream. It caught the ear of the miller, and his soul sunk within him as he beheld a dark cloud of smoke and black fragments scattered everywhere. A little spark had done the work—the mill had exploded. Poor Luman C——. The explosion had parted the building and opened the roof, carrying the profane swearer high through the opening into the air, and throwing him some distance into the mill-pond. The miller was the first to see the young man struggling, and ran to his aid. When the shore was gained, what a pitiful sight, and how changed the poor creature's words from what they were a few minutes before. "O, Mr. F——, I 'm a dead man. *Pray for my soul.*"

Quick as possible he was carried home and a physician brought. On account of his distress, the suffering man could not lie down. His strength of frame and voice was unimpaired. He sat on the bedside, black as a coal, the skin from his face and arms stripped away, all except two callous bunches hanging from the palms of his hands. And yet he spoke not a word of his bodily sufferings. It was the agony of the immortal spirit which absorbed his thoughts, his feelings, and his fears. Sitting there, his dark features distorted with intensity of pain, and his hands extended, he spoke to his fellow-workmen, and especially those whose wrong principles had poisoned his mind.

"See me, I am going away, and Oh, it is a lie that there is no punishment after death. I know it, I see it, I feel it already. God have mercy on me! O, don't believe these things. I tried to believe them, and Oh, they have deceived me. Don't, don't believe them; there is, O yes, there is a hell! I was afraid they would prove false, and Oh, they have betrayed me."

Such preaching melted all: even his profane companions were awed and trembled. He then looked on the minister with such an imploring look, it went to the pastor's soul. To another present, who was weeping, he said, "O, deacon F——, pray God to have mercy on me. O, pray that God will forgive me. O God—O Jesus, have mercy, have mercy!" Thus the night-shadows fell upon the poor sufferer, and poor Luman with a groan entered the "dark valley," and set out to meet his God.

Reader, be honest with your soul. Are *you* hugging a delusion? Perhaps friends have warned, and you have scoffed; the Holy Spirit has reproved, and you "have spoken stout words against him." Mal. 3:13. Are you grasping a lie in your right hand? Abandon it *now*, or it will by and by betray thee. Shun it ere it prove thy ruin, for "he that being often reproved hardeneth his neck, shall suddenly be destroyed, and that without remedy." Prov. 29:1.

S. L.

RESISTING THE HOLY SPIRIT.

Some years ago there was an interesting revival of religion in the place where I now labor in the ministry. In one school-district, the members of the church were much engaged, in connection with the pastor. Not a few were hopefully converted, and became active in the service of Christ. But there were three young men in that district who, though they attended many of the meetings, kept themselves aloof from the good work. They were exhorted and dealt with in kindness, but all to no purpose. One of them was dreadfully profane, and all of them treated the subject with ridicule. They lived through the precious season without any share in the blessing. Subsequently they removed from the place, and became settled in life.

A year or two ago the one that was so profane was on a fishing expedition, when he took cold, and was brought upon a sick-bed, from which he never arose. His friends were alarmed, and spoke to him about his soul, but he railed on them, and died with curses on his lips. What reason have men to regard the words of the apostle, "Beware therefore, lest that come upon you which is spoken of in the prophets: Behold, ye despisers, and wonder, and perish."

Another of the three young men living in an adjacent town, in his eagerness to accumulate property, exposed himself, fell sick, and died after a short illness, without hope.

I was called to visit a young man in the last stages of consumption. I found him near his end, but wholly insensible of his danger as a sinner out of Christ; he could not be aroused to a sense of his condition. He listened to a prayer; the next day his reason in a measure left him, and he died without any signs of repentance. This was the last of the three. How affecting to attend such a funeral.

These facts confirm the remark often made, that a revival of religion is a sealing time. Some are sealed to life, others are sealed to death. Those young men, to all human view, witnessed their last season of grace, received their last call, and rejected their last invitation of mercy. Oh how dangerous to resist the Spirit of God. M. T.

DEATH OF A MISER.

Some years since, there lived in the town of I——, which lies embosomed among the hills of Vermont, in the northern part of the state, an old man of some seventy years. He was a worldly man, emphatically so. His toil and care had been to accumulate corruptible things, and God had granted him his desires; he had lands, and silver, and gold. Still, they were of little use to him, for his spirit was so grasping and avaricious, that he would scarcely allow himself the necessaries of life.

The subject of religion was an unwelcome one to him; he gave no heed to its claims. And indeed, so long had he resisted the conviction of his understanding and conscience, that he was hardened beyond feeling, and as we feared, a reprobate. There had been many revivals in I——, some of them of great power and extent, but he had passed through them all apparently but little affected. He lived to make money; he loved it; and so absorbed was he in its pursuit, that he was utterly indifferent to what was passing around him, except as it told upon the object of his devotion. It was sad to see him, stricken and bowed with years, his eye dimmed by age, and his hand tremulous from nervous derangement; for you felt, as you gazed upon him, that his hopes and joys were all "of the earth, earthy."

Suddenly we missed him from the streets, and his accustomed places of resort, and were told that he was sick and must die. We hastened to his house, and entered the chamber of death. How dark and cheerless was that room. There was no Saviour there, lighting up by his presence the gloom, brightening the eye, and strengthening the heart by his faith, and blessed hopes. There lay the old man, groaning in the wretchedness of his spirit, not because he was a sinner, and was trembling at the thought of the eternal world to which he was hastening, but because he was about to leave his treasures—he could take none of his mortgages and bonds and acres and gold with him—they must all be left behind. For these he had sacrificed every thing, and the thought of an eternal separation from them was intolerable. Efforts to turn his thoughts in another direction were useless, for all his affections were fastened to this world, and he would not dislodge them.

But death was fast making him his prey; the dying man writhed in the agony of his soul, and looked imploringly to his nurse. She bent over him, and after catching his few and imperfectly uttered words, quickly brought from a chest standing near, a bag well filled with coin. This the dying man clasped convulsively in his hand, and straightway his spirit returned unto the God who gave it.

What a deathbed! Who would die in such a way? Gold in a dead man's hand! He would have it in life—he wished it in death. But the two were now separated—that on which his eye had feasted was no longer his.

What think you of such a death; rather, what think you of such a life?

Is it not preferable to have one's treasures so placed that when he dies he can go to them? Beware how you labor for the meat that perisheth, lest you become so fascinated, so deeply absorbed, as to beggar your soul for eternity.

F. B. W.

"I WAS NOT ONE OF THEM."

I am one of those pastors who continue the good old apostolical practice of visiting "from house to house" among my people. And although a most laborious, it is an exceedingly important and efficient way of doing good. It gives access to minds and hearts that can never be reached from the pulpit; it tends to bind pastor and people together, and it is richly suggestive of topics for public instruction.

On a damp and chilly day in the month of November, I went forth on a pastoral visitation among my people. It was my first regular visitation after my settlement among them. As the day was drawing towards its close, I entered a farm-house wearing externally and internally an air of comfort. Every thing was in pleasant preparation for my reception. On either side of a glowing fire sat the father and mother of the household, now well advanced in years;

and ranged between them were the other members of the family, the youngest child, then a lad of about fifteen years, holding his catechism in his hand. He could repeat it from beginning to end, showing that, as to the theory of religion, his education was not neglected. I went round the family group conversing with each as to their personal interest in the work of Christ for the salvation of men. Every thing was free, social, and pleasant; but while with an intelligent understanding of the plan of salvation, and while freely admitting that there was no way for them to heaven but through faith in Jesus Christ, I found, to my great grief, that parents and children were aliens from the commonwealth of Israel. After giving to each a word of instruction adapted to their circumstances, and to the views expressed by them in conversation, we bowed together before the high and lofty One; and having implored for them all temporal and spiritual good, I bade them farewell.

The father, whose natural strength many years had not impaired, and whose kind and gentle manners made him a favorite among his neighbors, followed me to the door, and closing it after him, stopped me on the porch. His countenance gave strong indications that there was something pressing upon his soul which he wished to communicate. Hoping that the Holy Spirit had blessed my visit to his conviction, I waited with anxiety to hear what he had to say. After a considerable pause, taking me by the hand, he thus addressed me:

"I thank you for this visit; although the first you have made us, I hope it will not be the last. I thank you for all the advice you have given us. And as you have but just commenced your labors among us as a minister, I wish to give you a word of advice, based on my own experience. Let us old people alone, for we are hopeless subjects, and devote your labors to the youth of your flock. Forty years ago, when Mr. A—— was our pastor, I was greatly anxious about my soul. Many were then converted, *but I was not one of them.* During the ministry of Mr. M—— I was often greatly anxious about my soul—I went to the conference-meeting—many were converted in the successive revivals enjoyed, *but I was not one of them.* And now, for years that are passed, I have not had a single feeling on the subject. I know that I am a lost sinner—I know that I can be saved only through Jesus Christ—I feel persuaded that when I die I shall go to hell for ever—I believe all you preach—I believe all you have said to me and my family, but I feel it no more than if I were a block of marble. And I expect to live and to die just as I am. So that my advice to you is to leave us old people to ourselves and our sins, for you cannot do us much good, and devote yourself to the work of seeking the conversion of the young."

And all this, and more, was said with a kind and pleasing bearing which forbade every thing like suspicion of his motives, and yet with a cool deliberateness which made me feel that the man was a mystery. After placing before him the fulness of the redemption which is in Christ Jesus, we parted.

I remembered the incident, and watched the progress of this man. His seat was rarely vacant in the sanctuary. To hear the word preached, he breasted many a storm which kept the professor of religion at home. I made him other visits; and while he admitted all I said, and freely confessed his lost state, I never witnessed in him the slightest ruffle of religious emotion. He was a true prophet of his own fate. He lived as he predicted; and so he died. And we laid him down in a hopeless grave, after having spent his threescore years and ten without repentance towards God, or faith in our Lord Jesus Christ, in the midst of a congregation over which God has often made windows in heaven.

The lessons taught by this incident are very obvious, highly important, and deeply impressive. To a few of these, the prayerful attention of the reader is earnestly requested.

Are you *advanced in life?* Are you approaching the verge of old age? Then ponder, unless you are a Christian, the many probabilities that you will never be converted. "Can a man be born again when he is old?" Being long habituated to certain ways of thinking and doing, the aged find it difficult to change. Old ways and things become, to a certain extent, sacred. Hence their attachment to old modes of dress and of living—to old habitations and associations. The old heathen die as they live. The aged papist dies as he lives. The most gross absurdities of his system of worship have become interwoven with his feelings on the subject of religion, and form the most sacred part of it. And the aged moralist, infidel, atheist, die as they live. Custom renders every thing easy. And the man who, through a long life, has been accustomed to hear and to assent to the truth of heaven with indifference, will, to a moral certainty, die as he lives. His habits are to him what his skin is to the Ethiopian—what his spots are to the leopard.

And the ground of the moral certainty that you will not be converted lies not in God, but in yourself. God is ever waiting and willing to be gracious; but you have been so long accustomed to neglect every call to work out your salvation, that there is no probability that you will now attend to it. But although your feet are on the borders of time, you have only to look to Jesus in true faith, to be prepared for eternity. At the eleventh hour of your life the gospel puts the cup of salvation into your trembling hand. O hasten to drink it, remembering that this hour is on the wing, and that when it ends you will be in the grave, where there is no work, nor device, nor knowledge, nor repentance.

Are you one of that large number who have been often convicted of sin without being converted; who have been often deeply impressed with divine truth without receiving "with meekness the ingrafted word, which is able to save your soul?" If so, then yours is an alarming state. You are passing through that process which has converted many a tender heart into a heart of steel. Of this process there are many illustrations. The young physician is excited, perhaps disgusted, the first time he witnesses a dissection; but he will soon use the knife upon the living or dead subject, without the least emotion. The young soldier, when he first treads the battle-field, is filled with fear and trepidation; but in the course of time the clangor of the war-trumpet is to him the sweetest music, and the field of his highest glory is the field of blood and carnage. And in a similar way, the heart that melts under the preaching of the gospel, and that trembles at the word of the Lord, becomes as hard as the flint, and as unimpressible. This state is gained by slow stages. Satan does not permit the heart to offend the judgment, by asking too much at once. He asks but here a little, and there a little. And by degrees the judgment is perverted, and the conscience is seared, and fear is overcome, and the warnings of God's word and providence lose their point and power—and the most awful truths of heaven, whose reality the mind never questions, fall as lightly upon the soul as does the snow drop upon the rock. Thus we pass on from youth, when the feelings, like the bosom of the ocean, are ruffled by the slightest zephyr, to old age, when the feelings are like the Dead sea, whose surface can scarcely be excited by the sweeping whirlwind, and which, if excited, soon relapses into its sullen stillness. And the longer the process is continued, the harder the heart becomes. If religious impressions, often made on your mind, have been as often erased, yours is a fearful state. If the slightest whisper of the Spirit yet calls you to the cross, go at once, lest when that whisper dies away upon your ear, the Spirit may take its flight, saying, "He is joined to his idols; I will hereafter let him alone." This will be sealing the instrument which consigns you to eternal death.

Are you yet *in your youth,* with the dew of the morning of your life sparkling on your green leaf? Then has this incident a most important lesson for you. If difficulties, many and great, impede the conversion of the aged, how important to secure your salvation while young. Many promises are now in your favor, but they are daily diminishing. Your heart, now easily impressed, is becoming harder and harder. You are now comparatively but little immersed in the world, but it is throwing daily a new fold around you. You should not be ignorant of the important truth, that the probabilities of your salvation are becoming fewer and weaker as your years roll on. It is an easy matter to break up the earth in April and May, and to plant in its bosom the good seed that bears fruit in autumn; but what power can cultivate it when congealed by the cold, and covered by the snows of December? Seize, O seize, then, the halcyon days of youth to prepare for old age, death, and eternity. Wait not until covered by the rust, and weakened by the infirmities of years. To-day, if you will hear His voice, harden not your heart. Opportunity, grace, mercy, heaven, eternal glory, are all upon the wing of the present hour; condemnation, hell, eternal despair, the worm that never dies, may all be in the train of the next. So improve your youth as not to be left to say in old age, "Many were converted, BUT I WAS NOT ONE OF THEM."

N. M.

www.ingramcontent.com/pod-product-compliance
Lightning Source LLC
LaVergne TN
LVHW021259110826
845150LV00003B/427

* 9 7 8 1 4 2 5 5 6 0 4 3 0 *